HOMELAND SECURITY
FOR POLICING

HOMELAND SECURITY FOR POLICING

Willard M. Oliver

Sam Houston State University
and
U.S. Army Reserves, Military Police Corps

Upper Saddle River, New Jersey

Library of Congress Cataloging-in-Publication Data

Oliver, Willard M.
  Homeland security for policing / Willard M. Oliver. — 1st ed.
    p. cm.
  Includes bibliographical references and index.
  ISBN 0-13-153466-1
  1. Internal security—United States. 2. Law enforcement—United States.
  3. Community policing—United States. I. Title.
  HV8141.O55 2006
  363.34—dc22

                                    2006015859

Editor-in-chief: Vernon R. Anthony
Executive Editor: Frank Mortimer, Jr.
Assistant Editor: Mayda Bosco
Editorial Assistant: Jillian Allison
Managing Editor: Mary Carnis
Production Editor: John Shannon/Laserwords
Production Liaison: Janice Stangel/Brian Hyland
Director of Manufacturing and Production: Bruce Johnson
Marketing Manager: Adam Kloza
Manufacturing Buyer: Cathleen Peterson
Manufacturing Manager: Ilene Sanford
Senior Design Coordinator: Cheryl Asherman
Printer/Binder: RR Donnelley and Sons
Cover Design: Cheryl Asherman
Cover Image: Brendan Smialowski

Pearson Education LTD.
Pearson Education Singapore, Pte. Ltd
Pearson Education, Canada, Ltd
Pearson Education-Japan

Pearson Education Australia PTY, Limited
Pearson Education North Asia Ltd
Pearson Educación de Mexico, S.A. de C.V.
Pearson Education Malaysia, Pte. Ltd

10 9 8 7 6 5 4 3 2 1
ISBN: 0-13-153466-1

Dedication

This book is dedicated in honor of those police officers who responded to the tragic events of September 11, 2001, in New York City, New York; Arlington County, Virginia; and Somerset County, Pennsylvania; and in memory of those police officers who made the ultimate sacrifice on that fateful day
(see Appendix A).

Contents

Preface

There has been too little assessment of actions that local and state police can take when facing an immeasurable threat such as terrorism.

—Juliette N. Kayyem,
Executive Director,
Executive Session on Domestic Preparedness,
John F. Kennedy School of Government,
Harvard University.[1]

On September 11, 2001, America entered into a new era, an era of terrorism.[2] On that same day, policing in America also entered a new era, an era of homeland security.[3] Although America had faced numerous terrorist attacks against its interests around the world, and several on its own soil, both domestic (the Oklahoma City Bombing) and international (the first World Trade Center Bombing), it was not until the Al-Qaeda terrorist highjackings that America truly understood the destructive nature of terrorism. It was also at that point that the threat of terrorism became real, and the need for protection and security against future threats, long held as the primary function of government, became a necessity. Although police in New York, Arlington County, Virginia, and Somerset, Pennsylvania, were among the first responders and remained throughout the recovery efforts, prior to 9-11 there was essentially no formal role for local and state police in regard to terrorism. In a post–9-11 world, that must change.

There is little doubt that local and state police will play a key role in homeland security. The newly created Department of Homeland Security makes this acknowledgment. The *National Strategy for Homeland Security* makes this acknowledgment. And numerous white papers have asserted this same notion, that police must and will play a significant role in securing the homeland. However, what has not been well defined is the exact nature of that role. As the opening quote denotes, despite the calls for police to play a role in homeland security, that role has been ill defined. Police agencies cannot and should not wait for that role to be defined by the federal government, as any plan from that level will not fully consider the needs and constraints of state and local police and their communities. Rather, police agencies must begin giving serious consideration to their role in homeland security.

The role of police in homeland security will maintain many of the elements of past policing practices, from the so-called traditional policing, to problem solving, to community-oriented policing. Yet, at the same time, policing will have to take on new roles and learn new tasks to adapt to an era of homeland security. These new roles will include information gathering, risk and threat assessments, intelligence analysis, preparation for mass disasters including weapons of mass destruction, risk management, information sharing both laterally and vertically, preemption of terrorism, and use of an incident command system under the national incident management system. Although elements of each of these will reflect past policing practices, concepts such as intelligence-led policing will reflect new challenges to law enforcement personnel.

The purpose of this book, then, is to present a framework for understanding the police role in homeland security. The book intends to present a fuller understanding of how the concept of homeland security developed, what it means for the police, and where within the scope of a national homeland security framework the police fit. Unlike past police restructuring, homeland security relies on cooperation with other local agencies, as well as state and federal police. Policing for homeland security is an integral web of dependency with these other agencies, not a new style of policing that can be adopted in singular fashion. Recognizing this, police must have a broad strategic focus for the adoption of homeland security to ensure that their goals and objectives are compatible and nest with other agency's strategic plans. In addition, how to operationalize the strategic concepts is equally important, which then tells us the tactics to be used and the training necessary for the police officers on the street. Although the scope of this book limits its ability to serve as a training manual, it is intended to present to the reader a more holistic understanding of policing for homeland security, what role the police will play in this new era, and the strategic, operational, and tactical considerations necessary to implement this new philosophy of policing.

ORGANIZATION OF THE BOOK

To understand the concepts of policing for homeland security, it is important to remember the origin of this new era in policing, namely the events of September 11th. Although the author believes remembering these events are important unto themselves, considering the police response that day helps to place the concepts of prevention, preparedness, response, and recovery in perspective. In addition, it also places into perspective the significant impact that the terrorist attacks had on America and American policing. This is the purpose of Chapter 1 of the book, to establish that policing today finds itself in an era of homeland security.

Although acknowledging that policing finds itself in an era of homeland security helps us to focus on the police role, understanding the history of homeland security and how it has developed since September 11th is equally important. As previously stated, policing for homeland security is not a program that police can add onto its department's organization and function autonomously, but rather is one that fits into a national framework that must be taken into consideration. Therefore, Chapter 2 will explore the history and current status of homeland security in America to again provide perspective.

However, to fully understand the role of police in homeland security, it is important that we first have a conceptual understanding of the strategies necessary for achieving homeland security. These can come from multiple sources, including national policy, the Department of Homeland Security, which is leading up homeland security operations, state policy, and policy recommendations from key professional organizations that help shape policy, such as the International Association of Chiefs of Police (IACP), the Police Executive Research Forum (PERF), and the Office of Community Oriented Policing Services (COPS). Second, it is imperative that we have an understanding of the operational level in homeland security, specifically detailing how best to deploy police personnel and resources to achieve these strategic goals. This requires an understanding of how best to organize the police for homeland security operations, as well as understanding the decision-making processes necessary to achieve these goals. Third, and finally, we must understand the tactics available, the equipment necessary, and the type of training needed to allow state and local police to conduct operations at the tactical level for homeland security. To this end, Chapter 3 of this book will review the strategy of homeland security as it relates to state and local policing, Chapter 4 will review the operational level concepts as they apply to policing and homeland security, and Chapter 5 will detail the tactical level methods and training necessary for police to achieve the goals and objectives of homeland security.

About the Author

Willard M. Oliver is an Associate Professor of Criminal Justice in the College of Criminal Justice at Sam Houston State University, Huntsville, Texas. He holds a Ph.D. and an M.A. in political science from West Virginia University and an M.S. and a B.S. in criminal justice from Radford University. Currently he serves as an instructor in the Incident Command Simulation Training Program (INCOSIT) for the Law Enforcement Management Institute of Texas (LEMIT); Huntsville, Texas. He also serves as a Major in the United States Army Reserves, Military Police Corps, with the 75th Training Division, Houston, Texas and is a decorated Veteran of the Persian Gulf War. He is a graduate of both the military police basic and advanced training (enlisted), both the military police basic and advanced officer training, the Combined Arms Services Support School, and Command & General Staff College. He is also a former police officer from the Washington, D.C., Metropolitan area. His research interests are centered on policing and public policy issues, and he is the author of numerous peer-reviewed journal articles, books, and magazine articles related to both topics. In his spare time he enjoys running and teaching martial arts.

Acknowledgments

The author would first like to thank the numerous people who have helped to educate and train the author throughout his policing and military careers. Dedicated soldiers and police officers have had a great influence upon me, and I am indebted to them for providing me an education at all three levels of military and police education, namely the strategic, operational, and tactical levels.

I would also like to thank several individuals who helped shape this book. Richard Ward, Dean of the College of Criminal Justice, for hiring me and providing me the opportunity to write such a book. Joe Serio, also of the College of Criminal Justice, for having faith in my ideas despite what he says. And to Frank Mortimer, the Criminal Justice Editor at Prentice Hall, whose faith in my ideas has allowed me a very respectable outlet. My thanks to all of you.

I would also like to acknowledge and thank the reviewers for their constructive comments, all of which helped to greatly improve the manuscript. They are as follows: Professor Edward G. Piper, Johns Hopkins University, Baltimore, MD; Professor Brian G. Onieal, John Jay College of Criminal Justice, New York, NY; Professor Vincent F. Benincasa, Hesser College, Manchester, NH; Professor Timothy R. Hart, College of Sequoias, Visalia, CA.

Finally, as always, the love and support of my family who give me the encouragement to see the ominous task of writing a book through. To my wife, Judy, and my three children, Paul, James, and Sarah. You are ever my reminder why both my current service in the military and policing for homeland security are so important.

Great harm has been done to us. We have suffered great loss.
And in our grief and anger we have found
our mission and our moment . . .
We will not tire, we will not falter, and we will not fail.

—President George W. Bush,
September 20, 2001

The only thing necessary for the triumph of evil is
for good men to do nothing.

—Edmond Burke,
Member of the British Parliament

CHAPTER 1

The Era of Homeland Security

Our nation has been put on notice: We are not immune from attack. We will take defensive measures against terrorism to protect Americans. Today, dozens of federal departments and agencies, as well as state and local governments, have responsibilities affecting homeland security.

President George W. Bush, September 20, 2001
(See Appendix B for full speech)

INTRODUCTION

On September 11, 2001, policing entered the era of homeland security. Prior to the attack on America by Osama bin Laden and his terrorist group, Al Qaeda, on that fateful day, policing in America recognized that various crime problems had international implications, but there was little acknowledgment of how these crimes would impact state and local police directly. Issues such as international and transnational crimes, particularly organized and white-collar crime, and both drug and human trafficking, were issues of concern, but generally concerns for either the federal government and their criminal justice assets or for the international community. The realization that global concerns, such as terrorism, were indeed a state and local concern changed on September 11, 2001. That day policing in America moved out of the community policing era and into the era of homeland security.

To understand how this came about, it is important to first review the threat that Osama bin Laden and his terrorist organization, Al Qaeda, posed to America prior to September 11th. In addition, reviewing the actual events of the attack helps place the significance of that day in better context. Perhaps more importantly, reviewing how the local police responded to the attacks provides us some insight into what the era of Homeland Security means for policing. Therefore, this chapter will review the threat, the attack, and the response to better understand the significance of the threat, see how that attack moved American policing into the era of Homeland Security, and provide the context for understanding the role state and local police will play in this new era.

1

BOX 1-1

TERRORISM TIME LINE (ABBREVIATED)
PRIOR TO FIRST WORLD TRADE CENTER (1993)

Kidnappings of U.S. Citizens in Colombia, January 31, 1993:
   Revolutionary Armed Forces of Colombia (FARC) terrorists kidnapped three U.S. missionaries.

Kidnapping of U.S. Businessmen in the Philippines, January 17–21, 1992:
   A senior official of the corporation Philippine Geothermal was kidnapped in Manila by the Red Scorpion Group, and two U.S. businessmen were seized independently by the National Liberation Army and by Revolutionary Armed Forces of Colombia (FARC).

Sniper Attack on the U.S. Embassy in Bonn, February 13, 1991:
   Three Red Army Faction members fired automatic rifles from across the Rhine River at the U.S. Embassy Chancery. No one was hurt.

Attempted Iraqi Attacks on U.S. Posts, January 18–19, 1991:
   Iraqi agents planted bombs at the U.S. ambassador to Indonesia's residence and at the USIS library in Manila.

U.S. Soldiers Assassinated in the Philippines, May 13, 1990:
   The New People's Army (NPA) killed two U.S. Air Force personnel near Clark Air Force Base in the Philippines.

U.S. Embassy Bombed in Peru, January 15, 1990:
   The Tupac Amaru Revolutionary Movement bombed the U.S. Embassy in Lima, Peru.

Assassination of U.S. Army Officer, April 21, 1989:
   The New People's Army (NPA) assassinated Colonel James Rowe in Manila. The NPA also assassinated two U.S. government defense contractors in September.

Pan Am 103 Bombing, December 21, 1988:
   Pan American Airlines Flight 103 was blown up over Lockerbie, Scotland, by a bomb believed to have been placed on the aircraft by Libyan terrorists in Frankfurt, West Germany. All 259 people on board were killed.

Attack on U.S. Diplomat in Greece, June 28, 1988:
   The defense attaché of the U.S. Embassy in Greece was killed when a car bomb was detonated outside his home in Athens.

Naples USO Attack, April 14, 1988:
   The Organization of Jihad Brigades exploded a car bomb outside a USO club in Naples, Italy, killing one U.S. sailor.

Kidnapping of William Higgins, February 17, 1988:
   U.S. Marine Corps Lieutenant Colonel W. Higgins was kidnapped and murdered by the Iranian-backed Hizballah group while serving with the United Nations Truce Supervisory Organization (UNTSO) in southern Lebanon.

Servicemen's Bar Attack, December 26, 1987:
> Catalan separatists bombed a Barcelona bar frequented by U.S. servicemen, resulting in the death of one U.S. citizen.

Bus Attack, April 24, 1987:
> Sixteen U.S. servicemen riding in a Greek Air Force bus near Athens were injured in an apparent bombing attack, carried out by the revolutionary organization known as November 17.

Berlin Discothèque Bombing, April 5, 1986:
> Two U.S. soldiers were killed and 79 American servicemen were injured in a Libyan bomb attack on a nightclub in West Berlin, West Germany. In retaliation U.S. military jets bombed targets in and around Tripoli and Benghazi.

Aircraft Bombing in Greece, March 30, 1986:
> A Palestinian splinter group detonated a bomb as TWA Flight 840 approached Athens airport, killing four U.S. citizens.

Airport Attacks in Rome and Vienna, December 27, 1985:
> Four gunmen belonging to the Abu Nidal Organization attacked the El Al and Trans World Airlines ticket counters at Rome's Leonardo da Vinci Airport with grenades and automatic rifles. Thirteen persons were killed and 75 were wounded before Italian police and Israeli security guards killed three of the gunmen and captured the fourth. Three more Abu Nidal gunmen attacked the El Al ticket counter at Vienna's Schwechat Airport, killing three persons and wounding 30. Austrian police killed one of the gunmen and captured the others.

Egyptian Airliner Hijacking, November 23, 1985:
> An EgyptAir airplane bound from Athens to Malta and carrying several U.S. citizens was hijacked by the Abu Nidal Group.

Achille Lauro Hijacking, October 7, 1985:
> Four Palestinian Liberation Front terrorists seized the Italian cruise liner in the eastern Mediterranean Sea, taking more than 700 hostages. One U.S. passenger was murdered before the Egyptian government offered the terrorists safe haven in return for the hostages' freedom.

Attack on a Restaurant in El Salvador, June 19, 1985:
> Members of the FMLN (Farabundo Marti National Liberation Front) fired on a restaurant in the Zona Rosa district of San Salvador, killing four Marine security guards assigned to the U.S. Embassy and nine Salvadorean civilians.

TWA Hijacking, June 14, 1985:
> A Trans-World Airlines flight was hijacked en route to Rome from Athens by two Lebanese Hizballah terrorists and forced to fly to Beirut. The eight crew members and 145 passengers were held for seventeen days, during which one American hostage, a U.S. Navy sailor, was murdered. After being flown twice to Algiers, the aircraft was returned to Beirut after Israel released 435 Lebanese and Palestinian prisoners.

Kidnapping of U.S. Officials in Mexico, February 7, 1985:
Under the orders of narcotrafficker Rafael Caro Quintero, Drug Enforcement Administration agent Enrique Camarena Salazar and his pilot were kidnapped, tortured, and executed.

Restaurant Bombing in Spain, April 12, 1984:
Eighteen U.S. servicemen were killed and 83 people were injured in a bomb attack on a restaurant near a U.S. Air Force base in Torrejon, Spain.

Kidnapping of Embassy Official, March 16, 1984:
The Islamic Jihad kidnapped and later murdered Political Officer William Buckley in Beirut, Lebanon. Other U.S. citizens not connected to the U.S. government were seized over a succeeding two-year period.

Naval Officer Assassinated in Greece, November 15, 1983:
A U.S. Navy officer was shot by the November 17 terrorist group in Athens, Greece, while his car was stopped at a traffic light.

Bombing of Marine Barracks, Beirut, October 23, 1983:
Simultaneous suicide truck-bomb attacks were made on American and French compounds in Beirut, Lebanon. A 12,000-pound bomb destroyed the U.S. compound, killing 242 Americans, while 58 French troops were killed when a 400-pound device destroyed a French base. Islamic Jihad claimed responsibility.

Naval Officer Assassinated in El Salvador, May 25, 1983:
A U.S. Navy officer was assassinated by the Farabundo Marti National Liberation Front.

Bombing of U.S. Embassy in Beirut, April 18, 1983:
Sixty-three people, including the CIA's Middle East director, were killed and 120 were injured in a 400-pound suicide truck-bomb attack on the U.S. Embassy in Beirut, Lebanon. The Islamic Jihad claimed responsibility.

Colombian Hostage-taking, April 8, 1983:
A U.S. citizen was seized by the Revolutionary Armed Forces of Colombia (FARC) and held for ransom.

Murder of Missionaries, December 4, 1981:
Three American nuns and one lay missionary were found murdered outside San Salvador, El Salvador. They were killed by members of the National Guard, and the killers are currently in prison.

Assassination of Egyptian President, October 6, 1981:
Soldiers who were secretly members of the Takfir Wal-Hajira sect attacked and killed Egyptian President Anwar Sadat during a troop review.

U.S. Installation Bombing, August 31, 1981:
The Red Army exploded a bomb at the U.S. Air Force Base at Ramstein, West Germany.

Grand Mosque Seizure, November 20, 1979:
200 Islamic terrorists seized the Grand Mosque in Mecca, Saudi Arabia, taking hundreds of pilgrims hostage. Saudi and French security forces retook the shrine after an intense battle in which some 250 people were killed and 600 wounded.

Iran Hostage Crisis, November 4, 1979:

> After President Carter agreed to admit the Shah of Iran into the United States, Iranian radicals seized the U.S. Embassy in Tehran and took 66 American diplomats hostage. Thirteen hostages were soon released, but the remaining 53 were held until their release on January 20, 1981.

Ambassador to Afghanistan Assassinated, February 14, 1979:

> Four Afghans kidnapped U.S. Ambassador Adolph Dubs in Kabul and demanded the release of various "religious figures." Dubs was killed, along with four alleged terrorists, when Afghan police stormed the hotel room where he was being held.

Assassination of Former Chilean Diplomat, September 21, 1976:

> Exiled Chilean Foreign Minister Orlando Letelier was killed by a car bomb in Washington.

Domestic Terrorism, January 27–29, 1975:

> Puerto Rican nationalists bombed a Wall Street bar, killing four and injuring 60; two days later, the Weather Underground claims responsibility for an explosion in a bathroom at the U.S. Department of State in Washington.

Ambassador to Cyprus Assassinated, August 19, 1974:

> U.S. Ambassador to Cyprus Rodger P. Davies and his Greek Cypriot secretary were shot and killed by snipers during a demonstration outside the U.S. Embassy in Nicosia.

Attack and Hijacking at the Rome Airport, December 17, 1973:

> Five terrorists pulled weapons from their luggage in the terminal lounge at the Rome airport, killing two persons. They then attacked a Pan American 707 bound for Beirut and Tehran, destroying it with incendiary grenades and killing 29 persons, including 4 senior Moroccan officials and 14 American employees of ARAMCO. They then herded 5 Italian hostages into a Lufthansa airliner and killed an Italian customs agent as he tried to escape, after which they forced the pilot to fly to Beirut. After Lebanese authorities refused to let the plane land, it landed in Athens, where the terrorists demanded the release of 2 Arab terrorists. In order to make Greek authorities comply with their demands, the terrorists killed a hostage and threw his body onto the tarmac. The plane then flew to Damascus, where it stopped for two hours to obtain fuel and food. It then flew to Kuwait, where the terrorists released their hostages in return for passage to an unknown destination. The Palestine Liberation Organization disavowed the attack, and no group claimed responsibility for it.

Consul General in Mexico Kidnapped, May 4, 1973:

> U.S. Consul General in Guadalajara, Terrence Leonhardy, was kidnapped by members of the People's Revolutionary Armed Forces.

Ambassador to Sudan Assassinated, March 2, 1973:

> U.S. Ambassador to Sudan, Cleo A. Noel, and other diplomats were assassinated at the Saudi Arabian Embassy in Khartoum by members of the Black September organization.

Munich Olympic Massacre, September 5, 1972:

> Eight Palestinian "Black September" terrorists seized eleven Israeli athletes in the Olympic Village in Munich, West Germany. In a bungled rescue attempt by West German authorities, nine of the hostages and five terrorists were killed.

"Bloody Friday," July 21, 1972:
> An Irish Republican Army (IRA) bomb attack killed eleven people and injured 130 in Belfast, Northern Ireland. Ten days later, three IRA car bomb attacks in the village of Claudy left six dead.

U.S. Agency for International Development Adviser Kidnapped, July 31, 1970:
> In Montevideo, Uruguay, the Tupamaros terrorist group kidnapped AID Police adviser Dan Mitrione; his body was found on August 10.

Ambassador to Brazil Kidnapped, September 3, 1969:
> U.S. Ambassador to Brazil Charles Burke Elbrick was kidnapped by the Marxist revolutionary group MR-8.

Ambassador to Japan Attacked, July 30, 1969:
> U.S. Ambassador to Japan, A. H. Meyer, was attacked by a knife-wielding Japanese citizen.

Ambassador to Guatemala Assassinated, August 28, 1968:
> U.S. Ambassador to Guatemala, John Gordon Mein, was murdered by a rebel faction when gunmen forced his official car off the road in Guatemala City and raked the vehicle with gunfire.

First U.S. Aircraft Hijacked, May 1, 1961:
> Puerto Rican born Antuilo Ramierez Ortiz forced at gunpoint a National Airlines plane to fly to Havana, Cuba, where he was given asylum.

Source: U.S. Army—Timeline of Terrorism, Available online at http://www.army.mil/terrorism

THE THREAT—AL QAEDA

Thomas Friedman, a columnist for the *New York Times*, argued in an op-ed piece that America in the 1990s experienced the growth of three bubbles, all of which burst at the beginning of the twenty-first century.[1] The three bubbles included the stock market, corporate governance, and terrorism. The first bubble burst when the various dot-com organizations became greatly inflated in the 1990s, and the stock market simply adjusted their values downward in 2000. The second bubble burst at about the same time, when a number of ethical lapses were allowed to go unchecked throughout the 1990s until the illegal activities of corporate firms Enron and Arthur Andersen were revealed. The third bubble burst on September 11, 2001, and resulted from the terrorism bubble that was allowed to grow during the 1990s.

The terrorism bubble, Friedman asserted, "started with the suicide bombings against U.S. troops in Saudi Arabia, was followed by attacks on the U.S. Embassies in East Africa and on the USS *Cole*, then ballooned with the rise of Palestinian suicide terrorism in Israel and finally peaked with Al Qaeda's attack on 9/11."[2] Friedman traced most of what led up to the third bubble as being the result of Osama bin Laden and the terrorist organization Al Qaeda's ability to grow in power unchecked during the 1990s. He explained that like the other two bubbles, "the terrorism bubble was the product of a kind of temporary insanity, in which basic norms were ignored and excessive behavior was justified by new theories."[3] The threat of Al Qaeda was ultimately what led to the bubble bursting and ushering in the post–September 11th world, or as Friedman calls it, the "post-bubble world."[4] Understanding the origin of this threat, namely Osama bin Laden and his terrorist network Al Qaeda, and how this threat developed is important to understanding what led us into the era of Homeland Security.

The Bubble Forms

Al Qaeda was founded by Osama bin Laden in Afghanistan in 1988.[5] Osama bin Laden was born in July 1957, the seventeenth of twenty sons of a Saudi construction magnate of Yemeni origin. Many Saudis were conservative Sunni Muslims, and bin Laden adopted militant Islamist views while studying at King Abdul Aziz University in Jeddah, Saudi Arabia. There he studied Islam under Muhammad Qutb, brother of Sayyid Qutb, the key idealogue of a major Sunni Islamist movement, the Muslim Brotherhood.[6] Another of bin Laden's instructors was a major figure in the Jordanian branch of the Muslim Brotherhood, Dr. Abdullah Azzam. Azzam has been identified by some experts as the intellectual architect of the *jihad* against the 1979–1989 Soviet occupation of Afghanistan and ultimately of Al Qaeda itself;[7] he cast the Soviet invasion as an attempted conquest by a non-Muslim power of sacred Muslim territory and people.

Bin Laden went to Afghanistan shortly after the December 1979 Soviet invasion and joined Azzam there. He reportedly used some of his personal funds[8] to establish himself as a donor to the Afghan *mujahedin* and a recruiter of Arab and other Islamic volunteers for the war. In 1984 Azzam and bin Laden structured this assistance by establishing a network of recruiting and fund-raising offices in the Arab world, Europe, and the United States. That network was called the *Maktab al-Khidamat* (Services Office), also known as *Al Khifah;* many experts consider the *Maktab* network to be the organizational forerunner of Al Qaeda. Another major figure who utilized the *Maktab* network to recruit for the anti-Soviet *jihad* was Umar Abd al-Rahman (also known as "the blind shaykh"), the spiritual leader of radical Egyptian Islamist group Al Jihad. Bin Laden also fought in the anti-Soviet war, participating in a 1986 battle in Jalalabad and, more notably, a 1987 frontal assault by foreign volunteers against Soviet armor. Bin Laden has said he was exposed to a Soviet chemical attack and slightly injured in that battle.[9]

During this period, most U.S. officials perceived the volunteers as positive contributors to the effort to expel Soviet forces from Afghanistan, and U.S. officials made no apparent effort to stop the recruitment of non-Afghan volunteers for the war. U.S. officials have repeatedly denied that the United States directly supported the volunteers, although the United States did covertly finance (about $3 billion during 1981–1991) and arm (via Pakistan) the Afghan *mujahedin* factions, particularly the Islamic fundamentalist Afghan factions, fighting Soviet forces. At this time, neither bin Laden, Azzam, nor Abd al-Rahman was known to have openly advocated, undertaken, or planned any direct attacks against the United States, although they were critical of U.S. support for Israel in the Middle East.

In 1988, toward the end of the Soviet occupation, bin Laden and Azzam began contemplating how, and to what end, to utilize the Islamist volunteer network they had organized. U.S. intelligence estimates of the size of that network was about 10,000 to 20,000, although not all of these necessarily supported or joined Al Qaeda terrorist activities.[10] Azzam reportedly wanted this "Al Qaeda" (Arabic for "the base") organization to become an Islamic "rapid reaction force," available to intervene wherever Muslims were perceived to be threatened. Bin Laden differed with Azzam, hoping instead to dispatch the Al Qaeda activists to their home countries to try to topple secular, pro-Western Arab leaders, such as President Hosni Mubarak of Egypt and Saudi Arabia's royal family. Some attribute their differences to the growing influence on bin Laden by the Egyptians in his inner circle, such as Abd al-Rahman, who wanted to use Al Qaeda's resources to install an Islamic state in Egypt. Another close Egyptian confidant was Dr. Ayman al-Zawahiri, operational leader of Al Jihad in Egypt. Like Abd al-Rahman, Zawahiri had been imprisoned but ultimately acquitted for the October 1981 assassination of Egyptian President Anwar Sadat, and he permanently left Egypt for Afghanistan in 1985. There, he used his medical training to tend to wounded fighters in the anti-Soviet war. In November 1989, Azzam was assassinated, and some allege that bin Laden might have been responsible for the killing to resolve this power struggle. Following Azzam's death, bin Laden gained control of the *Maktab*'s funds and organizational mechanisms. Abd al-Rahman later came to the United States and was convicted in October 1995 for terrorist plots related to the February 1993 bombing of the World Trade Center. Zawahiri stayed with bin Laden to serve as bin Laden's main strategist; he is believed to still be serving in that role today.

The Bubble Grows

The August 2, 1990, Iraqi invasion of Kuwait apparently turned bin Laden from a de facto U.S. ally against the Soviet Union into one of its most active adversaries.[11] Bin Laden had returned home to Saudi Arabia in 1989 after the completion of the Soviet withdrawal from Afghanistan that February. While back home, he lobbied Saudi officials not to host the 500,000 U.S. combat troops that defended Saudi Arabia from the Iraqi invasion and ultimately expelled Iraq from Kuwait in Operation Desert Storm (January 17–February 28, 1991). He argued instead for the raising of a "mujahedin" army to oust Iraq from Kuwait, but his idea was rebuffed as impractical, causing a falling out with Saudi leaders. He relocated to Sudan in 1991, buying property there that he used to host and train Al Qaeda militants—this time, for use against the United States and its interests, as well as for *jihad* operations in the Balkans, Chechnya, Kashmir, and the Phillipines. He remained there until the Sudanese government, under U.S. and Egyptian pressure, expelled him in May 1996; he then returned to Afghanistan and helped the Taliban gain and maintain control of Afghanistan. The Taliban would capture the capital, Kabul, in September of 1996.

Bin Laden and Zawahiri apparently believed that the only way to bring Islamic regimes to power was to oust from the region the perceived backer of secular regional regimes, the United States. During the 1990s, bin Laden and Zawahiri transformed Al Qaeda into a global threat to U.S. national security by engaging in a number of attacks against the United States and its interests. In 1992, Al Qaeda claimed responsibility for bombing a hotel in Yemen where 100 U.S. military personnel were awaiting deployment to Somalia for Operation Restore Hope. No one was killed. However, Al Qaeda was responsible for the tragedy that subsequently followed during this operation in Somalia. Al Qaeda claimed responsibility for arming Somali factions, who battled U.S. forces there

BOX 1-2

TERRORISM TIME LINE (ABBREVIATED)
FIRST WORLD TRADE CENTER (1993) TO SEPTEMBER 11, 2001

Philippines Hostage Incident, May 27, 2001:
  Muslim Abu Sayyaf guerrillas seized 13 tourists and 3 staff members at a resort on Palawan
  Island and took their captives to Basilan Island. The captives included three U.S. citizens:
  Guellermo Sobero and missionaries Martin and Gracia Burnham. Philippine troops fought
  a series of battles with the guerrillas between June 1 and June 3, during which nine
  hostages escaped and two were found dead. The guerrillas took additional hostages when
  they seized the hospital in the town of Lamitan. On June 12, Abu Sayyaf spokesman Abu
  Sabaya claimed that Sobero had been killed and beheaded; his body was found in October. The Burnhams remained in captivity until June 2002.

Manila Bombing, December 30, 2000:
  A bomb exploded in a plaza across the street from the U.S. Embassy in Manila, injuring
  nine persons. The Moro Islamic Liberation Front was likely responsible.

Helicopter Hijacking, October 12, 2000:
  In Sucumbios Province, Ecuador, a group of armed kidnappers led by former members of
  defunct Colombian terrorist organization the Popular Liberation Army (EPL) took
  hostage 10 employees of Spanish energy consortium REPSOL. Those kidnapped included
  five U.S. citizens, one Argentine, one Chilean, one New Zealander, and two French pilots,
  who escaped four days later. On January 30, 2001, the kidnappers murdered American
  hostage Ronald Sander. The remaining hostages were released on February 23 following
  the payment of $13 million in ransom by the oil companies.

Attack on USS *Cole*, October 12, 2000:
  In Aden, Yemen, a small dinghy carrying explosives rammed the destroyer USS *Cole*, killing
  seventeen sailors and injuring 39 others. Supporters of Osama bin Laden were suspected.

Church Bombing in Tajikistan, October 1, 2000:
  Unidentified militants detonated two bombs in a Christian church in Dushanbe, killing seven
  persons and injuring 70 others. The church was founded by a Korean-born U.S. citizen, and
  most of those killed and wounded were Korean. No one claimed responsibility.

Kidnappings in Kyrgyzstan, August 12, 2000:
  In the Kara-Su Valley, the Islamic Movement of Uzbekistan took four U.S. citizens hostage.
  The Americans escaped on August 12.

ELN Kidnapping, June 27, 2000:
  In Bogota, Colombia, ELN militants kidnapped a five-year-old U.S. citizen and his Colombian
  mother, demanding an undisclosed ransom.

RUF Attacks on U.N. Mission Personnel, May 1, 2000:
  On May 1 in Makeni, Sierra Leone, Revolutionary United Front (RUF) militants kidnapped
  at least 20 members of the United Nations Assistance Mission in Sierra Leone (UNAMSIL)
  and surrounded and opened fire on a UNAMSIL facility, according to press reports. The

militants killed five UN soldiers in the attack. RUF militants kidnapped 300 UNAMSIL peacekeepers throughout the country, according to press reports. On May 15 in Foya, Liberia, the kidnappers released 139 hostages. On May 28 on the Liberia and Sierra Leone border, armed militants released unharmed the last of the UN peacekeepers.

PLA Kidnapping, December 23, 1999:
Colombian People's Liberation Army (PLA) forces kidnapped a U.S. citizen in an unsuccessful ransoming effort.

Burmese Embassy Seizure, October 1, 1999:
Burmese dissidents seized the Burmese Embassy in Bangkok, Thailand, taking 89 persons hostage, including one U.S. citizen.

AFRC Kidnappings, August 4, 1999:
An Armed Forces Revolutionary Council (AFRC) faction kidnapped 33 UN representatives near Occra Hills, Sierra Leone. The hostages included one U.S. citizen, five British soldiers, one Canadian citizen, one representative from Ghana, one military officer from Russia, one officer from Kyrgystan, one officer from Zambia, one officer from Malaysia, a local bishop, two UN officials, two local journalists, and 16 Sierra Leonean nationals.

Shell Platform Bombing, June 27, 1999:
In Port Harcourt, Nigeria, armed youths stormed a Shell oil platform, kidnapping one U.S. citizen, one Nigerian national, and one Australian citizen and causing undetermined damage. A group calling itself "Enough is Enough in the Niger River" claimed responsibility. Further seizures of oil facilities followed.

ELN Hostage-taking, May 30, 1999:
In Cali, Colombia, armed ELN militants attacked a church in the neighborhood of Ciudad Jardin, kidnapping 160 persons, including six U.S. citizens and one French national. The rebels released approximately 80 persons, including three U.S. citizens, later that day.

ELN Hostage-taking, March 23, 1999:
Armed guerrillas kidnapped a U.S. citizen in Boyaca, Colombia. The National Liberation Army (ELN) claimed responsibility and demanded $400,000 ransom. On 20 July, ELN rebels released the hostage unharmed following a ransom payment of $48,000.

Hutu Abductions, March 1, 1999:
150 armed Hutu rebels attacked three tourist camps in Uganda, killed four Ugandans, and abducted three U.S. citizens, six Britons, three New Zealanders, two Danish citizens, one Australian, and one Canadian national. Two of the U.S. citizens and six of the other hostages were subsequently killed by their abductors.

FARC Kidnappings, February 25, 1999:
FARC kidnapped three U.S. citizens working for the Hawaii-based Pacific Cultural Conservancy International. On March 4, the bodies of the three victims were found in Venezuela.

Ugandan Rebel Attack, February 14, 1999:
A pipe bomb exploded inside a bar, killing five persons and injuring 35 others. One Ethiopian and four Ugandan nationals died in the blast, and one U.S. citizen working for

USAID, two Swiss nationals, one Pakistani, one Ethiopian, and 27 Ugandans were injured. Ugandan authorities blamed the attack on the Allied Democratic Forces (ADF).

Angolan Aircraft Downing, January 2, 1999:

A UN plane carrying one U.S. citizen, four Angolans, two Philippine nationals, and one Namibian was shot down, according to a UN official. No deaths or injuries were reported. Angolan authorities blamed the attack on National Union for the Total Independence of Angola (UNITA) rebels. UNITA officials denied shooting down the plane.

Armed Kidnapping in Colombia, November 15, 1998:

Armed assailants followed a U.S. businessman and his family home in Cundinamarca Department and kidnapped his 11-year-old son after stealing money, jewelry, one automobile, and two cell phones. The kidnappers demanded $1 million in ransom. On January 21, 1999, the kidnappers released the boy.

Colombian Pipeline Bombing, October 18, 1998:

A National Liberation Army (ELN) planted bomb exploded on the Ocensa pipeline in Antioquia Department, killing approximately 71 persons and injuring at least 100 others. The pipeline is jointly owned by the Colombia State Oil Company Ecopetrol and a consortium including U.S., French, British, and Canadian companies.

U.S. Embassy Bombings in East Africa, August 7, 1998:

A bomb exploded at the rear entrance of the U.S. Embassy in Nairobi, Kenya, killing 12 U.S. citizens, 32 Foreign Service Nationals (FSNs), and 247 Kenyan citizens. Approximately 5,000 Kenyans, 6 U.S. citizens, and 13 FSNs were injured. The U.S. Embassy building sustained extensive structural damage. Almost simultaneously, a bomb detonated outside the U.S. Embassy in Dar es Salaam, Tanzania, killing 7 FSNs and 3 Tanzanian citizens, and injuring 1 U.S. citizen and 76 Tanzanians. The explosion caused major structural damage to the U.S. Embassy facility. The U.S. Government held Osama bin Laden responsible.

Somali Hostage-takings, April 15, 1998:

Somali militiamen abducted nine Red Cross and Red Crescent workers at an airstrip north of Mogadishu. The hostages included a U.S. citizen, a German, a Belgian, a French, a Norwegian, two Swiss, and one Somali. The gunmen were members of a subclan loyal to Ali Mahdi Mohammed, who controlled the northern section of the capital.

FARC Abduction, March 21–23, 1998:

FARC rebels kidnapped a U.S. citizen in Sabaneta, Colombia. FARC members also killed 3 persons, wounded 14, and kidnapped at least 27 others at a roadblock near Bogota. Four U.S. citizens and one Italian were among those kidnapped, as well as the acting president of the National Electoral Council (CNE) and his wife.

Murder of U.S. Businessmen in Pakistan, November 12, 1997:

Two unidentified gunmen shot to death four U.S. auditors from Union Texas Petroleum Corporation and their Pakistani driver after they drove away from the Sheraton Hotel in Karachi. The Islami Inqilabi Council, or Islamic Revolutionary Council, claimed responsibility in a call to the U.S. Consulate in Karachi. In a letter to Pakistani newspapers, the Aimal Khufia Action Committee also claimed responsibility.

Yemeni Kidnappings, October 30, 1997:
Al-Sha'if tribesmen kidnapped a U.S. businessman near Sanaa. The tribesmen sought the release of two fellow tribesmen who were arrested on smuggling charges and several public works projects they claim the government promised them. They released the hostage on November 27.

Israeli Shopping Mall Bombing, September 4, 1997:
Three suicide bombers of HAMAS detonated bombs in the Ben Yehuda shopping mall in Jerusalem, killing eight persons, including the bombers, and wounding nearly 200 others. A dual U.S./Israeli citizen was among the dead, and 7 U.S. citizens were wounded.

Hotel Nacional Bombing, July 12, 1997:
A bomb exploded at the Hotel Nacional in Havana, injuring three persons and causing minor damage. A previously unknown group calling itself the Military Liberation Union claimed responsibility.

FARC Kidnapping, March 7, 1997:
FARC guerrillas kidnapped a U.S. mining employee and his Colombian colleague, who were searching for gold in Colombia. On November 16, the rebels released the two hostages after receiving a $50,000 ransom.

ELN Kidnapping, February 24, 1997:
National Liberation Army (ELN) guerrillas kidnapped a U.S. citizen employed by a Las Vegas gold corporation, who was scouting a gold mining operation in Colombia. The ELN demanded a ransom of $2.5 million.

Empire State Building Sniper Attack, February 23, 1997:
A Palestinian gunman opened fire on tourists at an observation deck atop the Empire State Building in New York City, killing a Danish national and wounding visitors from the United States, Argentina, Switzerland, and France before turning the gun on himself. A handwritten note carried by the gunman claimed this was a punishment attack against the "enemies of Palestine."

Venezuelan Abduction, February 14, 1997:
Six armed Colombian guerrillas kidnapped a U.S. oil engineer and his Venezuelan pilot in Apure, Venezuela. The kidnappers released the Venezuelan pilot on February 22. According to authorities, the FARC is responsible for the kidnapping.

Egyptian Letter Bombs, January 2–13, 1997:
A series of letter bombs with Alexandria, Egypt, postmarks were discovered at Al-Hayat newspaper bureaus in Washington, New York City, London, and Riyadh, Saudi Arabia. Three similar devices, also postmarked in Egypt, were found at a prison facility in Leavenworth, Kansas. Bomb disposal experts defused all the devices, but one detonated at the Al-Hayat office in London, injuring two security guards and causing minor damage.

Tupac Amaru Seizure of Diplomats, December 17, 1996:
Twenty-three members of the Tupac Amaru Revolutionary Movement (MRTA) took several hundred people hostage at a party given at the Japanese Ambassador's residence in Lima, Peru. Among the hostages were several U.S. officials, foreign ambassadors, and other diplomats, Peruvian Government officials, and Japanese businessmen. The group demanded

the release of all MRTA members in prison and safe passage for them and the hostage takers. The terrorists released most of the hostages in December but held 81 Peruvians and Japanese citizens for several months.

Abduction of US. Citizen by FARC, December 11, 1996:
Five armed men claiming to be members of the Revolutionary Armed Forces of Colombia (FARC) kidnapped and later killed a U.S. geologist at a methane gas exploration site in La Guajira Department.

Paris Subway Explosion, December 3, 1996:
A bomb exploded aboard a Paris subway train as it arrived at the Port Royal station, killing two French nationals, a Moroccan, and a Canadian and injuring 86 persons. Among those injured were one U.S. citizen and a Canadian. No one claimed responsibility for the attack, but Algerian extremists are suspected.

Red Cross Worker Kidnappings, November 1, 1996:
In Sudan a breakaway group from the Sudanese People's Liberation Army (SPLA) kidnapped three International Committee of the Red Cross (ICRC) workers, including a U.S. citizen, an Australian, and a Kenyan. On December 9 the rebels released the hostages in exchange for ICRC supplies and a health survey for their camp.

PUK Kidnapping, September 13, 1996:
In Iraq, Patriotic Union of Kurdistan (PUK) militants kidnapped four French workers for Pharmaciens Sans Frontieres, a Canadian United Nations High Commissioner for Refugees (UNHCR) official, and two Iraqis.

Sudanese Rebel Kidnapping, August 17, 1996:
Sudan People's Liberation Army (SPLA) rebels kidnapped six missionaries in Mapourdit, including a U.S. citizen, an Italian, three Australians, and a Sudanese. The SPLA released the hostages 11 days later.

Khobar Towers Bombing, June 25, 1996:
A fuel truck carrying a bomb exploded outside the U.S. military's Khobar Towers housing facility in Dhahran, killing 19 U.S. military personnel and wounding 515 persons, including 240 U.S. personnel. Several groups claimed responsibility for the attack.

Zekharya Attack, June 9, 1996:
Unidentified gunmen opened fire on a car near Zekharya, killing a dual U.S./Israeli citizen and an Israeli. The Popular Front for the Liberation of Palestine (PFLP) was suspected.

AID Worker Abduction, May 31, 1996:
A gang of former Contra guerrillas kidnapped a U.S. employee of the Agency for International Development (AID) who was assisting with election preparations in rural northern Nicaragua. She was released unharmed the next day after members of the international commission overseeing the preparations intervened.

West Bank Attack, May 13, 1996:
Arab gunmen opened fire on a bus and a group of Yeshiva students near the Bet El settlement, killing a dual U.S./Israeli citizen and wounding three Israelis. No one claimed responsibility for the attack, but HAMAS was suspected.

Dizengoff Center Bombing, March 4, 1996:
> HAMAS and the Palestine Islamic Jihad (PIJ) both claimed responsibility for a bombing outside Tel Aviv's largest shopping mall that killed 20 persons and injured 75 others, including 2 U.S. citizens.

HAMAS Bus Attack, February 26, 1996:
> In Jerusalem, a suicide bomber blew up a bus, killing 26 persons, including three U.S. citizens, and injuring some 80 persons, including three other U.S. citizens.

ELN Kidnapping, February 16, 1996:
> Six alleged National Liberation Army (ELN) guerrillas kidnapped a U.S. citizen in Colombia. After nine months, the hostage was released.

Athens Embassy Attack, February 15, 1996:
> Unidentified assailants fired a rocket at the U.S. Embassy compound in Athens, causing minor damage to three diplomatic vehicles and some surrounding buildings. Circumstances of the attack suggested it was an operation carried out by the 17 November group.

IRA Bombing, February 9, 1996:
> An Irish Republican Army (IRA) bomb detonated in London, killing 2 persons and wounding more than 100 others, including 2 U.S. citizens.

Tamil Tigers Attack, January 31, 1996:
> Members of the Liberation Tigers of Tamil Eelam (LTTE) rammed an explosives-laden truck into the Central Bank in the heart of downtown Colombo, Sri Lanka, killing 90 civilians and injuring more than 1,400 others, including 2 U.S. citizens.

Kidnapping in Colombia, January 19, 1996:
> Revolutionary Armed Forces of Colombia (FARC) guerrillas kidnapped a U.S. citizen and demanded a $1 million ransom. The hostage was released on May 22.

Saudi Military Installation Attack, November 13, 1995:
> The Islamic Movement of Change planted a bomb in a Riyadh military compound that killed one U.S. citizen, several foreign national employees of the U.S. government, and over 40 others.

Attack on U.S. Embassy in Moscow, September 13, 1995:
> A rocket-propelled grenade was fired through the window of the U.S. Embassy in Moscow, ostensibly in retaliation for U.S. strikes on Serb positions in Bosnia.

Jerusalem Bus Attack, August 21, 1995:
> HAMAS claimed responsibility for the detonation of a bomb that killed 6 and injured over 100 persons, including several U.S. citizens.

Kashmiri Hostage-taking, July 4, 1995:
> In India six foreigners, including two U.S. citizens, were taken hostage by Al-Faran, a Kashmiri separatist group. One non–U.S. hostage was later found beheaded.

Bombing of the Federal Building in Oklahoma City, April 19, 1995:
> Right-wing extremists Timothy McVeigh and Terry Nichols destroyed the Federal Building in Oklahoma City with a massive truck bomb that killed 166 and injured hundreds more in what was up to then the largest terrorist attack on American soil.

Attack on U.S. Diplomats in Pakistan, March 8, 1995:
> Two unidentified gunmen killed two U.S. diplomats and wounded a third in Karachi, Pakistan.

FARC Hostage-taking, September 23, 1994:
> FARC rebels kidnapped U.S. citizen Thomas Hargrove in Colombia.

Hebron Massacre, February 25, 1994:
> Jewish right-wing extremist and U.S. citizen Baruch Goldstein machine-gunned Moslem worshippers at a mosque in the West Bank town of Hebron, killing 29 and wounding about 150.

Attempted Assassination of President Bush by Iraqi Agents, April 14, 1993:
> The Iraqi intelligence service attempted to assassinate former U.S. President George Bush during a visit to Kuwait. In retaliation, the U.S. launched a cruise missile attack two months later on the Iraqi capital Baghdad.

World Trade Center Bombing, February 26, 1993:
> The World Trade Center in New York City was badly damaged when a car bomb planted by Islamic terrorists exploded in an underground garage. The bomb left 6 people dead and 1,000 injured. The men carrying out the attack were followers of Umar Abd al-Rahman, an Egyptian cleric who preached in the New York City area.

Source: U.S. Army—Timeline of Terrorism, Available on-line at http://www.army.mil/terrorism

in October 1993 and who killed 18 U.S. special operation forces in Mogadishu in October 1993, as depicted in the book and movie by the same title, *Black Hawk Down.*

Earlier that same year, Al Qaeda was involved in a more direct attack on the United States and its first on American soil. A growing body of information about central figures in the February 1993 bombing of the World Trade Center in New York City, particularly the reputed key bomb maker Ramzi Ahmad Yusef, suggests possible Al Qaeda involvement. As noted earlier, Abd Al-Rahman was convicted for plots related to this attack.

The next attack by Al Qaeda came in June of 1995, in Ethiopia, when operatives of Al Qaeda allegedly aided the Egyptian militant Islamic Group in a nearly successful assassination attempt against the visiting Egyptian President Hosni Mubarak. That fall, Al Qaeda would strike America in Saudi Arabia. The four Saudi nationals who confessed to a November 1995 bombing of a U.S. military advisory facility in Riyadh, Saudi Arabia, claimed on Saudi television to have been inspired by bin Laden. Five Americans were killed in that attack. In addition, it is commonly believed that another attack on Americans in Saudi Arabia that occurred the next year was also by Al Qaeda. Specifically, the 9/11 Commission report indicates that Al Qaeda might have had a hand in the June 1996 bombing of the Khobar Towers complex near Dhahran, Saudi Arabia, although FBI officials have attributed the attack primarily to Shiite Saudi dissidents working with Iranian agents. Nineteen U.S. airmen were killed.

The next attack that Al Qaeda is alleged to have been responsible for was the August 1998 bombings of U.S. embassies in Kenya and Tanzania, which killed about 300. On August 20, 1998, two weeks after the attacks, the United States launched a cruise missile strike against bin Laden's training camps in Afghanistan, reportedly missing him by a few hours. In July 1999 President Clinton imposed a ban on U.S. trade with Taliban-controlled Afghanistan and froze Taliban assets in the United States. Then, in December 1999, U.S. and Jordanian authorities separately thwarted related Al Qaeda plots against religious sites in Jordan and apparently against the Los Angeles International Airport. This prompted the issuance of UN Security Council Resolution 1333, on December 19, 2000, which banned any arms shipments or provision of military advice to the Taliban. The Clinton administration also pursued a number of covert operations against bin Laden during this same time frame of 1999–2000. Later, after President Bush entered the White House in January of 2001, nine months before the attacks of September 11th, his administration considered some new options, which included arming anti-Taliban opposition groups.[12]

The last significant attack by Al Qaeda before September 11th occurred in October 2000, when Al Qaeda activists attacked the USS *Cole* in a ship-borne suicide bombing while the *Cole* was docked at the harbor in Aden, Yemen. The ship was damaged, and 17 sailors were killed. The next attack and the bursting of the terrorism bubble came with the September 11, 2001, attacks. By this time, Al Qaeda had become a coalition of factions of radical Islamic groups operating throughout the Muslim world, mostly groups opposing their governments. Cells and associates have been located in over 70 countries, according to U.S. officials. Among the groups in the Al Qaeda coalition, virtually all of which are still active today, are the Islamic Group and Al Jihad (Egypt), the Armed Islamic Group and the Salafist Group for Call and Combat (Algeria), the Islamic Movement of Uzbekistan (IMU), the Jemaah Islamiyah (Indonesia), the Libyan Islamic Fighting Group (Libyan opposition), and Harakat ul-Majahedin (Pakistan, Kashmiri).

THE ATTACK: SEPTEMBER 11, 2001

Tuesday September 11 dawned temperate and nearly cloudless in the eastern United States.[13] Millions of men and women readied themselves for work. Some made their way to the Twin Towers, the signature structures of the World Trade Center complex in New York City. Others went to Arlington, Virginia, to the Pentagon. Across the Potomac River, the U.S. Congress was back in session. At the other end of Pennsylvania Avenue, people began to line up for a White House tour. In Sarasota, Florida, President George W. Bush went for an early morning run.

For those heading to an airport, weather conditions could not have been better for a safe and pleasant journey. Among the travelers were Mohamed Atta and Abdul Aziz al Omari, who arrived at the airport in Portland, Maine.

Boston: American 11 and United 175

Atta and Omari boarded a 6:00 a.m. flight from Portland to Boston's Logan International Airport.

When he checked in for his flight to Boston, Atta was selected by a computerized prescreening system known as CAPPS (Computer Assisted Passenger Prescreening System), created to identify passengers who should be subject to special security measures. Under security rules in place at the time, the only consequence of Atta's selection by

The Collapse of the World Trade Center Building, September 11, 2001. (*Source: AP Wide World Photos.*)

CAPPS was that his checked bags were held off the plane until it was confirmed that he had boarded the aircraft. This did not hinder Atta's plans.

Atta and Omari arrived in Boston at 6:45 a.m. Seven minutes later, Atta apparently took a call from Marwan al Shehhi, a longtime colleague, who was at another terminal at Logan Airport. They spoke for three minutes. It would be their final conversation.

Between 6:45 and 7:40, Atta and Omari, along with Satam al Suqami, Wail al Sherhi, and Waleed al Shehri, checked in and boarded American Airlines Flight 11, bound for Los Angeles. The flight was scheduled to depart at 7:45 a.m.

In another Logan terminal, Shehhi, joined by Fayez Banihammad, Mohand al Shehri, Ahmed al Ghamdi, and Hamza al Ghamdi, checked in for United Airlines Flight 175, also bound for Los Angeles. A couple of Shehhi's colleagues were obviously unused to travel; according to the United ticket agent, they had trouble understanding the standard security questions, and she had to go over them slowly until they gave the routine, reassuring answers. Their flight was scheduled to depart at 8:00 a.m.

The security checkpoints through which passengers, including Atta and his colleagues, gained access to the American 11 gate were operated by Globe Security under a contract with American Airlines. In a different terminal, the single checkpoint through which passengers for United 175 passed was controlled by United Airlines, which had contracted with Huntleigh USA to perform the screening.

In passing through these checkpoints, each of the hijackers would have been screened by a walk-through metal detector calibrated to detect items with at least the mental content of a .22 caliber handgun. Anyone who might have set off that detector would have been screened with a hand wand—a procedure requiring the screener to identify the metal item or items that caused the alarm. In addition, an X-ray machine would have screened the hijackers' carry-on belongings. The screening was in place to identify and confiscate weapons and other items prohibited from being carried onto a commercial flight. None of the checkpoint supervisors recalled the hijackers or reported anything suspicious regarding their screening.

As Atta had been selected by CAPPS in Portland, three members of his hijacking team—Suqami, Wail al Shehri, and Waleed al Shehri—were selected in Boston. Their selection affected only the handling of their checked bags, not their screening at the checkpoint. All five men cleared the checkpoint and made their way to the gate for American 11. Atta, Omari, and Suqami took their seats in business class. The Shehri brothers had adjacent seats in row 2, in the first-class cabin. They boarded American 11 between 7:31 and 7:40. The aircraft pushed back from the gate at 7:40.

Shehi and his team, none of whom had been selected by CAPPS, boarded United 175 between 7:23 and 7:28. Their aircraft pushed back from the gate just before 8:00.

Washington Dulles: America 77

Hundreds of miles southwest of Boston, at Dulles International Airport in the Virginia suburbs of Washington, D.C., five more men were preparing to take their early morning flight. At 7:15, a pair of them, Khalid al Mihdhar and Majed Moqed, checked in at the American Airlines ticket counter for Flight 77, bound for Los Angeles. Within the next 20 minutes, they would be followed by Hani Hanjour and two brothers, Nawaf al Hazmi and Salem al Hazmi.

Hani Hanjour, Khalid al Mihdhar, and Majed Moqed were flagged by CAPPS. The Hazmi brothers were also selected for extra scrutiny by the airline's customer service representative at the check-in counter. He did so because one of the brothers did not have photo identification nor could he understand English, and because the agent found both of the passengers to be suspicious. The only consequence of their selection was that their checked bags were held off the plane until it was confirmed that they had boarded the aircraft.

All five hijackers passed through the main terminal's west security screening checkpoint; United Airlines, which was the responsible air carrier, had contracted out the work to Argenbright Security. The checkpoint featured closed-circuit television that recorded all passengers, including the hijackers, as they were screened. At 7:18, Mihdhar and Moqed entered the security checkpoint.

Midhar and Moqed placed their carry-on bags on the belt of the X-ray machine and proceeded through the first metal detector. Both set off the alarm, and they were directed to a second metal detector. Mihdhar did not trigger the alarm and was permitted through the checkpoint. After Moqed set it off, a screener wanded him. He passed this inspection.

About 20 minutes later, at 7:35, another passenger for Flight 77, Hani Hanjour, placed two carry-on bags on the X-ray belt in the main terminal's west checkpoint and proceeded, without alarm, through the metal detector. A short time later, Nawaf and Salem al Hazmi entered the same checkpoint. Salem al Hazmi cleared the metal detector and was permitted through; Nawaf al Hazmi set off the alarms for both the first and second metal detectors and was then hand-wanded before being passed. In addition, his over-the-shoulder carry-on bag was swiped by an explosive trace detector and then passed. The video footage indicated that he was carrying an unidentified item in his back pocket, clipped to its rim.

When the local civil aviation security office of the Federal Aviation Administration (FAA) later investigated these security screening operations, the screeners recalled nothing out of the ordinary. They could not recall that any of the passengers they screened were CAPPS selectees. The 9/11 Commission asked a screening expert to review the videotape of the hand-wanding, and he found the quality of the screener's work to have been "marginal at best." The screener should have "resolved" what set off the alarm; and in the case of both Moqed and Hazmi, it was clear that he did not.

At 7:50, Majed Moqed and Khalid al Mihdhar boarded the flight and were seated in 12A and 12B coach. Hani Hanjour, assigned to seat 1B (first class), soon followed. The Hazmi brothers, sitting in 5E and 5F, joined Hanjour in the first-class cabin.

Newark: United 93

Between 7:03 and 7:39, Saeed al Ghamdi, Ahmed al Nami, Ahmad al Haznawi, and Ziad Jarrah checked in at the United Airlines ticket counter for Flight 93, going to Los Angeles. Two checked bags; two did not. Haznawi was selected by CAPPS. His checked bag was screened for explosives and then loaded on the plane.

The four men passed through the security checkpoint, owned by United Airlines and operated under contract by Argenbright Security. Like the checkpoints in Boston, it lacked closed-circuit television surveillance, so there is no documentary evidence to indicate when the hijackers passed through the checkpoint, what alarms may have been triggered, or what security procedures were administered. The FAA interviewed the screeners later; none recalled anything unusual or suspicious.

The four men boarded the plane between 7:39 and 7:48. All four had seats in the first-class cabin; their plane had no business-class section. Jarrah was in seat 1B, closest to the cockpit; Nami was in 3C, Ghamdi in 3D, and Haznawi in 6B.

The 19 men were aboard four transcontinental flights. They were planning to hijack these planes and turn them into large guided missiles, loaded with up to 11,400 gallons of jet fuel. By 8:00 a.m. on the morning of Tuesday, September 11, 2001, they had defeated all the security layers that America's civil aviation security system then had in place to prevent a hijacking.

The Hijacking of American 11

American Airlines Flight 11 provided nonstop service from Boston to Los Angeles. On September 11, Captain John Ogonowski and First Officer Thomas McGuinness piloted the Boeing 767. It carried its full capacity of nine flight attendants. Eighty-one passengers boarded the flight with them (including the five terrorists).

The plane took off at 7:59. Just before 8:14, it had climbed to 26,000 feet, not quite its initial assigned cruising altitude of 29,000 feet. All communications and flight profile data were normal. About this time the Fasten Seatbelt sign would usually have been turned off, and the flight attendants would have begun preparing for cabin service.

At that same time, American 11 had its last routine communication with the ground when it acknowledged navigational instructions from the FAA's air traffic control (ATC) center in Boston. Sixteen seconds after that transmission, ATC instructed the aircraft's pilots to climb to 35,000 feet. That message and all subsequent attempts to contact the flight were not acknowledged. From this and other evidence, the 9/11 Commission believes the hijacking began at 8:14 or shortly thereafter.

Reports from two flight attendants in the coach cabin, Betty Ong and Madeline "Amy" Sweeney, tell us most of what we know about how the hijacking happened. As it began, some of the hijackers—most likely Wail al Shehri and Waleed al Shehri, who were seated in row 2 in first class—stabbed the two unarmed flight attendants who would have been preparing for cabin services.

The 9/11 Commission does not know exactly how the hijackers gained access to the cockpit; FAA rules required that the doors remained closed and locked during flight. Ong speculated that they had "jammed their way" in. Perhaps the terrorists stabbed the flight attendants to get a cockpit key, to force one of them to open the cockpit door, or to lure the captain or first officer out of the cockpit. Or the flight attendants may just have been in their way.

At the same time or shortly thereafter, Atta—the only terrorist on board trained to fly a jet—would have moved to the cockpit from his business-class seat, possibly accompanied by Omari. As this was happening, passenger Daniel Lewin, who was seated in the row just behind Atta and Omari, was stabbed by one of the hijackers—probably Satam al Suqami, who was seated directly behind Lewin. Lewin had served four years as an officer in the Israeli military. He may have made an attempt to stop the hijackers in front of him, not realizing that another was sitting behind him.

The hijackers quickly gained control and sprayed Mace, pepper spray, or some other irritant in the first-class cabin to force the passengers and flight attendants toward the rear of the plane. They claimed they had a bomb.

About five minutes after the hijacking began, Betty Ong contacted the American Airlines Southeastern Reservations Office in Cary, North Carolina, via an AT&T airphone to report an emergency aboard the flight. This was the first of several occasions on 9/11 when flight attendants took action outside the scope of their training, which emphasized that in a hijacking they were to communicate with the cockpit crew. The emergency call lasted approximately 25 minutes, as Ong calmly and professionally relayed information about events taking place aboard the airplane to authorities on the ground.

At 8:19, Ong reported: "The cockpit is not answering, somebody's stabbed in business class—and I think there's Mace—that we can't breathe—I don't know, I think we're getting hijacked." She then told of the stabbings of the two flight attendants.

At 8:21, one of the American employees receiving Ong's call in North Carolina, Nydia Gonzalez, alerted the American Airlines operations center in Fort Worth, Texas, reaching Craig Marquis, the manager on duty. Marquis soon realized this was an emergency and instructed the airline's dispatcher responsible for the flight to contact the cockpit. At 8:23, the dispatcher tried unsuccessfully to contact the aircraft. Six minutes later, the air traffic control specialist in American's operation center contacted the FAA's Boston Air Traffic Control Center about the flight. The center was already aware of the problem.

Boston Center knew of a problem on the flight in part because just before 8:25 the hijackers had attempted to communicate with the passengers. The microphone was keyed, and immediately one of the hijackers said, "Nobody move. Everything will be okay. If you try to make any moves, you'll endanger yourself and the airplane. Just stay quiet." Air traffic controllers heard the transmission; Ong did not. The hijackers probably did not know how to operate the cockpit radio communication system correctly and thus inadvertently broadcast their message over the air traffic control channel instead of the cabin public-address channel. Also at 8:25, and again at 8:29, Amy Sweeney got through to the American Flight Services Office in Boston but was cut off after she reported someone was hurt aboard the flight. Three minutes later, Sweeney was reconnected to the office and began relaying updates to the manager, Michael Woodward.

At 8:26, Ong reported that the plane was "flying erratically." A minute later, Flight 11 turned south. American also began getting identifications of the hijackers, as Ong and then Sweeney passed on some of the seat numbers of those who had gained unauthorized access to the cockpit.

Sweeney calmly reported on her line that the plane had been hijacked; a man in first class had his throat slashed; two flight attendants had been stabbed—one was seriously hurt and was on oxygen whereas the other's wounds seemed minor; a doctor had been requested; the flight attendants were unable to contact the cockpit; and there was a bomb in the cockpit. Sweeney told Woodward that she and Ong were trying to relay as much information as they could to people on the ground.

At 8:38, Ong told Gonzalez that the plane was flying erratically again. Around this time Sweeney told Woodward that the hijackers were Middle Easterners, naming three of their seat numbers. One spoke very little English, and one spoke excellent English. The hijackers had gained entry to the cockpit, and she did not know how. The aircraft was in a rapid descent.

At 8:41, Sweeney told Woodward that passengers in coach were under the impression that there was a routine medical emergency in first class. Other flight attendants were busy at duties such as getting medical supplies while Ong and Sweeney were reporting the events.

At 8:41, in America's operations center, a colleague told Marquis that the air traffic controllers declared Flight 11 a hijacking and "think he's [American 11] headed toward Kennedy [airport in New York City]. They're moving everybody out of the way. They seem to have him on a primary radar. They seem to think that he is descending."

At 8:44, Gonzalez reported losing phone contact with Ong. About this same time Sweeney reported to Woodward, "Something is wrong. We are in a rapid descent . . . we are all over the place." Woodward asked Sweeney to look out the window to see if she could determine where they were. Sweeney responded: "We are flying low. We are flying very, very low. We are flying way too low." Seconds later she said, "Oh my God we are way too low." The phone call ended.

At 8:46:40, American 11 crashed into the North Tower of the World Trade Center in New York City. All on board, along with an unknown number of people in the tower, were killed instantly.

The Hijacking of United 175

United Airlines Flight 175 was scheduled to depart for Los Angeles at 8:00. Captain Victor Saracini and First Officer Michael Horrocks piloted the Boeing 767, which had seven flight attendants. Fifty-six passengers boarded the flight.

United 175 pushed back from its gate at 7:58 and departed Logan Airport at 8:14. By 8:33, it had reached its assigned cruising altitude of 31,000 feet. The flight attendants would have begun their cabin service.

The flight had taken off just as American 11 was being hijacked, and at 8:42 the United 175 flight crew completed their report on a "suspicious transmission" overheard from another plane (which turned out to have been Flight 11) just after takeoff. This was United 175's last communication with the ground.

The hijackers attacked sometime between 8:42 and 8:46. They used knives (as reported by two passengers and a flight attendant), Mace (reported by one passenger), and the threat of a bomb (reported by the same passenger). They stabbed members of the flight crew (reported by a flight attendant and one passenger). Both pilots had been killed (reported by one flight attendant). The eyewitness accounts came from calls made from the rear of the plane, from passengers originally seated further forward in the cabin, a sign that passengers and perhaps crew had been moved to the back of the aircraft. Given similarities to American 11 in hijacker seating and in eyewitness reports of tactics and weapons, as well as the contact between the presumed team leaders, Atta and Shehhi, the 9/11 Commission believes the tactics were similar on both flights.

The first operational evidence that something was abnormal on United 175 came at 8:47, when the aircraft changed beacon codes twice within a minute. At 8:51, the flight deviated from its assigned altitude, and a minute later New York air traffic controllers began repeatedly and unsuccessfully trying to contact it.

At 8:52, in Easton, Connecticut, a man named Lee Hanson received a phone call from his son Peter, a passenger on United 175. His son told him: "I think they've taken over the cockpit—An attendant has been stabbed—and someone else up front may have been killed. The plane is making strange moves. Call United Airlines—Tell them it's Flight 175, Boston to LA." Lee Hanson then called the Easton Police Department and relayed what he had heard.

Also at 8:52, a male flight attendant called a United office in San Francisco, reaching Marc Policastro. The flight attendant reported that the flight had been hijacked, both pilots had been killed, a flight attendant had been stabbed, and the hijackers were probably flying the plane. The call lasted about two minutes, after which Policastro and a colleague tried unsuccessfully to contact the flight.

At 8:58, the flight took a heading toward New York City.

At 8:59, Flight 175 passenger David Sweeney tried to call his wife, Julie. He left a message on their home answering machine that the plane had been hijacked. He then called his mother, Louise Sweeney, told her the flight had been hijacked, and added that the passengers were thinking about storming the cockpit to take control of the plane away from the hijackers.

At 9:00, Lee Hanson received a second call from his son Peter:

It's getting bad, Dad—A stewardess was stabbed—They seem to have knives and Mace—They said they have a bomb—It's getting very bad on the plane—Passengers are throwing up and getting sick—The plane is making jerky movements—I don't think the pilot is flying the plane—I think we are going down—I think they intend to go to Chicago or someplace and fly into a building—Don't worry, Dad—If it happens, it'll be very fast—My God, my God.

The call ended abruptly. Lee Hanson had heard a woman scream just before it cut off. He turned on a television, and in her home so did Louise Sweeney. Both then saw the second aircraft hit the World Trade Center.

At 9:03:11, United Airlines Flight 175 struck the South Tower of the World Trade Center. All on board, along with an unknown number of people in the tower, were killed instantly.

The Hijacking of American 77

American Airlines Flight 77 was scheduled to depart from Washington Dulles for Los Angeles at 8:10. The aircraft was a Boeing 757 piloted by Captain Charles F. Burlingame and First Officer David Charlebois. There were four flight attendants. On September 11, the flight carried 58 passengers.

American 77 pushed back from its gate at 8:09 and took off at 8:20. At 8:46, the flight reached its assigned cruising altitude of 35,000 feet. Cabin service would have begun. At 8:51, American 77 transmitted its last routine radio communication. The hijacking began between 8:51 and 8:54. As on American 11 and United 175, the hijackers used knives (reported by one passenger) and moved all the passengers (and possibly crew) to the rear of the aircraft (reported by one flight attendant and one passenger). Unlike the earlier flights, the Flight 77 hijackers were reported by a passenger to have box cutters. Finally, a passenger reported that an announcement had been made by the "pilot" that the plane had been hijacked. Neither of the firsthand accounts mentioned any stabbings or the threat or use of either a bomb or Mace, though both witnesses began the flight in the first-class cabin.

At 8:54, the aircraft deviated from its assigned course, turning south. Two minutes later the transponder was turned off, and even primary radar contact with the aircraft was lost. The Indianapolis Air Traffic Control Center repeatedly tried and failed to contact the aircraft. American Airlines dispatchers also tried, without success.

At 9:00, American Airlines Executive Vice President Gerald Arpey learned that communications had been lost with American 77. This was now the second American aircraft in trouble. He ordered all American Airlines flights in the Northeast that had not taken off to remain on the ground. Shortly before 9:10, suspecting that American 77 had been hijacked, American headquarters concluded that the second aircraft to hit the World Trade Center might have been Flight 77. After learning that United Airlines was missing a plane, American Airlines headquarters extended the ground stop nationwide.

At 9:12, Renee May called her mother, Nancy May, in Las Vegas. She said her flight was being hijacked by six individuals who had moved them to the rear of the plane. She asked her mother to alert American Airlines. Nancy May and her husband promptly did so.

At some point between 9:16 and 9:26, Barbara Olson called her husband, Ted Olson, the Solicitor General of the United States. She reported that the flight had been hijacked, and the hijackers had knives and box cutters. She further indicated that the hijackers were not aware of her phone call, and that they had put all the passengers in the back of the plane. About a minute into the conversation, the call was cut off. Solicitor General Olson tried unsuccessfully to reach Attorney General John Ashcroft.

Shortly after the first call, Barbara Olson reached her husband again. She reported that the pilot had announced that the flight had been hijacked, and she asked her husband what she should tell the captain to do. Ted Olson asked for her location and she replied that the aircraft was then flying over houses. Another passenger told her they were traveling northeast. The Solicitor General then informed his wife of the two previous hijackings and crashes. She did not display signs of panic and did not indicate any awareness of an impending crash. At that point, the second call was cut off.

At 9:29, the autopilot on American 77 was disengaged; the aircraft was at 7,000 feet and approximately 38 miles west of the Pentagon. At 9:32, controllers at the Dulles Terminal Radar Approach Control "observed a primary radar target tracking eastbound at a high rate of speed." This was later determined to have been Flight 77.

At 9:34, Ronald Reagan Washington National Airport advised the Secret Service of an unknown aircraft heading in the direction of the White House. American 77 was then 5 miles west-southwest of the Pentagon and began a 330-degree turn. At the end of the turn, it was descending through 2,200 feet, pointed toward the Pentagon and downtown Washington. The hijacker pilot then advanced the throttles to maximum power and dove toward the Pentagon.

At 9:37:46, American Airlines Flight 77 crashed into the Pentagon, traveling at approximately 530 miles per hour. All on board, as well as many civilian and military personnel in the building, were killed.

The Battle for United 93

At 8:42, United Airlines Flight 93 took off from Newark (New Jersey) Liberty International Airport bound for San Francisco. The aircraft was piloted by Captain Jason Dahl and First Officer Leroy Homer, and there were five flight attendants. Thirty-seven passengers,

BOX 1-3

REMARKS BY THE PRESIDENT AFTER TWO PLANES CRASH INTO WORLD TRADE CENTER EMMA BOOKER ELEMENTARY SCHOOL SARASOTA, FLORIDA SEPTEMBER 11, 2001, 9:30 A.M.

THE PRESIDENT: Ladies and gentlemen, this is a difficult moment for America. I, unfortunately, will be going back to Washington after my remarks. Secretary Rod Paige and the Lt. Governor will take the podium and discuss education. I do want to thank the folks here at Booker Elementary School for their hospitality.

Today we've had a national tragedy. Two airplanes have crashed into the World Trade Center in an apparent terrorist attack on our country. I have spoken to the Vice President, to the Governor of New York, to the Director of the FBI, and have ordered that the full resources of the federal government go to help the victims and their families, and to conduct a full-scale investigation to hunt down and to find those folks who committed this act.

Terrorism against our nation will not stand.

And now if you would join me in a moment of silence. May God bless the victims, their families, and America. Thank you very much.

including the hijackers, boarded the plane. Scheduled to depart the gate at 8:00, the Boeing 757's takeoff was delayed because of the airport's typically heavy morning traffic.

The hijackers had planned to take flights scheduled to depart at 7:45 (American 11), 8:00 (United 175 and United 93), and 8:10 (American 77). Three of the flights had actually taken off within 10 to 15 minutes of their planned departure times. United 93 would ordinarily have taken off about 15 minutes after pulling away from the gate. When it left the ground at 8:42, the flight was running more than 25 minutes late.

As United 93 left Newark, the flight's crew members were unaware of the hijackings of American 11. Around 9:00, the FAA, American, and United were facing the staggering realization of apparent multiple hijackings. At 9:03, they would see another aircraft strike the World Trade Center. Crisis managers at the FAA and the airlines did not yet act to warn other aircraft. At the same time, Boston Center realized that a message transmitted just before 8:25 by the hijacker pilot of American 11 included the phrase, "We have some planes."

No one at the FAA or the airlines that day had ever dealt with multiple hijackings. Such a plot had not been carried out anywhere in the world in more than 30 years, and never in the United States. As news of the hijackings filtered through the FAA and the airlines, it does not seem to have occurred to their leadership that they needed to alert other aircraft in the air that they too might be at risk.

United 175 was hijacked between 8:42 and 8:46, and awareness of that hijacking began to spread after 8:51. American 77 was hijacked between 8:51 and 8:54. By 9:00, the FAA and airline officials began to comprehend that attackers were going after multiple aircraft. American Airlines' nationwide ground stop between 9:05 and 9:10 was followed by a United Airlines ground stop. FAA controllers at Boston Center, which had tracked the first two hijackings, requested at 9:07 that Herndon Command Center "get messages to airborne aircraft to increase security for the cockpit." There is no evidence that Herndon took such action. Boston Center immediately began speculating about other aircraft that might be in danger, leading them to worry about a transcontinental flight—Delta 1989—that in fact was not hijacked. At 9:19, the FAA's New England regional office called Herndon and asked that Cleveland Center advise Delta 1989 to use extra cockpit security.

Several FAA air traffic control officials told the 9/11 Commission that it was the air carrier's responsibility to notify their planes of security problems. One senior FAA air traffic control manager said that it was simply not the FAA's place to order the airlines what to tell their pilots. The Commission believes that such statements did not reflect an adequate appreciation of the FAA's responsibility for the safety and security of civil aviation.

The airlines bore responsibility, too. They were facing an escalating number of conflicting and, for the most part, erroneous reports about other flights, as well as a continuing lack of vital information from the FAA about the hijacked flights. The 9/11 Commission found no evidence, however, that American Airlines sent any cockpit warnings to its aircraft that day. United's first decisive action to notify its airborne aircraft to take defensive action did not come until 9:19, when a United flight dispatcher, Ed Ballinger, took the initiative to begin transmitting warnings to his 16 transcontinental flights: "Beware any cockpit intrusions—Two a/c (aircraft) hit World Trade Center." One of the flights that received the warning was United 93. Because Ballinger was still responsible for his other flights as well as Flight 175, his warning message was not transmitted to Flight 93 until 9:23.

By all accounts, the first 46 minutes of Flight 93's cross-country trip proceeded routinely. Radio communications from the plane were normal. Heading, speed, and altitude ran according to plan. At 9:24, Ballinger's warning to United 93 was received in the cockpit. Within two minutes, at 9:26, the pilot, Jason Dahl, responded with a note of puzzlement: "Ed, confirm latest mssg plz—Jason."

The hijackers attacked at 9:28. While traveling 35,000 feet above eastern Ohio, United 93 suddenly dropped 700 feet. Eleven seconds into the descent, the FAA's air traffic control center in Cleveland received the first of two radio transmissions from the aircraft. During the first broadcast, the captain or first officer could be heard declaring "Mayday" amid the sounds of a physical struggle in the cockpit. The second radio transmission, 35 seconds later, indicated that the fight was continuing. The captain or first officer could be heard shouting: "Hey get out of here—get out of here—get out of here."

On the morning of 9/11, there were only 37 passengers on United 93—33 in addition to the 4 hijackers. This was below the norm for Tuesday mornings during the summer of 2001. But there is no evidence that the hijackers manipulated passenger levels or purchased additional seats to facilitate their operation.

The terrorists who hijacked three other commercial flights on 9/11 operated in five-man teams. They initiated their cockpit takeover within 30 minutes of takeoff. On Flight 93, however, the takeover took place 46 minutes after takeoff, and there were only four hijackers. The operative likely intended to round out the team for this flight, Mohamed al Kahtani, had been refused entry by a suspicious immigration inspector at Florida's Orlando International Airport in August.

Because several passengers on United 93 described three hijackers on the plane, not four, some have wondered whether one of the hijackers had been able to use the cockpit jump seat from the outset of the flight. FAA rules allow use of this seat by documented and approved individuals, usually air carrier or FAA personnel. The 9/11 Commission found no evidence indicating that one of the hijackers, or anyone else, sat there on this flight. All the hijackers had assigned seats in first class, and they seem to have used them. It is more likely that Jarrah, the crucial pilot-trained member of their team, remained seated and inconspicuous until after the cockpit was seized; and once inside, he would not have been visible to the passengers.

At 9:32, a hijacker, probably Jarrah, made or attempted to make the following announcement to the passengers of Flight 93: "Ladies and Gentlemen: Here the captain, please sit down keep remaining sitting. We have a bomb on board. So, sit." The flight data recorder (also recovered) indicates that Jarrah then instructed the plane's autopilot to turn the aircraft around and head east.

The cockpit voice recorder data indicate that a woman, most likely a flight attendant, was being held captive in the cockpit. She struggled with one of the hijackers who killed or otherwise silenced her.

Shortly thereafter, the passengers and flight crew began a series of calls from GTE airphones and cellular phones. These calls between family, friends, and colleagues took place until the end of the flight and provided those on the ground with firsthand accounts. They enabled the passengers to gain critical information, including the news that two aircraft had slammed into the World Trade Center.

At 9:39, the FAA's Cleveland Air Route Traffic Control Center overheard a second announcement indicating that there was a bomb on board, that the plane was returning to the airport, and that passengers should remain seated. Although it apparently was not heard by the passengers, this announcement, like those on Flight 11 and Flight 77, was intended to deceive them. Jarrah, like Atta earlier, may have inadvertently broadcast the message because he did not know how to operate the radio and the intercom. To the 9/11 Commission's knowledge, none of them had ever flown an actual airliner before.

At least two callers from the flight reported that the hijackers knew that passengers were making calls but did not seem to care. It is quite possible Jarrah knew of the success of the assault on the World Trade Center. He could have learned of this from messages being sent by United Airlines to the cockpits of its transcontinental flights, including Flight 93, warning of cockpit intrusion and telling of the New York attacks. But even without them, he would have certainly understood that the attacks on the World Trade Center would already have unfolded, given Flight 93's tardy departure from Newark. If Jarrah did know that the passengers were making calls, it might not have occurred to him that they were certain to learn what had happened in New York, thereby defeating his attempts at deception.

At least 10 passengers and 2 crew members shared vital information with family, friends, colleagues, or others on the ground. All understood the plane had been hijacked. They said the hijackers wielded knives and claimed to have a bomb. The hijackers were wearing red bandanas, and they forced the passengers to the back of the aircraft.

Callers reported that a passenger had been stabbed and that two people were lying on the floor of the cabin, injured or dead—possibly the captain and first officer. One caller reported that a flight attendant had been killed.

One of the callers from United 93 also reported that he thought the hijackers might possess a gun. But none of the other callers reported the presence of a firearm. One recipient of a call from the aircraft recounted specifically asking her caller whether the hijackers had guns. The passenger replied that he did not see one. No evidence of firearms or of their identifiable remains were found at the aircraft's crash site, and the cockpit voice recorder gives no indication of a gun being fired or mentioned at any time. The 9/11 Commission believes that if the hijackers had possessed a gun, they would have used it in the flight's last minutes as the passengers fought back.

Passengers on three flights reported the hijackers' claim of having a bomb. The FBI told the 9/11 Commission they found no trace of explosives at the crash sites. One of the passengers who mentioned a bomb expressed his belief that it was not real. Lacking any evidence that the hijackers attempted to smuggle such illegal items past the security screening checkpoints, the 9/11 Commission believes the bombs were probably fake.

During at least five of the passengers' phone calls, information was shared about the attacks that had occurred earlier that morning at the World Trade Center. Five calls described the intent of passengers and surviving crew members to revolt against the hijackers. According to one call, they voted on whether to rush the terrorists in an attempt to retake the plane. They decided and acted.

At 9:57, the passenger assault began. Several passengers had terminated phone calls with loved ones to join the revolt. One of the callers ended her message as follows: "Everyone's running up to first class, I've got to go. Bye."

The cockpit voice recorder captured the sounds of the passenger assault muffled by the intervening cockpit door. Some family members who listened to the recording report that they could hear the voice of a loved one among the din. The 9/11 Commission could not identify whose voices can be heard. But the assault was sustained.

In response, Jarrah immediately began to roll the airplane to the left and right, attempting to knock the passengers off balance. At 9:58:57, Jarrah told another hijacker in the cockpit to block the door. Jarrah continued to roll the airplane sharply left and right, but the assault continued. At 9:59:52, Jarrah changed tactics and pitched the nose of the airplane up and down to disrupt the assault. The recorder captured the sounds of loud thumps, crashes, shouts, and breaking glasses and plates. At 10:00:03, Jarrah stabilized the airplane.

Five seconds later, Jarrah asked, "Is that it? Shall we finish it off?" A hijacker responded, "No. Not yet. When they all come, we finish it off." The sounds of fighting continued outside the cockpit. Again, Jarrah pitched the nose of the aircraft up and down. At 10:00:26, a passenger in the background said, "In the cockpit. If we don't we'll die!" Sixteen seconds later, a passenger yelled, "Roll it." Jarrah stopped the violent maneuvers at about 10:01:00 and said, "Allah is the greatest! Allah is the greatest!" He then asked another hijacker in the cockpit, "Is that it? I mean, shall we put it down?" to which the other replied, "Yes, put it in it, and pull it down."

The passengers continued their assault and at 10:02:03, a hijacker said, "Pull it down! Pull it down!" The hijackers remained at the controls but must have judged that the passengers were only seconds from overcoming them. The airplane headed down; the control wheel was turned hard to the right. The airplane rolled onto its back, and one of the hijackers began shouting, "Allah is the greatest! Allah is the greatest!" With the sounds of the

BOX 1-4

REMARKS BY THE PRESIDENT UPON ARRIVAL AT BARKSDALE AIR FORCE BASE, LOUISIANA

THE PRESIDENT: I want to reassure the American people that the full resources of the federal government are working to assist local authorities to save lives and to help the victims of these attacks. Make no mistake: The United States will hunt down and punish those responsible for these cowardly acts.

I've been in regular contact with the Vice President, the Secretary of Defense, the national security team and my Cabinet. We have taken all appropriate security precautions to protect the American people. Our military at home and around the world is on high alert status, and we have taken the necessary security precautions to continue the functions of your government.

We have been in touch with the leaders of Congress and with world leaders to assure them that we will do whatever is necessary to protect America and Americans.

I ask the American people to join me in saying a thanks for all the folks who have been fighting hard to rescue our fellow citizens and to join me in saying a prayer for the victims and their families.

The resolve of our great nation is being tested. But make no mistake: We will show the world that we will pass this test. God bless.

passenger counterattack continuing, the aircraft plowed into an empty field in Shanksville, Pennsylvania, at 580 miles per hour, about 20 minutes' flying time from Washington, D.C.

Jarrah's objective was to crash his airliner into symbols of the American Republic, the Capitol or the White House. He was defeated by the alerted unarmed passengers of United 93.

THE RESPONSE: SEPTEMBER 11, 2001

New York, NY

The World Trade Center (WTC) complex was built for the Port Authority of New York and New Jersey.[14] Construction began in 1966, and tenants began to occupy its space in 1970. The Twin Towers came to occupy a unique and symbolic place in the culture of New York City and America.

The WTC actually consisted of seven buildings, including one hotel, spread across 16 acres of land. The buildings were connected by an underground mall (the concourse). The Twin Towers (1 WTC, or the North Tower, and 2 WTC, or the South Tower) were the signature structures, containing 10.4 million square feet of office space. Both towers had 110 stories, were about 1,350 feet high, and were square; each wall measured 208 feet in length. On any given workday, up to 50,000 office workers occupied the towers, and 40,000 people passed through the complex.

In New York City, the city government had ready at their disposal a number of plans for critical incidents that may have potentially occurred in the city, with the Office of Emergency Management and Interagency Preparedness (OEM) established to coordinate the workings of such agencies as the New York Police Department (NYPD), the Port Authority Police Department (PAPD), and the Fire Department of New York (FDNY). In 1996 Mayor Rudolph Giuliani created the Mayor's Office of Emergency Management, which had three basic functions. First, OEM's Watch Command was to monitor the city's key communications channels—including radio frequencies of FDNY dispatch and the NYPD—and other data. A second purpose of the OEM was to improve New York City's response to major incidents, including terrorist attacks, by planning and conducting exercises and drills that would involve multiple city agencies, particularly the NYPD and the FDNY. Third, the OEM would play a crucial role in managing the city's overall response to an incident. After OEM's Emergency Operations Center was activated, designated liaisons from relevant agencies, as well as the mayor and his or her senior staff, would respond there. In addition, an OEM field responder would be sent to the scene to ensure that the response was coordinated.

The OEM's headquarters was located at 7 WTC. Some questioned locating it both so close to a previous terrorist target (the 1993 bombing) and on the 23rd floor of a building (difficult to access should elevators become inoperable). There was no backup site. The site was activated shortly after the first plane hit the North Tower. However, after the South Tower was hit, an evacuation order was issued. Prior to its evacuation, no outside agency liaisons had reached OEM.

The NYPD on September 11 stood at 40,000 police officers and was led by Police Commissioner Bernard Kerik, whose duties were not primarily operational but who retained operational authority. Much of the NYPD's operational activities were run by the chief of department. In the event of a major emergency, a leading role would be played by the Special Operations Division. This division included the Aviation Unit, which provided helicopters for surveys and rescues, and the Emergency Services Unit (ESU), which carried out specialized rescue missions. The NYPD had specific and detailed standard operating procedures for the dispatch of officers to an incident's depending on the incident's magnitude.

The Port Authority of New York and New Jersey Police Department consisted of 1,331 officers, many of whom were trained in fire suppression methods as well as in law enforcement. The PAPD was led by a superintendent. There was a separate PAPD command for each of the Port Authority's nine facilities, including the World Trade Center.

As of September 11, the Port Authority lacked any standard operating procedures to govern how officers from multiple commands would respond to and then be staged and utilized at a major incident at the WTC. In particular, there were no standard operating procedures covering how different commands should communicate via radio during such an incident.

At 8:46:40, the hijacked American Airlines Flight 11 flew into the upper portion of the North Tower, cutting through floors 93 to 99. Within minutes, New York City's 911 system was flooded with eyewitness accounts of the events. Most callers correctly identified the target of the attack. Some identified the plane as a commercial airliner.

Numerous NYPD officers saw the plane strike the North Tower and immediately reported it to NYPD communications dispatchers.

At 8:58, while en route, the NYPD Chief of Department raised the NYPD's mobilization to level 4, thereby sending to the WTC approximately 22 lieutenants, 100 sergeants, and 800 police officers from all over the city. The Chief of Department arrived at Church and Vesey at 9:00.

At 9:01, the NYPD patrol mobilization point was moved to West and Vesey to handle the greater number of patrol officers dispatched in the higher-level mobilization. These officers would be stationed around the perimeter of the complex to direct the evacuation of civilians. Many were diverted on the way to the scene by intervening emergencies related to the attack.

At 8:50, the Aviation Unit of the NYPD dispatched two helicopters to the WTC to report on conditions and assess the feasibility of a rooftop landing or of special rescue operations. En route, the two helicopters communicated with air traffic controllers at the area's three major airports and informed them of the commercial airplane crash at the World Trade Center. The air traffic controllers had been unaware of the incident.

At 8:56, an NYPD ESU team asked to be picked up at the Wall Street heliport to initiate rooftop rescues. At 8:58, however, after assessing the North Tower roof, a helicopter pilot advised the ESU team that they could not land on the roof because "it is engulfed in flames and heavy smoke conditions."

Two on-duty NYPD officers were on the 20th floor of the North Tower at this time. They climbed to the 29th floor, urging civilians to evacuate, but did not locate a group of civilians trapped on the 22nd floor.

Just before 9:00, an ESU team began to walk from Church and Vesey to the North Tower lobby, with the goal of climbing toward and setting up a triage center on the upper floors for the severely injured. A second ESU team would follow them to assist in removing those individuals.

Numerous officers responded to help injured civilians and to urge those who could walk to vacate the area immediately. Putting themselves in danger of falling debris, several officers entered the plaza and successfully rescued at least one injured, nonambulatory civilian, and attempted to rescue others.

Also by about 9:00, transit officers began shutting down subway stations in the vicinity of the World Trade Center and evacuating civilians from those stations.

Around the city, the NYPD cleared major thoroughfares for emergency vehicles to access the WTC. The NYPD and PAPD coordinated the closing of bridges and tunnels into Manhattan.

The Port Authority's on-site commanding police officer was standing in the concourse when a fireball erupted out of elevator shafts and exploded onto the mall concourse, causing him to dive for cover. The on-duty sergeant initially instructed the officers in the WTC Command to meet at the police desk in 5 WTC. Soon thereafter, he instructed officers arriving from outside commands to meet him at the fire safety desk in the North Tower lobby. A few of these officers from outside commands were given WTC Command radios.

One Port Authority police officer at the WTC immediately began climbing stairwell C in the North Tower. Other officers began performing rescue and evacuation operations on the ground floors and in the PATH (Port Authority Trans-Hudson) station below the WTC complex.

Within minutes of impact, Port Authority police officers from the PATH, bridges, tunnels, and airport commands began responding to the WTC. The PAPD lacked written standard operating procedures for personnel responding from outside commands to the WTC during a major incident. In addition, officers from some PAPD commands lacked interoperable radio frequencies. As a result, there was no comprehensive coordination of PAPD's overall response.

At 9:00, the PAPD commanding officer of the WTC ordered an evacuation of all civilians in the World Trade Center complex because of the magnitude of the calamity in the North Tower. Also, at 9:00, the PAPD Superintendent and Chief of Department arrived separately and made their way to the North Tower.

In the 17-minute period between 8:46 and 9:03 a.m. on September 11, New York City and the Port Authority of New York and New Jersey had mobilized the largest rescue operation in the city's history. Well over a thousand first responders had been deployed, an evacuation had begun, and the critical decision that the fire could not be fought had been made. Then the second plane hit.

At 9:03:11, the hijacked United Airlines Flight 175 hit WTC (the South Tower) from the south, crashing through the 77th to 85th floors. What had been the largest and most complicated rescue operation in city history instantly doubled in magnitude.

Immediately after the second plane hit, the Chief of Department of the NYPD ordered a second Level 4 mobilization, bringing the total number of NYPD officers responding to close to 2,000.

The NYPD Chief of Department called for Operation Omega, which required the protection of sensitive locations around the city. NYPD headquarters were secured, and all other government buildings were evacuated.

The ESU command post at Church and Vesey streets coordinated all NYPD ESU rescue teams. After the South Tower was hit, the ESU officer running this command post decided to send one ESU team (each with approximately six police officers) up each of the Twin Towers' stairwells. While he continued to monitor the citywide SOD channel, which NYPD helicopters were using, he also monitored the point-to-point tactical channel that the ESU teams climbing in the towers would use.

Initial responders from outside PAPD commands proceeded to the police desk in 5 WTC or to the fire safety desk in the North Tower lobby. Some officers were then assigned to assist in stairwell evacuations; others were assigned to expedite evacuation in the plaza, concourse, and PATH station. As information was received of civilians trapped above ground-level floors of the North Tower, other PAPD officers were instructed to climb to those floors for rescue efforts. Still others began climbing toward the impact zone.

At 9:11, the PAPD superintendent and an inspector began walking up stairwell B of the North Tower to assess damage near and in the impact zone. The PAPD chief and several other PAPD officers began ascending a stairwell to reach the Windows on the World restaurant on the 106th floor, from which calls had been made to the PAPD desk reporting at least 100 people trapped.

The first NYPD ESU team entered the West Street–level lobby of the North Tower and prepared to begin climbing at about 9:15 a.m. They attempted to check in with the FDNY chiefs present, but were rebuffed. OEM personnel did not intervene. The ESU team began to climb the stairs. Shortly thereafter, a second NYPD ESU team entered the South Tower. The OEM field responder present ensured that they check in with the FDNY chief in charge of the lobby, as it was agreed that the ESU team would ascend and support FDNY personnel.

Many PAPD officers from different commands responded on their own initiative. By 9:03, the PAPD central police desk requested that responding officers meet at West and Vesey and await further instructions. In the absence of a predetermined command structure to deal with an incident of this magnitude, a number of PAPD inspectors, captains, and lieutenants stepped forward at around 9:30 to formulate an on-site response plan. They were hampered by not knowing how many officers were responding to the site and where those officers were operating. Many of the officers who responded to this command post lacked suitable protective equipment to enter the complex.

At 9:37, a civilian on the 106th floor of the South Tower reported to a 911 operated that a lower floor—the "90-something floor"—was collapsing. This information was conveyed inaccurately by the 911 operator to an NYPD dispatcher. The dispatcher further confused the substance of the 911 call by telling NYPD officers at the WTC complex that "the 106th floor is crumbling" at 9:52, 15 minutes after the 911 call was placed. The NYPD dispatcher conveyed this message on the radio frequency used in precincts in the vicinity of the WTC and subsequently on the Special Operations Division channel, but not on City Wide channel 1.

A third ESU team subsequently entered the North Tower at its elevated mezzanine lobby level and made no effort to check in with the FDNY command post. A fourth ESU team entered the South Tower. By 9:59, a fifth ESU team was next to 6 WTC and preparing to enter the North Tower.

By approximately 9:50, the officer running the ESU command post on Church and Vesey streets had a final radio communication with one of the ESU teams in the South Tower. The team then stated that it was ascending via stairs, was somewhere in the 20s, and was making slow progress because of the numerous descending civilians crowding the stairwell.

Three plainclothes NYPD officers without radios or protective gear had begun ascending either stairwell A or C of the North Tower. They began checking every other floor above the 12th for civilians. Only occasionally did they find any, and in those few cases they ordered the civilians to evacuate immediately. While checking floors, they used office phones to call their superiors. In one phone call an NYPD chief instructed them to leave the North Tower, but they refused to do so. As they climbed higher, they encountered increasing smoke and heat. Shortly before 10:00 they arrived on the 54th floor.

By 9:58, one PAPD officer had reached the 44th floor sky lobby of the North Tower. Also in the North Tower, one team of PAPD officers was in the mid-20s and another was in the lower 20s. Numerous PAPD officers were also climbing in the South Tower, including the PAPD ESU team. Many PAPD officers were on the ground floor of the complex—some assisting in evacuation, others manning the PAPD desk in 5 WTC or assisting at lobby command posts.

Throughout this period (9:03 to 9:59), a group of NYPD and Port Authority police officers, as well as two Secret Service agents, continued to assist civilians leaving the North Tower. They were positioned around the mezzanine lobby level of the North Tower, directing civilians leaving stairwells A and C to evacuate down an escalator to the concourse. The officers instructed those civilians who seemed composed to evacuate the complex calmly but rapidly. Other civilians exiting the stairs, who were either injured or exhausted, collapsed at the foot of these stairs; officers then assisted them out of the building.

When civilians reached the concourse, another NYPD officer stationed at the bottom of the escalator directed them to exit through the concourse to the north and east and then out of the WTC complex. This exit route ensured that civilians would not be endangered by falling debris and people on West Street, on the plaza between the towers, and on Liberty Street.

Some officers positioned themselves at the top of a flight of stairs by 5 WTC that led down into the concourse, going into the concourse when necessary to evacuate injured or disoriented civilians. Numerous other NYPD officers were stationed throughout the concourse, assisting burned, injured and disoriented civilians, as well as directing all civilians to exit to the north and east. NYPD officers were also in the South Tower lobby to assist in civilian evacuation. NYPD officers stationed on Vesey Street between West Street and Church Street urged civilians not to remain in the area and instead to keep walking north.

At 9:58:59, the South Tower collapsed in 10 seconds, killing all civilians and emergency personnel inside, as well as a number of individuals—both first responders and civilians—in the concourse, in the Marriott, and on neighboring streets. The building collapsed into itself, causing a ferocious windstorm and creating a massive debris cloud. The Marriott Hotel suffered signficant damage as a result of the collapse of the South Tower.

A member of the NYPD Aviation Unit radioed that the South Tower had collapsed immediately after it happened and further advised that all people in the WTC complex and nearby areas should be evacuated. At 10:04, NYPD aviation reported that the top 15 stories of the North Tower "were glowing red" and that they might collapse. At 10:08, a helicopter pilot warned that he did not believe the North Tower would last much longer.

Immediately after the South Tower collapsed, many NYPD radio frequencies became overwhelmed with transmissions relating to injured, trapped, or missing officers. As a result, NYPD radio communications became strained on most channels. Nevertheless, they remained effective enough for the two closest NYPD mobilization points to be moved further from the WTC at 10:06.

Just like most firefighters, the ESU rescue teams in the North Tower had no idea that the South Tower had collapsed. However, by 10:00 the ESU officer running the command post at Church and Vesey ordered the evacuation of all ESU units from the WTC complex. This officer, who had observed the South Tower collapse, reported it to ESU units in the North Tower in his evacuation instructions.

This instruction was clearly heard by the two ESU units already in the North Tower and the other ESU unit preparing to enter the tower. The ESU team on the 31st floor found the full collapse of the South Tower so unfathomable that they radioed back to the ESU officer at the command post and asked him to repeat his communication. He reiterated his urgent message.

The ESU team on the 31st floor conferred with the FDNY personnel there to ensure that they, too, knew that they had to evacuate, then proceeded down stairwell B. During the descent, they reported seeing many firefighters who were resting and did not seem to be in the process of evacuating. They further reported advising these firefighters to evacuate, but said that at times they were not acknowledged. In the opinion of one of the ESU officers, some of these firefighters essentially refused to take orders from cops. At least one firefighter who was in the North Tower has supported this assessment, stating that he was not going to take an evacuation instruction from a cop that morning. However, another firefighter reports that ESU officers ran past him without advising him to evacuate.

The ESU team on the 11th floor began descending stairwell C after receiving the evacuation order. Once near the mezzanine level—where stairwell C ended—this team spread out in chain formation, stretching from several floors down to the mezzanine itself. They used their flashlights to provide a path of beacons through the darkness and debris for civilians climbing down the stairs. Eventually, when no one else appeared to be descending, the ESU team exited the North Tower and ran one at a time to 6 WTC, dodging those who still were jumping from the upper floors of the North Tower by acting as spotters for each other. They remained in the area, conducting additional searches for civilians; all but two of them died.

After surviving the South Tower's collapse, the ESU team that had been preparing to enter the North Tower spread into chain formation and created a path for civilians (who had exited from the North Tower mezzanine) to evacuate the WTC complex by descending the stairs on the north side of 5 and 6 WTC, which led down to Vesey Street. They remained at this post until the North Tower collapsed, yet all survived.

The three plainclothes NYPD officers who had made it up to the 54th floor of the North Tower felt the building shake violently at 9:59 as the South Tower collapsed (although they did not know the cause). Immediately thereafter, they were joined by three firefighters from an FDNY engine company. One of the firefighters apparently heard an evacuation order on his radio, but responded in a return radio communication, "We're not fucking coming out!" However, the firefighters urged the police officers to descend because they lacked the protective gear and equipment needed to handle the increasing smoke and heat. The police officers reluctantly began descending, checking that the lower floors were clear of civilians. They proceeded down stairwell B, poking their heads into every floor and briefly looking for civilians.

Other NYPD officers helping evacuees on the mezzanine level of the North Tower were enveloped in the debris cloud that resulted from the South Tower's collapse. They struggled to regroup in the darkness and to evacuate both themselves and civilians they encountered. At least one of them died in the collapse of the North Tower. At least one NYPD officer from this area managed to evacuate out of 5 WTC, where he teamed up with a Port Authority police officer and acted as a spotter in advising the civilians who were still exiting when they could safely run from 1 WTC to 5 WTC and avoid being struck by people and debris falling from the upper floors.

At the time of the collapse of the South Tower, there were numerous NYPD officers in the concourse, some of whom are believed to have died there. Those who survived struggled to evacuate themselves in darkness, assisting civilians as they exited the concourse in all directions.

The North Tower collapsed at 10:28:25 a.m., killing all civilians alive on upper floors, an undetermined number below, and scores of first responders. The FDNY Chief of Department, the Port Authority Police Department Superintendent, and many of their senior staff were killed. Incredibly, 12 firefighters, 1 PAPD officer and 3 civilians who were descending stairwell B of the North Tower survived its collapse.

On September 11, the nation suffered the largest loss of life—2,973—on its soil as a result of hostile attack in its history. The FDNY suffered 343 fatalities—the largest loss of life of any emergency response agency in history. The PAPD suffered 37 fatalities—the largest loss of life of any police force in history. The NYPD suffered 23 fatalities—the second-largest loss of life of any police force in history, exceeded only by the number of PAPD officers lost the same day.

Mayor Guiliani, along with the Police and Fire commissioners and the OEM director, moved quickly north and established an emergency operations command post at the Police Academy. Over the coming hours, weeks, and months, thousands of civilians and city, state, and federal employees devoted themselves around the clock to putting New York City back on its feet.

Arlington, VA

At 9:37 a.m., the west wall of the Pentagon was hit by hijacked American Airlines Flight 77, a Boeing 757. The crash caused immediate and catastrophic damage. All 64 people aboard the airliner were killed, as were 125 people inside the Pentagon. One hundred six people were seriously injured and would be transported to area hopitals.[15]

At approximately 9:37 a.m., Arlington County Police Department (ACPD) Corporal Barry Foust and Officer Richard Cox, on patrol in south Arlington, saw a large American Airlines aircraft in steep descent on a collision course with the Pentagon.[16] They immediately radioed the Arlington County Emergency Communication Center (ECC). ACPD Headquarters issued a simultaneous page to all members of the ACPD with instructions to report for duty. Two-way pagers are standard issue only for the Emergency Response Team, hostage negotiators, members of the Special Weapons and Tactics (SWAT) team, and several command officials. Media reports of the attack alerted those who did not receive the pager message.

BOX 1-5

REMARKS OF ATTORNEY GENERAL JOHN ASHCROFT; SEPTEMBER 11, 2001

Today America has experienced one of the greatest tragedies ever witnessed on American soil.

These heinous acts of violence are an assault on the security of our nation and every American citizen.

We will not tolerate such acts and we will expend every effort and devote all necessary resources to bring the people responsible for these crimes to justice.

Now is the time for us to come together as a nation and offer our support and prayers for victims and their families, for the rescue workers and law enforcement, and for every one of us who has been changed forever by this horrible tragedy.

The following is a summary of the known facts surrounding today's incidents:

American Airlines flight 11 departed Boston for Los Angeles, was hijacked by suspects armed with knives. This plane crashed into the World Trade Center.

United Airlines flight 175 departed Boston for Los Angeles, was hijacked and crashed into the World Trade Center.

American Airlines flight 77 departed Washington Dulles for Los Angeles, was hijacked and crashed into the Pentagon.

United Airlines flight 93 departed Newark for San Francisco, was hijacked and crashed in Shanksville, Pennsylvania.

Crime scenes have been established by federal authorities in New York, Washington, D.C., Pittsburgh, Boston, and Newark.

The full resources of the Department of Justice, including the Federal Bureau of Investigation, the Immigration and Naturalization Service, the U.S. Attorneys offices, the U.S. Marshals Service, the Bureau of Prisons, the Drug Enforcement Administration and the Office of Justice programs, have been deployed to investigate these crimes and to assist victim survivors and victim families.

Thousands of FBI agents in all of the field offices across the country and in the international legats assisted by personnel from the other Department of Justice agencies are cooperating in this investigation.

The FBI has established a website where people can report any information about these crimes. That address is www.ifccfbi.gov.

The FBI is also in the process of establishing a toll free 800 number for the same purpose.

It takes courage to come forward in situations like this and I urge anyone with information that may be helpful to the authorities to use these resources.

The Office of Victims of Crime has established a toll free 800 for family and friends of victims. They can call 800-331-0075 to leave contact information for a future time when more information is available, to find out information about a victim or to find out information about the rights of victims and the services available to victim survivors and victim families.

The determination of these terrorists will not deter the determination of the American people. We are survivors and freedom is a survivor.

A free American people will not be intimidated or defeated. We will find the people responsible for these cowardly acts and justice will be done.

Local, regional, state, and federal agencies immediately responded to the Pentagon attack. In addition to county fire, police, and sheriff's departments, the response was assisted by the Metropolitan Washington Airports Authority, Ronald Reagan Washington National Airport Fire Department, Fort Myer Fire Department, the Virginia State Police, the Virginia Department of Emergency Management, the FBI, FEMA, a National Medical Response Team, the Bureau of Alcohol, Tobacco, and Firearms, and numerous military personnel within the Military District of Washington.[17]

The ACPD response to the incident was also immediate, with the on-duty shift engaged in minutes and most ACPD officers arriving on the scene within the first three hours.[18] Several ACPD senior officers were out of the county when the incident occurred. Chief Flynn was attending a conference in Atlantic City, New Jersey, where he was the featured speaker on the subject of racial profiling. Deputy Chief Holl was at a Virginia Police Corps meeting in Richmond, Virginia. Both Chief Flynn and Deputy Chief Holl immediately began driving back to Arlington. Deputy Chief John Haas was in Miami, Florida, participating in a police chief's assessment program and was unable to arrange immediate transportation back to Arlington. This delay turned out to be fortuitous. When Deputy Chief Haas reported for duty on Monday, September 17, he brought fresh leadership to a command section that had been continuously engaged for nearly a week.

Lieutenant Robert Medarios was the first ACPD command-level official to arrive on the scene; he assumed command of the ACPD response. Lieutenant Medarios quickly reached an agreement with a Defense Protective Service (DPS) official that the ACPD would assume responsibility for the outer perimeter. This was an important decision because the DPS exercises exclusive federal legislative jurisdiction at the Pentagon and its surrounding grounds. In these instances, the federal government acquires all the authority usually reserved by the state.

Lieutenant Medarios, Lieutenant Brian Berke, and Sergeant Jim Daly quickly assessed the road network conditions and identified 27 intersections that required immediate police posting. Sergeant Daly began organizing the staging area at Fire Station 5 and the adjacent park. The parking lot and adjacent field were cordoned off and guards posted around the perimeter. By 11:00 a.m., more than 100 law enforcement personnel had reported to the staging area representing the ACPD, Arlington County Sheriff's Office, Fairfax County Police Department, Alexandria Police Department, Arlington County Park Rangers, and the Immigration and Naturalization Service (INS). Officers were assigned to a particular post for 2 or 3 hours, given an hour of relief, then assigned to a different post to minimize boredom.

Many ACPD officers attempting to reach the Pentagon, including detectives who were responding from headquarters, found themselves fully engaged in rerouting traffic and clearing a path for fire, rescue, and medical units. Although they had difficulty reaching their intended destination, these officers knew precisely what needed to be done and acted on their own initiative, radioing to ACPD Headquarters their respective locations and activities. Detectives from the ACPD Vice Control Section assumed general patrol of the county away from the incident site to augment remaining officers in the event of a major criminal incident.

At 9:55, the incident commander ordered an evacuation of the Pentagon impact area because a partial collapse was imminent; it occurred at 9:57, and no first responders were injured.[19]

At about 10:15 a.m., Arlington County Fire Department Chief James Schwarz ordered a site-clearing evacuation because of the report of a second hijacked aircraft heading toward the Washington Metropolitan Area.[20] This was the first of three evacuations caused by reports of incoming aircraft, and the evacuation order was well communicated and well coordinated.[21] After this first evacuation, the ACPD incident command post (ICP) moved to an area beneath the I-395 overpass at Hayes Street and set up near the Arlington County Fire Department (ACFD) ICP to facilitate communications and coordination.[22]

At ACPD Headquarters, Captain Rich Alt, Captain Mary Gavin, Lieutenant Karen Hechenroder, and Administrative Assistant Barbara Scott began organizing the departmentwide response. Officers were being deployed throughout the county, and information had to be gathered regarding their locations and times of arrival so replacements could be scheduled and relief coordinated. The roll call room is a natural meeting place in the police department for gathering and distributing information. It became the home of the ACPD Incident Command System (ICS) staffing command for the duration of operations. The ACPD previously adopted the ICS as the appropriate response structure for large-scale incidents. Moreover, less than two weeks prior to the terrorist attack on the Pentagon, all ACPD command officers participated in routine recurring ICS training.

Shortly after Lieutenant Medarios assumed initial command at the incident site on September 11, Captain Rebecca Hackney arrived and took over as Incident Commander. Captain Hackney sketched the initial ACPD ICS assignments on a notepad. Acting Chief James Younger arrived, reviewed Captain Hackney's ICS assignments, then directed Captain Daniel Murray to be ACPD liaison to the ACFD ICP and Captain David Herbstreit to liaison with the FBI. By telephone, he spoke with Deputy Chief Holl, who was returning from Richmond, and requested that he respond directly to the incident site. Deputy Chief Holl arrived at about noon and took over as the ACPD incident commander. Deputy Chief Younger reported to the Arlington County Emergency Operation Center, as requested by the County Manager.

The ACPD loaned its mobile command post to the ACFD to serve as the initial ICP. The ACFD did not have a similar capability. Deputy Chief Holl worked out of the Watch Commander's Ford Expedition. The ACPD formulated a plan to screen pedestrian and vehicular traffic and assign ACPD representatives to the ACPD ICP, the FBI Command Post, Emergency Medical Services Control, the Arlington County EOC, and the Emergency Communication Center. Captain Murray reported to the ACFD ICP and told Chief Edward Plaugher he would remain with the ACFD throughout the fire and rescue operations.

Recognizing that minute-to-minute activities would be all consuming, early in the afternoon of September 11, Deputy Chief Holl assigned Lieutenant Steve Broadhurst to forecast the issues that would confront the department during the next 6 to 12 hours. Captain Roy Austin was assigned responsibility for department routine operations away from the incident site.

The Arlington County Sheriff's Office (ACSO) also immediately responded to the attack. Sheriff Beth Arthur and Chief Deputy Sheriff Mike Raffo were watching the World Trade Center attacks on television when they were notified that an airliner crashed into the Pentagon. They immediately headed to the Arlington County Emergency Operations Center (EOC). ACSO recall procedures were implemented, and an ICP was set up on the first floor of the courthouse building. The ICP was subsequently relocated to a large conference room in the Arlington County Detention Facility.

Some deputies not already on assignment rushed to the Pentagon, arriving in time to help rescue a few of the victims. Other deputies began directing traffic, as roadways became jammed.

One of the first actions taken by the ACSO was closing the courts and evacuating the judges and staff. This action was in consultation with the Arlington County judges, who approved the closure. This decision freed up approximately 20 deputies who were then able to assist with the response to the attack on the Pentagon.

Several factors facilitated the response to this incident and distinguished it from the far more difficult task in New York. There was a single incident, and it was not 1,000 feet above ground. The incident site was relatively easy to secure and contain, and there were no other buildings in the immediate area. There was no collateral damage beyond the Pentagon.[23] In the end, the emergency response at the Pentagon represented a mix of local, state, and federal jurisdictions and was generally effective.[24] It overcame the inherent complications of a response across jurisdictions because the ICS, a formalized management structure for emergency response, was in place in the National Capital Region on 9/11.

BOX 1-6

STATEMENT BY THE PRESIDENT IN HIS ADDRESS TO THE NATION SEPTEMBER 11, 2001, 8:30 P.M.

THE PRESIDENT: Good evening. Today, our fellow citizens, our way of life, our very freedom came under attack in a series of deliberate and deadly terrorist acts. The victims were in airplanes, or in their offices; secretaries, businessmen and women, military and federal workers; moms and dads, friends and neighbors. Thousands of lives were suddenly ended by evil, despicable acts of terror.

The pictures of airplanes flying into buildings, fires burning, huge structures collapsing, have filled us with disbelief, terrible sadness, and a quiet, unyielding anger. These acts of mass murder were intended to frighten our nation into chaos and retreat. But they have failed; our country is strong.

A great people has been moved to defend a great nation. Terrorist attacks can shake the foundations of our biggest buildings, but they cannot touch the foundation of America. These acts shattered steel, but they cannot dent the steel of American resolve.

America was targeted for attack because we're the brightest beacon for freedom and opportunity in the world. And no one will keep that light from shining.

Today, our nation saw evil, the very worst of human nature. And we responded with the best of America—with the daring of our rescue workers, with the caring for strangers and neighbors who came to give blood and help in any way they could.

Immediately following the first attack, I implemented our government's emergency response plans. Our military is powerful, and it's prepared. Our emergency teams are working in New York City and Washington, D.C. to help with local rescue efforts.

Our first priority is to get help to those who have been injured, and to take every precaution to protect our citizens at home and around the world from further attacks.

The functions of our government continue without interruption. Federal agencies in Washington which had to be evacuated today are reopening for essential personnel tonight, and will be open for business tomorrow. Our financial institutions remain strong, and the American economy will be open for business, as well.

The search is underway for those who are behind these evil acts. I've directed the full resources of our intelligence and law enforcement communities to find those responsible and to bring them to justice. We will make no distinction between the terrorists who committed these acts and those who harbor them.

I appreciate so very much the members of Congress who have joined me in strongly condemning these attacks. And on behalf of the American people, I thank the many world leaders who have called to offer their condolences and assistance.

America and our friends and allies join with all those who want peace and security in the world, and we stand together to win the war against terrorism. Tonight, I ask for your prayers for all those who grieve, for the children whose worlds have been shattered, for all whose sense of safety and security has been threatened. And I pray they will be comforted by a power greater than any of us, spoken through the ages in Psalm 23: "Even though I walk through the valley of the shadow of death, I fear no evil, for You are with me."

This is a day when all Americans from every walk of life unite in our resolve for justice and peace. America has stood down enemies before, and we will do so this time. None of us will ever forget this day. Yet, we go forward to defend freedom and all that is good and just in our world.

Thank you. Good night, and God bless America.

UNDERSTANDING THE THREAT

To understand the implications that the September 11th attacks had on policing, one must understand the threat behind the attack as well as the threat in a post–9-11 world. The threat that led to the September 11th attack, as previously detailed, came from Osama bin Laden and his terrorist network, Al Qaeda. This terrorist group was unique for the fact it was not a state-sponsored terrorist group, nor did it have a state to call its own. Although bin Laden had established his operations first in Sudan and later Afghanistan, political pressure removed him from the former, and military pressure removed him from the latter. Although it is believed that bin Laden has moved his operations into the mountains of Pakistan, Al Qaeda has continued to operate, increasing the number of its attacks by hitting "soft targets," such as nightclubs, synagogues, and train/subway stations.[25] In addition, most of the attacks since 9-11 have been on a much smaller scale. These attacks have included the Jemaah Islamiya (Indonesian affiliate) attack on a Bali nightclub, killing 180 (October 2002); the bombing of an Israeli-owned hotel and the related firing (and near miss) of shoulder-fired missiles at an Israeli passenger aircraft, both in Mombasa, Kenya (November 2002); suicide car bomb attacks against three housing compounds in Riyadh, Saudi Arabia, killing 20 people, including eight Americans (May 2003); a suicide bomb attack against five sites in Casablanca killing about 40 people (May 2003); and the bombing of a commuter train in Madrid, Spain, killing about 300 (March 2004).[26] Numerous smaller attacks have also been conducted against U.S. interests and personnel in Saudi Arabia, Turkey, East Asia, and other areas where Al Qaeda affiliates operate.

It has, however, been noted that no attacks have occurred on American soil since September 11th, which the Bush administration, as well as Thomas Friedman of the *New York Times*, have attributed to the work of the F.B.I., the C.I.A., and the Department of Homeland Security and for the fact that the fight has been brought to the Middle East in terms of both wars in Afghanistan and Iraq.[27] This, however, should not negate the emphasis of state and local police on homeland security, for Al Qaeda's history of attacks against U.S. interests has consistently retained a time lag between attacks. Al Qaeda has also been quite adept at adapting to the changing environment in which it finds itself, thus although our attention may be on airport security, this focus may very well leave other sectors vulnerable to attack. Therefore, it should be stated that although Al Qaeda has not carried out a direct attack on the United States since September 11th, it is true that their ability to survive and adapt continues to leave future attacks a reality.

Although Al Qaeda is assuredly the terrorist group of concern, it is important that police come to understand that they are not the only threat to homeland security. Other international terrorist organizations and extremist groups exist that perceive the United States as a target of interest.[28] In addition, other international crime problems cross countries, and thus transnational crimes such as drug trafficking, human trafficking, and the black market sales of both conventional weapons and weapons of mass destruction have become a threat to homeland security. Taken further, the United States also has its own domestic terrorism threats that are of concern, and past threats, such as organized crime and gangs, continue to pose a threat to homeland security. Just like these latter threats, good information and intelligence are the primary means by which police can make arrests; therefore, the key to dealing effectively with the threat of terrorism, both international and domestic, is having good information and intelligence and the ability to act on it. This is why understanding the threat America faces, not only from Al Qaeda, but other terrorist organizations, is critical to today's modern police.

Police, however, are better able to comprehend the threat of crime, rather than the threat of terrorism. Police operate in an environment of law-based violations and the enforcement of these laws. The fact that there are conceptual similarities between crime and terrorism provides for a better understanding of terrorism from a police perspective. First and foremost, it should be noted that terrorism is criminal in nature. According to McVey, "virtually all terrorist acts violate some criminal statutes of the host jurisdiction," making it "the easiest element for local law enforcement to appreciate."[29] In addition, it has been noted that both crime and terrorism are almost always the work of young males, similar to the majority of crimes, especially violent crimes.[30] And, at a more conceptual level, it has also been noted that both the terms *crime* and *terrorism* are often hard to define, are social constructs, and when committed, serve to undermine social trust.[31] From these viewpoints, terrorism is an issue with which police can play a role.

Crime and terrorism are different, however, in that the targets of terrorism are often symbolic, the terrorist's actions are almost always violent, terrorists are primarily seeking publicity, and their goals are largely political.[32] Unlike crime, there are few laws regulating terrorism, and the response to terrorism is not limited to the local level, but almost always rises to the highest levels of government.[33] In addition, unlike criminals who tend to commit crimes in a very similar manner (modus operandi), terrorists tend to adapt and innovate, thus making it more difficult to utilize traditional investigatory methods. Finally, although only some crime tends to operate within an organizational structure, terrorist groups almost always operate by some operational structure, even if the structural organization is not fully clear.

BOX 1-7

REMARKS BY THE PRESIDENT TO POLICE, FIREMEN AND RESCUE WORKERS MURRAY AND WEST STREETS, NEW YORK, NEW YORK SEPTEMBER 14, 2001

CROWD: U.S.A.! U.S.A.!

THE PRESIDENT: Thank you all. I want you all to know—

Q: Can't hear you.

THE PRESIDENT: I can't talk any louder. (Laughter.)

I want you all to know that America today—that America today is on bended knee in prayer for the people whose lives were lost here, for the workers who work here, for the families who mourn. This nation stands with the good people of New York City, and New Jersey and Connecticut, as we mourn the loss of thousands of our citizens.

Q: I can't hear you.

THE PRESIDENT: I can hear you. (Applause.) I can hear you. The rest of the world hears you. (Applause.) And the people who knocked these buildings down will hear all of us soon. (Applause.)

CROWD: U.S.A.! U.S.A.!

THE PRESIDENT: The nation sends its love and compassion to everybody who is here. Thank you for your hard work. Thank you for making the nation proud. And may God bless America. (Applause.)

CROWD: U.S.A.! U.S.A.!

Understanding the threat first entails understanding the ideological motivations behind terrorism. It then necessitates an understanding of the various groups and the threat they pose to America. Specifically, it entails not only a generic understanding of terrorism and terrorist groups, but also a continual update of potential threats and the potential targets, especially those in each police department's jurisdiction. But perhaps before any of this can occur, the police must first understand the impact that September 11th has had on policing and that because of that attack, the police now play a crucial role in the era of homeland security.

UNDERSTANDING THE ATTACK[34]

On September 11, 2001, when Al Qaeda terrorists hijacked four planes and attacked the World Trade Center buildings in New York City and the Pentagon in Arlington County, Virginia, little did anyone know that they would set in motion a new era of policing, namely the era of homeland security.[35] In the wake of 9-11 it has become evident that many state and local police agencies across the country have found themselves adapting to this new role in policing. Whether they have adopted the concepts of Homeland Security by force (e.g., New York City, Arlington County (VA), Washington, D.C.), by local circumstances (e.g., San Francisco, Chicago, Houston), by lure of grant dollars (e.g., City of Pine Bluff Police Department, Arkansas; Town of Kittery Police Department, Maine; Casper Police Department, WY), by state directive, or simply by local government and citizen demand, police agencies are beginning to wrestle with what homeland security means to their particular agencies. As one author has stated, the overriding question today for police management is, "What is the role of state and local law enforcement in a post–September 11 environment?"[36]

The new role in American policing in the post–September 11 environment is not only a response to the specific events on that fateful day, but they are also an amalgam of change brought about by various political, economic, and social factors in the United States. The political implications have been derived by the president winning a second term and his agenda focus on the "war on terrorism" and Homeland Security. In addition, Congress has played a major role in the passage of legislation that created the Department of Homeland Security and enacted the myriad laws encapsulated in the USA PATRIOT Act.

The economic factors that followed in kind are found in the spending by the national government, and to some degree by state governments, in the area of homeland security. Many government agencies have seen their budgets slashed while budgets for homeland security have risen. In fact, even police-related grant programs such as the Edward Bryne and COPS grants have seen their budgets drastically cut by the Bush administration, while funding for homeland security has continued to rise substantially.

No less important than the political and economic factors shaping the concepts of homeland security are the social factors. The social implications for the movement toward homeland security are derived from public concern regarding terrorism, which has moved from little to no concern in the pre–9-11 years to ranking as one of the three most important problems facing our country ever since.[37] Americans now agree that government should address the problems of terrorism and homeland/domestic security. This may be from a high level of concern that there will be another terrorist attack in the United States and that they or someone in their family could become a victim of terrorism. According to a recent Pew Research poll, since 9-11, 23 percent of respondents stated they were very worried, whereas an additional 44 percent have stated they are somewhat worried about another terrorist attack.[38] And, in a Gallup poll during the same time period, 9 percent of respondents have stated they were very worried, and an additional 29 percent have stated they are somewhat worried that they or a member of their family would fall victim to a terrorist act.[39] In fact, concern among Americans has risen so high that approximately half of Americans surveyed by the Pew Research Center stated that to "curb terrorism" they believe it will be necessary to "give up some of their civil liberties," and they favor the requirement that all citizens carry a national identification card.[40] It is perhaps not all too surprising, then, to find that over 81 percent of citizens favor government expanding under-cover activities to penetrate groups under suspicion, over 67 percent of citizens favor closer monitoring of banking and credit card transactions to trace funding sources, and over 54 percent favor law enforcement monitoring Internet discussions in chat rooms and other forums.[41] The movement toward the era of homeland security by police is not emerging in some police management vacuum, but rather it is coming about as part of a larger environmental change.

The movement to an era of homeland security in policing should also not be all too surprising. The previous paradigm[42] or epicycle[43] in policing that has lasted for well over 25 years has been the philosophy of community policing. It will later be noted that community policing moved through three generations of policy development, namely innovation (early 1980s), diffusion (late 1980s and early 1990s), and institutionalization, achieving this by the mid to late 1990s.[44] What typically follows the institutionalization of a policy is the process of disappearance, which generally takes the form of new innovations being integrated into the institutionalized model as a means of dealing with change. This eventually gives way to the new innovations and ideas beginning to stand more firmly on their own, thus giving rise to the new policy and diminishing the old.[45] We witnessed the adoption of "Homeland Security through Community Policing" in the wake of 9-11, but as the idea of a policing role in homeland security took shape, homeland security has been more recently thought of as its own distinct policy. As a result, Pelfrey's assertion in 1998 that "the current paradigm, community policing, will be refined . . . and may eventually be replaced by a different paradigm"[46] is possibly coming to fruition.

To understand the implications of the September 11th attack for state and local policing, it is necessary to explore this new era of policing by drawing on past conceptual frameworks of policing. To do so, we must look to the organizational strategies of policing used by Kelling and Moore to explain the three previous eras of policing, specifically the political, reform, and community eras.[47] As they once stated, "This concept can be used not only to describe the different styles of policing in the past and the present, but also to sharpen the understanding of police policy makers of the future."[48] Still further, we must draw on the previous work of Greene[49] and his comparison of various models of policing to compare and contrast the various social interactions and social components of American policing, by highlighting these same concepts under the homeland security form of policing.

BOX 1-8

The Four Eras of Policing Based on Organizational Strategy

Elements	Political Era	Reform Era	Community Era	Homeland Security Era
Authorization	Politics and law	Law and professionalism	Community support (political), law, professionalism	National/international threats (politics), law (intergovernmental), professionalism
Function	Broad social services	Crime control	Broad, provision of service	Crime control, antiterrorism/counterterrorism, intelligence gathering
Organizational design	Decentralized	Centralized, classical	Decentralized, task forces, matrices	Centralized decision making, decentralized execution
Relationship to environment	Intimate	Professionally remote	Intimate	Professional
Demand	Decentralized, to patrol and politicians	Centralized	Decentralized	Centralized
Tactics and technology	Foot patrol	Preventive patrol and rapid response to calls for service	Foot patrol, problem solving, etc.	Risk assessment, police operations centers, information systems
Outcome	Citizen political satisfaction	Crime control	Quality of life and citizen satisfaction	Citizen safety, crime control, antiterrorism

Adapted by author from Kelling, G. L. & Moore, M. H. (1988). "The Evolving Strategy of Policing." *Perspectives on Policing*, No. 4. Washington, D.C.: National Institute of Justice.

The Four Eras of Policing

According to researchers Kelling and Moore, American policing has moved through three distinct eras: the political, the reform, and the community eras.[50] In explaining these three distinct eras, the authors used the conceptual framework of "corporate strategy," which was defined as "the pattern of major objectives, purposes, or goals and essential policies and plans for achieving these goals."[51] Based on this framework, Kelling and Moore looked at police organizational strategies in seven topical areas: authorization, function, organization, demand, environment, tactics, and outcomes to distinguish how policing has evolved throughout American history. Authorization, the first of these seven dimensions, referred to the underlying source of authority given to the police. This was essentially the mandate for police operations. Function detailed the values, mission, and goals of the organization, which focused on the police role in society. Organization consisted of the structure, human resources, and management processes of an agency. Demand entailed the source of the demand for police services, whereas environment dealt with the varied relationship of the organization with those elements external to the agency. Tactics described the methods and technologies the organization used to obtain their goals, and outcomes are the results of these activities. By detailing the changes in policing across these seven dimensions throughout the history of American policing, Kelling and Moore were able to describe these three distinct eras in policing (see Box 1-8).

The first era of policing, the political era, began around the 1840s with the creation of the first bona fide police agencies in America. Although people recognized the need for a police force at the time, they were not sure of its role in society. As the political machines of the day had full control over the machinations of government, policing became part and parcel to the politics of the day. The authorization for the police during the political era was largely derived from these same political machines. Because no one was certain as to their specific function and for the fact few social agencies existed at the time, police delivered a broad array of services from dealing with criminals, to keeping immigrant workers in line and running soup kitchens. Although the organization of these early police had military overtones, they were largely decentralized in their deployment with poor supervision and little in the way of management. As a result of this and the strong political ties, the police were very intimate and close to the people they policed. The demands on these early police came first and foremost from the ward politicians, who made their demands for political gain, while the local citizens made their demands directly to the local beat cop. There was little in the way of tactics or technology at the time, although call boxes would later be a factor, so local beat officers and foot patrol was the overriding method of police delivery. The outcome of policing during the political era was largely aimed at implementing the political machine's will and keeping the citizens satisfied by officers maintaining some semblance of order. The political era, however, was not successful in any right as it was ill-suited for controlling crime, delivering social services, or maintaining control, for it was largely corrupt and often very brutal.

The time period of the 1920s through the 1970s is marked as the "reform era" by Kelling and Moore.[52] The political corruption and rampant brutality among the police, exacerbated by their ties to the local political machines, reached a zenith at the turn of the century, as citizens began calling for the reform of the police. Progressive police chiefs such as August Vollmer and professional-minded leaders like J. Edgar Hoover helped create a model of policing that would take decades to implement, but the changes would help reign in control of the police. The authorization of the police became more entrenched in the law, especially the criminal law, and rooted in the concept of police professionalism. Its function, stripped of all the social services, became centered on crime control. In addition, to rein in corruption it adopted a very paramilitary template formed around the classical hierarchical organizational method. The demand for police services was more centralized by directing calls toward the police station itself, and police became more professionally detached from the citizens they policed. The overriding methods of police deployment came about as a result of technology, police vehicles, and radios and emphasized preventive patrol and rapid response to the centralized calls for service. The outcome of policing was solely focused on crime control. The reform era was somewhat successful in removing corruption and brutality from policing through its centralized control and its move toward professionalism. However, the distancing of the police from the citizens generated new problems and conflicts, especially during the array of social changes that occurred during the 1960s.

This realization, that for police to effectively perform their job they need the assistance of the citizenry, led to the third era of policing, the "community era."[53] The authorization for the police, although still rooted in the law and professionalism, focused more heavily on local community support. To deal more effectively with crime, fear of crime, and disorder, police began focusing on those factors that contribute to crime by providing a broad array of services beyond the crime control methods of the previous era. The police organized themselves through a more decentralized geographical neighborhood identity method of policing and responded to the demands of these citizens by working more closely with them on a routine basis. The tactics employed included a return to foot patrols (and bicycle, horse, etc.) to enhance contact with citizens, and it used various problem-solving and geographical information systems to identify trends and solve underlying problems rather than symptoms. As a result, the focus of the community era was on the outcome of citizen satisfaction with the police and the quality of life of the local communities and neighborhoods. Although the community era has been marginally successful in reducing the fear of crime and increasing the quality of life, there is little evidence that its ability to control crime has had equal success, if any at all.

In terms of the era of homeland security, by applying the framework used by Kelling and Moore to describe the political, reform, and community eras, it helps clarify the direction of this new era in policing. The authorization for this era has largely come from the national and international threat that is terrorism, driven by the events of September 11, 2001. In addition, citizen awareness of the issue of terrorism reached a critical juncture on that day, and as a result, citizens have given authorization to the government to target terrorism and protect the home front.[54] Thus the authorization for policing is derived from the national and international threats, but it has played out through government and citizens giving this new role in policing legitimacy. In addition, the era is still marked by an adherence to the law, but more so in that intergovernmental law (and relations) are becoming an overriding concern. Professionalism of the police also continues to play a role in authorizing the police to take on this role in that police were and, in the event of future attacks, will continue to be the first responders and an integral part of the recovery process.

The function of police under homeland security is marked by a more focused concentration of its resources into crime control, for it is through crime control, enforcement of the criminal law, and traffic law that many potential threats can be exposed and intelligence gathered. In addition, police have begun to take on the role of antiterrorism by focusing on various passive measures that can reduce the vulnerabilities of their communities to future terrorist attacks. Much of this is being done through local threat assessments, intelligence gathering, and intergovernmental information sharing. Another added function of the police is counterterrorism, which are those offensive measures taken to respond to terrorist acts through the process of preparedness training, creation of emergency (and routine) operations centers, large-scale crisis intervention, and special reaction team training. Moreover, the collection, processing, and analysis of intelligence are also becoming a necessary and crucial function of the police in this current era.

The organizational design of the police agency would seem to entail another pendulum swing bringing it back to the centralized design. This is only partially the case. Although the era of homeland security would entail a more centralized organizational control, especially in dealing with information coming from the enhanced intergovernmental relations and information sharing, it primarily entails a centralized decision-making process. The actual execution of the organization will, like the community era, entail a decentralized and flexible approach. It is internal information sharing that will feed the centralized decision making, but it is the officer on the street that will execute these decisions with the flexibility of street-level decision making.

Because the demand on the organization will be somewhat more centralized, the demand for the agency's services will be more centralized as well. Hence, under the role of the police in homeland security the relationship to their environment will be professional. Unlike the professionally remote relationship that marked the reform era, policing under homeland security will not isolate themselves from the community, which is a crucial source of information and intelligence, but will by the nature of demand, function, and organizational design be professionally oriented.

Tactics and technology are perhaps one of the most critical areas due to the nature of homeland security concepts and one in which police are most deficient and for which they will remain on a learning curve for some time to come. The concepts of conducting risk assessments, intelligence gathering and processing, and developing large-scale crisis response, although not completely foreign to policing, will necessitate more training and education. The employment of tactics related to antiterrorism and counterterrorism is partially a continuation of past police practices, but with a wider array of information to process. It is the adoption of new technologies that police will need and the protection of these technologies that police will be engaged in for some time to come.

The outcome of homeland security continues to bear elements of previous eras—crime control, citizen satisfaction, and quality of life. However, the primary emphasis of this new era will be citizen safety and antiterrorism methods aimed at the mitigation of future attacks. Although crime prevention will also still be a desired outcome, preventing future terrorist acts is the new challenge to law enforcement in America.

The Five Models of Policing

A more recent analysis of policing styles comes from a leading researcher in the policing field, Jack R. Greene.[55] Greene articulated that there were currently (at the time of his writing) four models of policing in America. These four models included traditional policing, community policing, problem-oriented policing, and zero-tolerance policing. To clarify the differences among these four models, Greene compared them across 12 dimensions related to the "police role and function, interaction with the community, formal and social organization, and service delivery."[56] These dimensions consisted of the following: (1) focus of policing, (2) forms of intervention, (3) range of police activity, (4) level of discretion at line level, (5) focus of police culture, (6) locus of decision making, (7) communication flow, (8) range of community involvement, (9) linkage with other agencies, (10) types of organization and command focus, (11) implications for organizational change and development, and (12) measurement of success (see Box 1-9).[57] Although Greene acknowledges this typology was largely a heuristic device it does provide "a useful way to contrast and compare potentially differing paradigms of policing."[58]

BOX 1-9

COMPARISONS OF SOCIAL INTERACTIONS AND STRUCTURAL COMPONENTS OF VARIOUS FORMS OF POLICING INCLUDING HOMELAND SECURITY

Social Interaction or Structural Dimension	Traditional Policing	Community Policing	Problem-Oriented Policing	Zero-Tolerance Policing	Homeland Security Policing
Focus of policing	Law enforcement	Community building through crime prevention	Law, order, and fear problems	Order problems	Security, antiterrorism, counter terrorism, law and order
Forms of intervention	Reactive, based on criminal law	Proactive, on criminal, and administrative law	Mixed, on criminal, and administrative law	Proactive, uses criminal, civil, and administrative law	Proactive, on criminal law and for mitigation and preparedness
Range of police activity	Narrow, crime focused	Broad crime, order, fear, and quality-of-life focused	Narrow to broad—problem focused	Narrow, location and behavior focused	Broad, security, terrorism, crime, fear
Levels of discretion at line level	High and unaccountable	High and accountable to the community and local commanders	High and primarily accountable to the police administration	Low, but primarily accountable to the police administration	High and primarily accountable to the police administration
Focus of police culture	Inward, rejecting community	Outward, building partnerships	Mixed depending on problem, but analysis focused	Inward focused on attacking the target problem	Mixed depending on threat, threat-analysis focused
Locus of decision making	Police directed, minimizes the involvement of others	Community–police coproduction —joint responsibility and assessment	Varied, police identify problems, but with community involvement and interaction	Police directed, some linkage to other agencies where necessary	Police directed with linkage to other agencies

BOX 1-9

Social Interaction or Structural Dimension	Traditional Policing	Community Policing	Problem-Oriented Policing	Zero-Tolerance Policing	Homeland Security Policing
Communication flow	Downward from police to community	Horizontal between police and community	Horizontal between police and community	Downward from police to community	Downward from police to community
Range of community involvement	Low and passive	High and active	Mixed depending on problem set	Low and passive	Mixed depending on threat
Linkage with other agencies	Poor and intermittent	Participative and integrative in the overarching process	Participative and integrative depending on the problem set	Moderate and intermittent	Participative and integrative in the overarching process
Type of organization and command focus	Centralized command and control	Decentralized with community linkage	Decentralized with local command accountability to central administration	Centralized or decentralized but internal focus	Centralized decision making, decentralized exectuion
Implications for organizational change/development	Few, static organization fending off the environment	Many, dynamic organization focused on the environmental interactions	Varied, focused on problem resolution but with import for organization intelligence and structure	Few, limited interventions focused on target problems, using many traditional methods	Varied, focused on security and threat, but with import for intelligence and stucture

BOX 1-9

Social interaction or Structural Dimension	Traditional Policing	Community Policing	Problem-Oriented Policing	Zero-Tolerance Policing	Homeland Security Policing
Measurement of success	Arrest and crime rates, particularly serious Part I crimes	Varied, crime, calls for service, fear reduction, use of public places, community linkages and contacts, safer neighborhoods	Varied, problems solved, minimized, displaced	Arrests, field stops, activity, location-specific reductions in targeted activity	Arrests, field stops, intelligence gathering, mitigation, and preparedness

Adapted by author from Greene, J. R. (2000). "Community Policing in America: Changing the Nature, Structure, and Function of the Police." In *Criminal Justice 2000: Policies, Processes, and Decisions of the Criminal Justice System.* Vol. 3. Washington, D.C.: U.S. Department of Justice, Office of Justice Programs.

The traditional policing model is largely an early twentieth-century development, and like Kelling and Moore explained, it was primarily focused on crime control through law enforcement. By enforcing the criminal law after crimes occurred, it made the police largely a reactive organization with a very narrow focus. Gone were the social services provided in the nineteenth century, as other social service agencies came into creation and took over those various tasks. In addition, to overcome the past corruption and brutality, police were organized more along military lines with a strict chain of command, which did make them more accountable for their behaviors, but also distanced them from the citizens they policed. Police officers became a responsive agent of the police centralized bureaucracy, and they began taking their orders solely from the police hierarchy, thus making their interaction with community members and other social agencies extremely limited. Ultimately the measurement of success under traditional policing became focused on the number of arrests made and the ability to control the crime rate as exemplified by the Federal Bureau of Investigation's Uniform Crime Reports. The traditional policing model still exists today and for many agencies remains the primary model of policing.

The community policing model, largely derived from innovations in the 1980s, is primarily focused on building community partnerships and crime prevention. Although community policing still uses criminal law, it encompasses a wider scope of alternatives, including administrative and civil law, mediation and arbitration, as well as redirecting problems by working with other social service agencies. Police officers under community policing are more proactive, and they address not only problems of crime, but also of disorder, quality of life, and fear of crime. As police officers build these partnerships, they become coproducers of the solutions to various problems that plague specific neighborhoods and thus are more accountable to the citizens they serve. As a result, police are actively involved with the community, they communicate on a routine basis, and they work with other agencies in addressing crime and disorder. Organizationally, to achieve these ends, the police must be more decentralized. Finally, the outcomes of community policing are based on the needs of the specific neighborhoods policed.

Problem-oriented policing also came became a key model of policing in the 1980s through the work of Herman Goldstein. Problem-oriented policing is also focused on crime, disorder, and fear of crime and utilizes a variety of means to address these problems. What sets problem-oriented policing apart is that police may engage in problem solving without the support or assistance of the community. Police identify specific problems in the neighborhoods they police, they research these problems, then develop solutions. After a period of implementation they assess the solution's effectiveness on the problem. Therefore, problem-oriented policing is problem centered, thus depending on the type of problem and the possible solutions selected, police may or may not have much discretion, contact with citizens, or engagement with other social agencies. The organization implementing problem-oriented policing in many ways has to allow decentralized local commands, but demands accountability to the central administration. The measurement of success under problem-oriented policing, then, is really based on the police officer's ability to solve problems, reduce the impact of the problem, or potentially to displace and disperse the problem from a concentrated area.

The final model of policing articulated by Greene is zero-tolerance policing. Largely a 1990s derived model of policing, its focus is on both crime and disorder problems through proactive means and calling on criminal, civil, and administrative law. It does this by targeting a specific crime (e.g., prostitution, open-air drug markets) or disorder (e.g., panhandlers, graffiti) that occurs in a specific time and place and then concentrating police resources on this specific problem. Police engaging in zero-tolerance policing tend to have a narrow range of focus, based on the behavior(s) they are trying to address. There tends to be a highly centralized control over this type of policing, which means communication is driven by the hierarchy with limited community or other social service agency involvement. The measurement of success for zero-tolerance policing, like traditional policing, emphasizes such things as the number of arrests, tickets, or field stops, with the desired outcome being a reduction in the undesirable behavior in a specific location.

Turning to the new model of policing, by applying Greene's 12 dimensions of policing to homeland security assists in clarifying the current and future direction of homeland security. The focus of policing under homeland security has incorporated the concepts of security and both antiterrorism and counterterrorism into its primary focus. Recognizing and assessing the level of threat, incorporating security measures to prevent future terrorist acts, and developing methods of mitigating threats and responding to both threats and actual incidents have become part of policing under homeland security. Despite these additions, more traditional methods of law enforcement and the focus on law and order still remain an important focus of homeland security policing, as this type of activity can serve the function of security through both arrests or simply intelligence gathering. This is why the forms of intervention under this model of policing will remain very proactive and will draw on the criminal law for enforcement. Although new laws oriented toward dealing with the problem of terrorism will be applied, especially in the area of investigations (e.g., USA PATRIOT Act), for the average line officer the basic means of intervention will remain criminal and traffic violations, as well as routine field stops.

Based on the focus and both new and old forms of intervention, the range of police activity is clearly going to be very broad under homeland security. New security measures will include threat assessments and risk analysis, antiterrorism practices for both mitigation and preparedness, as well as counterterrorism and recovery practices in the event of an actual attack. This will be combined with a concentration on crime, disorder, and fear of crime, especially when associated with terrorism. Because of the concentration of many of these activities at the line officer level, discretion for these officers will have to remain high, but due to the nature of intelligence gathering and information dissemination, these officers will be held accountable by the police administration.

The focus of the police culture, due to the nature of the threat, will be mixed. Although certain threats or information dissemination by such agencies as the U.S. Department of Homeland Security, or the state equivalent, may create a "police only" information dissemination, police will have to continue an outward focus in regard to their own low-level intelligence gathering. Police will need to rely on citizen support in providing information either through traditional means or through partnerships previously formed under the community policing model. This also means that the police will have a mixed range of community involvement as some aspects of the threat analysis may preclude citizen involvement, whereas others may rely heavily on their input and expertise.

Police and citizen participation may be mixed based on the threat, but police will have to link with other agencies, both governmental and nongovernmental to implement nearly any type of security measure. This will include other public safety agencies such as fire and code enforcement, it will include those in the medical and mental health community, and it will draw heavily on such agencies as public works, water treatment, and transportation. Police agencies will need to have far greater linkage with these types of agencies then ever before for security reasons, and this type of lateral linkage will be just as important as the vertical linkage with state and federal agencies.

Organizationally, police departments under homeland security will incorporate a strong centralized command structure, but it will need to maintain a largely decentralized method of execution. Because intelligence gathering and information sharing will be critical not only for the processing of information beyond the police agencies themselves, but also for quickly disseminating intelligence down to line officers, centralized control through active command operations centers that can link with these other agencies, both vertically and horizontally, will be critical. Because information has to be processed and disseminated in real time, the centralized operations command center with a decision-making staff element will become the means of organizational control. However, line officers will still need the flexibility of discretion for the implementation of centralized information and orders, as well as for the means of gathering and disseminating information through routine police procedures.

Ultimately, the measurement of success under the Homeland Security model will entail the traditional methods of arrest, field stops, and traffic enforcement, but it will include the ability to gather, process, and disseminate intelligence information. In addition, it will entail the agency's ability to mitigate security threats and be prepared for the possibility of an attack. Simply stated, preventing terrorism, mitigating the impact that a terrorist attack would have, and responding effectively to a terrorist attack are the key outcomes of policing for homeland security.

Recovery effort from the attack on the Pentagon, Arlington County, Virginia. (*Source: Photo Courtesy of the Federal Emergency Management Agency [FEMA].*)

UNDERSTANDING THE RESPONSE

Understanding the threat that America faced prior to September 11, 2001, the attack itself, and the local police response on that day provides us the context in which to understand that policing has moved into a new era, an era of homeland security. Recognizing that the threat from Al Qaeda and other terrorist organizations, as well as from other transnational crimes, remains provides the basis for which homeland security is now important to state and local police agencies. In addition, learning from the police response to the 9-11 attacks gives us some understanding of the issues that police face, not only in preparing to respond to future attacks, but to prevent future attacks as well.

As Melchor Guzman has so succinctly explained,

> The roles and strategies of the police are shaped by the need of the times. In this time of terror, police are required to be more vigilant and perhaps more suspicious. They are required to be more proactive both in detecting and investigating acts of terrorism. The community policing roles that they have embraced for the last decade should be examined in the light of its opposing tenets to the demands of providing police service in a time of terror. The police should lean toward a more legalistic style and begin to apply their innate talent for sensing danger. This is the philosophical shift that circumstances demand. This is probably the role that the American people demand from their law enforcement officers.[59]

BOX 1-10

Train Bombing, Madrid, Spain, March 11, 2004:
Bombs were exploded simultaneously on commuter trains as they arrived at various train stations in Madrid. The bombings killed at least 192 people and wounded more than 1,400.

Restaurant Bombing in Baghdad, December 31, 2003:
A car bomb explosion outside Baghdad's Nabil Restaurant killed 8 persons and wounded 35. The wounded included 3 *Los Angeles Times* reporters and 3 local employees.

Grenade Attacks in Bogota, November 15, 2003:
Grenade attacks on two bars frequented by Americans in Bogota killed one person and wounded 72, including 4 Americans. Colombian authorities suspected FARC (the Revolutionary Armed Forces of Colombia). The U.S. Embassy suspected that the attacks had targeted Americans and warned against visiting commercial centers and places of entertainment.

Rocket Attack on the al-Rashid Hotel in Baghdad, October 26, 2003:
Iraqis using an improvised rocket launcher bombarded the al-Rashid Hotel in Baghdad, killing one U.S. Army officer and wounding 17 persons. The wounded included 4 U.S. military personnel and 7 American civilians. Deputy Secretary of Defense Paul D. Wolfowitz, who was staying at the hotel, was not injured. After visiting the wounded, he said, "They're not going to scare us away; we're not giving up on this job."

Bomb Attack on U.S. Diplomats in the Gaza Strip, October 15, 2003:
A remote-controlled bomb exploded under a car in a U.S. diplomatic convoy passing through the northern Gaza Strip. Three security guards, all employees of DynCorp, were killed. A fourth was wounded. The diplomats were on their way to interview Palestinian candidates for Fulbright scholarships to study in the United States. Palestinian President Arafat and Prime Minister Qurei condemned the attack, while the major Palestinian militant groups denied responsibility. The next day, Palestinian security forces arrested several suspects, some of whom belonged to the Popular Resistance Committees.

Car Bombings in Baghdad, October 12, 2003:
Two suicide car bombs exploded outside the Baghdad Hotel, which housed U.S. officials. Six persons were killed and 32 wounded. Iraqi and U.S. security personnel apparently kept the cars from actually reaching the hotel.

Hotel Bombing in Indonesia, August 5, 2003:
A car bomb exploded outside the Marriott Hotel in Jakarta, Indonesia, killing 10 persons and wounding 150. One of the dead was a Dutch citizen. The wounded included an American, a Canadian, an Australian, and two Chinese. Indonesian authorities suspected the Jemaah Islamiah, which had carried out the October 12, 2002, bombing in Bali.

Truck Bomb Attacks in Saudi Arabia, May 12, 2003:
Suicide bombers attacked three residential compounds for foreign workers in Riyadh, Saudi Arabia. The 34 dead included 9 attackers, 7 other Saudis, 9 U.S. citizens, and one

citizen each from the United Kingdom, Ireland, and the Philippines. Another American died on June 1. It was the first major attack on U.S. targets in Saudi Arabia since the end of the war in Iraq. Saudi authorities arrested 11 al-Qaida suspects on May 28.

Suicide Bombing in Haifa, March 5, 2003:

A suicide bombing aboard a bus in Haifa, Israel, killed 15 persons and wounded at least 40. One of the dead claimed U.S. as well as Israeli citizenship. The bomber's affiliation was not immediately known.

Assassination of an AID Official, October 28, 2002:

Gunmen in Amman assassinated Laurence Foley, Executive Officer of the U.S. Agency for International Development Mission in Jordan. The Honest People of Jordan claimed responsibility.

Ambush on the West Bank, September 18, 2002:

Gunmen ambushed a vehicle on a road near Yahad, killing an Israeli and wounding a Romanian worker. The al-Aqsa Martyrs' Brigades claimed responsibility.

Attack on a School in Pakistan, August 5, 2002:

Gunmen attacked a Christian school attended by children of missionaries from around the world. Six persons (two security guards, a cook, a carpenter, a receptionist, and a private citizen) were killed, and a Philippine citizen was wounded. A group called al-Intigami al-Pakistani claimed responsibility.

Bombing at the Hebrew University, July 31, 2002:

A bomb hidden in a bag in the Frank Sinatra International Student Center of Jerusalem's Hebrew University killed 9 persons and wounded 87. The dead included 5 U.S. citizens and 4 Israelis. The wounded included 4 U.S. citizens, 2 Japanese, and 3 South Koreans. The Islamic Resistance Movement (HAMAS) claimed responsibility.

Suicide Bombing in Jerusalem, June 19, 2002:

A suicide bombing at a bus stop in Jerusalem killed 6 persons and wounded 43, including 2 U.S. citizens. The al-Aqsa Martyrs' Brigades claimed responsibility.

Car Bombing in Pakistan, June 14, 2002:

A car bomb exploded near the U.S. Consulate and the Marriott Hotel in Karachi, Pakistan. Eleven persons were killed and 51 were wounded, including one U.S. and one Japanese citizen. Al Qaida and al-Qanin were suspected.

Hostage Rescue Attempt in the Philippines, June 7, 2002:

Philippine Army troops attacked Abu Sayyaf terrorists on Mindanao Island in an attempt to rescue U.S. citizen Martin Burnham and his wife Gracia, who had been kidnapped more than a year earlier. Burnham was killed but his wife, though wounded, was freed. A Filipino hostage was killed, as were four of the guerrillas. Seven soldiers were wounded.

Suicide Bombing in the West Bank, March 31, 2002:

A suicide bombing near an ambulance station in Efrat wounded four persons, including a U.S. citizen. The al-Aqsa Martyrs' Brigades claimed responsibility.

Suicide Bombing in Israel, March 27, 2002:

A suicide bombing in a noted restaurant in Netanya, Israel, killed 22 persons and wounded 140. One of the dead was a U.S. citizen. The Islamic Resistance Movement (HAMAS) claimed responsibility.

Suicide Bombing in Jerusalem, March 21, 2002:
A suicide bombing in Jerusalem killed 3 persons and wounded 86 more, including 2 U.S. citizens. The Palestinian Islamic Jihad claimed responsibility.

Car Bomb Explosion in Peru, March 20, 2002:
A car bomb exploded at a shopping center near the U.S. Embassy in Lima, Peru. Nine persons were killed and 32 wounded. The dead included two police officers and a teenager. Peruvian authorities suspected either the Shining Path rebels or the Tupac Amaru Revolutionary Movement. The attack occurred 3 days before President George W. Bush visited Peru.

Grenade Attack on a Church in Pakistan, March 17, 2002:
Militants threw grenades into the Protestant International Church in Islamabad, Pakistan, during a service attended by diplomatic and local personnel. Five persons, two of them U.S. citizens, were killed, and 46 were wounded. The dead Americans were State Department employee Barbara Green and her daughter, Kristen Wormsley. Thirteen U.S. citizens were among the wounded. The Lashkar-e-Tayyiba group was suspected.

Drive-by Shooting in Colombia, March 14, 2002:
Gunmen on motorcycles shot and killed two U.S. citizens who had come to Cali, Colombia, to negotiate the release of their father, who was a captive of the FARC. No group claimed responsibility.

Suicide Bombing in Jerusalem, March 9, 2002:
A suicide bombing in a Jerusalem restaurant killed 11 persons and wounded 52, one of whom was a U.S. citizen. The al-Aqsa Martyrs' Brigades claimed responsibility.

Suicide Bombing in the West Bank, March 7, 2002:
A suicide bombing in a supermarket in the settlement of Ariel wounded 10 persons, 1 of whom was a U.S. citizen.

Suicide Bombing in Jerusalem, January 27, 2002:
A suicide bomb attack in Jerusalem killed 1 person and wounded 100. The incident was the first suicide bombing made by a Palestinian woman.

Kidnapping of Daniel Pearl, January 23, 2002:
Armed militants kidnapped *Wall Street Journal* reporter Daniel Pearl in Karachi, Pakistan. Pakistani authorities received a videotape on February 20 depicting Pearl's murder. His grave was found near Karachi on May 16. Pakistani authorities arrested four suspects. Ringleader Ahmad Omar Saeed Sheikh claimed to have organized Pearl's kidnapping to protest Pakistan's subservience to the United States and had belonged to Jaish-e-Muhammad, an Islamic separatist group in Kashmir. All four suspects were convicted on July 15. Saeed Sheikh was sentenced to death, the others to life imprisonment.

Drive-by Shooting at a U.S. Consulate, January 22, 2002:
Armed militants on motorcycles fired on the U.S. Consulate in Calcutta, India, killing 5 Indian security personnel and wounding 13 others. The Harakat ul-Jihad-I-Islami and the Asif Raza Commandoes claimed responsibility. Indian police later killed two suspects, one of whom confessed to belonging to Lashkar-e-Tayyiba as he died.

Ambush on the West Bank, January 15, 2002:
Palestinian militants fired on a vehicle in Beit Sahur, killing one passenger and wounding the other. The dead passenger claimed U.S. and Israeli citizenship. The al-Aqsa Martyrs' Battalion claimed responsibility.

Attack on the Indian Parliament, December 13, 2001:
Five gunmen attacked the Indian Parliament in New Delhi shortly after it had adjourned. Before security forces killed them, the attackers killed 6 security personnel and a gardener. Indian officials blamed Lashkar-e-Tayyiba and demanded that Pakistan crack down on it and on other Muslim separatist groups in Kashmir.

Suicide Bombing in Haifa, December 2, 2001:
A suicide bomb attack aboard a bus in Haifa, Israel, killed 15 persons and wounded 40. HAMAS claimed responsibility for both this attack and those on December 1 to avenge the death of a HAMAS member at the hands of Israeli forces a week earlier.

Anthrax Attacks, October–November 2001:
On October 7 the U.S. Centers for Disease Control and Prevention (CDC) reported that investigators had detected evidence that the deadly anthrax bacterium was present in the building where a Florida man who died of anthrax on October 5 had worked. Discovery of a second anthrax case triggered a major investigation by the Federal Bureau of Investigation (FBI). The two anthrax cases were the first to appear in the United States in 25 years. Anthrax subsequently appeared in mail received by television networks in New York and by the offices in Washington of Senate Majority Leader Tom Daschle and other members of Congress. Attorney General John Ashcroft said in a briefing on October 16, "When people send anthrax through the mail to hurt people and invoke terror, it's a terrorist act."

Source: U.S. Army—Timeline of Terrorism, Available online at http://www.army.mil/terrorism

September 11th spawned a number of changes related to law enforcement as the concepts of homeland security were put into place. These events include everything from the creation of the USA PATRIOT Act, a sweeping piece of legislation that was drafted and signed into law within six weeks, and the creation of the Department of Homeland Security, the largest reorganization of the federal bureaucracy since World War II. Although many of the changes have occurred at the national level, they place the role of state and local police in homeland security in context and is therefore the subject of the next chapter.

CHAPTER 2

Homeland Security

*The enemies of freedom have no regard for the innocent, no concept of
the just and no desire for peace. They will stop at nothing to destroy our
way of life, and we, on the other hand, we stop at nothing to defend it.*

Secretary of Homeland Security Tom Ridge,
August 6, 2003

INTRODUCTION

The concepts of homeland security did not appear out of thin air in the wake of the terrorist attacks on September 11th, but rather were both an extension of the history of homeland security, spanning nearly 80 years, and a result of policies that had been circulating on Capitol Hill for nearly a decade. The first purpose of this chapter, then, is to provide a historical perspective regarding the evolution of homeland security, from its early conceptions in American history, through its more formal evolution during the two World Wars, and finally to the more definitive restructuring throughout the latter half of the twentieth century. Once insight is gained from the historical perspective of homeland security, it helps to place the post–September 11th changes in perspective. Therefore, the second purpose of this chapter is aimed at reviewing the legislative actions by Congress and the president and how the federal bureaucracy has realigned to fight terrorism in the post–9/11 world. Specifically it will look at the largest overhaul of the federal bureaucracy since President Truman realigned the executive branch to transition America from World War II to the Cold War. The overall intent of this chapter, and related to the two main purposes, is to convey an understanding of how America has and is realigning to fight this new war at the federal level, which serves to provide some key insights into the role that state and local police will play in this era of homeland security.

HISTORY OF HOMELAND SECURITY

The Founding Fathers, under the U.S. Constitution, established a system that gave the primary role of homeland security to state and local governments. The national government essentially played a secondary role in the preservation of the homeland unless the state and local governments became so overwhelmed that they could not longer effectively deal with the situation. This particular relationship was embodied in Article 4, Section 4, of the U.S. Constitution, which declared that "the United States shall guarantee to every state in this Union a Republican form of government, and shall protect each of them against invasion; and on application of the legislature, or of the executive (when the legislature cannot be convened) against domestic violence."[1] The first clause gave the federal government the power and responsibility to protect all the states in the Union from an invasion by outside forces of any type. The second clause allowed for the federal government, primarily through the actions of the president, to intervene in cases of domestic disturbances on request of the state government.[2] This was mostly likely inserted by the founders as a result of Shays' Rebellion in Pennsylvania, which occurred just prior to the Constitutional Convention convening.[3]

Although presidential involvement in the issue of domestic disturbances would evolve over time, there was a profound realization that local disturbances were best left to the state and local governments. Federal intervention in local disturbances, the founders agreed, should be a last resort. Madison would highlight this fact, partially to alleviate the fears of the Anti-Federalists, in the Federalist Papers, Number 43, when he explained,

> Insurrection in a State will rarely induce a federal interposition, unless the number concerned in them bear some proportion to the friends of government. It will be much better that the violence in such cases should be repressed by the superintending power, than that the majority should be left to maintain their cause by a bloody and obstinate contest. The existence of a right to interpose will generally prevent the necessity of exerting it.[4]

However, this is not to say that Madison did not recognize the importance of maintaining civil order and that government, including the national government, had the right to intervene. As Madison explained in Federalist Number 37,

> Energy in government is essential to that security against external and internal danger and to that prompt and salutary execution of laws which enter into the very definition of good government. Stability in government is essential to national character and to the advantage annexed to it, as well as to that repose and confidence in the minds of the people, which are among the chief blessings of civil society.[5]

It was, however, Alexander Hamilton, who recognized that granting the state and local governments primary dominion over the issue of administering criminal and civil justice would give them a vested power over the national government. He wrote in Federalist Number 17,

> There is one transcendent advantage belonging to the province of the State governments, which alone suffices to place the matter in a clear and satisfactory light—I mean the ordinary administration of criminal and civil justice. This, of all others, is the most powerful, most universal, and most attractive source of popular obedience and attachment. It is this which, being the immediate and visible guardian of life and property, having its benefits and its terrors in constant activity before the public eye, regulating all those personal interests and familiar concerns to which the sensibility of individuals is more immediately awake, contributes more than any other circumstance to impressing upon the minds of the people affection, esteem, and reverence towards the government. This great cement of society,

which will diffuse itself almost wholly through the channels of the particular governments, independent of all other causes of influence, would insure them so decided an empire over their respective citizens as to render them at all times a complete counterpoise, and, not unfrequently, dangerous rivals to the power of the Union.[6]

Although perhaps overstating the case of power granted to state and local governments through their control of the criminal justice system, the important aspect of this lengthy quote is the fact that Hamilton recognized it was the state and local governments who had primary domain over the issue of law and order and continue to do so today.[7] The national government was a very limited, almost nonexistent, partner. The legal historian Lawrence Friedman has stated that the federal government, in regard to crime and order maintenance, had started "from a baseline of close to zero."[8]

It is evident that the founding fathers and the federal system they created left the primary task of maintaining law and order to the state and local governments. A combination of Article four, Section four, which guaranteed the states a "republican form of government" and the tenth amendment, which reserved the rights not granted by the Constitution to the states, vastly limited the power of the national government to intervene in matters of a criminal nature. Although it could most assuredly deal with crime in its territories and in the District of Columbia, as well as on the "high seas," it could not become directly involved in criminal matters, unless called on by the state legislature or state executive when the legislature could not convene. It is clear, then, that crime, criminal justice, and homeland security were, in the traditional sense, a state and local government matter and that presidents were greatly limited in their ability to address this issue.

Over time this would slowly change as critical events occurred throughout our history, the issue of federalism more fully developed, and people began looking to the national government to solve such problems. The federal government would began to become more involved in issues of homeland security by various means of asserting federal authority. As Calder has explained, there are essentially three broad categories under which the federal government could intervene: "(1) incidents threatening the unity principle of the federal system of government; (2) incidents threatening the national security and involving foreign nations; and (3) incidents violating a federal law passed by Congress."[9] It was under these three categories that presidents would begin to expand the role of government in homeland security beyond that in which state and local governments continued to be primarily responsible.

It has been noted that one of the first cases of federal intervention in a disaster came in 1803, when three great fires swept through the town of Portsmouth, New Hampshire.[10] The town's ability to recover in the aftermath severely taxed both town and state, and the latter appealed to Congress for assistance. Congress introduced and passed legislation that would render financial assistance to the community. This was the first of what would become a common occurrence by which the national government would become involved in domestic disturbances.[11] Most of these early encounters consisted of natural disasters, such as the Johnstown (Pennsylvania) flood in 1889[12] or the San Francisco earthquake in 1906. In other cases, the national government responded to man-made disasters such as the great Chicago fire of 1871. And in still other cases the national government became involved in domestic disturbances through Article 4 Section 4 of the Constitution, commencing with the Whiskey Rebellion of 1794, and including such historical disturbances as the Dorr Rebellion of 1842, the Pullman Strike of 1894, the Detroit (Michigan) riots during World War II, and the race riots of the late 1960s.[13]

In terms of homeland security, however, little thought was given to the protection of the homefront until World War I. Prior to that time, America was largely isolated from the rest of the world and was protected by the two great oceans. America's entry into World War I would somewhat alter this notion, but not necessarily with any lasting effect. There was never truly any "concentrated, organized attempt to address the protection of the population because it was largely assumed that no one could launch any significant, direct attacks on the vast U.S. land mass."[14]

There was one minor effort to address the protection of the population when America entered World War I. Congress enacted the U.S. Army Appropriations Act, which included the establishment of the Council of National Defense (CND).[15] According to D.F. Houston, the Secretary of Agriculture at the time, "the council was charged with the duty of mobilizing military and naval resources, studying the location, utilization and coordination of railroads, waterways and highways, increase of domestic production for civil and military purposes, the furnishing of requisite information to manufacturers, and the creation of relations which would render possible the immediate concentration of national resources."[16] Related to this charge, the CND was also to create a War Industries Board that would encourage state governments to create state defense councils and in turn encourage local governments to create their own local defense councils.[17] These entities would be formed to provide for local security against external threats. Once the war ended in 1918, the program was largely discontinued and officially abolished in 1921. America returned to its isolationism.

During the Great Depression and the Dust Bowl years of the mid-1930s, America faced a number of emergencies that prompted Roosevelt to create the National Emergency Council within the confines of the White House. As America began to move more toward a war footing in the late 1930s, Roosevelt's concern shifted away from the natural emergencies and more toward the issue of national security. In 1939, "Roosevelt issued a statement on espionage requesting that all citizens, including state and local officials, turn over relevant information to the FBI."[18] The next year, Roosevelt would abolish the National Emergency Council and reconstitute it as the Office of Emergency Management, which would remain under the president in the White House. The next year, on May 20, 1941, just prior to America entering World War II, Roosevelt created the Office of Civil Defense (OCD) with New York City Mayor Fiorello La Guardia as its director. Roosevelt placed the OCD within the Office of Emergency Management.[19]

Like its predecessor from World War I, the OCD sought to have a nationwide network of Civil Defense councils that were established to protect the homeland from external threats to include the tasking as an early warning system, an entity to monitor the threat of espionage, and as a means of responding to attacks on the homefront. Eventually the OCD saw 44 states establish Civil Defense councils, and over 1,000 local defense councils were created. The OCD became primarily known for its local citizens, who were in charge of conducting air raid drills and preparing for another attack on American soil after the December 7, 1941, bombing of Pearl Harbor. By the end of World War II over ten million citizens had volunteered their time as part of the OCD.

After World War II, as America shifted from a hot war to a cold war, the status of the OCD was in question. Technically there was no need for the OCD, as it was largely based on the threat of another direct attack such as the one on Pearl Harbor. However, it did not take long to realize that the Cold War was just as serious as the hot war, as the threat of an attack by the Soviet Union became the direct attack that America feared. Toward this end, Truman created the National Security Resources Board (NSRB) in 1947, and it would assume all civil defense planning duties until 1950.[20] At the same time the Department of Defense also created an Office of Civil Defense Planning aimed at preparing civil defense plans from the military's perspective. This was renamed the Office of Civil Defense Liaison, as it would no longer be primarily responsible for civil defense plans, but would liaison with the NSRB.

The NSRB continued to function until 1953 as an office within the White House and under the authority of the Executive Branch.[21] However, because the issue of civil defense was becoming a primary concern of the American people, highlighted by the fact that the Soviet Union had tested an atomic bomb in 1949, Truman decided to do something more definitive. By signing Executive Order 10186[22] he created the Federal Civil Defense Administration (FCDA).[23] Because the newly named agency had no funding and because Congress wanted both a chance to engage in the politics of civil defense and have oversight authority regarding civil defense, it moved to pass legislation that would make the FCDA an independent agency of the federal government responsible for coordinating all civil defense planning. Congress passed a comprehensive bill known as the Civil Defense Act of 1950,[24] and one aspect of the bill was the creation of the FCDA, which came into existence on January 12, 1951. Both the NSRB and the Office of Civil Defense Planning under the Department of Defense were absorbed into this newly created independent agency. America now had a consolidated agency for coordinating all civil defense planning in the United States.

The only problem with the consolidated agency was determining what its primary function was. The Truman administration debated the proper role, and Congress debated the proper funding. Although there was an initiative to build bomb shelters, the funding was severely lacking. Although there was consideration for the creation of medical treatment capabilities for mass casualties, the funding was limited, thus limiting the stockpiles of medical supplies. In addition, mass evacuation plans were developed, but largely limited to federal considerations, such as Washington, D.C. In the end, states retained the basic responsibility for civil defense by developing local plans and coordinating among state and local officials. The FCDA did develop education materials and created school lesson plans teaching such things as "duck and cover" and the effects of radiation. Funding was also allocated for cities and towns to install warning sirens and in coordination with the FCC, the CONELRAD (CONtrol of Electronic RADiation) system was created, which was the early protege of the Emergency Broadcast System (EBS).

Despite having one agency responsible for civil defense planning, the responsibilities were dispersed across existing agencies and newly created agencies. In 1950 Congress passed the Federal Disaster Relief Act, which was designed to provide relief to states in times of disaster.[25] To this end, the Office of Defense Mobilization (EOP) was created in the White House to coordinate this type of relief. Although initially this was to deal with wartime activities, it would pick up disaster relief responsibilities through another Executive Order (10427). In 1953, under reorganization plan #3, the FCDA would focus on war threats and the ODM would concentrate on peacetime threats. Although the administration was trying to make wartime civil defense and peacetime civil defense (natural and man-made disasters) distinct from each other, the reality was they were highly related. If a city in America was attacked by the Soviet Union, its evacuation plans would be no different than if a natural disaster occurred. Recognizing this duplication of effort, once again under a reorganization plan (this time #1 dated July 1, 1958), both the functions of the FCDA and ODM were consolidated under the Office of Defense and Civilian Mobilization (ODCM). The name aptly showed both concerns merging together.

The ODCM was placed under the control of the Executive Office of the President. Leading up to this consolidation, America experienced the impact of several hurricanes, and each one necessitated an individual response from Congress to provide for disaster relief. Recognizing the inefficiencies associated with responding to disasters in this manner, the newly created ODCM looked to establish a standard method of response. To ensure that there was adequate funding for this standard response, Congress amended the Federal Civil Defense Act to provide matching grants to help states and local governments share the cost of civil emergencies.

In 1961, with the election of John F. Kennedy as president, once again administrative priorities necessitated organizational changes. Kennedy, "sensing that the overwhelming majority of state and local governments were doing little if anything to develop a sheltering capability, decided to make civil defense preparedness once again a central issue."[26] The Kennedy administration's take on the issue of war and peace preparedness was that the functions should be split. Hence the Office of Civil and Defense Mobilization was split into two agencies, the Office of Emergency Planning (OEP), an office within the White House for civil emergencies, and the Office of Civil Defense, under the Department of Justice, for civil defense.

This was only the beginning of the fragmentation of various services related to civil defense. Beginning in the late 1960s and moving into the 1970s, state governors began to pressure Congress to once again consolidate civil defense and emergency preparedness. The main motivational factor was most likely the ability to allow for the dual use of funds, thus freeing up more support and financial assistance to state and local governments, regardless of the type of emergency. Although the dual use of funds became a reality, the two entities were not consolidated but fragmented even further. On the civil defense side of the equation, the Office of Civil Defense in 1964 retained its name, but the U.S. Army was given primary responsibility. In 1972, this was moved back to the Department of Defense's responsibility with another name change to the Defense Civil Preparedness Agency.

On the emergency preparedness side of the equation, the Office of Emergency Planning (OEP) became the Office of Emergency Preparedness (still OEP) in 1968, which retained all of the previous preparedness functions, only losing the civil defense responsibilities. However, in the early 1970s, other agencies became responsible for various aspects of preparedness. The OEP became the Office of Emergency Preparedness, but still being the OEP it was thus changed to the Federal Preparedness Agency (FPA) in 1975. The new OEP and later FPS was placed under the General Services Administration (GSA), thus downplaying its importance to the Nixon administration. In addition, the Office of Telecommunication Policy, the Office of Science and Technology Policy, the Department of the Treasury, and the Federal Disaster Assistance Administration picked up various responsibilities, as did the Dam Safety Coordination office, the Earthquake Hazard Reduction office, the Consequence Management in Terrorism office, the Warning and Emergency Broadcast Agency, the Federal Insurance Administration, the National Fire Prevention and Control Administration, and the National Weather Service Community Preparedness Program. This fragmentation was also evident at the state level as well, as states attempted to align their respective agencies with the federal agencies dealing with particular aspects of civil defense and emergency preparedness. Clearly there was no single plan or any coordinated effort regarding civil defense or emergency preparedness throughout the 1970s, leaving the United States strategy toward civil defense and emergency management in total confusion.[27]

BOX 2-1

HISTORICAL ORGANIZATIONAL ANTECEDENTS OF THE DEPARTMENT OF HOMELAND SECURITY

National Defense Council	1917–1918
National Emergency Council	1933–1939
National Defense Council	1939–1941
Office for Emergency Management	1940–1950
Office of Civilian Defense	1941–1945
National Security Resources Board (National Security Act 1947)	1947–1949
Office of Civil Defense Planning (Department of Defense)	1948–1949
National Security Resources Board (White House)	1949–1953
Office of Civil Defense Liasison (Department of Defense)	1949–1950
Office of Defense Mobilization (Federal Civil Defense Act 1950)	1950–1953
Federal Civil Defense Administration	1950–1958
Office of Defense and Civilian Mobilization	1958
Office of Civil and Defense Mobilization	1958–1961
Office of Emergency Planning	1961–1968
Office of Civil Defense (Department of Defense)	1961–1964
Office of Civil Defense (U.S. Army)	1964–1972
Defense Civil Preparedness Agency (Department of Defense)	1972–1979
Office of Preparedness (General Services Administration)	1973–1975
Federal Preparedness Agency (General Services Administration)	1975–1979
Federal Emergency Management Agency (FEMA)	1979–2003
Department of Homeland Security (FEMA falls under DHS)	2003–present
U.S. Northern Command (Department of Defense)	2002–present

Sources: City of Fort Collins. (2005). *From Civil Defense to Emergency Management.* Retrieved July 12, 2005 from *http://www.ci.fort-collins.co.us/oem/civildefense.php*, Drabek, T. E. (1991). "The Evolution of Emergency Management." In *Emergency Management: Principles and Practices for Local Government.* Edited by Drabek, T. E. and Hoetmer, G. J., 3–29. Washington, D.C.: International City Management Association; Green, W. G. (2005). *Civil Defense and Emergency Management Organizational History.* Retrieved July 14, 2005 from *http://www.richmond.edu/~wgreen/Ecdflow.pdf;* The Tennessee Emergency Management Agency. (2005). "Tennessee Civil Defense History." Retrieved June 15, 2005 from *http://www.tnema.org/Archives /EMHistory/TNCDHistory10.htm*

In 1979, the Carter administration put an end to the confusion. The state governors had begun to call for a consolidation of federal emergency management in 1977, and they used the National Governors Association to make their demands known. In 1978, Carter submitted a reorganization plan to Congress, and debate ensued. Then, on March 28, 1979, the nuclear power plant at Three Mile Island began to malfunction, generating serious concern among the American people. Three days later, on March 31, 1979, President Carter signed Executive Order 12127, which established the Federal Emergency Management Agency (FEMA). An additional Executive Order (12148) mandated the consolidation of all the various agencies listed under this newly created agency.[28] Carter placed John Macy in charge of FEMA with the responsibility of unifying an agency that consisted of a number of varying agencies, under a number of different organizations, spread across Washington, D.C. Despite the consolidation being mandated by Executive Order, the reality was that FEMA remained a conglomerate of many different entities acting independent of one another.[29] In addition, "for many years the 'civil defense' and 'national security' planners were distinct from those that assisted state and local governments in preparing for and responding to disasters."[30] Macy argued that both emergency preparedness and civil defense activities shared many similarities and that responses to both would be roughly the same. As a result, Macy focused his efforts on the creation of the Integrated Emergency Management System (IEMS), which focused on the "direction, control and warning systems which are common to the full range of emergencies from small isolated events to the ultimate emergency—war."[31]

FEMA continued to face a number of problems in regard to its operations. A number of early crises and disasters included the contamination of Love Canal, the Cuban Refugee crisis, the Loma Prieta earthquake and Hurricanes Hugo in 1989 and Andrew in 1992. Each of these disasters only managed to highlight how woefully ill-prepared FEMA was in responding to disasters—its primary charge. Perhaps the most demoralizing emergency to FEMA was Hurricane Andrew; when FEMA could not adequately respond, President Bush placed the Secretary of Transportation in charge and mobilized the military to provide assistance. Several investigative reports by the General Accounting Office (GAO) revealed that FEMA was not able to coordinate or handle the management of catastrophic disasters and changes needed to be made.[32]

Upon taking office, President Clinton appointed James Lee Witt as the Director of FEMA, the first director to actually have a background in emergency management, having served as then-Governor Clinton's director of the Arkansas Office of Emergency Services.[33] Witt initiated sweeping reforms, attempting to address many of the criticisms laid out by the GAO in their investigations. He drew on the concepts of "reinventing government," concepts proposed by authors Osborne and Gaebler[34] and touted by then Vice-President Al Gore, such as customer service training and reorganizations, to break down and eliminate stovepipes by encouraging agencies within FEMA to begin communicating with one another. In addition, he encouraged the use of new technologies to better manage the vast amounts of information that occur during disasters. Moreover, Witt also began to improve the relationships and coordination, one of its primary functions, with state and local agencies. In the end, FEMA was also assisted by President Clinton elevating the FEMA director to cabinet-level status, thus giving Witt and his agency far more power inside the Beltway.[35]

FEMA was tested numerous times in the 1990s, including the first World Trade Center Bombing in 1993 and the Oklahoma City Bombing in 1995. Although they were successful, due to the nature of federalism in America, one defining question still remained: in the event of a disaster, who was the lead agency? Witt did not immediately claim the role for FEMA, having to recognize that first responders are local police and fire and that states have the right and responsibility under the Constitution to respond to such disasters.[36] However, as FEMA began to flex its muscle by way of newfound capabilities and resources, state directors began looking to FEMA to lead the way. FEMA's constraints, however, fell in the area of the amount of resources it was able to command. Other agencies with various related responsibilities often had greater resources, such as the Department of Justice and the Department of Defense. This created constraints regarding FEMA's ability to always assume the primary leadership role. Despite this political misgiving, whether FEMA wanted the role or not, it was fast becoming an administrative given.

In 2001, when President George W. Bush came into office, he appointed Joe M. Allbaugh as the new director of FEMA.[37] Within months FEMA's new director was faced with the greatest challenge in that organization's history, the terrorist attacks on September 11, 2001. The agency responded well under the circumstances and was able to provide both New York City and Arlington County, Virginia, with urban search and rescue support, give assistance in various lifesaving operations, meet individual and public assistance needs, implement human services and victims' assistance programs, and help with the removal of debris at ground zero.[38] Despite its success in responding to the terrorist attacks, there was still the realization that FEMA's resources and capabilities needed to be enhanced to protect the homeland, and within two years FEMA became one of the major components of the DHS.

In addition to the creation of the DHS, the Bush administration also expanded the U.S. military's focus on the world, by creating the U.S. Northern Command (NORTHCOM) in 2003.[39] NORTHCOM was devised to cover all North America, the only geographical area in the world that the Department of Defense did not cover at the time. Given the new command with a four-star general in charge, NORTHCOM became the primary command for homeland defense and was given authority, as specific in Article 1, Section 8, "to provide for calling forth the militia to execute the laws of the union, suppress insurrections, and repel invasions." Although the DHS assumed the emergency management and civil defense duties, any military considerations fell under U.S. Northern Command.

U.S.A. P.A.T.R.I.O.T. ACT 2001

In the immediate aftermath of the terrorist attacks on September 11, 2001, neither the DHS nor the U.S. Northern Command existed. Although consideration had been given prior to the attacks for a major bureaucratic reorganization, the plans were merely in the discussion stage within the executive and legislative branches. Other bills to address the issue of terrorist investigations, strengthen existing laws on terrorism, or create new laws were also under consideration at the time. When the hijacked planes struck the World Trade Center towers and the Pentagon, this moved any and all proposals from the consideration stage to placing them on the table for action. For example, one such bill, the

Combating Terrorism Act, had "proposed expanding the government's authority to trace telephone calls to include e-mails,"[40] thus expanding existing surveillance powers to include modern technological changes. According to O'Harrow, a reporter for the *Washington Post,* "it was hauled out and approved in minutes."[41]

Although from the time the bill was crafted to the time it was ultimately passed by Congress and signed into law was very short by Washington standards, the debate was nonetheless extremely intense. Much of the debate centered on the right balance between targeting the terrorists who had committed the attacks and balancing that with the civil liberties of all citizens to avoid government peering into the lives of everyday people.[42] The Bush administration, namely under the guidance of Attorney General John Ashcroft, pushed for expanded governmental powers. The chairman of the Judiciary Committee, Senator Patrick Leahy (D-VT), attempted to slow down the push toward expanding government powers of surveillance. American sentiments as represented through public opinion polls, however, "showed that most people were more than willing to trade off civil liberties and privacy protection for more security."[43] So, although the Democrats began drafting their own antiterrorism legislation (tentatively titled the Uniting and Strengthening America Act), many of the administration's policies were finding their way into the bill that was ultimately crafted. Although there were many similarities between the bills, the final bill went much further than the Democrats' bill. And although it was Dick Armey (R-TX) that began the discussion of placing a "sunset" provision in the bill, it was the Democrats that embraced the concept, thus making it more palatable for all concerned. As a result, the majority of the bill's new laws would have a four-year sunset, thus the provisions would expire at the end of 2005 unless renewed by Congress.

The bill, House Resolution 2975, originated in the House of Representatives and became widely known as the "Patriot Act." The official title, however, was the U.S.A. P.A.T.R.I.O.T. Act, which stands for "Uniting and Strengthening America By Providing Appropriate Tools Required to Intercept and Obstruct Terrorism." One month after the September 11th terrorist attacks, the Senate passed Senate Bill 1510, their version of the Patriot Act provisions. On that same day the House Judiciary Committee reported out an amended version of House Resolution 2975, and amendments were then offered by House members to this bill over the next several days.

On October 17, the U.S. Capitol and its lawmakers confronted a new terrorist threat—the anthrax attacks. This increased the urgency to get a final bill to the president's desk for his signature.[44] As a result, over the next several days, the House passed a clean bill (House Resolution 3162), which resolved the differences between their earlier bill and the Senate bill. The Senate agreed to the changes, and House Resolution 3162 and the U.S.A. PATRIOT Act[45] was sent to the president, who signed it on October 26, 2001, making it Public Law 107-56.

The U.S.A. PATRIOT Act has ten titles that provided for new powers for government to use against terrorists. In general, it gave federal officials greater authority to track and intercept communications, both for law enforcement and foreign intelligence-gathering purposes.[46] It vested the secretary of the treasury with regulatory powers to combat corruption of U.S. financial institutions for foreign money laundering purposes. It sought to further close our borders to foreign terrorists and to detain and remove those within our borders. It created new crimes, new penalties, and new

BOX 2-2

THE PRESIDENT: Good morning and welcome to the White House. Today, we take an essential step in defeating terrorism, while protecting the constitutional rights of all Americans. With my signature, this law will give intelligence and law enforcement officials important new tools to fight a present danger.

...The changes, effective today, will help counter a threat like no other our nation has ever faced. We've seen the enemy, and the murder of thousands of innocent, unsuspecting people. They recognize no barrier of morality. They have no conscience. The terrorists cannot be reasoned with. Witness the recent anthrax attacks through our Postal Service.

Our country is grateful for the courage the Postal Service has shown during these difficult times. We mourn the loss of the lives of Thomas Morris and Joseph Curseen; postal workers who died in the line of duty. And our prayers go to their loved ones.

I want to assure postal workers that our government is testing more than 200 postal facilities along the entire Eastern corridor that may have been impacted. And we will move quickly to treat and protect workers where positive exposures are found.

But one thing is for certain: These terrorists must be pursued, they must be defeated, and they must be brought to justice. And that is the purpose of this legislation. Since the 11th of September, the men and women of our intelligence and law enforcement agencies have been relentless in their response to new and sudden challenges.

We have seen the horrors terrorists can inflict. We may never know what horrors our country was spared by the diligent and determined work of our police forces, the FBI, ATF agents, federal marshals, Custom officers, Secret Service, intelligence professionals and local law enforcement officials, under the most trying conditions. They are serving this country with excellence, and often with bravery.

They deserve our full support and every means of help that we can provide. We're dealing with terrorists who operate by highly sophisticated methods and technologies, some of which were not even available when our existing laws were written. The bill before me takes account of the new realities and dangers posed by modern terrorists. It will help law enforcement to identify, to dismantle, to disrupt, and to punish terrorists before they strike.

For example, this legislation gives law enforcement officials better tools to put an end to financial counterfeiting, smuggling and money-laundering. Secondly, it gives intelligence operations and criminal operations the chance to operate not on separate tracks, but to share vital information so necessary to disrupt a terrorist attack before it occurs.

As of today, we're changing the laws governing information-sharing. And as importantly, we're changing the culture of our various agencies that fight terrorism. Countering and investigating terrorist activity is the number one priority for both law enforcement and intelligence agencies.

Surveillance of communications is another essential tool to pursue and stop terrorists. The existing law was written in the era of rotary telephones. This new law that I sign today will allow surveillance of all communications used by terrorists, including e-mails, the Internet, and cell phones.

As of today, we'll be able to better meet the technological challenges posed by this proliferation of communications technology. Investigations are often slowed by limit on the reach of federal search warrants.

Law enforcement agencies have to get a new warrant for each new district they investigate, even when they're after the same suspect. Under this new law, warrants are valid across all districts and across all states. And, finally, the new legislation greatly enhances the penalties that will fall on terrorists or anyone who helps them.

Current statutes deal more severely with drug-traffickers than with terrorists. That changes today. We are enacting new and harsh penalties for possession of biological weapons. We're making it easier to seize the assets of groups and individuals involved in terrorism. The government will have wider latitude in deporting known terrorists and their supporters. The statute of limitations on terrorist acts will be lengthened, as will prison sentences for terrorists.

This bill was carefully drafted and considered. Led by the members of Congress on this stage, and those seated in the audience, it was crafted with skill and care, determination and a spirit of bipartisanship for which the entire nation is grateful. This bill met with an overwhelming—overwhelming agreement in Congress, because it upholds and respects the civil liberties guaranteed by our Constitution.

This legislation is essential not only to pursuing and punishing terrorists, but also preventing more atrocities in the hands of the evil ones. This government will enforce this law with all the urgency of a nation at war. The elected branches of our government, and both political parties, are united in our resolve to fight and stop and punish those who would do harm to the American people.

It is now my honor to sign into law the USA Patriot Act of 2001.

procedural efficiencies for use against domestic and international terrorists. Although it is not without safeguards, critics contended some of its provisions went too far.[47] And although it grants many of the enhancements sought by the Department of Justice, others are concerned that it did not go far enough.[48]

The titles and provisions of the USA PATRIOT Act that apply to law enforcement begin with Title I, which was designed to enhance domestic security. It created funding for various counterterrorist activities, authorized the Department of Justice to request assistance from the Department of Defense regarding enforcing laws related to weapons of mass destruction (specifically nuclear, chemical, and biological weapons), and it defined presidential authority in regard to terrorist attacks.

Title II was aimed at enhancing surveillance procedures for law enforcement to specifically target terrorists. Although many of these provisions have been used against organized crime and drug syndicates, the broader applications to terrorists, as well as some of the new powers, created much of the controversy over the Patriot Act. This title is broad in that it allowed for the seizure of voice mail messages under a warrant, it authorized intelligence agencies and federal law enforcement agencies to share noncriminal information, it permitted pen registers and trap and trace orders of electronic communication such as e-mail, and it encouraged cooperation between law enforcement and foreign intelligence investigators.

Title III was directed toward money laundering and expanding the powers of law enforcement to work with banking institutions to bring down those laundering money for terrorism purposes. In addition, it prohibited laundering the proceeds from such things as cybercrime, supporting a terrorist organization, and using American credit cards fraudulently overseas. Title IV contained a number of provisions designed to prevent alien terrorists from entering the United States, particularly from Canada, to enable authorities to detail and deport alien terrorists and those who support them, and to monitor the movement of foreigners in the United States. Title V was aimed at removing obstacles to investigating terrorism, including such provisions as allowing for DNA collection in terrorist offenses, and it increased the dollar amount for rewards that the Department of Justice may authorize for wanted terrorists. Title VI provided funding for the victims of terrorism, specifically public safety officers and their families. Title VII was focused on increasing information sharing for critical infrastructure protection allowing for the expansion of the Regional Information Sharing System (RISS) to be used to enhance cooperation between federal, state, and local law enforcement agencies to address multijurisdictional terrorist conspiracies and activities.

Title VIII of the Patriot Act focused on the creation of new crimes and new penalties. The Act created new federal crimes for terrorist attacks on mass transportation facilities, for biological weapons offenses, for harboring terrorists, for providing terrorists material support, for misconduct associated with money laundering as previously mentioned, for conducting the affairs of an enterprise that affects interstate or foreign commerce through the patterned commission of terrorist offenses, and for fraudulent charitable solicitation. Although strictly speaking these were new federal crimes, they generally supplemented existing laws by filling gaps and increasing penalties. More specifically, the Act did exclusively increase penalties for certain crimes that terrorists might commit. It established an alternative maximum penalty for acts of terrorism, raised the penalties for conspiracy to commit certain terrorist offenses, envisioned sentencing some terrorists to lifelong parole, and increased the penalties for counterfeiting, cybercrime, and charity fraud. Title IX was aimed at improving intelligence gathering through cooperation between the director of the Central Intelligence Agency and the attorney general. And, finally, Title X was a set of miscellaneous provisions that aimed to provide safeguards against civil rights abuses, to create the First Responders Assistance Act, which would give grants to state and local governments to assist them in preventing and responding to terrorist attacks, and authorized grants through such previous grants as the Office for State and Local Domestic Preparedness Support of the Office of Justice Programs and the Crime Identification Technology Act of 1998, greater appropriations for the purposes of antiterrorism.[49]

The vast majority of the USA PATRIOT Act is clearly aimed at providing provisions for the federal government to deal with the issue of terrorism, in particular federal law enforcement. However, some of the provisions have direct bearing on state and local law enforcement, and although it is federally driven, the Patriot Act cannot be ignored by local law enforcement, for they do play a role in the Act's enforcement. That particular role and which provisions apply and how they apply are still being determined. In addition, the sunset provisions could potentially impact the future application of the Patriot Act's provisions. As of this writing, however, Congress has made some minor changes to the bill, but for all intents and purposes it would appear that the majority of the provisions within the USA PATRIOT Act will be renewed with 14 of the sunset provisions becoming permanent, and two, one related to business records and the other to roving wiretaps, are being given a 10-year extension.[50]

BOX 2-3

THE PRESIDENT'S STATE OF THE UNION ADDRESS JANUARY 29, 2002

. . . The next priority of my budget is to do everything possible to protect our citizens and strengthen our nation against the ongoing threat of another attack. Time and distance from the events of September the 11th will not make us safer unless we act on its lessons. America is no longer protected by vast oceans. We are protected from attack only by vigorous action abroad, and increased vigilance at home.

My budget nearly doubles funding for a sustained strategy of homeland security, focused on four key areas: bioterrorism, emergency response, airport and border security, and improved intelligence. We will develop vaccines to fight anthrax and other deadly diseases. We'll increase funding to help states and communities train and equip our heroic police and firefighters. We will improve intelligence collection and sharing, expand patrols at our borders, strengthen the security of air travel, and use technology to track the arrivals and departures of visitors to the United States.

Homeland security will make America not only stronger, but, in many ways, better. Knowledge gained from bioterrorism research will improve public health. Stronger police and fire departments will mean safer neighborhoods. Stricter border enforcement will help combat illegal drugs. And as government works to better secure our homeland, America will continue to depend on the eyes and ears of alert citizens.

THE HOMELAND SECURITY ACT 2002

Although the U.S.A. P.A.T.R.I.O.T. Act gave the federal government new tools with which to track down terrorists, it did not rectify the organizational structure of the federal government for dealing with homeland security. At the time of the September 11th attacks, the federal government had over 100 agencies with some form of responsibility for homeland security. In addition, there was no entity or individual responsible for coordinating the work of these agencies to protect the homeland. Not to mention the fact that many of the agencies also worked with their state and local counterparts through joint efforts, various programs, and task forces. The Bush administration realized this problem immediately and attempted to rectify it by establishing the Office of Homeland Security within the White House through E.O. 13228, which was signed on October 8, 2001. Bush then selected Pennsylvania Governor Tom Ridge to serve as its director.

Shortly thereafter, realizing the political relationship that an Office of Homeland Security would cause, Senator Lieberman (D-CT) introduced a bill (S. 1534) with Senator Arlen Specter (R-PA) to establish a "Department of National Homeland Security." The bill would have made the head of the department a member of the cabinet and the National Security Council. The political issue centered around the fact that an "office" within the White House is part of the president's staff of advisors and does not have to appear before Congress when requested. A department head is part of the bureaucracy, which both the president and Congress control, and thus when Congress calls a department head to appear at a hearing, they must respond to this request. Senator Lieberman proposed the bill so as not to lose

Congressional control over the issue of homeland security. The bill did develop, albeit slowly, through Congress as it proceeded from one committee to the next. In the meantime, Lieberman's fears were realized when Tom Ridge, after becoming director, essentially refused to appear before Congress. Political pressure was brought on the president, giving impetus to the creation of a DHS.[51]

On June 6, 2002, President Bush proposed the creation of a DHS, a proposal that would move beyond the coordination efforts of the Office of Homeland Security to a strong administrative structure for managing consolidated programs concerned with border security and effective response to domestic terrorism incidents. On June 18th, the president transmitted to the House of Representatives proposed legislation to establish the new department. It was then introduced by request of the president as House Resolution 5005 and sponsored by Speaker of the House Dennis Hastert (R-IL) and the Minority Leader Richard Gephardt (D-MO).

The difficulties related to coordinating a massive overhaul of the federal bureaucracy are that Congress has the authority to reorganize the bureaucracy and allocate budgets for each of the agencies. As the discussion for reorganization centered on the creation of a new agency, the DHS, the debate was focused on what agencies, or what pieces of an agency, would fall under this new department-level organization. In addition, to move these particular agencies or subagencies out of their current agency, it would take the approval of the related committees in Congress to approve such a move. Hence, if a subagency was to be moved out of the Department of Agriculture, the Agriculture committee in the House would have to approve it before the entire House could make a motion. By the end of the summer the coordination of such a movement was underway.

President George W. Bush signing the Homeland Security Act. (*Source: AP Wide World Photos.*)

On June 19, 2002, the Agriculture, Armed Services, and Energy and Commerce committees approved plans for the reorganization of the federal bureaucracy. In addition, the Ways and Means Committee, the committee that approves budgetary allocations, also approved of the bill on June 19. Debate then began in the Judiciary, Science, and Transportation committees, as they had more agencies being affected by the proposed bill. All three of these committees, by voice vote, gave approval to moving forward with the proposals. As a result, the House of Representatives began open debate on House Resolution 5005, the Homeland Security Act of 2002, on June 25. The next day, debate in the House ended after 26 amendments to the bill were proposed, considered, and many adopted. Some of these amendments included establishing an office for state and local government coordination, retaining FEMA as an independent agency with responsibility for natural disaster preparedness, response, and recovery, and preserving the Customs Service as a distinct entity within the Department of Homeland Security. That same day, June 26, 2002, the House voted on the bill, and it passed with a 295 to 132 vote. The bill then moved to the Senate, where it went through a similar process of debate followed by reconciliation with the House bill, which came on November 19, 2002.[52]

A week later, in the East Room of the White House, President Bush made his remarks before signing the bill into law. He stated that "with my signature, this act of Congress will create a New DHS, ensuring that our efforts to defend this country are comprehensive and united." He further stated that the act, "takes the next critical steps in defending our country" and that "the continuing threat of terrorism, the threat of mass murder on our own soil will be met with a unified, effective response."[53]

The Homeland Security Act of 2002 consists of 17 titles. Title I of the act established the DHS and created the position for the Secretary of Homeland Security to be appointed by the president with the consent of the Senate at to be a part of the president's cabinet. Specifically, this first title sets out the responsibilities of the new department, which include preventing terrorist attacks within the United States, reducing the vulnerability of the United States to terrorism at home, and minimizing the damage and assisting in the recovery from any attacks that may occur. The DHS's primary responsibilities correspond to the five major functions established by the bill: information analysis and infrastructure protection (Title II); chemical, biological, radiological, nuclear, and related countermeasures (Title III); border and transportation security (Title IV); emergency preparedness and response (Title V); and coordination with other parts of the federal government, with state and local governments, and with the private sector (Title VII).[54]

Title II of the act is focused on information analysis and infrastructure and creates a corresponding undersecretary to the secretary for this purpose. The duties of this office include (1) receiving and analyzing law enforcement information, intelligence, and other information to understand the nature and scope of the terrorist threat to the American homeland and to detect and identify potential threats of terrorism within the United States; (2) comprehensively assessing the vulnerabilities of key resources and critical infrastructures; (3) integrating relevant information, intelligence analyses, and measures; (4) developing a comprehensive national plan for security key resources and critical infrastructures; (5) taking or seeking to effect necessary measures to protect those key resources and infrastructures; (6) administering the Homeland Security Advisory System, exercising primary responsibility for public threat advisories, and providing specific warning information to state and local governments, and the private sector, as well as advice about appropriate protective actions and countermeasures; and (7) reviewing, analyzing, and making recommendations for improvements in the policies and procedures governing the sharing of law enforcement, intelligence, and other information relating to homeland security within the federal government and between the federal government and state and local governments. In addition, this title transferred several agency systems related to information analysis to the DHS and granted the agency access to intelligence.[55]

Title III of the act focuses on chemical, biological, radiological, and nuclear countermeasures. As in Title II, this title creates an undersecretary position whose responsibilities include (1) securing the people, infrastructure, property, resources and systems in the United States from acts of terrorism involving chemical, biological, radiological, or nuclear weapons or other emerging threats; (2) conducting a national scientific research and development program to support the mission of the department, including developing national policy and coordinating the federal government's (nonmilitary) efforts to counter these types of terrorist threats, including relevant research and development; (3) establishing priorities and directing and supporting national research and development and procurement of technology and systems for detecting, preventing, protecting against, and responding to terrorist attacks using chemical, biological, radiological, nuclear, or related weapons and materials, and for preventing the importation of such weapons and materials into the United States; and (4) establishing guidelines for state and local efforts to develop and implement countermeasures in this area. This title also transferred a number of programs from various existing departments focused on these type of agents and to coordinate these programs with the public-health sector and Department of Health and Human Services.[56]

Title IV of the Homeland Security Act created an undersecretary for border and transportation security whose primary duties include (1) preventing the entry of terrorists and the instruments of terrorism into the United States; (2) securing the borders, territorial waters, ports, terminals, waterways, and air, land, and sea transportation systems of the United States; (3) administering the immigration and naturalization laws of the United States, including the establishment of rules governing the granting of visas and other forms of permission to enter the United States to individuals who are not citizens or lawful permanent residents; (4) administering the customs laws of the United States; and (5) ensuring the speedy, orderly, and efficient flow of lawful traffic and commerce in carrying out these responsibilities. Most significantly, this title transferred the United States Customs Service, the Immigration and Naturalization Service (INS), and the Coast Guard, along with several other agencies, under the DHS.[57]

Title V of the Act created the position of undersecretary for emergency preparedness and response. This undersecretary is responsible for (1) helping to ensure the preparedness of emergency response providers for terrorist attacks, major disasters, and other emergencies; (2) establishing standards, conducting exercises and training, evaluating performances, and providing funds in relation to the Nuclear Incident Response Team; (3) providing the federal government's response to terrorist attacks and major disasters; (4) aiding the recovery from terrorist attacks and major disasters; (5) working with other federal and nonfederal agencies to build a comprehensive national incident management system; (6) consolidating existing federal government emergency response plans into a single, coordinated national response plan; and (7) developing comprehensive programs for developing interoperative communications technology and ensuring that emergency response providers acquire such technology. The agencies transferred to the DHS under this title include the FEMA and several elements of both the Department of Justice and the Department of Health and Human Services. In addition, the title also gave DHS the ability to command certain elements of both the Department of Energy and the Environmental Protection Agency as they relate to nuclear threats and incidents.[58]

Title VI dealt with the treatment of charitable trusts for members of the armed forces and other government organizations. Title VII of the Homeland Security Act dealt with the management of the new agency and created the undersecretary for management whose responsibilities include (1) budget and fiscal matters; (2) procurement; (3) human resources and personnel; (4) information technology and communications systems; (5) facilities, property, equipment, and other material resources; (6) security for personnel, information technology and communications systems, and material resources; and (7) identification and tracking of performance measures. This undersecretary position did not absorb control of any outside agencies or their subagency parts.[59]

Title VIII of the act deals with coordination with nonfederal entities, the inspector general, the United States Secret Service, and general provisions. This title specifies the responsibilities of the secretary of homeland security relating to coordination with state and local officials and the private sector to ensure adequate planning, equipment, training, and exercise activities, coordinating and, as appropriate, consolidating, the federal government's communications and communications systems relating to homeland security with state and local governments, directing grant programs for state and local government emergency response providers, and distributing warnings and information to state and local governments and to the public. This title also created the office of Inspector General, transferred the U.S. Secret Service from the Treasury Department to DHS allowing it to maintain itself as a distinct entity, and it allowed for advisory committees to be created by the secretary of homeland security.[60]

Title IX created the National Homeland Security Council within the Executive Office of the president, much akin to the National Security Council that deals with foreign affairs. Title X focused on information security for the new department, whereas Title XI primarily involved the transfer of the Bureau of Alcohol, Tobacco, and Firearms from the Department of Treasury to the Department of Justice. Title XII dealt with airline liability arising out of insurance claims resulting from acts of terrorism, and Title XIII focused on federal workforce improvement. Title XIV allowed for the arming of airline pilots as a security measure against terrorism, and title XV of the act dealt with the transition of the various agencies as well as the appropriations originally allocated to the agencies and how this would be dealt with when the DHS was formed. And, finally, titles XVI and XVII dealt with legal changes that were necessary to have conformity in the law regarding all of the changes being made with the creation of the new department.[61]

The signature of the Homeland Security Act of 2002 by President Bush entered the act into law as Public Law 107-296. More significantly, it would stand as the largest change in the U.S. bureaucracy since President Harry S Truman's overhaul as America entered the Cold War. Bush announced that Tom Ridge, currently serving as the Director of the Office of Homeland Security, would serve as secretary, that Navy Secretary Gordon England would become the deputy secretary for homeland security, and DEA Administrator Asa Hutchinson would become the undersecretary for border and transportation security. On January 24, 2003, 60 days after the signing of the Homeland Security Act, the DHS came into existence.

OFFICE/DEPARTMENT OF HOMELAND SECURITY

On September 20, 2001, when President Bush addressed both Congress and the nation in the wake of the terrorist attacks on the United States, he announced that he was creating the Office of Homeland Security and that he was appointing Tom Ridge as its director. On October 8, President Bush did just that, swearing in Ridge as an assistant to the president for dealing with issues related to homeland security (see Appendix C). The problems of having an executive office consisted not only of the political ramifications as previously detailed, but also centered on the fact that without its own budgetary allocations from Congress, the office would essentially be ineffective in trying to coordinate the numerous agencies responsible for securing the homeland. As a result, the Homeland Security Act of 2002 was passed that began the process of overhauling the federal bureaucracy to create the DHS. The department came into official existence on January 24, 2003, with Tom Ridge moving into the secretary's position, creating continuity in the transition from an office to a department. On March 1, 2003, nearly all the federal agencies were transferred into the DHS with the remaining agencies coming onboard June 1, 2003. Although some of the agencies remained intact and reported directly to the secretary for homeland security, most fell under the four new directorates: Border and Transportation Security, Information Analysis and Infrastructure Protection, Emergency Preparedness and Response, and Science and Technology. Secretary Ridge was given one year to develop a structural framework for organizing the 22 agencies absorbed and the over 179,000 employees. This was accomplished by August of 2004, but under the direction of the new secretary of homeland security, Michael Chertoff, it is undergoing revisions and is projected to reorganize again by the end of fiscal year 2005.

Vision, Mission, and Strategic Goals

In 2004, the DHS released its Strategic Plan that relayed its vision and mission statement and listed the key strategic goals to achieve this vision and implement its mission.[62]

Vision
Preserving our freedoms, protecting America . . . we secure our homeland.

Mission
We will lead the unified national effort to secure America. We will prevent and deter terrorist attacks and protect against and respond to threats and hazards to the nation. We will ensure safe and secure borders, welcome lawful immigrants and visitors, and promote the free flow of commerce.

Strategic Goals
Awareness—Identify and understand threats, assess vulnerabilities, determine potential impacts and disseminate timely information to our homeland security partners and the American public.

Prevention—Detect, deter and mitigate threats to our homeland.

Protection—Safeguard our people and their freedoms, critical infrastructure, property and the economy of our Nation from acts of terrorism, natural disasters, or other emergencies.

Response—Lead, manage and coordinate the national response to acts of terrorism, natural disasters, or other emergencies.

Recovery—Lead national, state, local and private sector efforts to restore services and rebuild communities after acts of terrorism, natural disasters, or other emergencies.

Service—Serve the public effectively by facilitating lawful trade, travel and immigration.

Organizational Excellence—Value our most important resource, our people. Create a culture that promotes a common identity, innovation, mutual respect, accountability and teamwork to achieve efficiencies, effectiveness, and operational synergies.

Core Values

Integrity. "Service before self."   Each of us serves something far greater than ourselves. To our nation, we represent the President and the Congress. To the world, seeking to visit or do business with us, we are often the first Americans they meet. We will faithfully execute the duties and responsibilities entrusted to us, and we will maintain the highest ethical and professional standards.

Vigilance. "Guarding America."   We will relentlessly identify and deter threats that pose a danger to the safety of the American people. As a Department, we will be constantly on guard against threats, hazards, or dangers that threaten our values and our way of life.

Respect. "Honoring our Partners."   We will value highly the relationships we build with our customers, partners and stakeholders. We will honor concepts such as liberty and democracy, for which America stands.

Office of the Secretary

The secretary of homeland security is a cabinet-level official within the executive branch. The first secretary of homeland security was Tom Ridge, and the second and current secretary is Michael Chertoff. The staff functions in the office of the secretary oversee activities with other federal, state, local, and private entities as part of a collaborative effort to strengthen America's borders, provide for intelligence analysis and infrastructure protection, improve the use of science and technology to counter weapons of mass destruction, and create a comprehensive response and recovery division. Within the office of the secretary multiple offices contribute to the overall homeland security mission.[63]

The Privacy Office of the U.S. Department of Homeland Security

The DHS Privacy Office is the first statutorily required Privacy Office at any federal agency whose mission is to minimize the impact on individual's privacy, particularly the individual's personal information and dignity, while achieving the mission of the DHS. It operates under the direction of the chief privacy officer, who is appointed by

BOX 2-4

MEET THE SECRETARY OF HOMELAND SECURITY: MICHAEL CHERTOFF

On February 15, 2005, Judge Michael Chertoff was sworn in as the second secretary of the Department of Homeland Security. Chertoff formerly served as United States Circuit Judge for the Third Circuit Court of Appeals.

Secretary Chertoff was previously confirmed by the Senate to serve in the Bush administration as assistant attorney general for the criminal division at the Department of Justice. As assistant attorney general, he helped trace the 9/11 terrorist attacks to the Al-Qaida network, and worked to increase information sharing within the FBI and with state and local officials.

Before joining the Bush administration, Chertoff was a partner in the law firm of Latham & Watkins. From 1994 to 1996, he served as special counsel for the U.S. Senate Whitewater Committee.

(Source: Photo Courtesy of the Department of Homeland Security.)

Prior to that, Chertoff spent more than a decade as a federal prosecutor, including service as U.S. Attorney for the District of New Jersey, First Assistant U.S. Attorney for the District of New Jersey, and Assistant U.S. Attorney for the Southern District of New York. As United States Attorney, Chertoff investigated and prosecuted several significant cases of political corruption, organized crime, and corporate fraud.

Chertoff graduated magna cum laude from Harvard College in 1975 and magna cum laude from Harvard Law School in 1978. From 1979–1980 he served as a clerk to Supreme Court Justice William Brennan, Jr.

Secretary Chertoff is married to Meryl Justin Chertoff and has two children.

Source: Department of Homeland Security website. (2005). Retrieved April 2005 from *http://www.dhs.gov/dhspublic/display?theme=11&content=4353.*

the secretary. Nuala O'Connor Kelly was appointed chief privacy officer of the DHS by Secretary Ridge on April 16, 2003.[64]

Office for Civil Rights and Civil Liberties

The mission of the Office for Civil Rights and Civil Liberties is to protect civil rights and civil liberties of American citizens and to support homeland security by providing the department with constructive legal and policy advice on the full range of civil rights and civil liberties issues the department will face. Specifically, the Office for Civil Rights and Civil Liberties provides legal and policy advice to departmental leadership on civil rights and civil liberties issues, investigates and resolves complaints filed by members of the public, provides leadership to the department's Equal Employment Opportunity Programs, and serves as an information and communication channel with the public. The office is led by Daniel Sutherland, Officer for Civil Rights and Civil Liberties, who provides legal and policy advice to the secretary and the senior officers of the department.[65]

Office of Counter Narcotics

The Office of Counter Narcotics is largely a liaison position with other agencies responsible for the coordination of drug control policy in the United States, particularly the White House Office of National Drug Control Policy (ONDCP). The purpose is to counter the narcotics trade, for many of the profits from illegal drugs are used to finance terrorism against the United States. The director of this office is a former Central Intelligence Agency employee, Roger Mackin, who is responsible for performing as the U.S. Interdiction Coordinator (USIC), a position within the ONDCP, with those of the newly established DHS Counter Narcotics Officer. The mission of this office is to ensure that all DHS counterdrug policies, initiatives, efforts, and resources are aligned with the President's National Drug Control Strategy. The director coordinates with department and agency heads, U.S. ambassadors and military commanders, interagency working groups, task forces, and coordinating centers having interdiction responsibilities. He will also review the assets committed by federal agencies for drug interdiction to ensure that they are sufficient and their use is properly integrated and optimized.

Office of General Counsel

The Office of General Counsel is a legal advisory office for the secretary of Homeland Security. In addition, the director of this office also advises other members of Homeland Security senior leadership on legal issues arising throughout the department, including those relating to immigration, customs enforcement, environmental compliance, international agreements, civil litigation, transportation security, labor and employment, incident management, public health, infrastructure protection, and intelligence sharing.

Office of Legislative Affairs

The Office of Legislative Affairs facilitates the development and advancement of the department's legislative agenda. The office focuses on providing members of Congress and Congressional staff information about departmental programs, policies, and initiatives on the impact of pending legislation on the department and through Congressional hearings, briefings, meetings, and other communications.

Office of National Capital Region Coordination

The Office of National Capital Region Coordination (NCRC) oversees and coordinates federal programs for and relationships with state, local, and regional authorities in the Washington, D.C., metropolitan area. The office's responsibilities include coordinating department activities relating to the NCR; coordinating to ensure adequate planning, information sharing, training, and execution of domestic preparedness activities in the NCR; and assessing and advocating for resources needed in the NCR.

Private Sector Office

The Office of the Private Sector provides the American business community with a direct line of communication to the DHS. The office works with businesses, trade associations, and other nongovernmental organizations to foster dialogue between the private sector and the department on the full range of issues and challenges faced by America's business sector. In addition to ensuring open communication between the department and the private sector, the office provides strategic guidance to the secretary on prospective policies and regulations and their impact and promotes public–private partnerships and best practices to improve the nation's homeland and economic security.

Office of Public Affairs

The Office of Public Affairs manages both internal and external communications for the DHS and all its 22 component agencies. More specifically, it serves as the public relations office coordinating all press releases, media press conferences, and public affair's requests.

Office of Security

The Office of Security protects and safeguards DHS personnel, property, facilities, and information. The Office of Security develops, implements, and oversees the department's security policies, programs, and standards; delivers security awareness training and education to department personnel; and provides security support to Homeland Security component agencies.

The Office of State and Local Government Coordination and Preparedness

The Office of State and Local Government Coordination and Preparedness is the federal government's lead agency responsible for preparing the nation against terrorism by assisting states, local and tribal jurisdictions, and regional authorities as they prevent, deter, and respond to terrorist acts. The office provides a broad array of assistance to America's first responders through funding, coordinated training, exercises, equipment acquisition, and technical assistance in support of implementing the national strategy for homeland security. The office is focused on implementing Homeland Security Presidential Directive-8, the establishment of a National Preparedness Goal that establishes mechanisms for improved delivery of federal preparedness assistance to state and local governments, and outlines actions to strengthen preparedness capabilities of federal, state, and local entities.

The Five Directorates

As previously detailed under the Homeland Security Act of 2002, five directorates were established to coordinate homeland security efforts regarding five key functioning areas: Border and Transportation Security (BTS), Emergency Preparedness and Response (EP&R), Information Analysis and Infrastructure Protection (IAIP), Science and Technology (S&T), and the Office of Management.

Border and Transportation Security (BTS)

Border and Transportation Security (BTS) is the largest of the five directorates and is focused on securing the nation's borders and transportation systems and enforcing the nation's immigration laws. The BTS absorbed the functions of six former federal agencies: the U.S. Customs Service, the INS enforcement division, the Animal and Plant Health Inspection Service, the Transportation Security Administration, the Office for Domestic Preparedness, and the Federal Protective Service.

Transportation Security Administration (TSA)   The Transportation Security Administration (TSA) was created in response to the terrorist attacks of September 11, 2001, as part of the Aviation and Transportation Security Act signed into law by President George W. Bush on November 19, 2001. TSA was originally in the Department of Transportation but was moved to the DHS in March 2003. TSA's mission is to protect the nation's transportation systems by ensuring the freedom of movement for people and commerce. In February 2002, TSA assumed responsibility for security at the nation's airports and by the end of the year had deployed a federal workforce to meet challenging Congressional deadlines for screening all passengers and baggage. TSA has also engaged in several programs aimed at enforcement including a canine program, training airline crews in self-defense, training pilots and flight deck crews in

BOX 2-5

DEPARTMENT OF HOMELAND SECURITY GOAL #1—AWARENESS

Objective 1.1—Gather and fuse all terrorism-related intelligence; analyze and coordinate access to information related to potential terrorist or other threats.

Objective 1.2—Identify and assess the vulnerability of critical infrastructure and key assets.

Objective 1.3—Develop timely, actionable, and valuable information based on intelligence analysis and vulnerability assessments.

Objective 1.4—Ensure quick and accurate dissemination of relevant intelligence information to homeland security partners, including the public.

Source: Department of Homeland Security. (2004). *Securing Our Homeland: U.S. Department of Homeland Security Strategic Plan.* Washington, D.C.: U.S. Department of Homeland Security.

firearms, and enhancing the screening of passengers and luggage through enhanced science technology.[66]

U.S. Customs and Border Protection (CBP)   U.S. Customs and Border Protection (CBP) is the unified border agency within the (DHS). The CBP combined the inspection workforce and broad border authorities of U.S. Customs, U.S. Immigration, Animal and Plant Health Inspection Service, and the entire U.S. Border Patrol. CBP includes more than 41,000 employees to manage, control, and protect the nation's borders, at and between the official ports of entry. CBP has two goals—antiterrorism and facilitating legitimate trade and travel into and out of the United States.

U.S. Immigration and Custom Enforcement (ICE)   The U.S. Immigration and Custom Enforcement (ICE) was created out of the functions, expertise, resources, and jurisdictions of several once-fragmented border and security agencies that were merged and reconstituted into ICE, the DHS's largest investigative bureau. The agencies that were either moved entirely or merged in part, based on law enforcement functions, included the investigative and intelligence resources of the U.S. Customs Service, the INS, the Federal Protective Service, and as of November 2003, the Federal Air Marshals Service. ICE is the investigative arm of the BTS, the operational directorate within the DHS tasked with securing the nation's borders and safeguarding its transportation infrastructure. The largest component within the DHS, BTS employs more than 100,000 men and women. ICE brings together more than 20,000 employees who focus on the enforcement of immigration and customs laws within the United States, the protection of specified federal buildings, and air and marine enforcement. By unifying previously fragmented investigative functions, ICE will deliver effective and comprehensive enforcement. ICE is led by an Assistant Secretary, who reports directly to the under secretary for BTS.

Federal Law Enforcement Training Center (FLETC)   The Federal Law Enforcement Training Center FLETC serves as an interagency law enforcement training organization for 81 federal agencies. The center also provides services to state, local, and international law enforcement agencies. The center is headquartered at Glynco, Georgia; however, the FLETC also operates two other residential training sites in Artesia, New Mexico, and Charleston, South Carolina. The FLETC also operates an in-service requalification training facility in Cheltenham, Maryland, for use by agencies with large concentrations of personnel in the Washington, D.C., area. The FLETC has oversight and program management responsibility for the International Law Enforcement Academy (ILEA) in Gaborone, Botswana, and supports training at other ILEAs in Hungary and Thailand. The center's parent agency, the Department of Homeland Security, supervises its administrative and financial activities. The FLETC director serves under the authority of the under secretary for border and transportation security.[67]

Emergency Preparedness and Response (EP&R)

The second directorate is the Emergency Preparedness and Response (EP&R), which is built on the foundation laid by the Federal Emergency Management Agency (FEMA), which ensures that our nation is prepared for incidents, whether natural disasters or terrorist assaults, and oversees the federal government's national response and recovery strategy. The undersecretary of Emergency Preparedness and Response also serves as the director of the Federal Emergency Management Agency, who reports directly to the Secretary of Homeland Security. Essentially the EP&R is FEMA.

Federal Emergency Management Administration (FEMA)   FEMA is part of the Department of Homeland Security's Emergency Preparedness and Response Directorate. FEMA has more than 2,600 full-time employees. They work at FEMA headquarters in Washington D.C., at regional and area offices across the country, the Mount Weather Emergency Operations Center, and the National Emergency Training Center in Emmitsburg, Maryland. FEMA also has nearly 4,000 standby disaster assistance employees who are available for deployment after disasters. Often FEMA works in partnership with other organizations that are part of the nation's emergency management system. These partners include state and local emergency management agencies, 27 federal agencies, and the American Red Cross.[68]

Information Analysis and Infrastructure Protection (IAIP)

The Information Analysis and Infrastructure Protection (IAIP) directorate performs the two functions implied within its name. To accomplish the first role, essentially aimed at reducing the vulnerability of the United States to terrorism and to detect, to prevent, and to respond to terrorist attacks, the Information Analysis and Infrastructure Protection was made a member of the Intelligence Community. IAIP's mission to disseminate information analyzed by the department to state and local government agencies and authorities and private-sector entities brings to the post–9/11 federal government a capability for the security and protection of the nation's domestic assets that did not previously exist.

The essential function of IAIP is mapping the vulnerabilities of the nation's critical infrastructure against a comprehensive analysis of intelligence and public source information. This function is unique to the federal government and fundamental to the nation's ability to better protect itself from terrorist attacks.

BOX 2-6

DEPARTMENT OF HOMELAND SECURITY GOAL #2—PREVENTION

Objective 2.1—Secure our borders against terrorists, means of terrorism, illegal drugs, and other illegal activity.

Objective 2.2—Enforce trade and immigration laws.

Objective 2.3—Provide operational end users with the technology and capabilities to detect and prevent terrorist attacks, means of terrorism, and other illegal activities.

Objective 2.4—Ensure national and international policy, law enforcement, and other actions to prepare for and prevent terrorism are coordinated.

Objective 2.5—Strengthen the security of the nation's transportation systems.

Objective 2.6—Ensure the security and integrity of the immigration system.

Source: Department of Homeland Security. (2004). *Securing Our Homeland: U.S. Department of Homeland Security Strategic Plan.* Washington, D.C.: U.S. Department of Homeland Security.

Office of Information Analysis (IA)   Within IAIP, the Office of Information Analysis (IA) performs the intelligence activities carried out within DHS. IA responsibilities are to (1) monitor, assess, and coordinate indications and warnings in support of the secretary of the DHS, who by Executive Order is responsible for implementing the Homeland Security Advisory System (HSAS); (2) access all information, assessments, analysis, and unevaluated intelligence relating to terrorist threats to the homeland; (3) maintain real-time intelligence connectivity to support situational awareness during implementation of protective measures and incident management; (4) assess the scope of terrorist threats to the homeland to understand such threats in light of actual and potential vulnerabilities of the homeland; (5) integrate threat information and analyses with vulnerability assessments from the DHS Office of Infrastructure Protection (IP) to identify priorities for protective and support measures by DHS, other agencies of the federal government, state and local government agencies and authorities, the private sector, and other entities; (6) respond to requirements from the assistant secretary for Infrastructure Protection for information analysis and intelligence requirements; (7) gather and integrate terrorist-related information from DHS component agencies, state and local government agencies and authorities, and private-sector terrorist-related reporting/information; process requests for information (RFI) from these component agencies, state and local government agencies and authorities and private-sector entities; and (8) disseminate threat information, intelligence and responses to RFI's to DHS component agencies, state and local government agencies and authorities, and private-sector entities.[69]

The Terrorist Threat Integration Center (TTIC)   The roles and functions of IAIP and the Terrorist Threat Integration Center (TTIC) are complementary and collaborative and enhance the national effort to detect, disrupt, and prevent terrorism. TTIC makes full use of all terrorist threat–related information and expertise available to the U.S. government and provides comprehensive all-source threat analysis to the president, to DHS, and to other federal agencies. IAIP provides intelligence analysts to the TTIC, who participates with analysts from other federal agencies in analyzing this all-source terrorist information. IAIP also provides TTIC with threat information gathered and integrated from DHS component agencies, state and local government agencies and authorities, and private-sector entities.

IAIP integrates all-source threat information and analysis received from TTIC and other agencies of the intelligence community with its own vulnerability assessments to provide tailored threat assessments, including priorities for protective and support measures to other agencies of the federal government, state and local government agencies and authorities, and private-sector entities. Finally, IAIP administers the HSAS to include exercising primary responsibility for public advisories.[70]

Homeland Security Operations Center (HSOC)　The Homeland Security Operations Center (HSOC) serves as the nation's nerve center for information sharing and domestic incident management—dramatically increasing the vertical coordination between federal, state, territorial, tribal, local, and private-sector partners. The HSOC collects and fuses information from a variety of sources every day to help deter, detect, and prevent terrorist acts. Operating 24 hours a day, 7 days a week, 365 days a year, the HSOC provides real-time situational awareness and monitoring of the homeland, coordinates incidents and response activities, and in conjunction with the DHS Office of Information Analysis, issues advisories and bulletins concerning threats to homeland security, as well as specific protective measures. Information on domestic incident management is shared with Emergency Operations Centers at all levels through the Homeland Security Information Network (HSIN).

The HSOC represents over 35 agencies ranging from state and local law enforcement to federal intelligence agencies. Information is shared and fused on a daily basis by the two halves of the HSOC that are referred to as the "Intelligence Side" and the "Law Enforcement Side." Each half is identical and functions in tandem with the other but requires a different level of clearance to access information. The "Intelligence Side" focuses on pieces of highly classified intelligence and how the information contributes to the current threat picture for any given area. The "Law Enforcement Side" is dedicated to tracking the different enforcement activities across the country that may have a terrorist nexus. The two pieces fused together create a real-time snapshot of the nation's threat environment at any moment.[71]

Office of Infrastructure Protection (IP)　The IAIP's other critical function, as performed by the Office of Infrastructure Protection(IP), is focused on securing the nation's 17 critical infrastructure and key resource sectors. Chemical facilities are one specific sector that is of significant focus for the department. Prior to the formation of DHS, responsibility for the nation's critical infrastructure was scattered over a patchwork of various federal agencies. With the creation of the department and Homeland Security Presidential Directive-7, DHS is the sector-specific agency responsible for coordinating the U.S. government's efforts to protect critical infrastructure across the chemical sector. The department develops and coordinates plans in close cooperation with its federal, state, local, tribal, and private-sector partners to aggressively reduce the nation's vulnerability to acts of terrorism in the chemical sector.[72]

Science and Technology (S&T)

The Directorate of Science and Technology (S&T) serves as the primary research and development arm of Homeland Security, using our nation's scientific and technological resources to provide federal, state, and local officials with the technology and capabilities to protect the homeland. The focus is on catastrophic terrorism—threats to the security of our homeland that could result in large-scale loss of life and major economic impact. S&T's work is designed to counter those threats, both by evolutionary improvements to current technological capabilities and development of revolutionary, new technological capabilities.

Office of National Laboratories   The Office of National Laboratories provides the nation with a unifying core of science, technology, and engineering laboratories, organizations, and institutions dedicated to securing the homeland. The mission of this office is to establish, develop, nurture, and sustain the people, places, programs, and capabilities of the Homeland Security Science and Technology Complex to: facilitate access and maximize capabilities of existing national assets; successfully execute research, development, testing, and evaluation programs; prevent technology surprise; and anticipate and deter future terrorist threats.[73]

Homeland Security Advanced Research Projects Agency (HSARPA)   The Homeland Security Advanced Research Projects Agency (HSARPA) is mainly responsible for issuing solicitations for research, for reviewing the research capabilities of both public and private entities that apply, and to manage the funding of the research. The HSARPA also conducts conferences and workshops related to their solicitations. Most of the solicitations to date have centered on biological and chemical agents as well as radiological and nuclear elements.[74]

BOX 2-7

DEPARTMENT OF HOMELAND SECURITY GOAL #3—PROTECTION

Objective 3.1—Protect the public from acts of terrorism and other illegal activities.

Objective 3.2—Reduce infrastructure vulnerability from acts of terrorism.

Objective 3.3—Protect against financial and electronic crimes, counterfeit currency, illegal bulk currency movement, and identity theft.

Objective 3.4—Secure the physical safety of the president, vice president, visiting world leaders, and other protectees.

Objective 3.5—Ensure the continuity of government operations and essential functions in the event of crisis or disaster.

Objective 3.6—Protect the marine environment and living marine resources.

Objective 3.7—Strengthen nationwide preparedness and mitigation against acts of terrorism, natural disasters, or other emergencies.

Source: Department of Homeland Security. (2004). *Securing Our Homeland: U.S. Department of Homeland Security Strategic Plan.* Washington, D.C.: U.S. Department of Homeland Security.

BOX 2-8

DEPARTMENT OF HOMELAND SECURITY GOAL #4—RESPONSE

Objective 4.1—Reduce the loss of life and property by strengthening nationwide response readiness.

Objective 4.2—Provide scalable and robust all-hazard response capability.

Objective 4.3—Provide search-and-rescue services to people and property in distress.

Source: Department of Homeland Security. (2004). *Securing Our Homeland: U.S. Department of Homeland Security Strategic Plan.* Washington, D.C.: U.S. Department of Homeland Security.

Office of Management

The under secretary for management is responsible for the budget, appropriations, expenditure of funds, accounting and finance, procurement, information technology systems, facilities, property, equipment, other material resources, and the identification and tracking of performance measurements relating to the responsibilities of Homeland Security. Key to the mission of the DHS is the success of its employees, and the Directorate for Management is responsible for ensuring that employees have clear responsibilities and means of communication with other personnel and management. An important resource for communications is the office of the Chief Information Officer, who is responsible for maintaining the information technology necessary to keep the more than 170,000 employees of DHS connected to and fully a part of the goals and mission of the department.[75]

Coast Guard

The Coast Guard became part of the DHS in March of 2003, but it was not absorbed under any of the five directorates. Rather, it was kept whole and intact with the Commandant of the Coast Guard reporting directly to the secretary of homeland security. In addition, prior to the move to DHS, the U.S. Coast Guard's powers and responsibilities increased after the passage of the Maritime Transportation Security Act of 2002.[76] According to the U.S. Coast Guard's *Maritime Strategy for Homeland Security*,[77] the Coast Guard now serves as the nation's "maritime first responder" and is a crucial and responsive element of the DHS. Its well-trained crews react to a wide variety of maritime disasters, such as plane crashes, groundings, bridge and waterway accidents, and other maritime calamities. The Coast Guard's specially trained National Strike Force teams around the nation provide a flexible and adaptive resource of the DHS, deploying swiftly to clean up oil spills and hazardous materials, provide assistance during natural disasters such as hurricanes and flooding, and work hand in hand with EPA, FEMA, state, local, and other key agencies to save lives and protect property.

The Coast Guard ensures that our maritime transportation system and its waterways are safe, as over 95 percent of U.S. trade comes by sea. Our waterways and maritime productivity depend on our nation's aids to navigation systems—buoys and markers, lighthouses,

BOX 2-9

DEPARTMENT OF HOMELAND SECURITY GOAL #5—RECOVERY

Objective 5.1—Strengthen nationwide recovery plans and capabilities.
Objective 5.2—Provide scalable and robust all-hazard recovery assistance.

Source: Department of Homeland Security. (2004). *Securing Our Homeland: U.S. Department of Homeland Security Strategic Plan.* Washington, D.C.: U.S. Department of Homeland Security.

and electronic navigation systems such as the Differential Global Positioning System (DGPS) along with Coast Guard Vessel Traffic Services in key ports—all combine to help keep our homeland waters safe, secure, and productive.

As the nation's lead agency for maritime law enforcement, Coast Guard vessels and aircraft constantly patrol both our offshore and coastal regions, "pushing our borders out" and extending our vigilance and awareness of potential approaching threats, enforcing U.S. immigration policies and customs laws, and stopping drug smugglers, all of which strengthen our nation's maritime homeland security. The Coast Guard interdicts thousands of illegal migrants each year, stops tons of drugs from reaching our streets and arrests hundreds of smugglers, and works tirelessly in interagency teams with its homeland security partners such as U.S. Customs, Immigration, Department of Defense, and state and local authorities to help identify threats far off our coasts and help secure our maritime borders and our homeland.

Specifically, the Coast Guard's mission includes (1) maritime safety: eliminate deaths, injuries and property damage associated with maritime transportation, fishing, and recreational boating. The Coast Guard's motto is Semper Paratus—(Always Ready), and the service is always ready to respond to calls for help at sea; (2) national defense: defend the nation as one of the five U.S. armed services. Enhance regional stability in support of the National Security Strategy, utilizing the Coast Guard's unique and relevant maritime capabilities; (3) maritime security: protect America's maritime borders from all intrusions by: (a) halting the flow of illegal drugs, aliens, and contraband into the United States through maritime routes; (b) preventing illegal fishing; and (c) suppressing violations of federal law in the maritime arena; (4) mobility: facilitate maritime commerce and eliminate interruptions and impediments to the efficient and economical movement of goods and people, while maximizing recreational access to and enjoyment of the water; and (5) protection of natural resources: eliminate environmental damage and the degradation of natural resources associated with maritime transportation, fishing, and recreational boating.[78]

U.S. Secret Service

The other agency that was transferred into the Department of Homeland Security intact, whose director reports directly to the secretary of homeland security, is the U.S. Secret

Service. Originally under the Department of the Treasury due to its responsibilities for investigating counterfeiting, the U.S. Secret Service was moved under the DHS. The U.S. Secret Service is mandated by statute and executive order to carry out two significant missions: protection and criminal investigations. The Secret Service protects the president and vice president, their families, heads of state, and other designated individuals; investigates threats against these protectees; protects the White House, Vice President's Residence, foreign missions, and other buildings within Washington, D.C.; and plans and implements security designs for designated National Special Security Events. The Secret Service also investigates violations of laws relating to counterfeiting of obligations and securities of the United States; financial crimes that include, but are not limited to, access device fraud, financial institution fraud, identity theft, computer fraud; and computer-based attacks on our nation's financial, banking, and telecommunications infrastructure.[79]

Office of Inspector General (OIG)

In addition to the U.S. Coast Guard and U.S. Secret Service, two other entities essentially stand alone in the DHS. The first is the Office of Inspector General (OIG). The inspector general is responsible for conducting and supervising audits, investigations, and inspections relating to the programs and operations of the department. The OIG is to examine, evaluate, and where necessary, critique these operations and activities, recommending ways for the department to carry out its responsibilities in the most effective, efficient, and economical manner possible. Specifically, the mission of the Inspector General's office is to serve as an independent and objective inspection, audit, and investigative body to promote effectiveness, efficiency, and economy in the DHS's programs and operations and to prevent and detect fraud, abuse, mismanagement, and waste in such programs and operations.[80]

BOX 2-10

DEPARTMENT OF HOMELAND SECURITY GOAL #6—SERVICE

Objective 6.1—Increase understanding of naturalization and its privileges and responsibilities.

Objective 6.2—Provide efficient and responsive immigration services that respect the dignity and value of individuals.

Objective 6.3—Support the U.S. humanitarian commitment with flexible and sound immigration and refugee programs.

Objective 6.4—Facilitate the efficient movement of legitimate cargo and people.

Source: Department of Homeland Security. (2004). *Securing Our Homeland: U.S. Department of Homeland Security Strategic Plan.* Washington, D.C.: U.S. Department of Homeland Security.

U.S. Citizenship & Immigration Services (USCIS)

The other entity that largely stands alone within the DHS is the Citizenship and Immigration Services (USCIS). The DHS has administered the nation's immigration laws since March 1, 2003, when the INS became part of DHS. Through the USCIS, DHS continues the tradition of processing immigrants into the country by administering services such as immigrant and nonimmigrant sponsorship, adjustment of status, work authorization and other permits, naturalization of qualified applicants for U.S. citizenship, and asylum or refugee processing. This function, along with immigration enforcement, was originally performed by the INS. These functions were split out with USCIS performing the administrative aspects of immigration law, whereas immigration enforcement became the responsibility of the Directorate of Border and Transportation Security. The USCIS states that the department tries to ensure that "America continues to welcome visitors and those who seek opportunity within our shores while excluding terrorists and their supporters."[81]

DHS, Six-Point Agenda—July 2005

In July of 2005, the DHS issued a six-point agenda for organizational change to ensure that the department's policies, operations, and structures are aligned in the best way to address the potential threats—both present and future—that face our nation. The six-point agenda is intended to guide the department in its current round of changes with the intent to (1) increase overall preparedness, particularly for catastrophic events; (2) create better transportation security systems to move people and cargo more securely and efficiently; (3) strengthen border security and interior enforcement and reform immigration processes; (4) enhance information sharing with our partners; (5) improve DHS financial management, human resource development, procurement, and information technology; and (6) realign the DHS organization to maximize mission performance.

Supporting the six-point agenda, the department has proposed to realign the DHS to increase its ability to prepare, prevent, and respond to terrorist attacks and other emergencies. These changes, according to Secretary Chertoff, will better integrate the department and give department employees better tools to accomplish their mission. These plans include the following.

Centralize and Improve Policy Development and Coordination

A new Directorate of Policy will be the primary departmentwide coordinator for policies, regulations, and other initiatives; ensure consistency of policy and regulatory development across the department; perform long-range strategic policy planning; assume the policy coordination functions previously performed by the BTS Directorate; and include the Office of International Affairs, Office of Private Sector Liaison, Homeland Security Advisory Council, Office of Immigration Statistics, and the Senior Asylum Officer.

Strengthen Intelligence Functions and Information Sharing

A new Office of Intelligence and Analysis will ensure that information is gathered from all relevant field operations and other parts of the intelligence community, analyzed with a

BOX 2-11

DEPARTMENT OF HOMELAND SECURITY GOAL #7—ORGANIZATIONAL EXCELLENCE

Objective 7.1—Protect confidentiality and date integrity to ensure privacy and security.

Objective 7.2—Integrate legacy services within the department improving efficiency and effectiveness.

Objective 7.3—Ensure effective recruitment, development, compensation, succession management, and leadership of a diverse workforce to provide optimal service at a responsible cost.

Objective 7.4—Improve the efficiency and effectiveness of the department, ensuring taxpayers get value for their tax dollars.

Objective 7.5—Lead and promote e-government modernization and interoperability initiatives.

Objective 7.6—Fully integrate the strategic planning, budgeting, and evaluation processes to maximize performance.

Objective 7.7—Provide excellent customer service to support the mission of the department.

Source: Department of Homeland Security. (2004). *Securing Our Homeland: U.S. Department of Homeland Security Strategic Plan.* Washington, D.C.: U.S. Department of Homeland Security.

mission-oriented focus, informative to senior decision makers, and disseminated to the appropriate federal, state, local, and private-sector partners. It will be led by a chief intelligence officer reporting directly to the secretary. The office is intended to be comprised of analysts within the former Information Analysis directorate and draw on expertise of other department components with intelligence collection and analysis operations.

Improve Coordination and Efficiency of Operations

A new director of Operations Coordination will conduct joint operations across all organizational elements, coordinate incident management activities, and use all resources within the department to translate intelligence and policy into immediate action. The Homeland Security Operations Center, which serves as the nation's nerve center for information sharing and domestic incident management on a 24/7/365 basis, will be a critical part of this new office.

Enhance Coordination and Deployment of Preparedness Assets

The Directorate for Preparedness will consolidate preparedness assets from across the department, facilitate grants and oversee nationwide preparedness efforts supporting first responder training, citizen awareness, public health, infrastructure, and cyber security and

DHS Organizational Chart

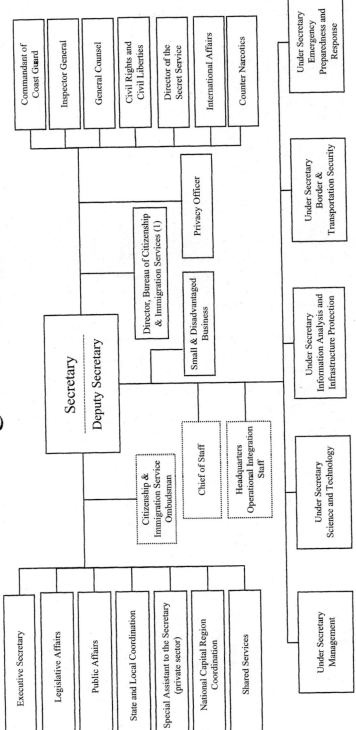

Secretary
─────────
Deputy Secretary

- Commandant of Coast Guard
- Inspector General
- General Counsel
- Civil Rights and Civil Liberties
- Director of the Secret Service
- International Affairs
- Counter Narcotics

- Executive Secretary
- Legislative Affairs
- Public Affairs
- State and Local Coordination
- Special Assistant to the Secretary (private sector)
- National Capital Region Coordination
- Shared Services

- Citizenship & Immigration Service Ombudsman
- Chief of Staff
- Headquarters Operational Integration Staff

- Director, Bureau of Citizenship & Immigration Services (1)
- Privacy Officer
- Small & Disadvantaged Business

- Under Secretary Management
- Under Secretary Science and Technology
- Under Secretary Information Analysis and Infrastructure Protection
- Under Secretary Border & Transportation Security
- Under Secretary Emergency Preparedness and Response

August 2004

Homeland Security

U.S. DEPARTMENT OF HOMELAND SECURITY

93

ensure proper steps are taken to protect high-risk targets, focus on cyber security and telecommunications, and will include a new Chief Medical Officer, responsible for carrying out the department's responsibilities to coordinate the response to biological attacks. Managed by an under secretary this Directorate will include infrastructure protection, assets of the Office of State and Local Government Coordination and Preparedness responsible for grants, training, and exercises, the U.S. Fire Administration, and the Office of National Capitol Region Coordination.[82]

Other Department Realignments

Other department realignments include the attempt to improve National Response and Recovery Efforts by focusing FEMA on its core functions. FEMA will report directly to the Secretary of Homeland Security. To strengthen and enhance our nation's ability to respond to and recover from man-made or natural disasters, FEMA will now focus on its historic and vital mission of response and recovery. It will integrate the Federal Air Marshal Service (FAMS) into Broader Aviation Security Efforts. The Federal Air Marshal Service will be moved from the ICE bureau to the TSA to increase operational coordination and strengthen efforts to meet this common goal of aviation security. The DHS will merge Legislative and Intergovernmental Affairs. This new Office of Legislative and Intergovernmental Affairs will merge certain functions among the Office of Legislative Affairs and the Office of State and Local Government Coordination to streamline intergovernmental relations efforts and better share homeland security information with members of Congress as well as state and local officials. And finally, the DHS plans to assign the Office of Security to the Management Directorate. The Office of Security will be moved to return oversight of that office to the Under Secretary for Management to better manage information systems, contractual activities, security accreditation, training, and resources.[83]

HOMELAND SECURITY AND POLICE

Just as the American federal bureaucracy was forced to realign itself in the wake of World War II with America's entry into the Cold War, the American federal bureaucracy has once again found itself realigning to fight a new war, a war on terrorism. The history of homeland security provides the perspective that although the federal government has been concerned about securing the homeland, the ultimate question has centered on how to best organize for such a complex problem. How we organize is how we manage, and it is clear that there has been much debate over how best to organize.[84] In the early twentieth century, much of the debate seemed to center on who was most responsible, the federal government or the state and local governments. Later, in the post–World War II era, it appeared that the debate centered around whether or not to combine the threat of terrorism with the threat of natural disasters. Although the response and recovery aspects of the two are vastly similar, the planning, preparedness, and prevention are not. Some presidents saw the two as highly related and combined the functions, whereas others saw them as separate responsibilities and, hence, divided the responsibilities among agencies. This ultimately led to the splintering and decentralization of duties, powers, and responsibilities, which resulted in little cohesion among the various concepts of homeland security. Although President Carter

Department of Homeland Security
Organization Chart
(proposed end state)

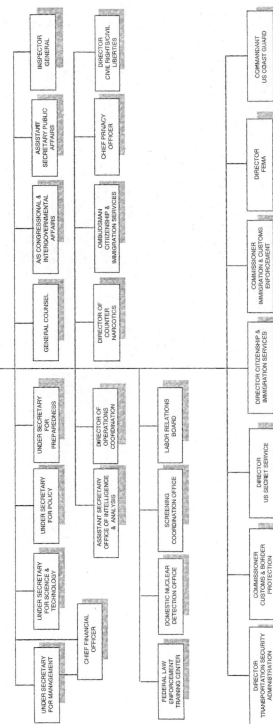
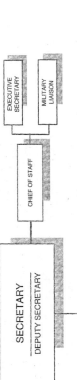

07-27-05

Department of Homeland Security
Organization Chart—Policy

(proposed end state)

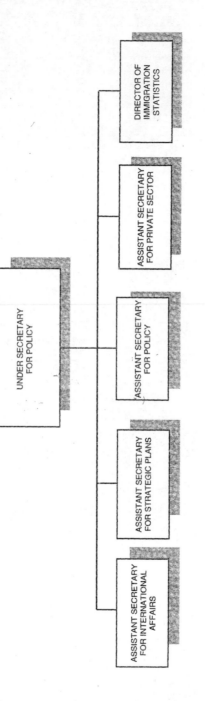

UNDER SECRETARY FOR POLICY

ASSISTANT SECRETARY FOR INTERNATIONAL AFFAIRS

ASSISTANT SECRETARY FOR STRATEGIC PLANS

ASSISTANT SECRETARY FOR POLICY

ASSISTANT SECRETARY FOR PRIVATE SECTOR

DIRECTOR OF IMMIGRATION STATISTICS

07-13-05

Homeland Security

Department of Homeland Security
Organization Chart—Preparedness

(proposed end state)

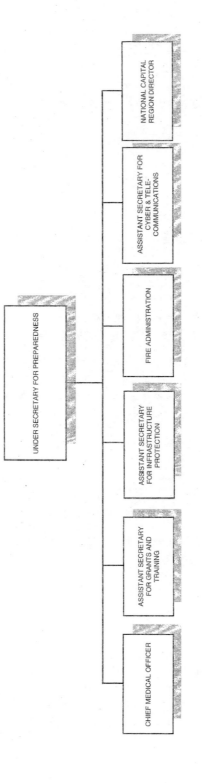

UNDER SECRETARY FOR PREPAREDNESS

CHIEF MEDICAL OFFICER

ASSISTANT SECRETARY FOR GRANTS AND TRAINING

ASSISTANT SECRETARY FOR INFRASTRUCTURE PROTECTION

FIRE ADMINISTRATION

ASSISTANT SECRETARY FOR CYBER & TELE-COMMUNICATIONS

NATIONAL CAPITAL REGION DIRECTOR

07-13-05

Homeland Security

97

brought the various agencies togther under FEMA, this centralized agency would take over a decade before it became fully capable in its ability to respond to disasters. And despite FEMA's admirable response to the September 11th attacks, it was clear that America's needs for securing the homeland far exceeded FEMA's capabilities.

In the 1990s, with several terrorists attacks on America's assets and interests, policies for securing the homeland were advocated. However, according to John Kingdon, three streams must converge together for action to be taken.[85] These three streams are the problem stream, the political stream, and the policy stream. Regarding terrorism and homeland security, the problem stream did exist and was identified by researchers, analysts, and Congressional staffers who work on public policy issues. These same people also generated policy solutions to the terrorism problem, which circulated among those on Capitol Hill. However, what was lacking was the political stream that would create the impetus for acting on the policies to address the problems. September 11th, sadly, created the political stream that galvanized the public and demanded action. As the three streams merged, Congress and the president were able to secure the passage of several comprehensive bills, including the USA PATRIOT Act and the Homeland Security Act of 2002.

The impact of these broad pieces of legislation is still being worked out. The USA PATRIOT Act gave sweeping powers to law enforcement to pursue terrorists, would-be terrorists, and those that finance and support terrorism. The controversy over whether the laws went too far and invaded civil rights or simply did not go far enough aside, the majority of the act's provisions that were due to sunset on December 31, 2005, apparently will be renewed,[86] for as of March 2006, Congress had only left to workout differences between the Senate and House renewal bills. And despite the sweeping laws that were implemented by the act, law enforcement officials are still determining how best to use these new powers to fight terrorism. Equally, despite the passage of the Homeland Security Act of 2002 and the creation of the DHS, the federal bureaucratic structure continues to reorganize. And, more specifically, the DHS is still reorganizing to enhance its capabilities, as is evidenced by the six-point agenda released July 2005.[87] The DHS is still trying to determine how best to organize to secure the homeland. This then begs the question, if the federal bureaucracy is still busy trying to organize itself, where does that leave state and local police and their role in homeland security? That is the subject of the next three chapters.

CONCLUSION

Historically, state and local governments have played a role in protecting the homeland, albeit not a role that has been consistently defined. In the aftermath of September 11th, there has been a near consensus that state and local police will play a role in homeland security, but that role has also been ill defined. Legislative acts such as the USA PATRIOT Act and the Homeland Security Act all cite the role of state and local police and have established numerous liaison positions, operations centers, and various entities to work with the agencies, but like the Department of Homeland Security, it is a mosaic of plans and actions, rather than a unified concept. Therefore, it is the intent of the next three chapters to draw on this mosaic to try and clarify the role of the police in homeland security. Specifically, the next three chapters will attempt to identify the strategic, operational, and tactical roles of state and local police agencies in homeland security.

CHAPTER 3

Police Strategy for Homeland Security

Strategy without tactics is the slowest route to victory. Tactics without strategy is the noise before defeat.

Sun Tzu (circa 500 BC)

INTRODUCTION

As reviewed in Chapter 1, America has moved into a new era, one often cited as the post–9/11 era. The events of that day have significantly changed not only America and its policies, they have also changed the world. Moreover, they have created new demands on federal, state, and local government and have transformed the responsibilities of the police. Although Homeland Security has become the overall umbrella under which policing and security in the post–9/11 world work, as reviewed in Chapter 2, the various organizational roles are still being worked out at the federal level, leaving less time for consideration of the role of state and local police. Although it is repeatedly stated that the police will play a role in homeland security and a very important role, defining that role has been limited. Recognizing that policing in the post–9/11 world has moved into an era of homeland security and that there is a stated role for state and local police, determining exactly what that role is becomes the concern of the rest of this book.

To understand the role of police in homeland security, as the opening quote denotes, it is important to have an understanding of the strategic objectives of homeland security to guide the tactics being used. Strategy provides the goals and objectives for achieving an end and the policies that will allow us to achieve these goals and objectives. In the case of homeland security, strategy determines the goals and objectives for securing the homeland and provides the framework for the formulation and implementation of policies aimed at achieving homeland security. These policies, then, become the basis for all operations and the use of actual tactics on the street. As Harold G. Campbell has explained, "The best defense against terrorism is offensive action, but knowing how and where to act is also of extreme importance."[1] Strategy provides us the framework to know how and where to act. Therefore, determining the proper strategy for state and local police in the pursuit of homeland security is the purpose of this chapter.

STRATEGIES FOR HOMELAND SECURITY

Strategy is the overall framework by which resources are used to achieve certain goals and objectives. A strategy must take into consideration a number of factors that not only shape and influence the development of the strategy, but also will be influenced by the adoption of the strategy itself. As Campbell has also stated, "Homeland security strategy development is, in fact, a comprehensive endeavor that must take into consideration a significant number of seemingly disassociated variables in order to maximize strategic options and foster the creation of an indomitable public policy."[2] He explained that the strategist must be able to understand and recognize critical level variables, to see the relationships between these variables, and to be able to plan for all eventualities. As he succinctly explained, "Strategic level security planners must see the entire battlefield and understand the complexities and interrelations of all the factors, if they are to anticipate the enemy's next move," and "like a Grandmaster in chess, the strategic security planner must be able to think twenty moves ahead in the game and have contingencies in place that serve to counter any moves made by their adversary or strike before the enemy is ready to act."[3] Many of these complexities and variables can be seen in the events that unfolded after 9/11 and can contribute to our understanding of the need for a policing strategy for homeland security.

The primary purpose of a strategy is usually derived from a particular threat. The threat may be one that has already attacked American interests, or it may be one that poses a future threat to national interests; thus strategy is created to prevent these situations from developing. In the case of homeland security, 9/11 was the attack that necessitated the development of a strategy for homeland security, but multiple threats continue to exist in today's post–9/11 world. These include potential future terrorist attacks by Al-Qaeda and other groups, the illegal drug trade, illicit arms and weapons of mass destruction (WMD) trafficking, international organized crime, and illegal immigration for criminal purposes. As various countries and groups continue to modernize and employ modern-day information technology, combined with the infrastructure for the movement of people and resources, America has become more vulnerable to attacks on its own soil. This was made clear to America on 9/11, thus creating the need for a strategy to secure the homeland.

Other considerations derived from 9/11 necessitated the development of a homeland security strategy in the United States. These include the political dimension, the use and need for greater technology, the need for better information coordination, as well as a more unified action among the various agencies responsible for security in the United States. The attacks on America created a need for the United States to meet the challenge of securing the homeland and to recognize the political environment in which this would have to operate. The various levels of government, from the federal government down to the local counties, cities, and tribal governments, create a complex political environment in which to work; thus a strategy to secure the homeland cannot exclude the various levels of government in the development of a strategy, as all levels of government are clearly going to be affected by an overall strategy.

The use of technology by Al-Qaeda and its operatives on 9/11 highlighted the fact that technology can be used against America and its interests. However, technology also serves to enhance our ability to organize, lead, and employ police officers with greater efficiency and effectiveness by providing the ability to inject quality information into the decision-making process. It also provides a number of tools that police officers can use to better perform their job. Because the United States does not have the monopoly on technology, using superior technology and giving officers the skills necessary to adapt this technology to their advantage is critical.

Closely related today to the use of technology is the use of information. As was highlighted from the 9/11 Commission's report, information was often available, but information was not readily shared. Because today's technology gives us the edge of having real-time information, any strategy today must take this into consideration to develop ways in which data can be shared. And, not only must agencies be willing to share information, but they must also be willing to act in a unified manner regarding this information. Therefore, any strategy must take into consideration the politically fragmented system and find ways to share information and unify these various agencies to work together.

BOX 3-1

HOMELAND SECURITY AND NATIONAL SECURITY

The Preamble to the Constitution defines our federal government's basic purpose as "... to form a more perfect Union, establish justice, insure domestic Tranquility, provide for the common defense, promote the general Welfare, and secure the Blessings of Liberty to ourselves and our Posterity." The requirements to provide for the common defense remains as fundamental today as it was when these words were written, more than two hundred years ago.

The *National Security Strategy of the United States* aims to guarantee the sovereignty and independence of the United States, with our fundamental values and institutions intact. It provides a framework for creating and seizing opportunities to strengthen our security and prosperity. The *National Strategy for Homeland Security* complements the *National Security Strategy of the United States* by addressing a very specific and uniquely challenging threat—terrorism in the United States—and by providing a comprehensive framework for organizing the efforts of federal, state, local, and private organizations whose primary functions are often unrelated to national security.

The link between national security and homeland security is a subtle but important one. For more than six decades, America has sought to protect its own sovereignty and independence through a strategy of global presence and engagement. In so doing, America has helped many other countries and peoples advance along the path of democracy, open markets, individual liberty, and peace with their neighbors. Yet there are those who oppose America's role in the world, and who are willing to use violence against us and our friends. Our great power leaves these enemies with few conventional options for doing us harm. One such option is to take advantage of our freedom and openness by secretly inserting terrorists into our country to attack our homeland. Homeland security seeks to deny this avenue of attack to our enemies and thus to provide a secure foundation for America's ongoing global engagement. Thus the *National Security Strategy of the United States* and The *National Strategy for Homeland Security* work as mutually supporting documents, providing guidance to the executive branch departments and agencies.

There are also a number of other, more specific strategies maintained by the United States that are subsumed within the twin concepts of national security and homeland security. The *National Strategy for Combating Terrorism* will define the U.S. war plan against international terrorism. The *National Strategy to Combat Weapons of Mass Destruction* coordinates America's many efforts to deny terrorists and states the materials, technology, and expertise to make and deliver weapons of mass destruction. The *National Strategy to Secure Cyberspace* will describe our initiatives to secure our information systems against deliberate, malicious destruction. The *National Money Laundering Strategy* aims to undercut the illegal flows of money that support terrorism and international criminal activity. The *National Defense Strategy* sets priorities for our most powerful national security instrument. The *National Drug Control Strategy* lays out a comprehensive U.S. effort to combat drug smuggling and consumption. All these documents fit into the framework established by the *National Security Strategy of the United States* and *National Strategy for Homeland Security*, which together take precedence over all other national strategies, programs, and plans.

Source: Office of Homeland Security. (2002). *National Strategy for Homeland Security*. Washington, D.C.: Office of Homeland Security, White House.

DEVELOPING A NATIONAL HOMELAND SECURITY STRATEGY FOR POLICE

Philip McVey decisively pointed out that the the primary dilemma facing law enforcement professionals is in regard to the development of a homeland security strategy for their police.[4] He stated that police executives could either do nothing and wait for direction from outside their agencies or they could do something that might possibly be wrong. Neither of these are attractive options for the development of a homeland security strategy or for the police to begin actively playing a role in homeland security. McVey articulated a third alternative and that is to start "with the basic realization that any proposal forthcoming from federal agencies will likely be only strategically general" and that ultimately, "each jurisdiction will have to interpret such a proposal according to the area's unique risk factors and operational capabilities."[5] He then argued that "given this, each agency must lay the necessary groundwork in preparation for those proposals by generating and incorporating into its individual administrative paradigm a basic understanding of the terrorist risks it faces and its own incident management capability."[6] In other words, he argued that each agency will ultimately have to establish its own strategic plan that will have to be continually updated and incorporate other strategies from other sources, whether the federal strategy, a state strategy, or a regional strategy, as well as other strategic plans where the police play an integral role.

As any strategy will generally draw from more than one source, this is also the case for a homeland security strategy. The most defined strategy to date comes from what was created by the Office of Homeland Security under then-director Tom Ridge, the *National Strategy for Homeland Security*.[7] The document was the product of eight months of consultation with a cross section of interested people who contributed to the formation of this national policy.

The opening preface by President Bush makes the argument that "this is a national strategy, not a federal strategy."[8] The document sets out the overall strategy for the entire nation as it relates to homeland security. It attempts to answer four basic questions: (1) What is homeland security and what missions does it entail? (2) What do we seek to accomplish, and what are the most important goals of homeland security? (3) What is the federal executive branch doing now to accomplish these goals and what should do in the future? and (4) What should nonfederal governments, the private sector, and citizens do to help secure the homeland?[9]

The document does address the role of state and local police in homeland security, but it is a much broader document attempting to focus on the broad array of homeland security issues facing America. Thus, the majority of the *National Strategy* is oriented toward the federal government and the various agencies responsible for homeland security. It is, however, the best place to start for developing an overall strategy for state and local law enforcement.

The second source for developing a strategy for Homeland Security comes from the joint efforts of the International City/County Management Association (ICMA) and the International Association of Chiefs of Police (IACP). Both of these associations have pulled together a number of articles that have looked at "best practices" for homeland security, especially as it relates to local police.[10] In addition, the IACP issued their own white paper, resulting from a project that brought together law enforcement leaders from across the country, titled *From Hometown Security to Homeland Security.*[11] The project was launched in November of 2004, and on May 17th of the next year, the IACP issued their white paper with a press release. The white paper was very critical of the *National Strategy for Homeland Security,* charging that the "national strategy" released in 2002 was developed by federal departments and agencies and that despite the assertions of Bush in the preface of the document, it was in fact a federal strategy, not a national strategy. The IACP argued that all levels of government, including local, tribal, state, and federal, should have participated in the development of the strategy to truly make it a *national* strategy.[12] A federally developed homeland security strategy, according to the IACP, that does not reflect the advice, expertise, or consent of public safety organizations at levels of government other than federal could be viewed as overly instructive and cumbersome and possibly impractical. The IACP advocated solving the problem by adopting a national, rather than a federal, approach to future homeland security planning and strategy development.[13]

The third document that is focused directly on policing's needs for a homeland security strategy comes from the Police Executive Research Forum and the Office of Community Oriented Policing Services document *Protecting Your Community From Terrorism: Strategies for Local Law Enforcement.*[14] This document was based on the findings of an executive session that was held in November of 2002, which included federal, state, and local law enforcement leaders. Through several days of discussion, these police executives provided their insight into possible strategies for fighting terrorism on the home front. Specifically they discussed the local–federal partnership, federal and local law enforcement needs, information sharing among agencies, and models of successful partnerships, and they developed a strategy for improving partnerships for the purpose of homeland security. A white paper was then published in 2003 detailing the strategic priorities for local law enforcement.

Finally, longtime policing scholar William V. Pelfrey has offered a "cycle of preparedness" for Homeland Security to establish a framework for preparing for terrorist attacks.[15] His article has adopted a broader framework that represents a solid strategy for local law enforcement to implement Homeland Security at the operational and tactical level.

President Bush and Vice President Cheney at the
University of the National Strategy for Homeland Security.
(*Source: AP Wide World Photos*)

National Strategy for Homeland Security

The *National Strategy for Homeland Security* defines "homeland security" as "a concerted
national effort to prevent terrorist attacks within the United States, reduce America's vulnerability to terrorism, and minimize the damage and recover from attacks that do occur."[16]
The *Strategy* makes the statement that the federal government does play a critical role in
homeland security, but the nature of American society and its governance demands a partnership among all levels of governments, as well as with the private sector and American
citizens. Therefore, the *Strategy*, it is again argued, is a national strategy, not a federal one.

As the focus of the *Strategy* is aimed at terrorism in the United States, it addresses
one of the more difficult problems in developing any strategy or policy aimed at terrorism, which is defining what terrorism means in the first place. The *Strategy* itself talks
about "characterizing" terrorism as "any premeditated, unlawful act dangerous to human life or public welfare that is intended to intimidate or coerce civilian populations
or governments."[17] Although this characterization may be helpful, what is more useful

is deriving a definition that can be used by police, but to do this, one must first arrive at a fuller understandiing of what is meant by the use of the term *terrorism*.

According to a leading scholar in the area of terrorism, White has explained that the term *terrorism*, although often defined, has no unified consensus regarding what constitutes terrorism.[18] White explained that the term itself is a very political term and is used to label certain groups as politically and socially unacceptable, thus allowing for governments to increase their legitimacy when using this label against certain groups, which becomes even more complicated when a legitimately recognized government uses terror as a means of ruling.[19] This can become even more problematic when we attempt to reach a consensus to determine what is meant by the threat of terrorism, how to legislate against terrorism, and more importantly, for the police, how to enforce the laws against terrorism. This ambiguity creates a problem for law enforcement in that it becomes difficult to separate common crimes from political crimes, it does not allow for comparison of the terrorist acts, and it makes it difficult to plan against such terrorist acts.[20] But, as McVey has explained, "It is crucial that a common definition of terrorism be developed within and between [law enforcement] agencies" and the definition "must be universally valid and must reliably serve the interests of local law enforcement jurisdictions by being both flexible and relevant."[21]

Despite the fact that there is little consensus regarding a unified definition of terrorism, that has not stopped many individuals from proposing a variety of definitions. One scholar, Jenkins, has explained terrorism as the use or threatened use of force designed to bring about political change.[22] Another scholar, Laqueur, has explained terrorism to be the use of illegitimate force to achieve a political objective by the targeting of innocent people.[23] Still another scholar has defined it as political violence in or against true democracies.[24] Although these and other scholarly definitions are beneficial, their focus is too often on the political and social aspects and not on the criminal aspects, which are of most concern to local law enforcement.

To derive a more acceptable definition for law enforcement, one can look to the writings of those in the law enforcement field. One such person, Friendlander, has defined terrorism as the use of force, violence, or threats thereof to attain political goals through fear, intimidation, or coercion.[25] Another source, the National Advisory Commission on Criminal Justice Standards and Goals, explains terrorism as violent, criminal behavior designed primarily to generate fear in the community, or a substantial segment of it, for political purposes.[26] Although both of these definitions draw on specific concerns for the police, their drawback is that they do not have the legal standing to serve as definitive definitions for the purposes of law enforcement.

The best place to turn for a useful definition of terrorism, as it relates to law enforcement, is the one currently used by the Federal Bureau of Investigation (FBI). The FBI's definition of terrorism is "the unlawful use of force and violence against persons or property to intimidate or coerce a government, the civilian population or any segment thereof, in furtherance of political or social objectives."[27] The benefit to this definition is the fact that it is already defined in the *Code of Federal Regulations* and is used by the FBI as the operational definition of terrorism. Further, the definition addresses the law enforcement aspect of terrorism largely because the FBI considers terrorists to be criminals and thus sees terrorism as a crime. As Dyson has explained, by referencing the "unlawful" use of force, it allows terrorism to be directly associated with criminal activity allowing for this type of illegal behavior to fall under the purview of the FBI.[28] And because the FBI is going to serve as the primary source of intergovernmental relations between local and federal law enforcement regarding issues of terrorism, if local law enforcement adopts the same definition, it resolves a number of definitional and operational problems.

The FBI also further elaborates on the definition of terrorism by dividing terrorism into two categories: domestic and international. The FBI, by way of the U.S. Code, defines domestic terrorism as "activities that involve acts dangerous to human life that are a violation of the criminal laws of the United States or of any state; appear to be intended to intimidate or coerce a civilian population; to influence the policy of a government by mass destruction, assassination, or kidnapping; and occur primarily within the territorial jurisdiction of the United States.[29] And international terrorism is defined by the FBI as "violent acts or acts dangerous to human life that are a violation of the criminal laws of the United States or any state, or that would be a criminal violation if committed within the jurisdiction of the United States or any state. These acts appear to be intended to intimidate or coerce a civilian population; influence the policy of a government by intimidation or coercion; or affect the conduct of a government by mass destruction, assassination or kidnapping and occur primarily outside the territorial jurisdiction of the United States or transcend national boundaries in terms of the means by which they are accomplished, the persons they appear intended to intimidate or coerce, or the locale in which their perpetrators operate or seek asylum."[30]

The FBI's definition of terrorism and the two categories of domestic and international terrorism provide a readily available and working definition of terrorism. Adopting them for local law enforcement purposes will assist not only in the law enforcement intergovernmental relations, but will also assist in law enforcement's understanding of the threat of terrorism. It will also assist in the development of a more unified national strategy for policing in an era of homeland security.

The *National Strategy* then proceeds to describe prevention as the first priority for homeland security. The first strategic goal of homeland security is to deter all potential attacks by detecting them before they strike, deny them from entering the United States and obtaining the instruments of terror, and take "decisive action" to eliminate the threat they pose. The second strategic goal is to reduce America's vulnerability to terrorism. This goal acknowledges the open and free society that we have in America makes this task difficult, and when we shore up one particular area against terrorism, such as airport security, terrorists can adapt and exploit another area of weakness, such as trains and subway transportation. Therefore, as the *National Strategy* articulates, "we must constantly balance the benefits of mitigating this risk against both the economic costs and infringements on individual liberty that this mitigation entails."[31] Finally, the third strategic objective for homeland security is to minimize the damage and recover from attacks that do occur. This strategic objective faces the reality that it is not a matter of *if* but *when* future attacks will occur in the United States and establishes the objective of preparedness for such attacks as one of the primary strategic goals.

Along with these three overarching objectives, the *National Strategy* establishes a number of principles necessary to achieve these objectives. First, it requires responsibility and accountability of the various agencies responsible for protecting the homeland. Although the emphasis is largely on the Department of Homeland Security (DHS), there is the recognition that all the bureaucratic agencies taking part in the security of the nation will have to act responsibly and be held accountable for their actions. Second, it is intent on mobilizing our entire society, not just federal agencies, but federal, state, and local governments, as well as the private sector. Third, it demands that we manage risk and allocate resources judiciously.

BOX 3-2

THE FEDERAL BUREAU OF INVESTIGATION'S DEFINITION OF TERRORISM

. . . the unlawful use of force and violence against persons or property to intimidate or coerce a government, the civilian population or any segment thereof, in furtherance of political or social objectives.

Source: Federal Bureau of Investigation (2002). *Terrorism in the United States: 2000/2001.* Washington, D.C.: U.S. Government Printing Office. The definition is derived from [18 U.S.C. § 2331(1).

This principle is focused on the use of risk assessment to prioritize America's vulnerabilities and thus allocate more funding to those areas that face the greatest risk. The fourth principle is to seek opportunity from adversity. This principle is focused on dual usage of terrorism preparedness by finding multiple uses for the methods and resources employed to fight terrorism. The fifth principle is that preparedness should be measured to ensure that agencies are achieving the proper level of performance and that these efforts, the sixth principle, should be sustained over the long term. Finally, the seventh and last principle is that efforts should be made to constrain government spending. These seven principles are intended to guide the implementation of the *National Strategy's* three primary objectives to ensure that it is done in a proper fashion.

Threat and Vulnerability

The *National Strategy* then turns to the need to understand the threat America faces and its vulnerabilities. They succinctly state that one fact dominates all homeland security threat assessments, and that is "terrorists are strategic actors."[32] Terrorists choose their targets based on weaknesses and vulnerabilities they observe, and they then move to exploit those weaknesses. Unlike criminals who tend to maintain a particular modus operandi where past behavior predicts future behavior, terrorists tend to learn and adapt to the strategic environment, making them far more difficult to protect against. In the 9/11 attack, terrorists exploited America's vulnerability of airline security. In the wake of the attacks, America has bolstered airport security by federalizing the baggage screeners, enhancing rules and regulations, and controlling access points throughout the airport process. Although this has been very important to protecting against future and similar airline attacks, terrorists recognize that this sector has been target-hardened and thus will select more vulnerable targets for future attacks. Because America is such a free and open society with a very large, diverse, and mobile citizenry, other vulnerabilities exhibit themselves. These include schools, sporting arenas, concerts, office buildings, high-rise residence, and various places of worship. Protecting America's homeland becomes very difficult when one recognizes that the very thing that makes America great also exposes it to potential attacks.

The *National Strategy* highlights this very thought when it reviews five key elements of American life: democracy, liberties, security, economy, and culture. American democracy promotes a very open society that is based on the rule of law. Terrorists tend to operate outside the rules of law and can exploit America's form of democracy. American liberties are the safeguards of individuals against an oppressive government, but terrorists can use these rights to help achieve their own ends. It also raises the possibility that to prevent terrorism in the United States, we may have to trade some of our liberties for more security, thus sacrificing some of what makes America great. The *National Strategy* does recognize this dilemma, for it addresses the issue of security, a primary reason for government to exist in the first place, and it acknowledges that although the federal government has tried to promote security in a global setting, "we have relied primarily on law enforcement and the justice system to provide for domestic peace and order." In addition, two other things that have made America so great are its free market economy and its diverse culture, but terrorism threatens both of these by its intent on damaging our economy and dividing our diverse nation. In a larger sense, these are the threats that terrorism poses to America.

In a more direct sense, terrorism poses a number of threats to America based on the means of attack available. Perhaps the most common threat cited by the news media and government is the threat of weapons of mass destruction, for which the acronym WMD has become part of America's vocabulary. It is true that nuclear, radiological, chemical, and biological weapons do pose a theat. The breakup of the Soviet Union and the proliferation of nuclear capabilities in such countries as Iran and North Korea have increased the availability of radiological materials that could be used in a "dirty bomb" (the use of radiological material in a conventional bomb). In addition, chemical attacks are real threats, for the attack in 1995 in the Tokyo subway has proven how threatening such an attack can be. Moreover, biological attacks can be just as threatening, whether to humans directly or by way of attacking our food sources such as farm produce or livestock. The anthrax attacks immediately following 9/11 demonstrate not only the dangers of such an attack, but they also highlight the fear that these weapons can generate.

Although WMD do pose a serious threat, so do attacks by conventional means. Attacks through car and truck bombs, kidnapping and hostage-taking, and suicide bombings all remain a threat in the United States. The 2005 bombings in the England subway stations highlight the amount of damage and fear such conventional means could have in America. In addition, terrorists have also found ways to exploit technology, in particular the Internet and cell phone communications, to further their attacks. Attacks on the computer systems themselves, whether through worms, viruses, or other means, can have a crippling effect on America's reliance on technology. And finally, it is recognized that terrorists tend to be innovators and may devise new methods of attack that haven't been fully recognized as viable options or truly possible methods of attack. Although some intelligence reports suggested planes could be hijacked and turned into missiles and Tom Clancy integrated this concept into one of his novels, the reality is that few people truly recognized this as a viable threat to America until it happened.

The *National Strategy* also states that the primary threat to America regarding terrorism was Al-Qaeda. The fact that Osama bin Laden and many of his immediate followers are still alive and operating, as well as the threat of Al-Qaeda cells operating on their own in various countries, still poses the greatest threat to America. There are, however, other terrorist groups sympathetic to Al-Qaeda, other international terrorist groups, and even individuals within the United States (as evidenced by the 1995 bombing of the Murrah Federal Building in Oklahoma City) that also pose a threat to America and should be considered in any homeland security strategy.

Organizing for a Secure Homeland

The *National Strategy* recognizes that America has over 87,000 different jurisdictions, consists of over 280 million people, and has a very large private sector ranging from international corporations down to family-run stores. In addition, it is acknowledged that "state, county, municipal, and local governments fund and operate the emergency services that would respond in the event of a terrorist attack,"[33] just as they did on September 11th. How best then to organize for homeland security has been a key concern in developing a strategy for homeland security. Although the *National Strategy* recognizes the various governments, it primarily deals with the federal executive branch and its organization for homeland security. As detailed in the previous chapter, the White House created the Office of Homeland Security and ultimately, through Congressional legislation, the DHS. The *Strategy* also looks to the role that the Department of Defense has taken in regard to homeland security and the creation of Northern Command to oversee military operations in the United States. And it looks to other federal departments and agencies outside the DHS that play a key role, such as the Justice Department, the Federal Bureau of Investigation, and the Central Intelligence Agency. It then discusses intergovernmental coordination and the request by the president that every state create a single Homeland Security Task Force (HSTF) to coordinate homeland security practices between the federal and local governments. It is very clear that under this strategic plan, the national government sees its role as leading on homeland security and encouraging state and local governments to cooperate.

Intelligence and Warning

The *National Strategy* states that intelligence and information analysis is critical to the mission of securing the homeland and that it is not a separate function, but an integral part of the overall strategy. It establishes a framework of four interrelated categories of intelligence and information and then sets out three categories of actions that can follow from intelligence analysis, thus creating "actionable intelligence." The first category of analysis is tactical threat analysis. According to the *National Strategy,* actionable intelligence is essential for preventing acts of terrorism. The timely and thorough analysis and dissemination of information about terrorists and their current and potential activities allow the government to take immediate and near-term action to disrupt and prevent terrorist acts. It also provides a useful warning to specific targets, security and public safety professionals, or the general population.

The second category is strategic analysis of the enemy. Intelligence agencies, it is argued, must have a deep understanding of the organizations that may conduct terrorist attacks against the United States. Knowing the identities, financial and political sources of support, motivation, goals, current and future capabilities, and vulnerabilities of these organizations assist in preventing and preempting future attacks. Intelligence agencies can support the long-term strategies to defeat terrorism by understanding the roots of terrorism overseas and the intentions and capabilities of foreign governments to disrupt terrorist groups in their territories and to assist the United States.

The third category is vulnerability assessment. These assessments are an integral part of the intelligence cycle for homeland security. They allow planners to project the consequences of possible terrorist attacks against specific facilities or different sectors of the economy or government. These projections allow authorities to strengthen defenses against different threats. Such assessments are informed by the use of tools such as computer modeling and analysis.

The fourth category is threat-vulnerability integration. Mapping terrorist threats and capabilities—both current and future—against specific facility and sectoral vulnerabilities will allow authorities to determine which organization poses the greatest threats and which facilities and sectors are most at risk. It will also allow planners to develop thresholds for preemptive or protective action.

The three types of action that can result from the four categories of intelligence analysis listed are tactical prevention, warning and protection, and strategic response. Tactical prevention attempts to use intelligence analysis when it uncovers evidence of terrorist planning by moving to preempt potential attacks. Warning and protective action draws on general knowledge of a possible attack, without the specifics to be able to employ tactical prevention. This allows for security to be upgraded in any affected sector and encourages citizens to be on a higher state of awareness. Finally, strategic response is aimed at refining the strategies used based on a continual update of intelligence information and analysis. This is to prepare for both immediate and long-term strategic planning.

To achieve these strategic goals, the *National Strategy* is highly focused on the national government's assets. It looks to enhancing the analytic capabilities of the FBI, building new capabilities within the DHS, implementing the Homeland Security advisory system, using dual-use analysis to prevent attacks, and using "red team" techniques, which utilizes intelligent knowledge of the potential threats to war game possible actions by the terrorists and to determine how the government would respond.

Border and Transportation Security

The *National Strategy* next focuses on several broad strategic areas that support the primary goals of homeland security, the first being border and transportation security. The *Strategy* recognizes that "virtually every community in America is connected to the global transportation network by the seaports, airports, highways, pipelines, railroads, and waterways that move people and goods into, within, and out of the Nation,"[34] hence border and transportation security are key concerns for any homeland security strategy. The initiatives necessary to ensure the protection of this network consist of the call for ensuring accountability in border and transportation security, which the *National Strategy* places in the hands of the newly formed DHS. The document also argues for the creation of "smart borders," a border management system that uses modern technology to track people and goods coming into the country and where those people and goods go after entry. Once again, the primary responsibility for the deployment of smart borders in the document lies with the DHS. There is some mention that this department would enter into law enforcement databases the names of high-risk aliens who remain in the United States longer than authorized and, when warranted, deport illegal aliens, but this is inherently a top-down approach.

The discussion of border and transportation security also focuses on increasing security of international shipping containers, implementing the Aviation and Transportation Security Act of 2001, recapitalizing the U.S. Coast Guard to enhance its mission of border security, and to reform immigration services. Again, all these are primarily federal government initiatives that, although having direct bearing on local law enforcement, do not necessarily present a particular role for the police.

Domestic Counterterrorism

If there is a section of the *National Strategy for Homeland Security* that speaks best to the role of local law enforcement, it is assuredly the police role in domestic counterterrorism. The section opens by explaining that "the attacks of September 11 and the catastrophic loss of life and property that resulted have redefined the mission of federal, state and local law enforcement authorities" and that "while law enforcement agencies will continue to investigate and prosecute criminal activity, they should now assign priority to preventing and interdicting terrorist activity within the United States."[35] The *Strategy* further explains that effectively reorienting law enforcement organizations to focus on counterterrorism objectives requires decisive action in a number of areas and that "much work remains to be done before law enforcement agencies can collectively pursue the counterterrorism mission with maximum effect."[36] The document discusses such things as information sharing and coordination of operational activities at all levels and recognizes that "the federal government needs to do a better job of utilizing the distinct capabilities of state and local law enforcement to prevent terrorism by giving them access, where appropriate, to the information in [the] federal databases, and by utilizing state and local information at the federal level."[37] The document acknowledges the success of some FBI-led Joint Terrorism Task Forces before discussing the major initiatives it sees as implementing the strategy of domestic counterterrorism.

The first major initiative is the call for an expansion and improvement of FBI-led Task Forces. It then discusses the facilitation of apprehending potential terrorists by expanding the FBI's National Crime Information Center (NCIC) databases to address terrorism, by having the FBI create a consolidated terrorism watch list, and for the FBI to obtain biographical data on suspected terrorists from foreign law enforcement agencies and to enter any fingerprint data into the FBI's Integrated Automated Fingerprint Identification System.

The second major initiative is to continue ongoing investigations and prosecutions of terrorists. Here the document acknowledges the important role that state and local law enforcement play in investigating such crimes as selling false driver's licenses, certificates for transporting hazardous material, and both passports and visas that may be used to further terrorist goals. It also states that local law enforcement plays an important role in reporting unusual behavior and any security anomalies. Although it recognizes the importance of state and local law enforcement in this section, it does not necessarily state a specific role for it to play in domestic counterterrorism beyond what policing already does as a matter of course.

The section on domestic counterterrorism also mandates the complete restructuring of the FBI to emphasize preventing terrorist attacks, for the federal agencies to target and attack terrorist financing, and for the Department of Justice to track foreign terrorists and help bring them to justice. All these, again, are federal government–related endeavors without any specification of a role for state and local governments.

BOX 3-3

POLICING FOR HOMELAND SECURITY: THE MIAMI-DADE POLICE DEPARTMENT

Phillip Davis, Sam Houston State University

Miami-Dade County, anchored by its seaport and airport, remains the North American gateway to Latin America and the Caribbean. The county is represented by over 2 million residents and continues to stand as the meeting ground for numerous multinational businesses and banks.

Because of these unique qualities, Miami remains a high-risk threat area of terrorism. In addition to producing mass casualties, an attack on the county can damage critical infrastructure, disrupt essential services, and cause severe nationwide economic loss. Miami-Dade County's Comprehensive Emergency Management Plan encompasses an all hazards approach to preparedness and protection of our community. As part of the approach, the county has developed a Domestic Preparedness Strategy (DPS) built on the National Strategy for Homeland Security and the State of Florida's Domestic Security Strategy. The DPS assesses the county's local ability to meet state and federal identified homeland security objectives. Miami-Dade County's funding of homeland security is allocated strategically to achieve the following goals:

Goal 1: Preparedness—achieve a readiness posture that reduces the impact of terrorism

Goal 2: Response—meet the community's terrorism response needs

Goal 3: Recovery—utilize resources to facilitate the community's recovery from terrorism disasters

Goal 4: Mitigation—reduce the community's vulnerabilities to terrorism hazards; prevent the occurrence of avoidable incidents

The county, with cooperation from its municipalities, has produced an extensive list of projects that are based on the assessment of threats and vulnerabilities. To date, Miami-Dade County has approximately $280 million in homeland security needs, while its municipalities have approximately $9 million in homeland security needs. Less than 12 percent, or $80 million, of all county funding applied for from state and federal governments over the past three years has been received.

The county's progress in utilizing funds over the past year includes training first responders, educating the community on terrorism, and obtaining much needed disaster response equipment. Homeland security priorities for the 2004–2005 fiscal year include funding projects such as: securing the Port (Seaport Department, $7 million) and guarding against the threat of terrorism for the county's drinking water (Water & Sewer Department, $85 million).

Source: Miami-Dade County Homeland Security Briefing Book (2004–2005). Retrieved from *http://www.miamidade.gov/Homeland/library/Homeland%20Security%20Briefing%20Book.pdf*

Protecting Critical Infrastructure and Key Assets

The *National Strategy* next emphasizes the need to protect critical infrastructure in America and to safeguard key assets. It details the numerous sectors that are vulnerable to attacks, including agriculture, food, water, public health, emergency services, government, defense industrial base, information and telecommunications, energy, transportation, banking and finance, the chemical industry, and postal and shipping. It then recognizes that government has only a limited amount of resources, and it faces the quandary of determining what must be protected. Once again, the *National Strategy* acknowledges the importance of state and local governments, as well as the private sector, to achieve this strategic goal.

The major initiatives for protecting the critical infrastructure in America are to unify these efforts under the DHS with the creation of a directorate aimed at this particular goal (see Chapter 2). It recommends that the department build a complete and accurate assessment of America's critical infrastructure and to develop a national infrastructure protection plan. It is recognized that to achieve these extremely complex goals, it will have to enable effective partnerships with state and local governments and the private sector. The emphasis here is actually with all levels of government cooperating with the private sector, as the *Strategy* states that the private sector controls 85 percent of America's infrastructure, making this task even more difficult. The primary responsibility for security and addressing public safety risks is placed on the private sector's shoulders, but it is recognized that often government at all levels may have the technical expertise that the private sector lacks. The key, the *Strategy* argues, is to enable, not inhibit, the private sector's ability to carry out its protection responsibilities. The *Strategy*, however, looks to the DHS as offering a single contact and coordinating point for coordinating infrastructure protection and developing a centralized plan.

This section also encourages that cyberspace be secured, that the best analytic and modeling tools be used to develop protective solutions, all of which will cost enormous amounts of money that only the federal government may be able to incur. And it encourages agencies to protect against "inside threats," attacks from its own personnel, and to partner with the international community to protect against "outside threats."

Defending Against Catastrophic Threats

The section of the *National Strategy* that deals with defending against catastrophic threats is primarily focused on the threat of WMD. Overall this section emphasizes the role of the federal government by focusing on the DHS's role in securing against such threats, as well as the role of the Departments of State, Energy, and Defense. The major initiatives under this section include preventing terrorist use of nuclear weapons through better sensors and procedures; detecting chemical and biological materials and attacks; improving chemical sensors and decontamination techniques; developing broad spectrum vaccines, antimicrobials, and antidotes; to harness the scientific knowledge and tools to counter terrorism; and to implement the Select Agent Program, which is the registration of laboratories that deal with hazardous materials.

There is little regarding state and local government in this section of the *National Strategy*, but the one place where state and local governments are invoked raises a very complicated issue for policing. The section falls under the detecting chemical and biological materials and attacks discussion and explains, "The ability to quickly recognize and report biological and chemical attacks will minimize casualties and enable first responders to treat the injured effectively." It succinctly states that "local emergency personnel and health providers must first be able to diagnose symptoms."[38] As police officers are always going to be first responders to any type of terrorist attack, their ability to recognize the type of attack and report it will be critical to launching a quick response. Perhaps more importantly, the faster a police officer can recognize an attack and identify it as such, the faster they will be able to protect themselves and other first responders, thus launching a more successful response.

Emergency Preparedness and Response

The second area that has clear implications for state and local law enforcement falls in the *National Strategy's* objective of emergency preparedness and response. Like the section on domestic counterterrorism, there is a distinct acknowledgment to the role that local police will play in a terrorist attack. It states that "America's first line of defense in the aftermath of any terrorist attack is its first responder community—police officers, firefighters, emergency medical providers, public works personnel, and emergency management officials."[39] It recognizes the three million first responders in the United States that serve at the state and local level, including those serving in specially trained positions, such as hazardous materials teams, search-and-rescue units, bomb squads, and special weapons and tactics units. Despite this acknowledgment, it points to the importance of the DHS and the Federal Emergency Management Administration (FEMA) and the role they play in responding to major emergencies.

The major initiatives outlined in this section include the goal of integrating separate federal response plans into a single all-discipline incident management plan and creating a national incident management system. Both of these would be centralized under the DHS. The *Strategy* does recognize that the Incident Management System is already widely spread throughout state and local governments, hence the federal government through the DHS sees its role as one of ensuring federal grants are in place to continue the promotion of this system to state and local governments. It also encourages all state and local governments to "regularly update their own homeland security plans, based on their existing emergency operation plans, to provide guidance for the integration of their response assets in the event of an attack."[40] Moreover, it urges agencies to work with their neighbors to establish and sign mutual aid agreements to facilitate cooperation among agencies during an actual emergency.

Another major initiative that falls under the purview of local law enforcement is the call to improve tactical counterterrorist capabilities. According to the *National Strategy:*

> With advance warning, we have various federal, state, and local response assets that can intercede and prevent terrorists from carrying out attacks. These include law enforcement, emergency response, and military teams. In the most dangerous of incidents, particularly when terrorists have chemical, biological, radiological, or nuclear weapons in their possession, it is crucial that the individuals who preempt the terrorists do so flawlessly, no matter if they are part of the local SWAT team or the FBI's Hostage Rescue

Team. It is crucial that these individuals be prepared and able to work effectively with each other and with other specialized response personnel. Finally, these teams and other emergency response assets must plan and train for the consequences of failed tactical operations.[41]

The section on emergency preparedness and response also encourages seamless communications among all responders to ensure that the response does not break down due to disparate communication systems. Again, it encourages the DHS to work with state and local governments to achieve this particular goal. In addition, it also sets the goals of preparing health-care providers for catastrophic terrorism, augmenting America's pharmaceutical and vaccine stockpiles, and preparing for chemical, biological, radiological, and nuclear decontamination as goals under preparedness. Moreover, it addresses plans for military support to civil authorities, building the citizen corps to assist in terrorism-related responses, and building a national training and evaluation system. However, all these goals are DHS led, working with other federal agencies and state and local constituents.

Law

The *National Strategy* cites the USA PATRIOT Act as being an important step in ensuring that the nation is prepared to prosecute terrorism under the law, but encourages a detailed review of the legal aspects of terrorism to ensure the proper laws are in place to allow for terrorist-related investigations and prosecutions. This is the one section in the *National Strategy* that identifies different major initiatives for federal and state governments. The major initiatives listed under the federal government consist of, again, ensuring the critical infrastructure for information sharing among federal agencies exists and that this information and intelligence can be properly shared with law enforcement agencies at the state and local level. It also sets the goals of expanding existing extradition authorities, reviewing authority for military assistance in domestic security, and giving the president the ability to reorganize the administration to better organize for homeland security (this authority lapsed in 1984 and has not been renewed).

The major initiatives for the states include coordinating suggested minimum standards for state driver's licenses, enhancing market capacity for terrorism insurance, training for prevention of cyberattacks, suppressing money laundering, ensuring continuity of the judiciary, and reviewing quarantine authority. In nearly all of these "state" initiatives, there is somewhat of a suggestion that federal standards be created. In terms of driver's license "minimum standards," there is a discussion that the "federal government, in consultation with state government agencies and non-governmental organizations, should support state-led efforts to develop suggested minimum standards," leading one to the conclusion that this is more a federal initiative. The ability to enhance market capacity for terrorism insurance, much like flood insurance, is going to need federal support; training for cyberattacks lists the FBI as taking the lead; and suppressing money laundering focuses on the USA PATRIOT Act, a federal law. Finally, most recently, the Bush administration has called for a military role in the event of an outbreak of the pandemic influenza in the United States.[42] Despite the categorization of "state" initiatives, it would appear these are more federal initiatives that require some coordination with current state law.

Science and Technology

The *National Strategy* also emphasizes the importance of science and technology for securing the homeland and is very realistic in its understanding that much of the development in these two areas lies in the private sector. Although the federal government can be involved in terms of funding and developing federal guidelines and standards, most of the development will occur in the private sector. Because the ability of the federal government to marshal resources is far greater than state and local governments, there is little in the way of a direct role for state and local governments under this part of the *National Strategy*.

The major initiatives for the development of science and technology for homeland security included the development of chemical, biological, radiological, and nuclear countermeasures; developing systems for detecting hostile intent; and applying biometric technology to identification devices. It also encourages improving the technical capabilities of first responders, coordinating research and development of the homeland security apparatus, and establishing a national laboratory for homeland security. There is also a call for soliciting independent and private analysis for science and technology research, essentially grants for private-sector development. The *Strategy* also cites the establishment of some mechanism for producing prototype technologies, conducting demonstrations and pilot deployments of these prototypes, and ensuring the system allows for the creation of high-risk, high-payoff homeland security research. These latter goals are focused on the promotion of innovation within the homeland security concept. Finally, the document calls for the DHS to establish the standards for all homeland security technology, once again calling for the DHS to take the lead role.

Information Sharing and Systems

It became readily clear in the aftermath of the terrorists attacks on September 11th that not only did agencies within the federal government not share information horizontally, but there was also a large weakness in sharing information vertically, among federal, state, and local governments. In fact, even before September 11th, there was evidence of a lack of interoperability between agencies in other terrorist attacks such as the 1993 World Trade Center bombing, the 1995 Oklahoma City bombing, and the 1999 Columbine school shootings. The latter truly highlighted the problem when the response to the Columbine shootings consisted of 23 local and county law enforcement agencies, 2 state and 3 federal law enforcement agencies, 6 local fire departments, and 7 local emergency medical services, most of which had incompatible communication procedures and equipment. Clearly any strategic plan for homeland security must address these issues, and it is imperative that any strategy for policing for homeland security must work toward enhancing communication.

The *National Strategy* recognizes that any expansion of information systems engages in a delicate balance of providing information that is both proper and legal with that of providing not only illegal and improper information, but wrong information as well. Therefore, the *National Strategy* invokes five principles to guide any strategic expansion of information systems for homeland security purposes. The first is to balance homeland security concerns with citizens' right to privacy. The second is to view the homeland security community, consisting of federal, state, and local governments, as one entity. Third, they state that information should be captured at the source, then used many times to support multiple requirements, rather than compartmentalizing information at the source and not sharing it with others. The fourth principle is to create databases of record that can serve as trusted sources of information. And the final principle is that homeland security information should provide a dynamic tool for those attempting to prevent or counter terrorism in the homeland.

The major initiatives for information sharing and systems consist of improving the sharing of information across the federal government and then moving to share information across state and local governments, as well as with private industry and citizens when warranted. In regard to sharing information with state and local governments, specifically the police, the document states that the FBI and other federal agencies are augmenting the information available in their crime and terrorism databases such as the National Crime Information Center and the National Law Enforcement Telecommunication systems. They also request that state and local governments use a secure intranet to increase the flow of classified federal information to state and local agencies. And it states that the federal government should make an effort to remove classified information from some documents so that the information can be distributed to state and local authorities. They explain that the "effort will help state and local law enforcement officials learn when individuals suspected of criminal activity are also under federal investigation and will enable federal officials to link their efforts to investigations being undertaken by the states."[43] Interestingly enough, the *Strategy* makes no mention of enhancing the number of state and local law enforcement officers that have security clearances so as to have access to classified material.

Other initiatives under the information sharing section included the call to adopt common "meta-data" standards for electronic information relevant to homeland security, to ensure reliable public health information, and to improve public safety emergency communication. Although the majority of public safety emergency communication is in the hands of the first responders, found at the local level, this section speaks more to the DHS and its initiatives. It does mention the creation of a tactical wireless infrastructure to support first responders at federal, state, and local law enforcement levels, but this is largely a technology pursuit that is being led by the DHS.

International Cooperation

As we are fighting a global war on terrorism, to protect the homeland there is the need for international cooperation not only in the investigation process, but in the political and economic realms as well. Here it is clear the federal government, not only through the DHS, but also in other federal agencies, must take the lead to support the mission of homeland security. To this end, some of the major initiatives are to combat fraudulent travel documents, increase the security of international shipping containers, help foreign nations fight terrorism, and improve cooperation in response to attacks.

The one initiative that has the most direct bearing on state and local law enforcement is the goal of intensifying international law enforcement cooperation. Although this is clearly a Department of Justice and FBI–led initiative, cooperation at this level can have a decisive impact on the state and local level, for information obtained from other countries could provide a key element to state and local law enforcement in pre-venting and/or preparing for a terrorist attack. Once again, the important element in regard to this type of information sharing between nations is that once received, it is shared with state and local police.

Costs of Homeland Security

Perhaps the most difficult aspect of adding the responsibility of homeland security to state and local police are the costs of this added role. This section does list some princi-ples to guide the allocation of homeland security costs, such as balancing benefits and costs, federal regulations on state and local governments, and the issue of federalism and cost sharing. There are no major initiatives under this section. Rather, it speaks to the costs of se-curing the homeland and the costs of recovering from attacks. There is simply a recognition that the federal government will have to pay more, but so too will state and local gov-ernments and the private sector. For economic recovery it speaks to various federal plans that support state and local government in the event of a terrorist attack, but gen-erally focuses on broader themes such as restoring the financial markets and national economic recovery.

IACP's Principles for a Nationally Coordinated Homeland Security Strategy

In May of 2005, the International Association of Chiefs of Police (IACP) issued a white paper titled *From Hometown Security to Homeland Security: IACP's Principles for a Locally Designed and Nationally Coordinated Homeland Security Strategy.*[44] In that document they explained that as the terrorist attacks of the 1990s occurred, the United States did not significantly alter its security strategy, but then again, neither did law enforcement agencies. They argued that although law enforcement most cer-tainly learned from those incidents, they "did not dramatically adjust their policing philosophies."[45] In the wake of the September 11th attacks, they argued that all agen-cies, at the federal, state, and local levels, rapidly shifted their attention toward the is-sue of homeland security. Everyone realized that homeland security would be a national issue, one that had to be addressed not just by the federal government, but by all levels of government. President Bush's own opening statements in the *National Strategy for Homeland Security,* released in 2002, when he stated, "This is a national strategy, not a federal strategy,"[46] emphasized this fact.

The IACP, however, argued that despite the passage of the USA PATRIOT Act, the creation of the DHS, programs supporting state and local governments, as well as the talk of creating a "national" plan, the reality is the national plan is a top-down driven federal plan. The majority of the *National Strategy,* according to the IACP, has focused on the federal government's role in homeland security, particularly the DHS, and when it does invoke state and local agencies, it has the tendency of focusing on what the federal government wants state and local agencies to do. The IACP explained that despite statements to the contrary, the *National Strategy* was primarily created by the federal government with a federal government perspective. They thus argued that the *National Strategy* "was developed without sufficiently seeking or incorporating the advice, expertise, or consent of public safety organizations at the state, tribal, or local level."[47]

Recognizing the deficiencies within the *National Strategy*, the IACP called for the development of a new homeland security strategy, one that would incorporate the perspective of state, tribal, and local public safety agencies, as they will remain the first line in prevention and the first responders to any homeland security plan. Although the IACP is currently working on the development of the strategic goals and objectives critical to state, tribal, and local law enforcement, they did identify five key principles that should continue to guide the development and implementation of a truly national homeland security strategy.

The IACP identified the first principle as a play on the former Speaker of the House Tip O'Neil's statement that "all politics is local," by stating that "all terrorism is local." The IACP clearly states that regardless of the global and international connections, any actual terrorism attack is going to occur at the local level, and it will be local first responders that will deal with the attack. The IACP thus succinctly stated "that it is imperative that as homeland security proposals are designed, they must be developed in an environment that fully acknowledges and accepts the reality that local authorities, not federal, have the primary responsibility for preventing, responding to and recovering from terrorist attacks."[48]

The second principle that the IACP articulates is "that the prevention of terrorist attacks must be viewed as the paramount priority in any national, state, tribal, or local homeland security strategy."[49] The IACP argued that the majority of state and local initiatives by the federal government have centered on the police responding to and participating in the recovery of a terrorist attack. The strategic goal of prevention is largely left to the federal government and its assets, mostly through the Department of Homeland Security and Justice domestically and the Department of State and Defense globally, to thwart any future attacks. The IACP believes that law enforcement can and do play a critical role in preventing terrorism, just as they do in preventing crimes or traffic accidents. A truly national strategy would recognize this fact and integrate it into the goals and objectives focused on the prevention of future terrorist attacks.

The third principle, and reflective of the title of the document, is "hometown security is homeland security." The IACP explained that by way of law enforcement's duties to protect their communities against crime, it is a natural extension that they should also protect their communities against terrorism. If law enforcement agencies each protect their hometown, this will cover the majority of communities, leaving the federal government responsible for issues related to overseas, on federal property, and along our borders. The IACP argued, however, that the federal government has not enhanced resources for local law enforcement, but rather has cut them by way of reductions in the Local Law Enforcement Block Grant Program, the Edward Byrne Memorial Grants, and the Office of Community Oriented Policing Services. The IACP believes this is a move in the wrong direction, and "if our homeland security efforts are to have any chance of succeeding, it is absolutely vital for Congress and the administration to make the necessary resources available that will allow law enforcement agencies to mount effective anticrime programs, which will also serve as effective antiterrorism programs."[50]

The fourth principle the IACP puts forth is largely a reiteration of their largest complaint regarding the *National Strategy for Homeland Security,* in that it is more of a federally coordinated strategy for homeland security than a nationally coordinated strategy. The IACP argues that since September 11th, the emphasis has remained on what the Departments of Homeland Security, Justice, and Defense, are doing to address homeland security. Although there is often discussion about local law enforcement, they are seen more as an effect than a cause. If the federal government creates a regulation for homeland security (the cause) then the local police will have to implement it (the effect). Or if the DHS establishes information-sharing procedures with local law enforcement, the DHS is the cause and the police are the effect. Local police are rarely seen as being the cause of homeland security, only the effect, the ones who execute the policies and procedures. According to the IACP, "a truly national effort will ensure that all levels of government, local, tribal, state, and federal, are participating in the policy design and development process as <u>full and equal partners</u>"[51] (emphasis in the original).

The fifth and final principle articulated by the IACP is the importance of bottom-up engineering; the diversity of the state, tribal, and local public safety community; and noncompetitive collaboration. Although these sound like numerous principles, the element that underlies each of them is the concept that any homeland security strategy should draw from a broad base of resources. In other words, like the concept of community policing, one size does not fit all. America's communities and law enforcement agencies are too diverse to adopt a cookie-cutter approach to homeland security. Rather, any homeland security strategy should first draw on the diversity by collaborating to determine the best strategies for prevention, response, and recovery, and then develop a homeland strategy that all agencies can draw on. To do this, they encourage bottom-up engineering or, more simply put, tapping into the knowledge of those on the front lines of the war on terror, those that are in fact securing the homeland, and those that have been and will be first responders in the future. Police officers bring a unique perspective and insight into the issues of security and prevention and should not be ignored. This is the same for police agencies, regardless of size or jurisdiction, as this diversity can bring further insights into the process of developing a national strategy. And finally, the IACP argues that resources for homeland security should not be competitive in nature emphasizing only large urban areas, but rather should be noncompetitive and that grants should not be given to large urban areas at the expense of protecting smaller jurisdictions throughout the United States.

These five principles are intended to guide the development of a national strategy, which the IACP is now working to develop, one that will "address critical areas of need, such as the development of prevention and response plans, hiring and training needs, and resource and funding strategies."[52] Their goal is to incorporate the views of federal, state, tribal, and local law enforcement to develop a strategic blueprint and to "identify, collect, and disseminate best practices and innovations in areas such as intelligence gathering and information sharing, threat assessment, deployment strategies, equipment needs and standards, and public-private partnerships."[53] In doing so, the IACP intends to reach out beyond just members of the law enforcement community and attempt to solicit input from all public safety agencies, including fire and emergency services.

Santa Ana Police Department morning briefing. (*Source: PhotoEdit Inc.*)

Homeland Security Best Practices—ICMA

As alluded to in their white paper, the IACP has in fact already advanced the concept of identifying, collecting, and disseminating best practices and innovations when the ICMA published its collection of articles entitled *Homeland Security: Best Practices for Local Government.*[54] Numerous articles written by police chiefs and others from the IACP were featured in this publication that attempted to identify successful practices of local government, particularly local law enforcement, for homeland security. The book was organized in the same manner as FEMA organizes its strategic goals, namely mitigation, preparedness, response, and recovery. The document serves not entirely as a strategic plan, but it is organized in such a manner as to, in the words of the IACP, create a blueprint for a strategic model.

The editor recognizes, like others, that on September 11th, the people that responded to the terrorist attacks were primarily from local governments, not federal agencies or the military. To discuss emergency management, they use the federal framework of mitigation, preparedness, response, and recovery. Mitigation is defined as those efforts to prevent man-made or natural disasters or to lessen their effects. Preparedness looks at how well government is readied to respond to disasters of all types, including terrorist attacks. Response deals with the government's actual reaction to such disasters, and recovery focuses on the ability of government to clean up debris, restore the environment, rebuild infrastructure, and reinstate public services to its citizens. Using this framework, the collection of articles then details various concepts necessary to achieve these overarching goals, similar to strategic planning.[55]

Mitigation

Under the mitigation section, several of the authors deal with the issue of information gathering, developing intelligence, and then sharing both information and intelligence. Police officers on a routine basis collect information, whether through field interviews and "routine" traffic stops or by more formal investigations into reported crimes. This information is collected and maintained by agencies in a variety of manners, but not necessarily in a way that coverts information (raw data) into intelligence (analyzed data). Although police departments prior to the 1970s typically maintained intelligence units, most were disbanded in the 1960s and 1970s due to the civil rights movement and a series of laws, rules, and regulations regarding the maintenance of police intelligence. In addition, many of these laws prevented or limited the sharing of such information, so unless agencies had bona fide crime information, raw data and even analyzed data, unless it pertained directly to known criminal activity, could not be shared.

There was a distinct realization that in the post–September 11th environment, this was detrimental to agencies attempting to prevent future terrorist attacks, and there has been a call for change. To effectively mitigate future attacks, police officers need to be able to collect information, analyze that information, and distribute it through various information systems. In addition, this type of information and intelligence contributes to an agency's ability to engage in threat assessments, the analysis of potential threats to a particular community and that government's ability to counter such a threat. Threat assessments assist agencies in determining the allocation of resources, but lacking information and analyzed information (intelligence), governments cannot make the necessary analysis for threat assessments. Therefore, to mitigate or prevent future terrorist attacks, it is argued that police must find legal means by which they can collect, analyze, and disseminate information and intelligence. Many have come to call this strategic goal "intelligence-driven" policing.

One particular article in this section by Douglas Bodrero[56] makes the argument that intelligence gathering and analysis and threat assessments are a critical goal to preventing future terrorist attacks. But, he also stated there are three other critical steps to prevention, and they include training to understand the threat and prepare for it, to develop or continue working with terrorism task forces and working groups, and that state and local agencies should develop counterterrorism plans, and that these should continually be updated to address changes in the intelligence environment and the recognition of new threats.

Preparedness

Under the preparedness section there is a common theme among the articles, that in order to be adequately prepared for a terrorist attack, it is imperative that agencies make the determination of who is to be in charge before any incident occurs. This can be done through the task force or working group process, or by way of mutual aid agreements between neighboring agencies. In addition, there is the consistent call for all such emergencies to be handled through the Emergency Operations Centers (EOC) concept. The EOC should be located in an easily accessible location, should have predetermined staffing, and should be exercised on a regular basis, so that when called on, the EOC can begin managing an incident in the immediate aftermath of an attack and carry it through both the response and recovery stages.

Another theme that runs through this section is the focus on the broader picture, specifically the different sectors of the community that will be affected. This includes such sectors as fire and emergency medical services, the medical community itself, public works, the private sector, and others. Each of these will play a critical role during the response and recovery phases, and therefore their participation in the preparedness stage is critical. In addition, one of the key tasks during this stage is the development of plans. One particular plan emphasized in this section was that for the evacuation of high-rise buildings, but other plans are needed as well. One only has to look to the mass evacuation of Houston, Texas, as Hurricane Rita swept toward its coast in September of 2005, to understand that plans were not fully in place to make the major highways and interstates one-way leaving Houston. This emphasizes the need for continual planning to address any eventuality that may occur. And plans, once put in place, must be continually updated as environment, threat, and intelligence change over time.

Response

The section related to response has one primary theme running through the various articles and that is the ability in a terrorist attack to communicate and share information during the actual incident. It is noted that although there is the common issue of police, fire, and emergency medical services responding to an attack and needing to communicate, other entities such as public works will be a crucial element with which to communicate. In addition, although much of the focus is on internal and cross-agency communication, there is also a strong need to communicate with the public. This is often not factored into the plan or if it is, during a response it is only with some delay that public notifications are made. Despite the history of the public emergency broadcast system, it was not invoked after the attacks on September 11th, and public notifications are usually only made through press conferences. Real-time or close to real-time information should be given to citizens to allow them to react in a proper and informed manner, rather than relying on rumor and innuendo that often surface in the event of a major incident.

In addition, in the immediate aftermath of a major incident the one source of information for citizens to notify government is through the dispatch centers, which often become overloaded during a crisis. A key part of the communications process is citizens calling dispatchers and dispatchers notifying public safety personnel of critical information. If this system breaks down or becomes overloaded, coordination in the response phase becomes quickly ineffective. Strategic goals and planning in this regard are critical to the response phase.

One innovative means for assisting in the response phase is the use of geographic information systems. The article by Russ Johnson details how the New York Office of Emergency Management (OEM) had a storehouse of geographic information on transportation systems, subway services, power grids, operational and staging areas available, and areas of personnel services, particularly food and water stations. In addition, geographic mapping also allows for visual blueprints of various key buildings, such as malls, schools, and courthouses that can provide key information to not only the emergency operation center personnel for planning purposes, but also to those officers that are the first responders. The use of this technology should most assuredly be part of any strategic homeland security plan.

Recovery

The recovery section deals primarily with planning for the worst-case scenarios such as stress management, particularly critical incident stress, and how to deal with line-of-duty deaths. Although many agencies have developed these types of plans over time, those agencies that do not have these in place should make it an integral part of their planning. The successful cleanup of disaster sites, the restoration of public services, and the rebuilding of infrastructures all deal with more physical elements of the recovery process, what this particular section reminds the strategic planners of is the mental elements of the recovery process.

Strategies for Local Law Enforcement—COPS and PERF

As previously described, in November of 2002, the Police Executive Research Forum, a widely known and respected police think tank, drew on a grant from the Office of Community Oriented Policing Services to conduct an executive session aimed at developing some broad strategic goals related to policing for homeland security. The executive session included a cross section of federal, state, and local law enforcement, collaborating together to identify key law enforcement strategies that were seen as the immediate priorities of police for engaging in homeland security. They identified seven priorities, which consisted of promoting effective local–federal partnerships, security clearances and information sharing, joint terrorism task forces, FBI strategies, intelligence, multijurisdictional information sharing, and training and awareness. Although many of these are highly related, the premise behind each will be discussed.

The first priority listed was the promotion of effective local–federal partnerships through information exchange and access. Many of the local agencies felt that communication with federal agencies tended to be a one-way street, local to federal, but not the other way around. The call was to build this relationship through processes and protocols, much in the way that the various joint task forces have operated. The priority also incorporated partnerships not only between federal and local agencies, but also with the media and the community. However, put simply, greater cooperation across all levels of officials and across sectors is critical to a successful homeland security strategy.

The second priority listed included security clearances and information sharing. The purpose of enhancing local–federal partnerships is to increase information exchanges, but in many cases the information that the federal government has is classified and therefore cannot be shared with local law enforcement unless they have clearances. In addition, even if one individual in the agency has a clearance, he or she may not be able to share that information within the police department due to the information being classified. The executive committee recognized this as an obstacle that must be overcome. Simply making police agencies aware of the security clearance dilemma and the process for applying for a security clearance can alleviate suspicions, but further administrative cooperation and streamlining of the process may be necessary to ensure that information and intelligence can be shared so that it may be acted on.

The third priority was the enhancement of joint terrorism task forces. Although these have been in existence since the first one in New York in 1980, they are few and far between and do not necessarily create a perfect solution. The executives all agreed that the joint task forces on terrorism generally lacked "the structure, appropriate number of analysts and administrative personnel to support investigations and other critical resources." Therefore, although they are held up as solid models for local and federal partnerships, they are not perfect. In addition, they cited the fact that in many cases the task forces are redundant, as there are often overlapping task forces, and that too many task forces would become unwieldy and would drain resources.

The fourth priority was related to FBI strategies, which attempted to recognize the goals and responsibilities of the FBI and how they differ from local law enforcement. Ultimately, this section was dedicated to enhancing local police and FBI cooperation by having each recognize the legal, political, and economic restraints that the other faces.

The firth priority was the collection, analysis, and dissemination of intelligence. Here there was the recognition that information sharing must be maintained, but that the FBI ultimately was the primary source for channeling information and intelligence. A key recommendation was that law enforcement agencies at all levels be given the assistance and training to develop intelligence units, a function most have not performed since the 1960s. And, once again, there was the call for the FBI to feed information back down to local agencies so that they may incorporate the available intelligence into their threat assessments and homeland security planning, recognizing again the constraints of classified material.

The sixth priority was multijurisdictional information sharing that focused on information sharing between not only the federal and local agencies, but also between federal, state, and local agencies that all share a similar geographical area. Finally, the seventh priority was to ensure that state and local agencies receive the proper training, not only for their line officers, but for their executives and midlevel managers as well.

A Framework to Prepare for Terrorist Threats

More recently, in 2005, Dr. William V. Pelfrey, longtime scholar of policing, wrote an article titled, "The Cycle of Preparedness: Establishing a Framework to Prepare for Terrorist Threats."[57] In this article, Pelfrey identified the fact that our numerous governmental agencies at all levels must not only prepare for terrorist threats, but also simultaneously plan for natural disasters. Although this may seem like an impossible task, he argued that by breaking down the concept of preparedness into its various components, it will be easier to prepare for the homeland security role. He explained that it is an accepted proposition that we must prepare for these eventualities. He stated what is most critical is identifying "a strategic framework that provides governmental and non-governmental entities the ability to prepare in stages."[58] He, therefore, proposed a strategic framework, which he labeled the "cycle of preparedness" to guide agencies toward this end.

Pelfrey explained that he sees the overall concept of homeland security as one of preparedness. He used the concept of preparedness as an umbrella term for many of the concepts previously stated under the other strategic plans reviewed. He then labeled these particular concepts as phases and titled them prevention, awareness of attack, response, recovery. He sees these four phases as a cyclical process, primarily emphasizing the first phase, prevention, until an attack or natural disaster occurs. At that point, the concept preparedness moves through the next three phases until returning to prevention.

In terms of the first phase, prevention, Pelfrey draws heavily on the Office for Domestic Preparedness' *Guidelines for Homeland Security 2003*[59] to articulate what elements make up the strategic goal of prevention. He quoted the *National Strategy for Homeland Security* stating the prevention consists of such objectives as "deterring all potential terrorists from attacking America through our uncompromising commitment to defeating terrorism wherever it appears," "detect terrorists before they strike," "prevent them and their instruments of terror from entering our country," and "take decisive action to eliminate the threat they pose."[60] Prevention, then, according to Pelfrey "is the process of identifying the risks associated with terrorism most likely to affect the security, safety, and well-being of the community and eliminating or mitigating those risks through all legal means."[61] To strategically apply the concepts of prevention, Pelfrey asserted that we must focus on the specific objectives of protection, deterrence, preemption, and mitigation. The key is to protect citizens, deter terrorism, take action against known terrorists' activity, and to work toward reducing the harm an attack will cause by being prepared to respond promptly.

To more fully operationalize these concepts (the subject of the next chapter), Pelfrey focused on two distinct elements necessary under the prevention phase. He drew these elements from the *Office of Domestic Preparedness Guidelines*, and they include collaboration and information sharing.[62] Collaboration focuses on the numerous governmental and police agencies working together both laterally and vertically, between neighboring and overlapping jurisdictions, including the private sector, as well as between federal, state, and local agencies. Information sharing is focused on the "process of gathering, storing, analyzing, and disseminating data, information, and intelligence between and among different agencies, organizations, and individuals, on a need-to-know basis, for the common purpose of foreseeing or recognizing terrorist threats, actions, and behaviors."[63] The combination of these two concepts, collaboration and information sharing, are thus the key elements to preventing future terrorist attacks.

The second phase of the preparedness cycle is awareness of an attack. Although intuitively one might think this phase is rather simplistic and ultimately recognizable, this is not always the case. In general, most people treated the first plane into the World Trade Center as a very serious accident. However, when the second plane flew into the World Trade Center it became very clear to all that it was, in fact, a terrorist attack. Some type of biological agent introduced into the food supply such as mad cow disease, could potentially be treated as a natural occurrence and never fully recognized as a terrorist attack. The key to this phase is recognizing an attack for what it truly is, for until we recognize an attack has occurred, we cannot launch the appropriate response. As Pelfrey stated, "The speed of the recognition is the key to the mediation of the harm."[64] And once an attack is recognized for what it is, we can begin to quickly transition to the next phase: response.

The third phase of Pelfrey's cycle of preparedness is the response phase. Citing the *National Strategy for Homeland Security*,[65] Pelfrey stated that the following passage, which describes emergency preparedness is really about response:

> We need a comprehensive national system to bring together and command all necessary response assets quickly and effectively. We must equip, train, and exercise many different response units to mobilize for any emergency without warning . . . to create

and employ a system that will improve our response to all disasters, both manmade and natural."[66]

Pelfrey then breaks down the necessary elements of the response, consisting of the strategies of "containment of the scene, control of the scene, management of the incident, and identification of the perpetrators, keeping in mind that preservation of life is the first priority of response."[67] Once the initial response is achieved, the routine that follows will be the transition to the next phase, that of recovery.

The fourth phase is the recovery phase. Regardless of whether man-made or natural, recovery can be seen as the "process of rehabilitating, restoring, and repairing the harm done."[68] Pelfrey makes the argument that like the other phases, planning and training must go into the recovery phase, which will determine how recovery will be handled by the agencies involved. And like the other phases, this phase must be managed properly for it to succeed. In addition, one other strategic consideration during this phase is the protection of those working during the recovery phase. One only has to look at the thousands of workers at ground zero at the World Trade Center working amidst the unstable rumble, often in no more protection than street clothes, to recognize the importance of this strategic concern.

After working through the four phases of the cycle of preparedness, Pelfrey then articulated the need for true preparation in advance for each of the four phases. He created a matrix that factors in each of the four phases and its goals and objectives and then crosses those with the need for planning, training, equipping, exercising, evaluating, and revisions based on the evaluations. By breaking each of the phases down into elements and ensuring that each of the preparedness considerations are met, it allows managers to implement this strategic plan in a rational and doable manner. Working through each of these considerations for each of the goals and objectives of preparedness will help ensure that the strategic plan is truly operationalized.

BOX 3-4

STRATEGY CHECKLIST

1. Align the strategic objectives that support state and urban area goals to the seven national priorities. This does not require an update to existing objectives if those objectives already reflect the National Priorities. However, the alignment of those objectives to the national priorities should be clearly articulated.

   Does the strategy address Regional Collaboration?
   Does the strategy address the National Incident Management System?
   Does the strategy address information sharing and collaboration?
   Does the strategy address interoperable communications?
   Does the strategy address police as first responder safety?

2. Describe the strategies, goals, and objectives within the framework of the mission areas: prevent, prepare, protect, respond, recover, assess.

Does the strategy address prevention?
Does the strategy address preparedness?
Does the strategy address protection?
Does the strategy address response?
Does the strategy address recovery?
Does the strategy address assessment?

3. Local jurisdictions participation in the strategic planning process.

Does the strategic process include participation from local jurisdictions?

4. Address citizen preparedness and volunteer efforts.

Does the strategy appropriately address citizen preparedness and volunteer efforts?

5. Regionalization and mutual aid.

Does the strategy address multiple agencies?
Does the strategy address regionalization?
Does the strategy address mutual aid agreements?

Source: Adapted from Department of Homeland Security. (2005). *State and Urban Area Homeland Security Strategy: Guidance on Aligning Strategies with the National Preparedness Goal.* Available online at http://www.ojp.usdoj.gov/odp/docs/StrategyGuidance_22JUL2005.pdf

Downloaded on August 15, 2005.

A COHESIVE STRATEGY FOR HOMELAND SECURITY

The move to a new era of policing, the era of homeland security, necessitates a strategic plan for the implementation of such a broad and sweeping change in law enforcement. The development of a strategy provides police agencies with the policy or framework with which to operationalize the myriad concepts associated with homeland security. The dilemma, however, as McVey has pointed out, is whether or not to wait for a strategy to be handed down or develop one's own without any sense of whether one is planning strategically in the right direction.[69] Responding to the first option, McVey sums it up nicely when he states that "fortunately, there is a third alternative for local law enforcement" and "it begins with the basic realization that any proposal forthcoming from federal agencies will likely be only strategically general."[70] In fact, not only was the *National Strategy for Homeland Security* strategically general, as the IACP pointed out, it was largely a federal strategy aimed at what the federal government can do to implement homeland security. In fact, there is nothing inherently wrong with this, as the federal government's strategic plan should emphasize federal activity. The only complaint is that it was sold as an all-encompassing national strategy, rather than a federal strategy. And so, McVey explained that "each jurisdiction will have to interpret such a proposal according to the area's unique risk factors and operations capabilities" and thus "each agency must lay the necessary groundwork in preparation for those proposals by generating and incorporating into its individual administrative paradigm a basic understanding of the terrorist risks it faces and its own incident management capability."[71] Simply put, each agency or a grouping of agencies (such as those in a metroplex environment), should develop their own strategic plan for homeland security.

To develop a strategic plan, it is important to draw on as many sources as possible for its creation. Despite the federal leanings toward the *National Strategy for Homeland Security,* it should not be ignored as being useless to a local police department, but rather a police department's strategic plan should incorporate elements of the *National Strategy.* In fact, a local strategic plan should be nested into the larger *National Strategy,* thus finding ways of being linked to one another to ensure the implementation of similar goals and fostering both collaboration and information sharing. Yet, as McVey pointed out, it must fit the needs, risks, and threats particular to the jurisdiction and police department of concern. Thus the next question is, Where to start?

Drawing on all of the previous documents that have focused on strategic goals and objectives, an underlying consistency exists that provides a framework for the development of a strategic plan. Beginning with these particular elements and incorporating those factors that are particular to a police department's jurisdiction will allow for the generation of a strategic plan to oversee any police department's move to homeland security.

The strategic goals of homeland security would appear to consist of five overarching goals, and they are Prevention, Preparedness, Response, Recovery, and Assessment/Adaptation. Every document reviewed has focused heavily on the concept of prevention. In fact, drawing on the IACP white paper, they stated that it was the IACP's belief "that the prevention of terrorist attacks must be viewed as the paramount priority in any national, state, tribal, or local homeland security strategy."[72] The *National Strategy* was also in accordance with the IACP in that it stated, "The first priority of homeland security is to prevent terrorist attacks."[73] Therefore, any strategic plan must begin with this goal and order its strategic applications around it. As Pelfrey has stated, some of the key strategic applications for prevention include protection, deterrence, and preemption.[74] Agencies should look to ways of altering the environment to protect people from terrorism (e.g., target hardening and Crime Prevention Through Environmental Design (CPTED) principles), they should implement means for deterring potential terrorists, and they should rapidly and forcefully preempt any terrorist attacks once detected. And, as *The Office for Domestic Preparedness Guidelines* explained, prevention and deterrence should focus on collaboration, information sharing, threat recognition, risk management, and intervention. Each of these strategic applications work toward the goal of prevention.

The second strategic goal should be that of preparedness. Unlike prevention, preparedness is the realization that a future attack or natural disaster is inevitable and that the agency should be prepared to respond to such an event. The strategic applications under preparedness include "proper planning, resource allocation, training and simulated disaster response exercises . . . to ensure that skills, equipment and other resources can be effectively coordinated when an emergency occurs."[75] Much of the strategic application is working through mutual aid agreements, determining which agency in a multiagency metroplex would be officially in charge, the emergency operation center command structure, governmental resources that can be drawn on, personnel readiness, and ensuring that plans and standard operating procedures are put into place. Each of these strategic applications works toward the goal of preparedness.

The third strategic goal is response. Incorporated within response is Pelfrey's third phase, and that is the importance of threat recognition. Once a threat is recognized, initiating the initial response to a terrorist attack is the next strategic goal. Strategic applications of the goal of response, beyond threat recognition, include the mechanism for issuing appropriate warnings and information to the public, accessing the proper personnel to initiate the response, ensuring the proper incident management and coordination with other police and government agencies. In addition, "other important aspects of the response phase include search-and-rescue operations, evacuations according to established procedures, damage assessments, and the proper handling of fatalities."[76] Response is focused on the various elements of the agency having the capabilities necessary to perform their function in a terrorist attack or natural disaster and being able to adequately deploy in such an environment. Each of these strategic applications works toward the goal of response.

The fourth strategic goal is that of recovery. Once the initial response is made and the event moves from the crisis mode to that of managing the scene, the agency will move into the recovery phase. This phase will include such things as "the cleanup of debris, the restoration of the environment, the reinstitution of public services, and the rebuilding of the public infrastructure."[77] The strategic application for recovery has to do with that ability to manage in this environment, especially under the strain of limited resources and personnel. Providing security and traffic control for the area that was impacted becomes a key concern during the response phase. In addition, part of the goal is providing protection to those officers engaging in the recovery effort, both physically and mentally. In the former case, the proper equipment must be on hand to work through the recovery phase and in the latter, the necessary counseling must be provided to effectively deal with the critical incident stress officers will face. Each of these strategic applications works toward the goal of recovery.

Finally, the last strategic goal is that of assessment. Although often subordinated to a final strategic application within the recovery phase, assessment here is detailed as its own strategic goal. Each agency should have the mechanisms in place to adequately assess how effective an agency was during the response to a true attack or natural disaster, regardless of scale, as well as the ability to assess effectiveness through simulated exercises, whether computer simulated or hands-on field exercises. Incorporating feedback obtained from action reviews and lessons learned must find their way into the strategic application under prevention, awareness, response, and recovery.

In addition to the strategic goals, a number of strategic objectives also underlie and support each of the strategic goals. Each of these in their own right must be addressed by police agencies and become an integral part of the strategic plan to move an agency into the era of homeland security. These objectives include organization, collaboration, intelligence, information/intelligence sharing, law, and science and technology. Agencies must determine how best to organize for homeland security. This will be largely determined by the level of personnel and resources available, the size of the jurisdiction and agency, resources available, threat and risk assessments, and a host of other factors influencing the agency. Whether this means restructuring the organization, centralizing the command or certain elements of command, or adding a new division to the agency must be determined by the capabilities and constraints of each agency. Central to the organizational considerations, however, should be the ability to achieve the strategic goals for homeland security. One element of organization that will more than likely fit into any plan is the reliance on the Incident Management System and the use of an incident command center.

Collaboration again cannot be ignored for its importance in working not only with other governmental agencies within one's own jurisdiction, but also with neighboring jurisdictions as well. In addition, collaborations with other regional agencies are important as is developing working relations under the concepts of homeland security with state and federal agencies. Although clearly collaboration is important in regard to the goal of prevention, it is also critical in all of the strategic goals.

Intelligence gathering and analysis is also a critical objective for law enforcement and one that has not been used by many departments over the previous 30 years. However, if policing for homeland security is to concentrate primarily on prevention, it will largely be driven by intelligence. Information must be collected and analyzed before it becomes intelligence. Having a means of data collection and the ability to analyze the data is critical to developing intelligence. Once this intelligence becomes available, the ability to disseminate to the agencies or units that are tasked with responding to threats and preempting strikes is critical to the success of the prevention goal. Therefore, drawing on both the collaboration and intelligence objectives necessitates the emphasis of yet another key objective, and that is information and intelligence sharing. Once information is attained or data has been analyzed into usable intelligence, some mechanism must exist to move the intelligence both laterally and vertically.

Also undergirding the strategic goals are the objectives of the law and both science and technology. In many cases the strategic goals of homeland security may run into problems with the law. For instance the creation of intelligence units within police departments may potentially be blocked by laws passed in the 1960s and 1970s. These types of impediments must be dealt with prior to the strategic goals being accomplished. In addition, laws may need to be created to support investigations into terrorism or to apply the law to the situation of terrorism. In addition, the application of both science and technology may be a necessary element for achieving the strategic goals, as it is technology that may provide the proper solution to achieving these goals.

CONCLUSION

As policing moves into this new era of homeland security and faces challenges hitherto unfaced in America, there is a clear and present need for a strategic plan to guide police agencies' implementation of homeland security. The federal government has issued its *National Strategy for Homeland Security,* but there has been criticism that it is much too focused on the federal government and not the nation as a whole. In addition, other writings exist that have focused on the strategic goals of homeland security, but they have presented little in the way of a complete framework from which to work. Drawing on Pelfrey's "Cycle of Preparedness" can provide a good starting point for developing a strategy, but it is important that local agencies, when developing their own strategic plan, look to multiple sources for the development of its own plan. Although a locally developed strategic plan is critical for the implementation of homeland security policy, it must be compatible with strategic plans at the federal, state, and local levels, so as to avoid conflicts in its implementation. Basing a strategic plan on the common themes presented in the strategic documents provides five goals: Prevention, Preparedness, Response, Recovery, and Assessment; as well as six strategic objectives: organization, collaboration, intelligence, information/intelligence sharing, law, and science and technology. Taken together, these five strategic goals and the various strategic objectives provide the necessary framework for which police departments can begin developing a useful strategy for homeland security. Drawing on these strategies, police can then begin to look at police operations for homeland security, the subject of the next chapter.

CHAPTER 4

Police Operations for Homeland Security

It is essential to relate what is strategically desirable to what is tactically possible with the forces at your disposal. To this end it is necessary to decide the development of operations before the initial blow is delivered.

Field Marshal Bernard Montgomery

INTRODUCTION

The operational level of policing is a transitional realm between good police strategy and tactics. It is where police management translates strategic goals and objectives writ large into a plan of action. It is moving from a general theory of how best to deal with securing the homeland, to a practical method that is aimed at achieving these goals. It is in essence the process by which the homeland security strategy is translated into operational plans for tactical action. Although it retains some aspects of being a science, because we do not deal with definitives in the police operational environment, it is in large part an art. It is the operational art of employing police officers to obtain the strategic goals and objectives by properly planning and directing officers on the street. It also includes the necessary planning to ensure that officers are prepared for all eventualities so that the police agency may achieve their strategic goals.

Police operations in the past have not entirely adhered to the strategic-operational-tactical process for the deployment of its police. Operational planning has generally been very limited and is usually found through simple policies in the standard operating procedures. In fact, police operations have largely been handled by the dispatchers with management intervention only in the event of a significant incident such as a hostage situation, bank robbery, or murder scene. Police operations under homeland security present a far more dynamic method of police planning, command, and conduct of police operations. It looks to reconceptualize how police departments organize and manager their assets, it looks to risk assessment and threat assessments to determine how assets should be deployed, and it draws on police intelligence for the actual deployment of these police assets. Drawing on these three concepts, it presents a far more advanced method of police operations, one that bridges the gap between homeland security strategy and street-level tactics.

The purpose of this chapter, then, is to understand police operations for homeland security by defining operations and analyzing it under the homeland security concept. It will then discuss police organization and management for homeland security, specifically looking at police planning, incident command, and partnering with other agencies through mutual aid agreements and joint task forces. It will further discuss the concept of operational planning through risk and threat assessments to develop plans and determine the allocation of police resources. And, finally, it will review the process of turning police information into usable and actionable intelligence for intelligence-led policing.

POLICE OPERATIONS FOR HOMELAND SECURITY

Historically, police operations have been grounded in traditions that date back to the late 19th and early 20th centuries. As police operations developed with the teaching and writing of August Vollmer, O. W. Wilson, and others, it began to take on more defined, albeit simplistic, methods. Traditionally, patrol officers responded to crimes and calls for service. Traffic units would handle any traffic offenses and would issue tickets. And detectives would investigate crimes. It was not until the 1960s that, according to Cordner, Gaines, and Kappeler, a slow revolution occurred in the way that police services were delivered.[1] The police community relations era, brought on by a number of social events such as the civil rights movement and protests over the Vietnam War, became the subject of focus for the police as the traditional methods of the past conflicted heavily with the environment of the 1960s. Police departments across the United States began implementing changes to its methods of police operations to deliver its services under these new concepts.

The primary methods of police operations, however, continued largely unchanged. The only true changes were appendages added to the organizational structure focused on specialized police services, ranging from team-policing units to special weapons and tactics (SWAT) units. It was not until the 1980s and 1990s that police operations began to see significant changes as a result of the community-oriented policing movement.[2] Police officers were now being assigned to permanent beats in neighborhoods and being required to partner with citizens to identify and solve problems. In addition, elements of crime prevention began to become a primary emphasis of police operations under this new model of policing. These concepts were seen as not only an operational change, but also as the adoption of a new philosophy of policing.

Despite several incidents that may have served as warning signs of what was to come, such as the first World Trade Center Bombing and the Oklahoma City Bombing, it was not until September 11th that police operations began to take on the consideration of adding homeland security to its operational functions. Dealing with terrorists was not often considered a standard police operation. Yet, it is not just terrorist bombings that have necessitated the move toward homeland security. The increasingly global society within which we live has generated numerous problems of global and transnational crimes. Ranging from organized crime and drug cartels to the abduction of women and children from other countries for the purposes of prostitution, the crimes have highlighted the impact that global crimes can have on local communities. In addition, the rapid spread of technology, specifically the Internet, has generated a whole new means of criminal activity and offenses that must be dealt with by local police, despite the fact that many of these crimes are occurring at the national or international level. Today's global society and the criminal elements inherent in it have necessitated changes in police operations.

Understanding what is meant by police operations under the concepts of homeland security is the first step in understanding the changes demanded in today's environment. As police operations have no definitive concept of linking strategy with tactics, it is perhaps necessary to turn to a bureaucratic agency that has a long history of dealing with the operational art and that is the military. Drawing on the military's conceptual understanding of operations without the language of war, it defines it as

> the level . . . at which . . . major operations are planned, conducted, and sustained to accomplish strategic objectives within . . . operational areas. Activities at this level link tactics and strategy by establishing operational objectives needed to accomplish the strategic objectives, sequencing events to achieve the operational objectives, initiating actions, and applying resources to bring about and sustain these events. These activities imply a broader dimension of time and space than do tactics; they ensure the logistics and administrative support of tactical [police] forces, and provide the means by which tactical successes are exploited to achieve strategic objectives.[3]

The intent here is not to apply a military model to policing, but to draw on aspects of operational activities that would be complimentary to policing for homeland security. In this case, police operations would be the level at which police responses and activities are planned, conducted, and sustained to achieve the strategic goals of homeland security reviewed in Chapter 3. Police operations would then determine, based on the strategic goals and objectives, what the operational objectives would be, how these can be accomplished, and it would determine how police assets, both personnel and equipment, could be deployed to achieve these objectives. This deployment of personnel and equipment also dictates what tactics police need to learn and be ready to use in the event the operational plans are put into motion.

The definition of operations also speaks to the "broader dimension of time and space," which focuses on the necessity for operational planning to think in terms of how long these plans will realistically take and what type of space is needed to accomplish these objectives. Time and space also denote constraints that must be factored into any plan. For instance, if New York City in a terrorist threat is to secure all bridges leading into and out of the island, it must consider the time necessary to move assets into place, but it must also think it terms of space, which may be the size of the bridge, the number of bridges, as well as the waterways under the bridges. Hence police operational planning in this case must ensure that the logistical and administrative support exists for the tactical forces (the police) to be able to achieve this strategic objective.

Another way of considering this is the concept of operational challenges, first denoted by the former Chairman of the Joint Chiefs of Staff, General Colin Powell. Powell explained that any operation must consider certain challenges, and these include (1) What political and social conditions (objectives) must be produced in the operational area to achieve the strategic goals? (Ends); (2) What sequence of actions is most likely to produce that condition? (Ways); How should the resources of the [police] be applied to accomplish that sequence of actions?; and (3) What is the likely cost or risk to the [police] in performing that sequence of actions?[4] Using these operational challenges the planning process should always exhibit a clear strategic aim. It must determine what is to be achieved by this strategic aim, it should identify the operational objectives, determine the steps necessary to achieve the objectives, and it must organize and apply the resources to accomplish each of these steps. These operational challenges hold true not only in operational planning, but also in the case of a significant event.

To apply these operational concepts to policing for homeland security, it is not necessary to scrap the traditions that have long built up through policing's history. Rather, we must continue to build on the framework that exists, but policing must apply new methods of doing business to prepare itself for this new role. Namely, it must begin to either adopt some of the changes that have circulated throughout policing or, where adopted, it must continue to adapt these concepts to the homeland security role. First and foremost it must look at the organizational structure and management of police. A number of concepts that already existed can be readily adopted or adapted, including decision-making processes, incident command structures, CompStat, mutual aid agreements, and Joint Task Forces. Second, it must utilize the methods of risk and threat assessment to more adequately develop its plans for homeland security. And, third, because risk and threat assessments are intelligence driven and these assessments factor into the planning process, information gathering, intelligence analysis, and sharing of both information and intelligence are critical to today's intelligence-led policing. It is to these three concepts that we now turn.

ORGANIZATION AND MANAGEMENT FOR HOMELAND SECURITY

Police organization in America has generally reflected the traditional aspects of police operations. As police operations have focused on patrol, traffic, and investigations, police organization has generally reflected this operational style by creating patrol, traffic, and investigation divisions, as well as an administrative division for managing the functions of the department. The patrol division has traditionally consisted of three to four shifts, centered on three eight-hour shifts for 24-hour coverage, and sometimes a fourth shift that serves as a power shift to overlay the busiest times for police calls-for-service, the late evening to early morning time frame. The traffic division has generally been a weekday coverage system for those time periods when traffic is at its peak, and investigations, like patrol, have generally adhered to a 24-hour coverage cycle with skeletal crews in the early morning hours.

Police management in America has generally consisted of shift commanders and midlevel management, sergeants that manage the police work in the field. The shift command has typically been a highly administrative entity, whereas field supervisors have served as the basic method of police officer oversight. For the most part, however, police management does not necessarily manage but rather administers. What typically drives the police department are calls-for-service, received by the "police operations center" dispatchers, who then allocate departmental resources by sending one or two police officers to the scene. Command of the scene then reverts to the police officers in the field and remains as such until a field supervisor supercedes the authority of the officer. This latter case is rare and usually only involves serious incidents that need to be coordinated, such as a hostage situation or bank robbery. It is an even rarer case when the actual shift commander supersedes the field supervisor's authority to take command of a situation. Therefore, police management cannot necessarily be defined as managing police assets, but rather serves as the administrator of police rules and regulations.

Mark H. Moore, a well-respected scholar of policing, has made a similar argument in a book entitled, *Impossible Jobs in Public Management.*[5] As he explained, "Police leadership is . . . handicapped by a startling lack of operational control over officers" and that departments function "under a carefully constructed illusion of control created to satisfy citizen demands for accountability."[6] Moore cites the focus on policies and procedures, a strict chain-of-command, and an emphasis on training as the mechanisms for police leadership appearing to have strict control over its officers. However, as Moore outrightly explains,

> The reality is quite different, however. For the most part, the police operate on their own. Although they must be responsive to dispatchers, they tell the dispatchers when they are available for service and where they are located. Their supervisors are often absorbed with other duties and cannot always find them. Supervisors respond to calls with the officers only on the most important occasions. As a practical matter, although the written procedures and hierarchical structure create deterrents for misconduct, the officer controls most of the information about his or her whereabouts and activities, and that fact defeats the effectiveness of these control arrangements.[7]

The drawback to this method of police management is largely found within the police decision-making process. Dispatchers generally make isolated decisions to allocate police resources. Police officers in the field make isolated decisions of how to properly handle a situation. These officers then direct departmental assets for solving the call-for-service. Throughout this process, the officer reports back to dispatch, which is "monitored" by police supervisors in the field and those at the police station. At no time, on a typical call, are there decisions being made by anyone other than individual actors based on the individual's environment as presented.

In the event of a crisis, officers continue to make decisions and communicate with dispatch, who in turn makes decisions for the allocation of resources. At this point, field supervisors intervene to collect as much information to make decisions and determine how to allocate resources. This is often slowed by the fact that they are in a situation where they have to be "brought up to speed" to understand the nature of the incident. They are essentially attempting to gather facts from both the officer on the scene and the dispatcher to once again make what is largely an isolated decision. It is not until the event becomes a major incident that any type of staffing system is summoned to move the organization into incident management.

Once an agency moves into the incident command system form of management, there is often a significant lag time between the commencement of the incident and the incident command system's ability to effectively manage the crisis. These time lags consist of personnel being off-duty, not always in communication with the department when off-duty, and because the incident command center tends to be at a specific location, which requires activation. Although several personnel from the incident command system may be available to take control of the situation, once again the decision-making process follows largely the same format, an isolated individual making decisions based on information being fed to him or her from the field and dispatch. It is not until the full incident command system is up and running that decisions are made with the greatest amount of input from the staff or management team operating the incident command center. In the case of another terrorist attack or a significant natural disaster, this is far too long a lag time for effective decision making to be obtained.

The National Commission on Terrorist Attacks Upon the United States in their *9/11 Commission Report,* stated that

> The attacks on 9/11 demonstrated that even the most robust emergency response capabilities can be overwhelmed if an attack is large enough. Teamwork, collaboration, and cooperation at an incident site are critical to a successful response. Key decisionmakers who are represented at the incident command level help to ensure an effective response, the efficient use of resources, and responder safety.[8]

The 9/11 Commission concluded that "emergency response agencies nationwide should adopt the Incident Command System (ICS)."[9] It is their belief that by using the ICS in critical incidents that what will ultimately be improved is the decision-making process. The problem, however, is that even if practiced on a regular basis, the lag time of having a fully operational ICS is too great a time when it comes to a critical incident. Therefore, what is needed is a full-time, fully staffed ICS that manages police resources on a routine basis. The ICS would become the method for routine police operations, which would conduct centralized planning, and all decision making would be preformed by the ICS staff. Despite the ICS implementing centralized planning, agencies would continue utilizing decentralized execution, thus continuing to rely on the professionalism and discretion of the officers on scene. What is needed, then, is an entirely new way of thinking about police decision making.

Problem-Oriented Policing

Herman Goldstein, in his seminal book *Problem-Oriented Policing,*[10] has documented that research into policing prior to the 1970s was greatly lacking. There were images of what the police did and then there were the realities, but the gulf between these was not well understood. Research coming out of the 1970s demonstrated that not only were the problems of policing a result of poor management, they were also a result of the complexities of the police role in society. It was found that police operational methods (e.g., preventative patrol, investigations, and rapid response) were not as successful at deterring or solving crime as conventional wisdom held. There was the realization that the police do far more than enforce the law and deal with criminal matters, despite an over-reliance on the criminal law. Perhaps most important was the recognition of policing's broad use of discretion when dealing with problems on the street.

What Herman Goldstein noticed was that police decision making was driven by calls-for-service and was isolated within the frame of the incident itself. In other words, when the police responded to a call, they treated the incident as if it had neither a past nor a future, and that it was an isolated incident. Even when officers acknowledged that they would often go back to the same address and deal with the same problems, they still did not treat the incident as the symptoms of a problem, but rather the problem itself. The goal was to deal with it as quickly and professionally as possible and move on to the next problem. Goldstein thus argued that a more rational method of dealing with problems—substantive problems—should be the goal of policing.

Goldstein's solution was the adoption of what he called "problem-solving" or "problem-oriented policing."[11] The goal is to begin analyzing calls-for-service and attempting to label the underlying problem, not the symptoms of the problem. Linking problems with other incidents may reveal the substantive problem that underlies the calls-for-service. These can then be more effectively dealt with through the development of alternatives and the implementation of a possible solution, tailor-made to the problem under consideration. The goal of problem-oriented policing was thus focused on the ability to strengthen the police decision-making process and to increase the accountability of the police to the public it serves. As Goldstein explained,

> This process, of course, is clear when alternatives require the approval of a mayor, city manager, city council, or legislature. It is less clear when the police administrator is the sole decision maker. But numerous opportunities exist for clarifying these processes so that a higher degree of accountability is achieved. This improved accountability, in [Goldstein's] opinion, can best be achieved by having police administrators assume a greater responsibility for decisions that, either by design or default, are already theirs to make. They are in the best position to weigh alternative responses to citywide problems. They are most likely to have the staff and resources required to conduct analyses, to implement policies, and to achieve conformity with them. Administrators are also in the best position to determine the latitude of decision making that can be delegated to officers on the street and the methods by which this decision making can be reviewed.[12]

Despite the call for administrators to take more responsibility in the decision-making process, the concepts of problem-oriented policing have largely developed into a method of police service delivery. This has especially been true with the application of the SARA model of policing, which is a hands-on adaptation of Goldstein's concept that stands for scanning, analysis, response, and assessment.[13] Officers are taught to use the SARA model to look for incidents that might be related in the beats they police (scanning), to begin analyzing the problem by the collection of as much data as possible, to then develop potential means of effectively dealing with the problem (analysis) and implementing the response (response), and finally, to evaluate the response for its effectiveness (assessment).

Combined with the concepts of community-oriented policing, officers have been encouraged to problem solve with citizens in the neighborhoods they police. However, most problem solving tends to be officer initiated and officer conducted.[14] Police administration is often brought into play when officers develop solutions that require the use of additional police assets, such as personnel or equipment. On a daily basis, however, police administration generally only functions to manage the process by ensuring that officers are engaged in problem-solving cases, that they report on the status of their problem-oriented policing cases, and that they turn in final reports on completion. Rather than managing the problem-solving cases themselves, police administrators tend to only manage the paperwork that tracks the problems. As one author has concluded, "problem solving policing, no matter how well conceived or designed, cannot succeed unless the individual designated to take the lead in solving problems has the requisite knowledge, skills, authority and discretion to intelligently identify problems and construct viable tactical responses, as well as the organizational power

Chief Daryl Gates of the Los Angeles P.D., one of the
creator's of COMPSTAT. *(Source: AP Wide World Photos)*

to marshal and apply resources to address them."[15] In other words, line officers are
not the proper level for solving substantive problems; the proper level lies, as Goldstein stated, with police administration. So, despite the calls for a more engaged police administration in the decision-making process, Goldstein's problem-oriented policing
developed simply into a method of policing, a tactic without good operational control,
support, or guidance.

The one concept in policing history that did develop into a system by which police administrators were forced to take on a more dynamic role in police decision making was the
implementation of CompStat by Police Commissioner William Bratton of the New York City
Police Department. CompStat recognized that the police commanders with a field perspective are "in a better position than beat officers to understand and harmonize the agency's
overall policies with the particular social dynamics operating within their geographic com-
pass."[16] In other words, the NYPD's application of CompStat was the first attempt in policing history where an agency attempted to place the responsibility of decision making where
it should be, with police management.[17]

CompStat

CompStat was created by the New York City Police Department under Police Commissioner William Bratton in the early 1990s.[18] Bratton's Deputy Commissioner, Jack Maple, is often the person credited as being the brainchild behind the concept.[19] The term *CompStat* has generally been said to have been derived from the concept of "compare statistics" or "compare stats," which was then shortened to CompStat. It was developed because police precinct reporting to the police headquarters in the New York City Police Department (NYPD) was dreadfully slow and was often three to six months old by the time it was fully collected and received. Bratton and Maple argued that the inability to have up-to-date and timely crime statistics was an impediment to good decision making for solving crime problems across the city.[20] Precinct commanders were then ordered to obtain current crime statistics on the seven major crime categories, and they were to report to a meeting of precinct commanders with the police commissioner. These meetings would evolve into the process of implementing CompStat.[21]

The precinct commanders would meet with Bratton and his staff to discuss the major crime concerns in their precincts and what they were doing to address the problems. At first the precinct commanders did not know what to expect, but once the process began with monthly meetings, the requirement became that they must be prepared to discuss the crimes that were occurring in their precincts and the methods they were using to address the problems. Failure to do so could possibly mean removal as a precinct commander. Those that were successful with their presentations were then held accountable for reducing the higher crime problems in their respective jurisdictions. Ultimately what was developed was a system of command profiles that tracked the capabilities of precinct commanders and special unit commanders (such as detective squad supervisors and narcotics supervisors) to determine their success in reducing crime. Again, those that demonstrated poor performance were removed and those that demonstrated high success were promoted.

The CompStat meetings eventually developed from low-tech paper handouts to a more high-tech conference room, emphasizing computer technology, video monitors, with projection screens. Data was presented via presentation software, and crime mapping data was presented, showing crimes over the previous month. Eventually, this command and control center became dubbed the "war room," and the department was essentially run through this method of command and decision making. In addition to the precinct commanders, other staff members were mandated to attend, despite the fact that they may not have to actually present. Their presence at these meetings allowed "for the immediate development of integrated plans and strategies" and gave precinct commanders the ability to "get on-the-spot commitments for the resources and assistance he or she need[ed] from ancillary and operational units."[22] Bringing together the high-level administrators, staff, and precinct commanders who were thus being held accountable for the actions of their subordinates brought police management and leadership to a vastly different level and attempted to overcome many of the criticisms of police management.

One realization after CompStat had been running was its lack of operational implementation. Although crime statistics were reviewed, trends and relationships discussed, and possible solutions generated, there was no mechanism for actually assigning responsibility or

BOX 4-1

COMPSTAT AS A MANAGEMENT APPROACH

Larry Hoover, Sam Houston State University

The notion that CompStat is a management approach instead of a strategy or even a set of strategies should not be quickly dismissed. Indeed, it should be noted that CompStat is strikingly similar to the generic principles of organizational success articulated by Peters and Waterman in their classic work, *In Search of Excellence.*

* **A bias for action** (immediate and definitive response to crime trends);
* **Close to the customer** (responsive to citizen complaints of crime problems);
* **Autonomy and entrepreneurship** (delegation to precinct commanders with innovation expected);
* **Productivity through people** (tough minded accountability);
* **Hands-on, value-driven** (the police can control crime, and we are here to do so);
* **Stick to the knitting** (crime control, not quality of life);
* **Simple form, lean staff** (back in uniform, back to patrol); and
* **Simultaneous loose-tight properties** (monitored at headquarters, but implemented at the precinct level with precinct-to-precinct variation).

Source: Reprinted with permission from Hoover, L. T. (2004). "CompStat as a Strategy: A Texas Persepctive Part I—Conceptual Framework." *TELEMASP Bulletin* 11(4): 1–7.

implementing the solutions. The solution was the creation of a post-CompStat meeting that the high-ranking officers would attend to work out these types of operational issues. However, this was not a full-time operational unit, but rather an additional staff meeting to ensure proper coordination.[23]

The goals and objectives of CompStat reached far beyond anything policing had seen throughout its history.[24] It was a unique method for attempting to manage the issue of crime, holding management accountable, and coordinating the numerous police elements into a communicative decision-making process. Vincent Henry, in his book on CompStat, perhaps explains the overall strategy behind CompStat best. He explains that

> CompStat meetings permit executives and managers to monitor practically every aspect of the agency's activities—from fulfilling the primary mission of reducing crime and making the city's streets safer to closely observing and controlling virtually every systemic change instituted in the agency's systems, practices, structures and culture. CompStat meetings are, in a sense, a window through which the department's executives and managers can glimpse every aspect of its operations as well as the process and directions of every change taking place. They are also a mechanism by which the agency's operations and practices can be continually assessed and fine-tuned to ensure their continued success, and through which important messages can be subtly or overtly transmitted and reinforced.[25]

For all intents and purposes, what CompStat in New York City was able to do was to apply an administrative process by which police decision making was being conducted at the executive level, rather than at the street level. Police leadership was actually beginning to both lead and manage the department.

The greatest deficiency to the CompStat process for department decision making, however, was actually the same factor that created CompStat in the first place, the lack of good current data. Although CompStat took what was often spotty records three to six months old and brought them up-to-date with monthly presentations, the one-month lag time was a deficiency in allowing the police department to operate in real time. Although many of the crime problems an agency faces are long term, many are not. The once-a-month format continued to demonstrate a significant lag time. The NYPD, after moving through a period of unscheduled surprise meetings, eventually went to weekly and then twice weekly meetings to address this problem. The process, however, was still largely reactive.

CompStat would further evolve in both the NYPD, as well as the Los Angeles Police Department, where William Bratton would assume the role of Police Chief. Ultimately, what Compstat has come to focus on are four key principles.[26] The first principle is the call for timely and accurate intelligence to determine how best to use police resources. The second principle was the use of effective tactics to ensure that the methods being deployed by the department are the most effective for the problem at hand. The third principle is the use of rapid deployment to move resources where they are needed most through a strong operational plan. And finally, the fourth principle is to relentlessly follow up and assess whether or not the tactics used were the most appropriate to use that information for future deployments of police personnel and resources. Operational planning, however, was still largely relegated to the weekly CompStat meetings.

In August of 2002, in the wake of the 9-11 terrorist attacks, Chief Charles H. Ramsey of the Washington, D.C., Metropolitan Police instituted the CompStat process in his department and made it a daily occurrence. For 90 minutes each weekday morning, the Washington, D.C., police force's top commanders and detectives would meet in a similar "war room" to review the latest crimes and disorder in Washington, D.C. The purpose was to bring management up-to-date on the latest intelligence, develop solutions to any serious problems, and begin the process of communication and interaction to solve those problems.[27] By moving to a daily briefing, it allowed the department to operate in near real time insofar as police decision making at the executive level can be conducted. What is lacking, however, is an executable staff system that can implement the plans and operations coming from the daily meetings, as well as being prepared to react to major incidents. This is still left largely to the purview of the dispatchers and police officers in the field.

To fully implement a real-time police decision-making process at the administrative level it is necessary to continue the daily CompStat briefings, but it must be the responsibility of the CompStat players to continue the planning process outside these briefings. In other words, the staff must continue to work these operational issues together to produce the final operational plan that will deploy officers tactically. More importantly, when a major incident does occur, if this staff is already operating 24/7, there is no need to initiate the emergency operations center, as it is already in place and operational. Although

BOX 4-2

CRITICAL COMPONENTS OF COMPSTAT

Larry Hoover, Sam Houston State University

* Most Critical Component = Some kind of Discretionary Quick Deployment Resource.
* Specificity, or Targeted Enforcement, is an essential component.
* Multiple units are typically employed for Tactical Response.
* In large agencies, CompStat should be conducted both at headquarters and substation level.
* Geographic Information System Display is very useful, but is only an enhancement.
* An experienced GIS operator who can instantly modify the display (e.g., zoom or overlay multiple family dwellings) is essential if GIS is to be useful.
* CompStat is as much about values and motivations as it is strategy.

Source: Reprinted with permission from Hoover, L. T. (2004). "CompStat as a Strategy: A Texas Persepctive Part II—Texas Practices." *TELEMASP Bulletin* 11(5): 1–15.

it may be staffed only with the primary players on each shift, the time it takes to respond to an incident is far less than if the emergency operations center is vacant or staffed by only one or two officers. In addition, it places full control of police operations in the hands of the police staff, it allows for the maximum amount of information to provide for the best information and intelligence to make informative decisions, and it forces police management to actually lead the department, rather than feigning leadership, as was previously discussed.

Incident Command/Emergency Operations Center as Police Operations

Prior to the events of September 11th and the actions of the Bush administration, exactly how the emergency operation center should work would most likely have been best left up to each individual department. A number of factors go into the determination of how best to organize such an entity. The so-called war room methods are generally a given, but space constraints, location, the proper personnel that need to be present, technology, and budget constraints, among other factors, all contribute to the determination of how best to organize. Questions revolve around whether or not the emergency operation center should be colocated with the police dispatch, at the police headquarters, or should the department purchase a mobile headquarters that can move closer to the scene? Other questions revolve around the proper staffing, who should be in command, what key players and staff members should have authorization to the emergency operations center, and how these entities communicate to one another. Still other questions center around the mechanisms for communication and information, such as television screens, computers, handwritten messages, e-mails, whiteboards, phone lines, or just plain old-fashioned shouting. All these issues generally had to be resolved, and many of these resulted in failures. In some cases state-of-the-art command centers were poorly located, such as was seen on September 11th, where the emergency operation center was located in one of the World Trade Center towers and proved inaccessible. In other cases, large and expensive recreational vehicles were purchased and equipped to be "close to the scene," making them more of a liability than an asset. And often these centers were seldom trained on or seldom used, and when used created an impediment due to unfamiliarity with the technology and equipment. All that hopefully will have ceased on February 28, 2003.

President Bush, on February 28, 2003, issued Homeland Security Presidential Directive Number 5, calling for the standardization of the National Incident Management System (NIMS) and the use of the ICS for all emergency operations.[28] NIMS provides a consistent framework for entities at all jurisdictional levels to work together to manage domestic incidents, regardless of cause, size, or complexity. The goal is to promote interoperability and compatibility among the federal, state, and local agencies and to provide a core set of guidelines, standards, and protocols for command and management, preparedness, resource management, communications and information management, supporting technologies, and both the management and maintenance of NIMS.[29] By creating a standardized system for managing incidents, it allows for greater ease of cross-boundary communication and helps to foster the multijurisdictional efforts that are often necessitated by major incidents. A good example of the need for this system was Hurricane Katrina, which devastated the New Orleans area, but was not merely relegated to the city of New Orleans. Or the following Hurricane Rita, that struck the Texas shores, which necessitated multiple jurisdictions to handle the evacuation of Galveston and Houston. In sum, it avoids the problem cited by one law enforcement official that "we co-locate on a regular basis, but we don't have the ability to communicate."[30]

The primary aspect of the NIMS for police command is the use of the ICS.[31] The ICS was developed in the aftermath of a devastating wildfire in California. During 13 days in 1970, 16 lives were lost, 700 structures were destroyed, and over one-half million acres burned. The overall cost and loss associated with these fires totaled $18 million per day. Although all the responding agencies cooperated to the best of their ability, numerous problems with communication and coordination hampered their effectiveness. As a result, the Congress mandated that the U.S. Forest Service design a system that would make a quantum jump in the capabilities of Southern California wildland fire protection agencies to effectively coordinate interagency action and to allocate suppression resources in dynamic, multiple-fire situations.

The California Department of Forestry and Fire Protection (CDF), the Governor's Office of Emergency Services (OES); the Los Angeles, Ventura, and Santa Barbara County Fire Departments; and the Los Angeles City Fire Department joined with the U.S. Forest Service to develop the system. This system became known as FIRESCOPE (FIrefighting RESources of California Organized for Potential Emergencies).

In 1973, the first "FIRESCOPE Technical Team" was established to guide the research and development design. Two major components came from this work, the ICS and the Multi-Agency Coordination System (MACS). The FIRESCOPE ICS is primarily a command and control system delineating job responsibilities and organizational structure for the purpose of managing day-to-day operations for all types of emergency incidents.

By the midseventies, the FIRESCOPE agencies had formally agreed on ICS common terminology and procedures, then conducted limited field testing of ICS. By 1980, parts of ICS had been used successfully on several major wildland and urban fire incidents. It was formally adopted by the Los Angeles Fire Department, the CDF, and the OES and endorsed by the State Board of Fire Services.

Also during the 1970s, the National Wildfire Coordinating Group (NWCG) was chartered to coordinate fire management programs of the various participating federal and state agencies. By 1980, FIRESCOPE ICS training was under development. Recognizing that in addition to the local users for which it was designed, the FIRESCOPE training could satisfy the needs of other state and federal agencies, the NWCG conducted an analysis of FIRESCOPE ICS for possible national application.

By 1981, ICS was widely used throughout Southern California by the major fire agencies. In addition, the use of ICS in response to nonfire incidents was increasing. Although FIRESCOPE ICS was originally developed to assist in the response to wildland fires, it was quickly recognized as a system that could help public safety responders provide effective and coordinated incident management for a wide range of situations, including floods, hazardous materials accidents, earthquakes, and aircraft crashes. It was flexible enough to manage catastrophic incidents involving thousands of emergency response and management personnel. By introducing relatively minor terminology, organizational and procedural modifications to FIRESCOPE ICS, the NIIMS ICS became adaptable to an all-hazards environment.

Although tactically each type of incident may be handled somewhat differently, the overall incident management approach still utilizes the major functions of the ICS. The FIRESCOPE board of directors and the NWCG recommended national application of ICS. In 1982, all FIRESCOPE ICS documentation was revised and adopted as the National Interagency Incident Management System (NIIMS). In the years since FIRESCOPE and the NIIMS were blended, the FIRESCOPE agencies and the NWCG have worked together to update and maintain the Incident Command System Operational System Description. This document would later serve as the basis for the NIMS ICS.

The NIMS ICS is readily adaptable to policing and in fact has already been implemented in numerous departments across the country. One of the benefits of the Arlington County Police Department's efficient response on September 11th, stemmed from a number of the command staff having received ICS training.[32] In addition, as a result of the HSPD-5, the Department of Homeland Security (DHS) has begun training police departments in the use of the ICS. Because HSPD-5 provides a framework for emergency incident command, it takes little additional effort to incorporate the concepts of ICS as a permanent fixture of police-level command. In other words, ICS should be the method of dealing with the daily routine of policing. Combined with the management capabilities of CompStat, its ability to operate in real time and manage the police department's personnel and resources, as well as being operational prior to a major incident, the ICS system is the most appropriate method for police management and leadership in a post–9-11 world.

The actual operational methods of the ICS consist of the command staff and the general staff.[33] The command staff has four positions, with the primary position being the Incident Commander. The Incident Commander then has three special staff personnel that report directly to him or her and assist in the command of the ICS. These positions include the Public Information Officer (PIO), the Safety Officer (SO), and the Liaison Officer (LO). The PIO is responsible for interfacing with the public, media, and/or other agencies with incident-related information requirements.

The SO monitors incident operations and advises the Incident Commander on all matters related to operational safety, including the health and safety of emergency response personnel. The SO is ultimately responsible to the Incident Commander, but he or she does have the emergency authority to stop and/or prevent unsafe acts during incident operations.

The LO is the point of contact for representatives of other government agencies, nongovernmental agencies (such as the Red Cross), and/or private companies.

Other possible command staff personnel may include a police chaplain, the Internal Affairs Inspector, and possibly the lead legal counsel for the department. These additional staff are generally left to the discretion of the Incident Commander. Finally, other members that are related to the command staff that may be present in the ICS are the assistants for the various staff members.

The General Staff includes incident management personnel who represent the major functional elements of the ICS, and these include the Operations Section Chief, Planning Section Chief, Logistics Section Chief, the Finance/Administration Section Chief, and the Information and Intelligence Officer. The Operations Section is responsible for all activities focused on reduction of the immediate hazard, saving lives and property, establishing situational control, and restoration of normal operations. The Operational Section Chief will establish an operational plan and will specify the tactical objectives necessary to carry out the operational plan. The Operational Section Chief will obviously have a staff of his or her own to assist in the development of incident plans and orders, but the actions of the Operation Section lie with the Chief and ultimately the Incident Commander.

The Planning Section of the General Staff collects, evaluates, and disseminates incident situation informational and intelligence to the Incident Commander and incident management personnel. The Planning Section also prepares status reports, displays situation information, maintains status of resources assigned to the incident, and develops and documents the Incident Action Plan based on guidance from the Incident Commander.

The Logistics Section is responsible for all support requirements needed to facilitate effective and efficient incident management. These support requirements include ensuring that the proper supplies, food, technology, and medical services are available to the responders.

The Finance/Administration Section of the General Staff is established when the agency involved in incident management requires finance and other administrative support. These needs may include cost/benefit analysis, procurement requirements, and compensation/claims issues.

The Information and Intelligence Section provides analysis and sharing of both information and intelligence during an incident. Intelligence can include national security or classified information but also can include operational information from open sources such as risk assessments, medical intelligence, weather information, structural designs of buildings, blueprints of various facilities, and hazardous chemical information.

In a major incident these staffs must come together to determine the operational plan and specifically the tactical objectives that will accomplish the operational plan in support of the overall strategy. The Incident Commander drawing on the input of the two staff elements is then in a position to make informative decisions by gaining input from the various sections as the operations proceed. This method has been proven to be highly effective in a number of settings, ranging from the U.S. military to political campaigns. More recently it has become a mainstay of decision making for special-interest groups to respond faster to any actions or language that may go against their particular issue, and even Wal-Mart has created a similar mechanism to deal with negative publicity. But again, the concept of only activating this in the event of major incidents slows down the effectiveness of such an operation. To move to a "full-time" ICS it would necessitate some administrative changes.

Moving to a full-time ICS would mean that each of the sections, except the Operations and Finance/Administration Sections, would require at least one staff member to be on duty at all times. The PIO, SO, and LO of the command staff would need to have someone subordinate, an assistant, to staff these positions around the clock, having the capability of calling back the primary officer in a major incident. The Planning, Logistics, and Information/Intelligence Sections would also have to maintain at least a skeleton crew on duty at all times. The Finance/Administration would be able to serve on call as the ICS would not necessarily need this individual or staff until a major incident. Finally, the shift commander could serve as the "Incident Commander" during that particular shift with his or her management personnel serving as the Operations Section Chief and Staff controlling the tactical deployment of officers.

The actual facility may be colocated with police dispatch, but with technological capabilities, that is not mandatory. However, consideration should be given to security when selecting a location, and a secondary site should be identified in case of the disabling of the primary ICS. It is from this facility that the ICS should be used to develop and disseminate operational orders, manage information, maintain staff estimates regarding personnel and equipment, and both control and assess operations. Information must be channeled to the ICS, and all orders should be processed through the ICS. Dispatch will retain its function, but it will be overseen by the Operations Section. Information must also be available to all those involved in the ICS; therefore, computer imaging, plasma screens on the walls, and a databank of television monitors would provide for as much information as possible for the staff to make decisions.

The use of other technologies should be considered as well, especially those technologies that the ICS can access and those that give the ICS more enhanced real-time information to contribute to the decision-making process. Three examples include closed-circuit cameras, geographic information systems with global positional satellites, and crime prevention through environmental design (CPTED). In the case of closed-circuit television cameras, the research is still somewhat mixed as to whether or not they reduce crime.[34] In some cases they have been found to reduce crime, in some cases they have displaced crimes, and in others they have proven useful in investigations. A recent survey conducted by the International Association of Chiefs of Police found that 80 percent of police departments reported used some form of closed-circuit televisions, many of which

BOX 4-3

HOMELAND SECURITY OPERATIONS CENTER (HSOC)

Phillip Davis, Sam Houston State University

The Homeland Security Operations Center (HSOC) serves as the nation's nerve center for information sharing and domestic incident management—dramatically increasing the vertical coordination between federal, state, territorial, tribal, local, and private-sector partners. The HSOC collects and fuses information from a variety of sources every day to help deter, detect, and prevent terrorist acts. Operating 24 hours a day, seven days a week, 365 days a year, the HSOC provides real-time situational awareness and monitoring of the homeland, coordinates incidents and response activities, and, in conjunction with the DHS Office of Information Analysis, issues advisories and bulletins concerning threats to homeland security, as well as specific protective measures. Information on domestic incident management is shared with Emergency Operations Centers at all levels through the Homeland Security Information Network (HSIN).

HSOC Structure

The HSOC represents over 35 agencies ranging from state and local law enforcement to federal intelligence agencies. Information is shared and fused on a daily basis by the two halves of the HSOC that are referred to as the "intelligence side" and the "law enforcement side." Each half is identical and functions in tandem with the other but requires a different level of clearance to access information. The "intelligence side" focuses on pieces of highly classified intelligence and how the information contributes to the current threat picture for any given area. The "law enforcement side" is dedicated to tracking the different enforcement activities across the country that may have a terrorist nexus. The two pieces fused together create a real-time snapshot of the nation's threat environment at any moment.

Source: U.S. Department of Homeland Security, Homeland Security Operations Center Fact Sheet.
Source: http://www.dhs.gov/dhspublic/display?theme=30&content=3813

were located in police cars, interrogation rooms, and access to courts and other government buildings.[35] While 63 percent of the respondents found these cameras useful in investigations and 54 percent said they were helpful in gathering evidence, only 20 percent reported they helped to reduce crime. Incorporated into the ICS operation center, however, they may also provide additional information for informative decisions, something not fully appreciated to date. Therefore, despite the controversy often surrounding them, the use of these cameras will most likely continue and could prove invaluable to the ICS system.[36]

The second example is the use of geographic information systems (GIS) and global positioning satellites (GPS).[37] In the case of GIS, with the various layers of geographic information available to police, ICS command centers can draw on this type of information through a computer tabletop screen in both daily routine patrol and major incidents. The impact of weather on certain areas prone to flood can give law enforcement an

BOX 4-4

DEPARTMENT OF HOMELAND SECURITY INCIDENT MANAGEMENT ROLE

Interagency Incident Management Group (IIMG)

Phillip Davis, Sam Houston State University

The IIMG is a headquarters-level group comprised of senior representatives from DHS components, other federal departments and agencies, and nongovernmental organizations. The IIMG provides strategic situational awareness, synthesizes key intelligence and operational information, frames operational courses of action and policy recommendations, anticipates evolving requirements, and provides decision support to the secretary of Homeland Security and other national authorities during periods of elevated alert and national domestic incidents.

   Quick Response. During incidents such as Hurricane Isabel, the December 2003 Orange Alert, and the blackout in New York City, the IIMG was "stood-up" in less than 90 minutes and hosted assistant secretary-level members of the represented agencies to provide strategic leadership.

Source: U.S. Department of Homeland Security, Homeland Security Operations Center Fact Sheet.
Source: http://www.dhs.gov/dhspublic/display?theme=30&content=3813

idea of where to move citizens to safe locations. In the event of a major incident, it can help the ICS staff determine where best to stage operations, alternate locations for managing a situation, and methods of ingress and egress from the incident. Coupled with the capability of global positioning satellites, if all police vehicles incorporated a GPS receiving device, it would allow the command center, and specifically the Operations Section, to know the location of police assets at all times.[38] This can help the ICS command and general staff make decisions of how best deploy officers tactically in the event of a major incident, based on their real-time location. The U.S. military has been using a very similar system in both Iraq and Afghanistan known as "blue-force tracker," giving the command tactical operations center the capability of controlling actions on the battlefield. A similar system would support the operational goals of a full-time ICS.

   The third example, CPTED has moved from a concept to a technological approach to preventing crime. CPTED concepts also lend themselves to preventing terrorism or reducing the harm caused by terrorist incidents, based on architectural design of buildings and streets, as well as the placement of such things as streetlights, landscaping, traffic control devices, sidewalks, parks, and other recreational areas. Using CPTED can assist in risk assessments and can have both a strategic and operational application to Homeland Security policing.[39]

Police Decision-Making Process

The confluence of a full-time ICS police center, alongside the organizational staff structure to compliment it, combined with the CompStat format of daily briefings, lends itself to a

NYPD Officers from the Bronx, NY undergoing In-Tac (In-Service Tactical) training in a classroom. (*Source: NYPD Photographic Unit*)

police decision-making process that can operate in real time. What is, in essence, being advocated is the implementation of CompStat full-time. Ultimately the goal of conducting operations in this manner is to utilize the staff to create good operational plans, make informative decisions during crises, and to deploy the police tactically in a manner that will best accomplish the operational objectives. By achieving these objectives, it allows the department to achieve its strategic goals of policing in an era of homeland security. And, overall, it places the management of the police department in the hands of the police department's leadership, advocating for centralized decision making and decentralized execution.

To achieve this level of operations, the police must use a mechanism to adequately deal with not only the daily routine operations, but also with major incidents as they arise. The staff format is the structure, but what is also needed is a process of decision making for the full-time ICS staff to receive information on situations, work through a process of developing good operational plans, then directing the tactical deployment from the police command center or "war room." Once again, the development of the problem-solving methods articulated by Goldstein and CompStat as developed by Bratton lend themselves readily.

The ICS should monitor the dispatch calls for services as a means of early warning that an incident is developing. The Operations Section would obviously be responsible for monitoring both radio and computer traffic to this regard. In addition, officers on the street can communicate their observations, thus providing for further input they more readily identify a situation developing. Once information begins to enter the ICS command center, the staff must identify the possible threats and begin to mobilize police officers on patrol, discretionary quick response units, special police units, detectives, or other personnel deemed appropriate. This does not simply mean that all available officers are dispatched to the scene as is common; it simply means that officers are made aware of a situation developing.

Once officers are mobilized, then the staff must begin the process of analyzing the situation with the information currently available. Specific information that is lacking must be identified and attempts to obtain that information made. It is during this time period that a tentative plan is made. Ideally, the ICS staff can draw on plans that previously existed within the Planning Section and modify these to fit the situation at hand. These standard operating procedures allow for a baseline for planning operations and can be updated in the after-action analysis that should be conducted. Regardless, the situation must be analyzed, and the Incident Commander and his or her staff should identify the threat and develop the basic who, what, when, where, and how the situation will be handled. The staff must also consider the key tactical tasks that must be conducted, what the goal or end-state of the operation is to be (Operations Officer), and they must constantly consider the constraints under which they operate (Liaison and Logistics Officers) and the risks posed by the operation (Safety Officer).

In addition to the key tasks cited earlier, the Incident Commander and his or her staff must develop various courses of action for dealing with the problem or incident. These courses of action must be distinguishable from one another, and they must be feasible to the operational capabilities of the department as well as from a legal standpoint. The various courses of action must also conform to the overall strategic goals of the department, and they must be acceptable in terms of a cost and benefit analysis, where the costs of resources and risks do not outweigh the benefits of the course of action. If each course of action satisfies these requirements, then the agency must analyze each of the courses of action for their positive and negative ramifications independently, and then they must compare them against one another. Although staff input into selecting the best course of action is highly desirable and should be the norm, ultimately the decision lies with the Incident Commander. Once the particular course of action is selected, the ICS staff must then began to put the final plan together based on the option selected.

Once a tentative plan is put into place, the ICS staff must began issuing the operational orders to the various units on standby, and they must be directed. The order must consider all the input from the various sections, including the identification of the threat and personnel responding to the threat, the operational plan, and the logistics and communication coordination necessary to achieve the tactical objectives. It must also assign responsibility to subordinate leaders, those in the field, to ensure that the tactical aspects of the plan will be implemented. And, as new information or intelligence becomes available and officers on the scene communicate updated information, the ICS staff must remain flexible enough to adapt its plans to the situation.

Although this form of decision making can be sped up to handle major crises that occur without warning, such as 9-11, it can also be used in terms of crime trend analysis and problem solving in the same format as CompStat. Although the process does become highly abbreviated, it is still suggested that each of the steps, identification of the situation, analysis, course of action development/analysis/comparison, and operational orders developed, would all remain a part of the process.

Finally, drawing on the cycle of preparedness identified by William V. Pelfrey, it is imperative that the ICS staff, after any incident, exercise, or implementation of a response to crime trends, evaluate its success.[40] At a minimum, an after-action review should be conducted, one that allows all the members of the staff to assess what went well and what went poorly. The key is to identify ways of improving the police response in the future to similar incidents. All this should be captured by the Planning Section to then be incorporated into standing plans. As Pelfrey articulated, the process should be one of constant planning, training, equipping, exercising, evaluating, and revising.[41] And, in the case of a major incident, a formal after-action report should be made available in a published format that not only all of those working within the agency may benefit, but those from other police agencies may benefit as well. A good example of this is the Arlington County Police Department's After-Action Report from their response on September 11th.[42]

Although there are numerous operational considerations when it comes to police operations under homeland security, three major factors will clearly influence operations and operational planning. These considerations include multijurisdictional partnerships, both risk and threat assessments, and law enforcement intelligence. Each of these will be expounded on in detail.

BOX 4-5

HAYWARD POLICE DEPARTMENT AND HOMELAND SECURITY

Hayward is a municipality near San Francisco with a population of about 144,600. Its police department has almost 200 sworn officers. After receiving a Department of Homeland Security grant, the Hayward Police Department created a full-time detective position focused specifically on homeland security issues. By contacting the Financial Investigations Program (FIP) of the California Department of Justice's Bureau of Narcotics Enforcement, the Hayward Police Department was able to access FinCEN data regarding suspicious financial transactions. The department requests reports on suspicious activity by ZIP Code and received 450 suspicious activity reports. An analysis of the reports revealed links to an outlaw motorcycle gang, possible organized crime groups, and terrorist financing.

As a result, the Hayward Police Department is conducting a joint investigation with the U.S. Bureau of Immigration and Customs into a subject with ties to terrorist financing and who has laundered more than $100 million during a three-year period.

The Hayward Police Department also has been able to access investigative and analytic support from the U.S. Department of Justice's FIP, including access to a wide range of commercial databases. One outcome of this work is the improved relationship between the police department and its local financial institutions. The institutions now contact the police proactively about suspicious financial activity reports, cutting the lag time between when a suspicious activity occurs and when police learn about it.

As a result of this success in the financial investigative area, the Hayward Police Department new requests a FinCEN check on every subject who is investigated for possible terrorist connections.

Source: Peterson, M. (2005). *Intelligence-Led Policing: The New Intelligence Architecture.* Washington, D.C.: Bureau of Justice Assistance, p. 23.

PARTNERSHIPS

The call for partnerships under homeland security has been very strong in post–9-11. It has differed from the community policing era in that the demands for partnerships are now primarily focused on partnering with other police departments, as well as state and federal law enforcement agencies, whereas under community policing, it was primarily about the police partnering with the community. Although this should not be diminished under the era of homeland security, as partnerships are assuredly still needed with citizens, the media, nongovernmental agencies, and other governmental agencies, the focus is on the coordination of police services across jurisdictional boundaries. Whether this is through enhanced mutual aid agreements, networking, data sharing, communication, or the implementation of the ICS unified command, partnerships are an important operational aspect of homeland security, and they begin with the mutual aid agreements.

Historically, law enforcement mutual aid agreements have been used most often on a limited basis for the sharing of personnel and resources to establish multiagency investigative teams and task forces.[43] Typically, the enabling agreement between jurisdictions takes the form of memorandums of understanding. Such agreements are limited in scope and purpose to address specific crime problems that cut across jurisdictional boundaries. Most familiar to law enforcement agencies are automatic mutual aid agreements in which units from neighboring jurisdictions are automatically dispatched to incident scenes. These are interlocal agreements that are usually basic contracts or even informal agreements. Mutual agreements for homeland security, however, should be more formalized than these types of agreements and should be designed to provide a wide range of services and resources to afflicted jurisdictions over longer periods.

Law enforcement has long recognized that such multijurisdictional, multiagency operations reap major benefits in combating broad-based criminal activities that cut across jurisdictional boundaries. For example, contiguous jurisdictions have successfully used major case squads in a variety of contexts for decades. In the early 1980s, the Federal Bureau of Investigation (FBI) set up a Joint Terrorism Task Force (JTTF) in New York City to serve as a link for regional operations among federal, state, and local agencies. The JTTF, as well as the Joint Drug Task Forces, soon spread to other major cities nationwide and have been widely hailed as effective partnerships.

In light of these successful interjurisdictional enterprises, it is not surprising that the same collaborative approach has been taken in local, state, and national attempts to address the threats of international and domestic terrorism. The utility of these agreements was demonstrated dramatically during and immediately following the events surrounding September 11, 2001, when well-orchestrated mutual aid agreements among regional agencies in New York and interstate agreements among other adjoining states were activated to deal with the cataclysmic events and aftermath of that day. Fire companies, law enforcement officers, other first responders, and a wide variety of other assistance were brought from throughout New York State as well as from far-flung regions of the country. In New York State, such personnel were activated under regional mutual aid agreements to assist at the scene. They also were used to backfill positions of first responders in jurisdictions surrounding New York City that were temporarily vacated by those who were directly engaged in rescue efforts at the World Trade Center so that fire and law enforcement services could continue unabated in these surrounding jurisdictions.

For these and other reasons, President George W. Bush launched the National Mutual Aid and Resource Management Initiative to assist first responders outside major metropolitan agencies in establishing mutual aid agreements or in renewing and refining existing agreements. The key concepts of this initiative are to establish preincident agreements, develop protocols for response, identify resources available for response, and to ideally create an automated resource management system that can track these resources. As part of the effort to ensure that America is prepared for future attacks and can mitigate the damage caused by such an attack, police agencies, in support of the strategies for homeland security, are encouraged to give operational consideration to mutual aid agreements to develop their partnerships with other agencies.

Mutual aid agreements should be regarded as another form of law enforcement partnership. Mutual aid may have been conceived primarily to respond to disasters and emergencies, but it also is well suited for preventing such occurrences. The organizational and collaborative approaches developed through mutual aid agreements bring together key decision makers who can share information that serves their individual and collective interests on many levels. This may be derived through shared intelligence. Local law enforcement officials can obtain a great deal about terrorist and other criminal activity in general and assist in identifying threats that are common local or regional concerns. It may come from the training received by one agency in the region that can be shared with officers in partnership with other agencies in the region through the train-the-trainer approach or similar means. There is also the case that these partnerships may assist in potential target identification and developing law enforcement agency threat assessments. Local law enforcement agencies that work closely together to identify regional threats, share intelligence, and work constructively to develop mutual aid agreements are more likely to prevent an emergency or disaster and to mitigate the damage caused by one.

Mutual aid agreements codify an understanding between two or more entities to provide support in a given context. Parties to agreements can include two, three, or more response agencies, private organizations, hospitals, public utilities, governments, and virtually any type of organization that can bring resources to bear during an emergency. Such agreements may be as expansive or as limited as the parties desire. Because of the varying levels of jurisdictions there are several types of mutual aid agreements, and they include (1) automatic mutual aid, where units from neighboring jurisdictions are automatically dispatched to the scene; (2) mutual aid, where neighboring jurisdictions agree to assist in incidents when requested to do so by another agency; (3) regional mutual aid, where agencies from a particular region, when called on, can assist local units for extended period of times; (4) statewide mutual aid, where agencies across the entire state and state-level resources can be called on to assist in a catastrophic event; and (5) interstate agreements, where out-of-state assistance can be utilized to assist in the recovery phase of a significant event. Depending on the geographical nature of the jurisdictions, both risk and threat assessments, and the level at which the mutual aid agreements are being negotiated, will determine the type of mutual aid agreement under consideration.

It is recommended that a committee be established to create or update mutual aid agreements. A wide variety of stakeholders should be involved in drafting a mutual aid agreement. The committee members should negotiate the agreement and approve it or recommend its approval on behalf of their respective organizations. Jurisdictions must determine who needs to be at the negotiating table so that the agreement will be as inclusive and responsive as possible. The respective heads of the law enforcement agencies involved should be included, as well as potentially the heads of other emergency response agencies, emergency management agencies, elected officials, and legal representatives. The committee should determine the boundaries of the agreement, the needs of each agency, what resources (personnel, equipment, etc.) they can bring to the table, and what stipulations they have on the agreement. Once this is ironed out, the parties should work with their agencies' stakeholders and legal advisors to craft the mutual aid agreement. These agreements can then be brought to future meetings to merge the various drafts into one document. The preference is to present the documents on-screen and edit "live" while everyone can read and review the language. Once the committee approves, the heads of agencies should be briefed for their input, and ultimately the agreement should be signed by all interested parties.

As the mutual aid agreement is signed, it is essential that the agreement turn into an operation plan. Therefore, it is critical that the agreement address as many factors as possible so that the operational plan can be drawn up. Considerations should include (1) department officials who are authorized to request assistance from other participating law enforcement agencies should be clearly identified; (2) the agreement must set forth the circumstances under which assistance may be granted; (3) it should specify the acceptable methods by which requests for assistance may be transmitted between agencies; (4) it should specify the forms of assistance that are to be rendered; (5) it should specify the extent and duration of any assistance rendered between jurisdictions; (6) it should detail under what circumstance assistance can be withdrawn; (7) command and control issues must be addressed in the agreements; (8) financial responsibility for the provision of services must be clearly defined; (9) claims for reimbursement must be established in the agreement, addressing the costs of personnel, equipment, supplies, and the record keeping process; (10) it should include conditions and procedures for the withdrawal of a participating agency from the agreement itself; (11) it should identify whether the agreement will be binding on subsequent agency chief executives; (12) it should deal with an agency's inability to respond to a request as not forming the basis of a breach of contract; (13) it should not contain provisions for summoning state or federal aid; (14) it should define the responsibilities of chief executive officers; and (15) it should provide for the inclusion of other public and private entities in prevention, preparation, and response to regional emergencies.[44] All these factors should be addressed in the mutual aid agreement, so that the operational plan can be properly developed.

The operational plan should consider the process by which mutual aid is obtained. Normally, a request for assistance begins at the line level when a supervisor becomes aware of a situation that may require assistance from a participating law enforcement agency. All such communications must receive approval of the chief law enforcement officer of the agency or a designated officer who has been delegated authority to make such decisions in the absence or on behalf of the chief executive officer. All initial requests should be sent through the law enforcement agency's communications center and routed to the authorized in a timely manner.

After a request is filed, a decision to provide assistance must be made by the law enforcement agency contacted for assistance. Agencies that participate in the plan are not legally obligated to provide assistance if doing so would unreasonably diminish the safety and welfare of their community. Once a decision has been make on deployment, personnel or units should be dispatched through the emergency communications center. Dispatchers should prohibit on- or off-duty units who are listening in from self-dispatching to the incident scene. This can be a common practice in emergency situations, but it is unacceptable. Self-dispatch can create chaos at an incident scene.

The incident commander is responsible for making initial and ongoing assessments of the personnel and resource requirements necessary to adequately address and control the emergency. Personnel and resources should report to a preestablished staging area or one identified by the incident commander. In the event that multiple jurisdictions are affected by the incident, under the NIMS, the use of a unified command is implemented.[45] This unified command can be one aspect of the mutual aid agreement and operational plan, which should address the possibility that an event may cover multiple jurisidictions, a single jurisdiction with multiagency involvement, or multiple jurisdictions with multiagency involvement. The unified command allows agencies to work together effectively without affecting individual agency authority, responsibility, or accountability. It does this by providing guidelines to enable agencies with different legal, geographic, and functional responsibilities to coordinate, plan, and interact effectively. This allows for both joint planning and joint execution, while attempting to avoid duplication of effort and general inefficiencies.

RISK ASSESSMENT AND RISK MANAGEMENT

In the aftermath of 9-11, the Heritage Foundation put together a Homeland Security Task Force to begin looking at the priorities of federal, state, and local governments in regard to the entire scope of Homeland Security issues.[46] One of the working groups of this task force focused on intelligence and law enforcement. Its number one stated priority was to "require the Office of Homeland Security to direct the assessment of threats to critical assets nationwide."[47] It argued that the key steps to accomplishing this priority consisted of assessing the threats, identifying critical targets, determining their vulnerabilities, and assessing risk. What should naturally follow, they urged, is the establishment of a national strategy to protect the homeland based on the national assessments. Although this is highly encouraged, local agencies cannot and should not wait for a national identification of risks and how to manage these risks. Each law enforcement agency should begin the process of conducting risk assessments to help develop their own risk management plan. Any risk assessment or management plan conducted at the regional, state, or federal level can simply be factored into the assessments already conducted by the local agency. The only drawback to this is that many law enforcement agencies have either not conducted these types of assessments in decades or they never have conducted these assessments at all. Therefore, it is necessary for law enforcement agencies under homeland security to learn what each of these assessments, threat, criticality, vulnerability, and ultimately risk, entails, and how they are conducted.

To understand the concept of threat assessments, it is important first to understand the concept of threat. Roper defines a threat as "any indication, circumstance or event with the potential to cause loss or damage to an asset" in the case of "the intention and capability of an adversary to undertake actions that would be detrimental to U.S. interests."[48] To be helpful in assessing vulnerability and risk, threats need to be characterized in some detail.[49] Important characteristics include type (e.g., insider, terrorist, military, hurricane, tornado), intent or motivation, triggers (i.e., events that might initiate an attack), capability (e.g., skills, specific knowledge, access to materials or equipment), methods (e.g., use of individual suicide bombers, truck bombs, assault, cyber), and trends (i.e., what techniques have groups used in the past or experimented with). Information useful to characterize the theat can come from the intelligence community, law enforcement intelligence units (see next section), specialists, news reports, analysis and investigations of past incidents, received threats, or "red teams" whose purpose is to "think" like a terrorist. Threat assessment typically also involves assumptions and speculation because information on specific threats may be scant, incomplete, or vague.

Once potential threats have been identified (both generically, e.g., terrorists, and specifically, e.g., Al-Qaeda) and characterized, a threat assessment estimates the "likelihood of adversary activity against a given asset or group of assets."[50] The DHS defines a threat assessment as

> a systematic effort to identify and evaluate existing or potential terrorist threats to a jurisdiction and its target assets. Due to the difficulty in accurately assessing terrorist capabilities, intentions, and tactics, threat assessments may yield only general information about potential risks.[51]

However, it should be noted that these assessments for law enforcement purposes must consider the full spectrum of threats, such as natural disasters, criminal activity, and major incidents, as well as any terrorist activity.

Focusing more specifically on the possibility of a terrorist attack, the likelihood of an attack is generally considered a function of at least two parameters.[52] The first is whether or not the asset represents a tempting target based on the goals and motivations of the adversary (i.e., Would a successful attack on that asset further the goals and objectives of the attacker?). The second is whether the adversary has the capability to attack the asset by various methods. Other parameters to consider include past history of such attacks against such targets by the same adversary or by others, the availability of the asset as a target (e.g., Is the location of the target fixed or does it change and how would the adversary know of the target's existence or movement?). The asset's vulnerability to various methods of attack (risk assessments) may also affect the attractiveness of the asset as a target.

To conduct a threat assessment, law enforcement must draw on these characterizations of the threat, consider the parameters, and draw on as many sources as possible. Threat assessments must be compiled from comprehensive and rigorous research and analysis.[53] Law enforcement cannot function unilaterally. Threat assessments that do not incorporate the knowledge, assessments, and understanding of state, local, and private organizations and agencies with the potential threats being assessed are inherently incomplete. For example, a threat assessment of water district facilities should include the most comprehensive data available from local police, sheriff, and fire departments; health services; emergency management organizations; and other applicable local, state, and federal agencies that may be affected by an attack on the water district's infrastructure. The threat assessments should also assimilate germane, open-source, or nonproprietary threat assessments, as well as intelligence information. Lastly, the assessment must provide a high level of awareness and understanding regarding the changing threat and threat environment faced by a government entity.

Essential data to collect for analysis prior to conducting a threat assessment include (1) the type of adversary, whether or not it is a terrorist, employee, or other; (2) category of adversary, such as foreign or domestic, terrorist or criminal; (3) objective of each type of adversary, examples include theft, sabotage, or mass destruction; (4) the number of adversaries expected for each category, for instance single suicide bomber or multiples, one or more terrorist cells, gang or gangs; (5) target selected by adversaries, such as critical infrastrucutre, government buildings, symbolic structures such as monuments; (6) the type of planning activities required to accomplish the objective, for example long-term casing, photography, monitoring of police patrols; (7) most likely or "worst-case" time an adversary could attack, when facility is fully staffed, rush hour, holidays; (8) range of adversary tactics, such as force, deceit; and (9) the capabilities of the adversary, their knowledge, motivations, skills, weapons, and equipment.[54]

It should also be clear that a threat assessment need not be static in time.[55] Threats (i.e., the likelihood that an adversary may attack) may rise and fall over time, depending on events, anniversary dates, an increase in capabilities, or the need for the adversary to reassert itself. Intelligence may detect activity that indicates preattack activity or a lull in such activity, or an explicit threat may be made. This is why continual updates of threat assessments must be made to keep them relevant to police operations. To this end, law enforcement executives must ensure that an officer or unit is trained and assigned to identify potential targets and can recommend enhancements for security at those targets.[56] The proper individual, under the staff process previously described, to assign this responsibility to is the Information and Intelligence Officer and his or her staff. However, action must be taken by all departments, including those with limited resources. Ideally, the entire patrol force should be trained to conduct intelligence gathering and reporting for the Intelligence staff to adequately conduct updates on their threat assessments.

In addition to assessing threats, it is also important that agencies conduct what are known as criticality and vulnerability assessments. The former attempts to identify key targets in a jurisdiction, whereas the latter attempts to determine how weak these targets are in relation to an attack. The DHS defines criticality assessments as

> a systematic effort to identify and evaluate important or critical assets within a jurisdiction. Criticality assessments help planners determine the relative importance of assets, helping to prioritize the allocation of resources to the most critical assets.[57]

The Department defines vulnerability assessments as

> the identification of weaknesses in physical structures, personnel protection systems, processes, or other areas that may be exploited by terrorists. The vulnerability assessments also may suggest options to eliminate or mitigate those weaknesses.[58]

These two assessments combined will give us an idea as to which assets present the greatest targets to the terrorists and which are most vulnerable to their attacks.

The measure of criticality, or asset value, determines the ultimate importance of the asset. Loss of life and/or damage to essential assets are of paramount concern to law enforcement executives. Loss of symbolic targets, which can result in the press coverage that terrorists seek, is also important, as it can destroy people's faith in the ability of law enforcement and government to protect the public.

Assessing criticality can at times involve some degree of subjectivity. Assessment may rely on the intimate knowledge of law enforcement agency professionals and their colleagues in other government agencies to gauge the importance of each potential target. However, clear objective thought must prevail when loss of human life is possible. Certain facilities are inherently vulnerable and should be addressed as critical infrastructure or key assets of law enforcement. These include transportation facilities, public utilities, public and government facilities, financial and banking institutions, defense-related centers, and health-care facilities, as well as cyber/information technology.[59] However, not every asset is as important as another. To focus assessment resources, all the methodologies reviewed suggest that the assessment should focus on those assets judged to be most critical. Criticality is typically defined as a measure of the consequences associated with the loss or degradation of a particular asset. The more the loss of an asset threatens the survival or viability of its owners, of those located nearby, or of others who depend on it (including the nation as a whole), the more critical it becomes.[60]

The consequences can be categorized in a number of ways, including economic, environmental, health, and technological. The immediate impact can have tremendous implications for not only the local jurisdiction, but again, across the country. However, although the immediate impact is important, so too is the amount of time and resources required to replace the lost capability. And another issue is that the loss of particular assets may create secondary effects, which can begin affecting other areas of infrastructure. For example, the loss of electric power can lead to problems in the supply of safe drinking water. Therefore, integral to the criticality assessment is a determination of all these factors when ranking those assets that present attractive targets to terrorists and ranking them by their criticality, the impact, that their loss or damage would have on the local community.

Once the facilities and assets have been identified as being potential targets and their criticality determined, the next assessment is to determine their vulnerability. Roper defines vulnerability as a "weakness that can be exploited to gain access to a given asset."[61] Weaknesses, like criticality, can be categorized in a number of ways: physical (e.g., accessibility, relative locations, visibility, toughness, strength), technical (e.g., susceptible to cyberattack, energy surges, contamination), operational (e.g., policies, procedures, personal habits), or organizational (e.g., would taking out police headquarters severely disrupt operations). Existing countermeasures may already exist to address these weaknesses. A vulnerability assessment must evaluate the reliability and effectiveness of those existing countermeasures in detail. For example, security guards may provide a certain degree of deterrence against unauthorized access to a certain asset. However, to assess their effectiveness, a number of additional questions may need to be asked. For example, how many security guards are on duty? Do they patrol or monitor surveillance equipment? How equipped or well trained are they to delay or repulse an attempt to gain access? Have they successfully repulsed any attempt to gain unauthorized access before?[62]

Vulnerabilities are assessed by the analyst against specific attacks. There are three steps to assessing vulnerabilities.[63] The first is to determine how an adversary could carry out a specific kind of attack against a specific asset (or group of assets). The second is to evaluate existing countermeasures for their reliability and their effectiveness to deter, detect, or delay the specific attack. And third, estimate current state of vulnerability and assign it a value. To measure the vulnerability, it is important to look at four areas: (1) Is the target available (i.e., is it present and/or predictable as it relates to the adversary's ability to plan and

BOX 4-6

CRITICAL INFRASTRUCTURE AND KEY RESOURCE SECTORS

Agriculture and food

Public health and health care

Drinking water

Wastewater treatment system

Energy

Banking and finance

National monuments and icons

Defense industrial base

Information technology

Chemical

Transportation systems

Emergency services

Postal and shipping

Dams

Government facilities

Commercial facilities

Nuclear reactors, materials, and waste

Source: U.S. Department of Homeland Security. (2005). *State and Urban Area Homeland Security Strategy: Guidance on Aligning Strategies with the National Preparedness Goal.* Available online at *http://www.ojp.usdoj.gov/odp/docs/StrategyGuidance_22JUL2005.pdf;* downloaded on August 15, 2005.

operate)? (2) Is it accessible (i.e., how easily can the adversary get to or near the target? (3) What are the "organic" countermeasures in place (i.e., what is the existing security plan, communication capabilities, intrusion detection systems, guard force)? and (4) Is the target hard (i.e., based on the target's design complexity and material construction characteristics, how effectively can it withstand the attack)?

Once the Information and Intelligence officer and his or her staff has conducted threat assessments and both criticality and vulnerability assessments, it is important that they combine this information into a risk assessment. Risk implies uncertain consequences to which Roper defines risk as the ". . . probability of loss or damage, and its impact."[64] The DHS defines risk assessment as "essentially an estimate of the expected losses should a specific target/attack scenario occurs."[65] Therefore, risk assessments factor in the threat by asking how likely it is that an adversary will attack those identified assets, it factors in criticality by asking what is the likely impact if the asset is lost or harmed by the threat, and it factors in vulnerability by asking what are the most likely vulnerabilities that the adversary or adversaries will use to target the identified asset.[66]

Risk assessments can be either qualitative or quantitative in nature. Threat assessments can be categorized as consisting of five categories: negligible, low, medium, high, and critical.[67] The presence of a terrorist group, its capabilities, intent, and history, all combine to determine the threat assessment levels. These levels can then be converted into numerical numbers ranging from 1 to 5, with the higher value being the more serious threat. Both criticality and vulnerability can also be measured in a very similar way, using the qualitative terms and turning them into numeric values. The comprehensive results of each of these assessments can be summarized into a risk statement with an adjectival or numeric rating. The risk equation used in most systems is expressed in this basic formula:

$$\text{Risk} = \text{Threat} \times \text{Vulnerability} \times \text{Criticality}$$

In this equation, risk is defined as the extent to which an asset is exposed to a hazard or danger. Threat times vulnerability represents the probability of an unwanted event occurring, and criticality equals the consequence of loss or damage to the critical infrastructure or key asset. Using this methodology allows the Information and Intelligence officer the ability to determine what assets face the greatest risk, thus allowing for an agency to engage more realistically in risk management.

Risk management is essentially the process of using risk assessments to identify and prioritize risk reduction activities. It is the decision-making process inherent in determining which assets to secure, the methods and resources used to address the security, and the cost-benefit calculus associated with those decisions.[68] Risk assessments help determine which assets to secure by weighting them toward those facing the higher risk. However, despite having an adjectival or numeric weighting it is still imperative that which key assets are going to be secured go through the decision-making process, as there are other factors involved. In addition, the decision-making process is also used to identify ways to reduce risk. Risks can be reduced in a number of ways: by reducing threats (e.g., through eliminating or intercepting the adversary before they strike), by reducing vulnerabilities (e.g., target hardening), or by reducing the impact or consequences (e.g., building backup systems or isolate facilities from major populations).[69] Countermeasures include physical security (fencing, camera surveillance, seismic monitoring devices, barricades), cybersecurity (firewalls, antivirus software, secure computer networks), personnel security, and other proactive methods that industry uses to secure critical infrastructure and key assets.[70] Countermeasures, such as expansion of agency staffing, installation of equipment and new technology, or target hardening, must be evaluated or tested periodically to ensure that improvements are actually working as intended.

For each potential countermeasure the cost-benefit for risk reduction should be determined.[71] More than one countermeasure may exist for a particular asset, or one countermeasure may reduce the risk for a number of assets. Multiple countermeasures should be assessed together to determine their net effects. The analysts should also assess the feasibility, acceptability, and suitability of each countermeasure. Although cost effectiveness is usually the recommended measure for setting priorities, it is imperative that these decisions go through the CompStat-like decision-making process, as decision makers may use other measures. Finally, it is imperative that the process be thought of as a continual process and one that should constantly be updated as new information and intelligence is obtained. As police intelligence may very

BOX 4-7

COMPARISON OF COMPSTAT AND INTELLIGENCE-LED POLICING

CompStat	Commonalities	Intelligence-Led Policing
* Single jurisdiction	* Each has a goal of prevention	* Multijurisdiction
* Incident driven	* Each requires organizational flexibility	* Threat driven
* Street crime and burglary	* Each requires consistent information input	* Criminal enterprises and terrorism
* Crime mapping	* Each requires a significant analytic component	* Commodity flow; trafficking and transiting logistics
* Time sensitive (24-hour feedback and response)	* "Bottom-up" driven with respect to operational needs	* Strategic
* Disrupt crime series (e.g., burglary ring)		* Disrupt enterprises
* Drives operations: patrol, tactical unit, & investigators		* Drives operations: JTTF, organized crime investigations, task forces
* Analysis of offender MOs		* Analysis of enterprise MOs

Correlated goals and methodologies make both concepts complement each other.

Source: Carter, D. (2002). *Law Enforcement Intelligence: A Guide for State, Local, and Tribal Law Enforcement Agencies.* Washington, D.C.: U.S. Department of Justice, p. 43.

well alter the equations of risk assessment, thus altering the risk management plan, it is imperative that the police intelligence process be as well defined as the risk management process.

POLICE INTELLIGENCE

Perhaps the greatest clarion call of policing for Homeland Security has been the call for increased focus on intelligence-driven policing and police intelligence units.[72] According to Professor Doug Moore, who specializes in the area of security, at the time of 9-11 there were probably only 50 to 100 police departments that had the ability to collect information for international terrorism, but that most of those collecting information did not have the capability for analysis.[73] He bluntly stated that at the time, police needed to update their criminal analysis capabilities. Adding on the intelligence analysis component would stress most agencies who did not have the training or resources to be able to conduct this type of police intelligence. And even if they did, he highlighted the fact that at the time, most local polices faced the problem of sharing information. Although these issues have not been fully resolved, work is being done at the federal, state, and local levels to address these specific problems to improve local policing's ability to collect information, analyze that information, and then share it with the appropriate agencies.

According to Peterson, introducing intelligence-led policing into law enforcement is problematic for a number of reasons.[74] First, many agencies do not understand what intelligence is or how to manage it. Second, agencies must work to prevent and respond to day-to-day crime at the same time they are working to prevent terrorism. Third, the realities of funding and personnel resources are often obstacles to intelligence-led policing. She concludes that although the current intelligence operations of most law enforcement agencies prevent them from becoming active participants in the intelligence infrastructure, this problem is not insurmountable.

A number of the homeland security grants have focused on this specific issue (see Chapter 2). In addition, the DHS and numerous police associations have made this a key strategic priority (see Chapter 3). Moreover, several recent publications by the U.S. Department of Justice have detailed the importance of intelligence-led policing, and they have laid the groundwork for perhaps one of the most important elements of policing for homeland security.[75] Intelligence then, is a key part of police operations for homeland security and must become an integral part of the process.

There are essentially two broad purposes for an intelligence function within a law enforcement agency: prevention and planning/resource allocation.[76] The first purpose, prevention, includes gaining or developing information related to threats of terrorism or crime and using this information to apprehend offenders, harden targets, and use strategies that will eliminate or mitigate the threat. The second purpose is planning and resource allocation. The intelligence function provides information to decision makers about the changing nature of threats, the characteristics and methodologies of threats, and emerging threat idiosyncracies for the purpose of developing response strategies and reallocating resources, as necessary, to accomplish effective prevention.

Despite the many definitions of the word *intelligence* that have been promulgated over the years, the simplest and clearest is "information plus analysis equals intelligence."[77] This formula clarifies the distinction between collected information and produced intelligence. It notes that without analysis, there is no intelligence. Intelligence is not what is collected, it is what is produced after collected data is evaluated and analyzed. Therefore, information may be defined as "pieces of raw, unanalyzed data that identifies persons, evidence, events or illustrates processes that indicate the incidence of a criminal event or witnesses or evidence of a criminal event,"[78] whereas law enforcement intelligence may be defined as "the product of an analytic process that provides an integrated perspective to disparate information about crime, crime trends, crime and security threats, and conditions associated with criminality."[79] Law enforcement intelligence analysis, therefore, should be done by a trained intelligence professional, and under the decision-making staff structure described earlier it will fall to the Information and Intelligence officer and his or her staff. This intelligence will then tell the staff everything they need to know to make informed decisions and develop courses of action.

Intelligence is often denoted as falling into one of three categories; strategic, operational, and tactical intelligence.[80] Strategic intelligence deals with the "big-picture" issues such as planning and manpower allocation. Operational intelligence is sometimes used to refer to intelligence that supports long-term investigations into multiple, similar targets. Operational intelligence is concerned primarily with identifying, targeting, detecting, and intervening in criminal activity. Tactical intelligence contributes directly to the success of specific investigations. It directs immediate action. Once again, strategic intelligence, like police strategy, guides the operational plan by allowing police executives to think about how best to structure the department and organize for homeland security. Operational intelligence provides police operations, the concern of this chapter, with how to effectively use this intelligence to act on it. Tactical intelligence is the type of intelligence that the police department can use to deploy its resources and will help drive police tactics in the field.

Historically, policing actually began moving toward the use of intelligence units in the 1970s. The original blueprint for intelligence work was published by the Law Enforcement Assistance Administration of the U.S. Department of Justice in 1971.[81] In 1973, the National Advisory Commission on Criminal Justice Standards and Goals made a strong statement about intelligence. It called on every law enforcement agency and every state to immediately establish and maintain the capability to gather and evaluate information and to disseminate intelligence in a manner that protects every individual's right to privacy while it curtails organized crime and public disorder.

When first instituted, intelligence units within law enforcement departments were not governed by policies that protected civil liberties and prevented intelligence excesses.[82] During the 1970s, a number of intelligence units ran afoul of good practices, and as a result, some agencies shut down their intelligence functions voluntarily, by court order, or from political pressure. In 1976, in response to the problem of intelligence abuses, standards were developed that required a criminal predicate for subjects to be entered in criminal intelligence files. Guidelines were then developed, but most agencies either avoided starting up intelligence units again or they relied on other initiatives such as the Regional Information Sharing System (RISS) that shared "information" and avoided the term *intelligence*. Although there was some development in enhancing the area of law enforcement intelligence analysis, it was not until 9-11 that the necessity of these units was recognized.

Intelligence is critical for the decision-making process, planning, targeting, and crime prevention. Gathering information and deciding what to do with it are common occurrences in law enforcement operations. Law enforcement officers and managers are beset by large quantities of information, yet decisions are often based on information that may be incomplete, inaccurate, or misdirected. The move from information gathering to informed decision making depends on the intelligence/analytic process and results in a best estimate of what has happened or what will happen.

Intelligence is also critical to effective planning and subsequent action. In many law enforcement agencies, planning and subsequent action is performed without an understanding of the crime problems facing the jurisdiction and without sufficient operation input. In these instances, planning bears no resemblance to analysis or intelligence. Instead it relates only to funding issues and operational constraints.

Targeting and prioritization are other critical roles of intelligence, as seen earlier with risk management. Law enforcement agencies with tight budgets and personnel reductions or shortages must use their available resources carefully, targeting individuals, locations, and operations that promise the greatest results and the best chances for success.

The final area in which intelligence is critical is crime prevention. Using intelligence from previous crimes in local and other jurisdictions, indicators can be created and shared among law enforcement agencies. Comparing the indicators from local neighborhoods, analysts can anticipate crime trends and agencies can take preventive measures to intervene or mitigate the impact of those crimes.

The actual intelligence process consists of six steps: planning and direction, collection, processing/collation, analysis, dissemination, and reevaluation.[83] The first step, planning and direction, is key to the intelligence process. Effective planning assesses existing data and ensures that additional data collected will fill any gaps in the information already on file. As one federal manager put it, "Don't tell me what I know, tell me what

BOX 4-8

NATIONAL ADVISORY COMMISSION ON CRIMINAL JUSTICE STANDARDS AND GOALS (NAC) AND POLICE INTELLIGENCE

In 1971, the National Advisory Commission on Criminal Justice Standards and Goals (NAC) was created to make recommendations for increased efficacy of the entire criminal justice system. "For the first time national criminal justice standards and goals for crime reduction and prevention at the state and local levels" were to be prepared. Included in the commission's report were recommendations directed at establishing and operating intelligence functions for state and local law enforcement agencies. These recommendations included the following:

Establishing Intelligence Functions

* Each state should develop a centralized law enforcement intelligence function with the participation of each police agency within the state.
* States should consider establishing regional intelligence networks across contiguous states to enhance criminal information-sharing processes.
* Every local law enforcement agency should establish its own intelligence function in accordance with its respective state's intelligence function.

Intelligence Function Operations

* Each state and local intelligence function should provide support to federal agencies.
* Operational policies and procedures should be developed for each local, state, and regional intelligence function to ensure efficiency and effectiveness.
* Each agency should have a designated official who reports directly to the chief and oversees all intelligence operations.
* Each agency should develop procedures to ensure the proper screening, securing, and disseminating of intelligence-related information.

Source: Carter, D. (2002). *Law Enforcement Intelligence: A Guide for State, Local, and Tribal Law Enforcement Agencies.* Washington, D.C.: U.S. Department of Justice, pp. 30–31; National Advisory Commission on Criminal Justice Standards. (1971). *Report of the Task Force on Organized Crime.* Washington, D.C.: U.S. Department of Justice.

I don't know."[84] To be effective, then, intelligence collection must be planned and focused, its methods must be coordinated, and its guidelines must prohibit illegal methods of obtaining information. Inaccurate collection efforts can result in a flawed result, regardless of the analytical skills used. Planning also requires an agency to identify the outcomes it wants to achieve from its collection efforts. This identification directs the scope of the officers' and detectives' investigations—for example, a straightforward inquiry to identify crime groups operating in a jurisdiction or a more complex inquiry to determine the likelihood that criminal extremists will attack a visiting dignitary.

The second step of the intelligence process is collection. Intelligence analysis requires collecting and processing large amounts of information. Data collection is the most labor-intensive aspect of the intelligence process. Traditionally, it has been the most emphasized segment of the process, with law enforcement agencies and prosecutors dedicating significant resources to gathering data. New technology and new or updated laws have supported this emphasis. Historically, the following have been the most common forms of data collection used in intelligence units: physical surveillance, electronic surveillance, confidential informants, undercover operators, newspaper records, and public records. To a large degree, most of these forms of data collection are very familiar to law enforcement.

The third step is processing and collation. This step involves sifting through available data to eliminate useless, irrelevant, or incorrect information and to put the data into a logical order. This organization makes it easier to identify relationships among entities and uncover relevant information. Today, collation is performed using sophisticated databases for retrieving and comparing data and many have text-mining capabilities. This step also involves evaluating the data being entered. Information placed into an intelligence file is evaluated for the validity of the information and the reliability of its source. And, information placed into an intelligence system must meet a standard of relevance in that it must be relevant to criminal activity.

The fourth step of the intelligence process is analysis. Analysis converts information into intelligence. Analysis, then, is quite simply a process of deriving meaning from data. The analytical process tells what information is present or missing from the facts or evidence. In law enforcement intelligence operations, data are analyzed to provide further leads in investigation, to present hypotheses about who committed a crime or how it was committed, to predict future crime patterns, and to assess threats facing a jurisdiction. Thus, analysis includes synthesizing data, developing inferences or conclusions, and making recommendations for action based on the data and inferences. These inferences constitute the finished intelligence product. This final product should identify the targeted consumer of the information (patrol officers, administrators, task force members, etc.), convey the critical information clearly, identify time parameters wherein the intelligence is actionable, and provide recommendations for specific courses of action.[85] It is important to remember that the analyst *recommends* but does not direct or decide on policy alternatives to minimize crime problems.

The fifth step of the process is dissemination. This requires getting intelligence to those who have the need and the right to use it in whatever form is deemed most appropriate. Intelligence reports kept within the intelligence unit fail to fulfill their mission. Those who need the information are most often outside the intelligence unit; therefore, the current dissemination protocol is to share by rule and to withhold by exception. It is here that the sharing of intelligence within, between, and across law enforcement agencies becomes critical for operational planning and tactical execution to have any meaning. One impediment that must be overcome in regard to the dissemination of intelligence is the lack of proper security clearances among the law enforcement community. It is time that all qualifying law enforcement officers in the United States obtain at a minimum a secret clearance to overcome these impediments. Those in the command staff should be considered for top secret clearances. Officers now designated to secure our homeland should not be left out of this step for the excuse that they don't have the proper security clearance.

The sixth and final step is reevaluation. This is the task of examining intelligence products to determine their effectiveness. Part of this assessment comes from the consumers of intelligence, that is, the managers, investigators, and officers to whom the intelligence is directed. One way to reevaluate intelligence is to include a feedback form with each product that is disseminated. Another way is to have the staff assess the "useability" of the intelligence reports in terms of their decision making, operational planning, and tactical execution. Did the reports present actionable intelligence, and how good was it?

The responsibility for the intelligence process once again falls to the Information and Intelligence Officer and his or her staff. As David Carter has explained, "State, local and tribal law enforcement will be its most effective when a single source in every agency is the conduit of critical information, whether it is the Terrorist Intelligence Unit of the Los Angeles Police Department, the sole intelligence analyst of the Lansing, Michigan Police Department, or the patrol sergeant who understands the language of intelligence and is the information sharing contact point in the Mercedes, Texas Police Department."[86] By having the Intelligence Officer handle all the intelligence information for the agency, he or she can control what is coming in and what is going out from the unit. More importantly, that individual than brings an enormous amount of knowledge, experience, and intelligence to the decision-making process so that well-informed decisions are made by

BOX 4-9

HOMELAND SECURITY OPERATIONS BY EXAMPLE: THE HOUSTON POLICE DEPARTMENT

Phillip Davis, Sam Houston State University

The Houston, Texas, Police Department has established a plan for any potential acts of terrorism. The plan is divided into two stages: crisis management and consequence management. During the crisis management phase of operations, the Houston Police Department will be in command of all responses to the terrorist incident. This includes all command and control of the investigation and whatever tasks are necessary to prevent the event from escalating. The consequence management phase of operations, however, is commanded by the Houston Office of Emergency Management. This phase of operations is primarily concerned with managing whatever negative effects have been created by the terrorist incident.

Source: The City of Houston. Houston Office of Emergency Management. *Annex V Terrorism Incident Response & Management Plan.* Retrieved from *http://www.houstontx.gov/oem/ANNEX%20V%202002.pdf*

the staff. Although it is important that this individual have a strong voice on the police decision-making process, by having them as only a member of the staff, it prevents final decisions being made simply on the recommendation of one individual.

CONCLUSION

Strategy drives operations. A police strategy for homeland security should then drive police operations for homeland security. This would necessitate that police leadership have a strong operational control over its police force. Yet, as Mark Moore has explained, "Police leadership is . . . handicapped by a startling lack of operational control over officers," and departments function "under a carefully constructed illusion of control created to satisfy citizen demands for accountability."[87] Due to this lack of operational control and capability for centralized decision making, police operations and police management under homeland security must change.

What is promising is the development of both CompStat and the ICS. By merging these two systems together into a full-time, staff-driven, operational control system, police departments will be better organized to deal with issues of homeland security, consisting of both natural disasters and terrorist threats and attacks. Centralized decision making through an informed staff, driven by a homeland security strategy, will establish a strong system of police operations. A system that can establish strong centralized plans, coupled with decentralized execution, will adapt well to the modern environment of policing for homeland security. Combined with an emphasis on partnerships, the ability to manage risk, and the capability of intelligence-led policing, today's modern police departments will operationally be prepared to deal with all threats, natural, criminal, and terroristic.

CHAPTER 5

Police Tactics for Homeland Security

One must change one's tactics every ten years if one wishes to maintain one's superiority.

Napoleon Bonaparte

INTRODUCTION

The tactical level of policing is about how the police are deployed. It is where police operations, after developing its operational plan, puts the plan into motion in support of the overall strategy. It is no longer the process of strategizing or planning, but one of action. This is the level that deals with the police officer on the street, the special tactical units available, and any other asset that can be deployed by the operational command to work an actual incident. Police tactics should be determined by the strategic goals of the organization and based on the operational planning for the possible incidents that may occur. Through good police intelligence, combined with threat and risk assessments, the tactics necessary for homeland security may continually change and need updating. If Al-Qaeda no longer looks to airports and airplanes as a viable means of attack, but instead adopts simultaneous suicide bombings in train and metro stations, the type of tactics necessary to defeat this threat will change. As the opening quote insinuates, one will have to change tactics to stay prepared for changing threats.

To change tactics and adapt to emerging threats in an era of homeland security, police departments will have to continually give consideration to changing its tactics, but more importantly, it will have to give consideration to changing and updating its training. To change one's tactics, one must learn new knowledge, new skills, and train to perfect both. Changes in tactics are good and beneficial to an organization, but it must be able to adequately deploy these tactics. Consideration must be given to the line officer's education, training, skills, capabilities, and equipment. Once the proper tactical changes are identified, then training and exercises must become part of the process of preparing an agency for homeland security.

A recent recommendation by the International Association of Chiefs of Police (IACP) highlights the necessity to change tactics to adapt to new threats, but it also highlights the need for certain knowledge, skills, equipment, and training on the part of the police. In the wake of the London train bombings by suicide bombers in July of 2005, there was a definitive acknowledgment to the fact that Al-Qaeda was beginning to target trains and underground transportation systems through suicide bombers. The IACP recommended that police officers confronting suicide bombers should take a head shot, rather than traditionally aiming for the torso.[1] Their reasoning was to prevent the detonation of bombs through a shot to the torso because that is generally where the bombs are strapped to the body. In addition, a shot to the head stands a greater chance of immediately disabling the bomber, thus preventing them from self-detonating the bomb. Bruce Hoffman, a terrorist expert at the Rand Corporation, has pointed out that "the police standard operating procedure of addressing a suspect and telling him to drop their weapon and put their hands up or freeze, is not going to work with a suicide bomber."[2] He tersely concludes that officers who use this tactic will essentially be signing their own death warrant.[3]

The IACP has also offered information on potential details that may identify possible suicide bombers, such as suspicious individuals wearing heavy clothing, walking with an unusual gait, evident irritability, excessive sweating, or obvious tunnel vision.[4] These types of clues may provide law enforcement with the means of identifying potential terrorists and give them the advantage of recognizing a threat in advance of the terrorist act.

The recognition of new threats is beneficial to law enforcement operations. Providing the means of identifying possible suicide bombers and how to appropriately deal with them is assuredly beneficial for adjusting police tactics in response to suicide bombings. Yet, what will become critical in this case is instructing officers on this tactical change, training them to adapt to this new threat, and ensuring that they are exercised on this realistic scenario. Officers must be trained on the cues of what to look for, to understand the methods the suicide bombers are using, and to be aware of multiple threats and simultaneous or near-simultaneous attacks. Therefore, they must be trained to act quick and respond to other potential locations that are at risk. In addition, they must be trained on how to accurately take a head shot, which is not something police have traditionally been trained to do. Repetitive training on this specific tactic is critical to the police ability to respond to such a terrorist threat. Finally, it should be noted that scenarios and exercises should also be used to allow officers the opportunity to test their abilities in these new tactics to ensure that if the real case presented itself, they would make the proper decision and perform this new tactic efficiently and effectively.

This chapter, then, is about the consideration of police tactics necessary for line officers to carry out police operations in support of the homeland security strategy. To this end, the tactics reviewed here are those tactics that are derived directly from the police operations chapter (Chapter 4) as conceptualized by the overall homeland security strategy (Chapter 5). It should be clear that these tactics are only considerations for state, local, and tribal police and do not, and essentially cannot, cover all the police tactical considerations for homeland security because the current environment is far too dynamic to create a definitive list. The purpose of this chapter is to consider police tactics in light of police operations and the overall strategy for homeland security. Therefore, this chapter will first define what is meant by police tactics more fully and then discuss various tactical considerations to draw attention to those areas in need of improved police tactics for this era of homeland security.

BOX 5-1

TACTICAL INTERVENTION CONSIDERATIONS

Jurisdictions seeking to improve "intervention" to stop terrorists before they can execute a threat should

1. Train personnel to recognize threats and threatening cues and to respond appropriately to suspects preparing for attacks.
2. Train law enforcement personnel in tactical capabilities with special teams of law enforcement, emergency response, and military resources to respond quickly and appropriately in a potential terrorism event with the objective of intervening in an impending attack.
3. Articulate and disseminate the legal criteria for making cases, conducting wiretaps, and conducting surveillance on suspected WMD terrorists through general training and specific tactical training within law enforcement to ensure familiarization with: conspiracy statutes, search and seizure requirements, Foreign Intelligence Surveillance Act (FISA) requirements, established legal criteria and procedures for intervention in suspicious circumstances and events, Standard Operating Procedures (SOPs) for observing people and targets at high threat locations, laws that protect public safety information, and contact lists and contact information for legal opinions and assistance.
4. Establish preservice and in-service training in legal, tactical, and strategic aspects of policing in the WMD terrorism environment to enhance the ability to apprehend terrorists.
5. If indicated in an analytical risk management model, develop plans for preboarding searches for mass transit vehicles in the event of a credible threat.
6. As indicated in an analytical risk management model, establish plans and needs assessments for deployment of resources to meet known or anticipated threats to preempt or deter events.
7. Facilitate a prosecutorial and judicial structure, process, collaboration, and expertise that enhances successful prosecution of WMD terrorism.
8. Exercise processes for collecting and entering investigative intelligence and retrieving information, to result in the successful intervention and arrest of terrorists.
9. Articulate the legal requisites for authorities to isolate and decontaminate to reduce spread of suspected diseases or agents.
10. Include in risk management plan the collateral implications to the private sector in a WMD event intervention and have plans to coordinate mitigation.

Source: Office of Domestic Preparedness. (2003). *The Office For Domestic Preparedness Guidelines for Homeland Security June 2003: Prevention and Deterrence.* Washington, D.C.: U.S. Department of Homeland Security.

TACTICS DEFINED

Tactics is the employment of police assets into critical incidents. It includes the ordered arrangement and maneuver of police officers in relation to each other, the terrain, and the threat to engage the police to quickly restore order. It is also the realm of close fights, where police officers are in direct and immediate confrontation with suspects. In policing for homeland security, it should be the operational-level staff command that sets the term of the type of tactical response and provides the resources necessary to achieve success. Tactical success is then measured by the ability to restore order and how well the action achieved the operational intent and plan.

Police tactics have also been described as a means of achieving "operational strategy."[5] According to P. K. Manning, a long-respected scholar of American policing, "tactics are the specifics of strategies, techniques for gaining control in face-to-face encounters or issue-oriented team situations."[6] He further explains that "tactics implies a degree of cognitive preconception of the stages or steps by which a given general line of action is implemented."[7] What Manning is delineating here are the relationships between strategy, operations, and tactics. Moving strategy to operational planning and then to tactical action is the key to successful implementation of a homeland security strategy. What Manning is essentially echoing are the ancient writings of Sun Tzu, who stated in his treatise on war that "strategy without tactics is the slowest route to victory," whereas "tactics without strategy is the noise before defeat."[8] Police tactics for Homeland Security, then, must be driven by the overall strategy to properly prepare the police for using homeland security tactics. And, it is critical that the police are prepared tactically to take on the challenges of protecting the homeland to defeat the terrorist threat. Therefore, like the opening quote by Napoleon suggests, it is time for the police to update their tactics in preparation for their role in homeland security.

Because tactics do fall into the realm of police action, police tactics should focus specifically on the education, training, and equipping of line police officers. Tactical considerations should focus on the numerous terrorist scenarios that police officers may face and train them to react accordingly. A suicide bomber at a train station is going to necessitate a very specific response, including the recognition of the threat, an elimination of that threat, and the awareness that there may be other attacks that will occur simultaneously or near-simultaneously. Compared with a sarin attack on a subway system, as occurred in Tokyo in 1995, this will necessitate a different type of response. Here officers will need to have the ability to recognize the attack for what it is, be properly equipped to respond to the attack so as not to become a victim themselves, and know what to look for in terms of investigatory evidence. Various considerations regarding the tactics necessary for the police to learn will be considered throughout the rest of this chapter; however, it should be noted that it is not the intent of this chapter to provide the full breadth and depth of knowledge necessary under homeland security. It is merely aimed at serving to highlight various factors that police officers must consider based on a general understanding of police strategy and operations for homeland security.

BOX 5-2

TACTICAL AWARENESS

In August of 2004, a Charlotte-Mecklenberg police officer noticed an individual filming an intersection in the city who, on spotting the officer, stopped filming and walked away. The officer had the presence of mind to stop the individual and inquire as to his destination. After some questioning, the individual, by the name of Kamran Akhtar, agreed to be questioned at the local FBI office. Akhtar claimed to be in the United States legally and was a tourist. It turns out Akhtar had been requested to leave the country in 1998 because he had illegally entered the United States, by way of Mexico, in 1991. Investigators watched the video that was in the recorder Akhtar was using and found 40 minutes of video showing banks, high-rise buildings, and light rail facilities in Houston, Dallas, Atlanta, New Orleans, and Charlotte, North Carolina, where he was stopped. After arresting him for immigration charges, a warrant was secured to search his apartment, where additional video of buildings and dams from Las Vegas to Austin were found. As this tactically aware officer demonstrates, police officers are truly on the front line of tactical intelligence gathering.

Source: Lezon, D. (2004). "Man Who Filmed Sites in U.S. Cities to Stay in Custody." *Houston Chronicle,* August 14: A13.

Kanas City TAC team *(Source: 911 Pictures. Photo by Mikael Karlsson)*

THREAT AWARENESS

The early identification of a terrorist event utilizing a weapon of mass destruction is critical to the protection of police officers and other first responders and their ability to save the lives of those people directly affected by the attack.[9] This early identification requires all persons involved in the initial response (911 operators, dispatchers, police officers, and supervisors) to be well informed and alert to the key indicators of a biological, chemical, or radiological attack.

The first source of information will most likely come in the form of information provided via emergency calls to 911.[10] The 911 operators should be alerted by any of following types of information: large volumes of calls reporting sick or injured persons with no known reason; numerous persons reporting similar illness, signs, and symptoms; numerous calls from the same general geographic area or large gathering of people such as a sporting event; symptoms indicative of an exposure such as drooling, tearing, shortness of breath, difficulty breathing, irritation of eyes, nose, throat, and/or skin; report of an explosion with no structural damage; reports of unexplained liquids; reports of unusual odors such as mowed grass, garlic, bitter almonds; reports of a release of a spray or aerosol; unexplained dead animals; and/or discarded Personal Protection Equipment (PPE) such as masks and gloves.

Police officers responding to any mass casualty scene need to be alert for key indicators that a weapon of mass destruction has been used.[11] These key indicators are the same as those indicated earlier and include multiple casualties with similar signs/symptoms, multiple casualties with no visible injuries other than being sick, widely dispersed casualties indicating a possible aerial dispersal of an agent, and unusual odors in the area. If police officers identify any of these indicators on scene, they must be trained to move away from the scene, something that generally runs counter to police officer instinct, until they can don PPE, otherwise they will become victims of the agent, thus inhibiting rather than succoring an adequate response. As Buerger and Levine pointed out, "officer safety at the point of discovering a suspected biological, chemical, or nuclear device reflects a new dimension."[12] This is clearly not a routine element of a patrol officer's duties, but an area where training officers will become critical if they are to know how to respond to such a scenario.

One key aspect of officer safety is the recognition that terrorists often use coordinated attacks. According to Houghton and Schachter, "since 1983, half of the 14 terrorist incidents with 100 or more fatalities were coordinated ones."[13] To educate officers on this threat, Houghton and Schachter stated that coordinated terrorist attacks tend to "fall into three main categories: (1) parallel device attacks, where participants use more than one device simultaneously or almost simultaneously in the same location; (2) secondary attacks, where the initial assault is followed by one or more additional attacks in the same location, typically targeting responders; and (3) multiple dispersed attacks, where groups stage simultaneous or near-simultaneous ones at different locations."[14] They make several recommendations to deal specifically with this reality. The first is to avoid centralizing equipment, but rather decentralizing it across a police agency's jurisdiction. This provides more flexibility in responding and avoids the possible liability of the centralized equipment site becoming a target or compromised by being close to ground zero. In addition, they, like others, make the tactical recommendation that the organization prevent the deployment of all resources—officers and equipment—to a terrorist scene to avoid a significant loss to a secondary device or from a dispersed weapon of mass destruction. This is the key to an incident command center controlling the deployment of police resources at all times (see Chapter 4).

Law enforcement officers should also be observant for possible methods of disseminating a weapon of mass destruction. In the case of either a biological or chemical attack, there are multiple ways in which these agents can be disseminated. The only two key characteristics of a biological or chemical dissemination device are an agent source (any type of container capable of holding a liquid, gas, or powder) and a dissemination mechanism. Dissemination mechanisms can vary from the very crude to the sophisticated. Examples include the normal evaporation of a liquid (the method used in the Tokyo subway attack), a blower or fan to aid in the spread and evaporation of an agent, a pressurized spray-release similar to pesticide canisters, or an explosive device. Because there is no specific profile of what a dissemination device looks like, police officers should be alert to certain visual indicators such as unusual liquids, damp or wet items abandoned, out of place items such as a pesticide sprayer in a subway, or items with spray nozzles.

The early identification of a weapons of mass destruction attack is essential to officer safety and survival. Failure to recognize an attack can result in the first responding officers becoming casualties themselves. No police call can produce a more urgent response than one of an officer down or in need of assistance; however, failure to recognize the incident for what it is can result in additional officers racing to the scene to become casualties. Key issues to consider include the immediate loss of contact with officers already on the scene, officers reporting signs or symptoms of agent exposure, distress calls indicating medical problems rather than some type of physical attack, and automatic distress signals such as the panic button on a radio, especially when this comes from the area of a 911 call.

The actions of the first law enforcement officer on the scene sets the stage for the remainder of the response, including the safety of all responding officers. The first priority must be self-protection.[15] Officers arriving on a mass casualty scene where a weapon of mass destruction was used must notify dispatch and the police command staff for them to begin mobilizing the necessary resources. The officers must protect themselves with PPE prior to entering the area, and they should consider maintaining a safe distance and approaching from upwind, so as to avoid contamination. Once PPE is donned, the officers should be careful when moving about the scene to avoid breaches in the PPE and possible exposure to the agent, such as walking through a liquid contaminant. If this should happen, officers should be decontaminated immediately, which necessitates a decontamination center being established relatively quickly. If officers become casualties, again, proper protection by the responding officers should be donned prior to assisting the officer, otherwise, additional officers will become casualties, thus multiplying the impact of the attack.

First responding officers must quickly define the perimeter of the attack and isolate the area. Both an inner perimeter and an outer perimeter should be established. The outer perimeter will most likely be quite large and will necessitate police to serve a traffic control function as well as security for the decontamination site. The inner perimeter will still be a large area and will consist of the initial isolation area around the site of the attack, but will have to be expanded to include all areas downwind of the site. Law enforcement will most likely perform crowd control, access into and out of the area, providing security for the decontamination corridor, will prevent those contaminated from leaving the area until decontaminated, and will coordinate with both EMS and the local fire department. Consideration must also be given to those working inside the inner perimeter, as the ability to work long term in the full PPE is limited. Rotations should be quickly established to ensure seamless police functions inside both perimeters.

Additional considerations for local law enforcement include the designation of a collection area for victims that must be identified and located far enough away from the contaminated area. In addition, law enforcement officers must identify an area for law enforcement officers to stage that is upwind of the incident scene. It must be far enough away that neither the contaminated area nor the victim collection area intrudes on its safety, otherwise cross contamination will render all of these officers ineffective. In addition, the decontamination site must be located in an area far enough away from the inner perimeter to avoid continued exposure after decontamination, but it must be close enough to be able to control the movement of individuals who have been exposed. A decontamination corridor should be established to move people to the decontamination site and, once processed through, to move them into a safe area.

Police command and control, as well as security, will be critical at the decontamination site. Although decontamination will be conducted by others, the crowd control and security of the site will be the responsibility of the police.[16] Law enforcement will have to assist in the collection of contaminated individuals and the movement of these people to the decontamination site. Once there, the collection of their personal belongings will potentially fall to the police. As the decontamination process will require full disrobement, the police will have to enforce this, as many people will refuse to disrobe or place their valuables in another's possession. Police will also have to screen for evidence, as individuals in the contaminated crowd may be potential suspects. If any evidence is collected, decisions must be made of how best to secure the item and whether or not to decontaminate, which could possible destroy some of the evidence. In addition, screening for secondary devices must also be conducted at this time. Police officers will also have to consider their own personal belongings and equipment and how such items as their firearms will be secured during the decontamination process and how they will be reequipped. Moreover, how officers will secure new PPE for reentry into the contaminated area must also be considered in advance.

Up to this point, most of the focus in the event of a weapons of mass destruction (WMD) attack, such as a chemical or biological attack, has been on securing the scene and handling the victims. One of the primary functions of law enforcement is to conduct criminal investigations, and that will also have to be considered in light of the difficult situation such an attack will create. Police officers must also be looking for perpetrators. Field interviews will have to be done as quickly as possible, but will be difficult under the circumstances. Witness statements will be crucial in helping to identify possible suspects. There is also the potential that the key suspect or suspects may be in the crowds that form after an attack. It is most likely that if any of them survived, they will be the most severely injured or ill individuals, as they will have been at ground zero. Officers will also have to consider asking questions that relate to the type of explosions, liquids, or mists that witnesses saw and the types of symptoms people are experiencing to assist in the identification of the type of attack. Moreover, officers will have to try to identify any individuals that left the scene prior to being decontaminated, as they will become a risk to anyone with whom they come in contact. Finally, officers should consider the collection of any audiovisual devices that may have captured the suspects and the actual attack.

WEAPONS OF MASS DESTRUCTION (WMD)

In relation to threat awareness, it is not only critical that police officers, police staff, and police leaders be familiar with the threat of weapons of mass destruction, but they must also have a grounded knowledge in the different types, their capabilities, delivery systems, and how an actual attack would likely progress. This knowledge is key for many elements of the homeland security strategy, ranging from prevention and preparedness to response and recovery. Although space is limited here to provide the full range of knowledge and education on WMD, a brief overview can demonstrate some of the tactical knowledge that is necessary to prepare police officers to respond, work, and survive in a WMD environment.

The term *weapons of mass destruction* is actually a former Soviet military term that was euphemistically used to denote nuclear, chemical, and biological weapons.[17] It is now widely used, despite debate over its appropriateness, and its definition has broadened to include radiological weapons. In addition, toxin weapons are sometimes included as a separate category or as part of either the biological or chemical categories. A brief review of these different types of WMD follows.

Biological weapons are pathogens that cause disease and illness in infected humans.[18] Because the pathogens multiply within the victim, a small initial amount of pathogen is sufficient to cause infection. As a consequence, biological weapons require much less material than chemical weapons to produce equivalent causalities and generally take longer to produce side effects. Biological weapons include diseases that are primarily incapacitating, such as Q fever, as well as those that are lethal, such as smallpox. Some biological weapons are contagious pathogens, such as smallpox, and have the potential to spread the effects of an attack by traveling from victim to victim. The symptoms from a biological weapon attack would require some time to develop, so a covert biological attack might not be recognized for several days.

Toxin weapons are primarily illness-inducing chemicals formed from living creatures, such as bacteria, fungi, plants, and animals.[19] Toxins range in effect from disabling to acutely toxic. The most deadly compound currently known, botulinum toxin, is a bacterial toxin. Toxins are more potent than chemical weapons, requiring less material to produce equivalent casualties, but they are not self-reproducing, so more material is required than for a biological weapon. Symptoms from toxin exposure typically occur on a timescale intermediate between chemical and biological weapons, generally appearing over the course of several hours.

Chemical weapons are chemical compounds that have a strong, deleterious effect on the human body, even when encountered in small doses.[20] The different types of chemical weapons include vesicants, which blister and burn on contact; choking agents, which cause lung damage; and nerve agents, which interfere with the nervous system and may lead to death. The effects from chemical weapons may occur very quickly after exposure, on the order of minutes to hours. Military planners categorize chemical

BOX 5-3

CHEMICAL AGENTS

Type	Agent	Physical State	Signs & Symptoms	Odor	Decontamination	Persistence
Nerve	GA/GB/GD	Liquid	Pinpoint pupils Salivation Tearing Vomiting Twitching Convulsions	Fruity	Remove all clothing; flush with soap & volumes of water	Minutes–days
Nerve	VX	Oily	S/a	Sulfur	S/a	Days–weeks
Blister	mustard	Liquid	Eye pain Reddened skin Large blisters	Garlic	S/a	Days–years
Blister	lewisite	Liquid	Eye pain Burning lungs Bee sting blisters Gray skin	Geraniums	S/a	Hours–days
Blood	hydrogen cyanide	Gas	Bright red lips Red skin Headache Gasping Nausea	Bitter almonds	S/a	Minutes
Blood	cyanogen cloride	Gas	S/a	S/a	S/a	S/a
Choking	phosgene	Gas	Coughing Choking Pneumonia	New mown hay	S/a	S/a
Choking	chlorine	Gas	Coughing Choking	Bleach	S/a	S/a

Source: U.S. Army Solider and Biological Chemical Command's Improved Respond Program. (2003). *Law Enforcement Officers Guide for Responding to Chemical Terrorist Incidents*. Washington, D.C.: U.S. Army Solider and Biological Chemical Command, Homeland Defense Business Unit. Available online at http://www.mipt.org/pdf/leofficersguideChemicalIncidents.pdf, downloaded June 2004.

agents into four classes: nerve, blister, choking, and blood agents.[21] This categorization groups chemicals by the effects they cause to those exposed to them. The nerve and blister agents are predominately only manufactured and used by militaries as weapons, but both choking agents and blood agents include chemicals widely used in industrial processes.

Chemical weapons affecting the nervous system are called nerve agents.[22] Nerve agents do not occur naturally. Rather, they are man-made compounds that require manufacture and isolation for high toxicity and purity. Most nerve agents belong to a group of chemicals called organophosphates. Organophosphates have a wide range of toxicity, and some are commercially employed as insecticides, though these are significantly less toxic than those developed as chemical weapons. Nerve agents are mainly liquids.

The first nerve agent developed for military use, called Tabun or GA, was made in Germany in the 1930s. Following this discovery, a series of nerve agents similar to Tabun was developed. This series, known as the G-series, includes the weapons sarin (GB) and Soman (GD). In the late 1940s, another series of nerve agents, the V-series, was invented in England. Both the British and the U.S. chemical weapons programs investigated these compounds. The United States manufactured and stockpiled VX. A related compound, V-gas, was manufactured and stockpiled by the Soviet Union. Military use of nerve agents has been rare. Nerve agents were not used during World War I or World War II. During the 1980–1988 Iran–Iraq war, Iraq used nerve agents against Iranian troops and later against members of the Kurdish population in northern Iraq.

National chemical weapons programs have produced nerve agents for decades. The technological barriers for a terrorist group to synthesize these agents might be overcome by using commercially available equipment, though there would be appreciable danger to the manufacturer due to the extreme toxicity of these compounds. Nerve agent production requires the use of toxic chemicals during synthesis and specialized equipment to contain the nerve agent produced. Of the nerve agents, VX has been identified as the most difficult to manufacture.

Nerve agents are extremely dangerous and can enter the body through the lungs or by skin contact, though for the G-series nerve agents, the inhalation toxicity is significantly greater than the dermal toxicity. Of the nerve agents, VX is the most deadly and Tabun is the least deadly, though all are exceedingly toxic.

Nerve agents interfere with the nervous system, causing overstimulation of muscles. Victims may suffer nausea and weakness and possibly convulsions and spasms. At high concentrations, loss of muscle control, nervous system irregularities, and death may occur. The action of nerve agents can be irreversible if victims are not quickly treated.

Two drugs, atropine and pralidoxime chloride, are used as antidotes for nerve agents. Atropine prevents muscle spasms and allows the body time to clear the nerve agent. Pralidoxime chloride limits the effects of nerve agent exposure by reversing the agent's action. Both of these drugs were issued to U.S. troops during the Persian Gulf War in the form of an antidote kit called the Mark I. Diazepam (Valium) may be used to reduce convulsions and seizures brought on by exposure to nerve agents.

The treatment window for nerve agent exposure is agent-dependent. Some agents quickly and irreversibly react to enzymes within the body, whereas others require a much longer time to permanently bind to these enzymes. The most effective treatment occurs before such permanent binding has taken place. Soman, for example, is permanently bound within minutes, whereas Tabun is not and can be treated up to several hours after exposure. Prophylactic use of some compounds, such as pyridostigmine bromide, may create a larger window for effective treatment for some nerve agents.

Blister agents, also known as vesicants, are chemicals that cause painful blistering of the skin. Although such blistering is not generally lethal, the excruciating pain caused by the blister agents requires full body protection against these chemicals. Militarily, blister agents produce casualties and reduce the combat effectiveness of opposing troops by requiring them to wear bulky protective equipment. The most common blister agent is mustard agents, which include nitrogen- and sulfur-based compounds. Mustard agents are oily liquids that range in color from a very pale yellow to dark brown, depending on the type and purity, and have a faint odor of mustard, onion, or garlic. These liquids evaporate quickly, and their vapors are also injurious.

Blister agents are not naturally occurring compounds. Mustard agents, for example, were first developed in the late 1800s. During World War I, both sides in the conflict used these weapons against their enemies, and the mustard-type blister agent produced the greatest number of chemical casualties during World War I, though fewer than 5 percent of these casualties died. Many countries have stockpiled blister agents in their chemical weapon inventories. Mustard agent was also reportedly used in the Iraq–Iran war. The United States is currently destroying its stockpile of blister agents.

Production of blister agents is considered less complicated than that of nerve agents. Like nerve agents, it requires the use of some toxic chemicals and specialized equipment to contain the agent produced. The most common blister agents have many different methods for their production published in the open literature.

Blister agents can enter the body through the lungs or by contact with the skin or eyes. Some can penetrate through normal clothing material, causing burns in areas that were covered by cloth. Although blister agents react quickly on skin contact, their symptoms may be delayed. In the case of mustard agent, damage occurs within one to two minutes of exposure, but symptoms do not manifest for several hours. As even low concentrations of vaporized blister agent quickly causes damage, it is unlikely that agents will be removed from the skin prior to injury.

The initial symptoms of blister agent exposure are a reddening of the skin, resembling sunburn, combined with pain in the effected area. Swelling, blisters, and lesions may then develop, depending on the degree of exposure. Systemic symptoms such as malaise, vomiting, and fever may also develop in extreme cases. Exposure to large amounts of liquid mustard agent may prove fatal.

The eyes are also very sensitive to blister agents. At high vapor exposures, great pain, corneal damage, and scarring between the iris and lens may occur. The most severe eye damage is often caused by liquid agent, either from contact with airborne droplets or by self-contamination of the eyes from contaminated clothing or body parts.

Victims inhaling blister agents may suffer damage to their lungs. Although a single, low-level exposure will likely produce only temporary impairment, high concentrations or repeated exposures may cause permanent damage. Inhalation victims may have symptoms ranging from mild bronchitis to blistering of the lungs.

Damage from blister agent exposure, lesions, and other skin irritations is symptomatically treated. Hospitalization may be required for respiratory tract injuries. Victims who suffer severe lung damage may require mechanical ventilation. An additional complication after exposure to large amounts of mustard agent is a general weakening of the whole immune system. Because of these systemic effects, special precautions must be taken against opportunistic infections in the case of exposure to high concentrations of mustard agent.

Chemicals that act on the lungs, causing difficulty in breathing and, potentially, permanent lung damage are known as choking agents. Examples of choking agents include chlorine, ammonia, and phosgene. Choking agents have historically been used during wartime and are sometimes encountered during industrial accidents. Choking agents are generally gases that have marked odors and may color the surrounding air.

Many choking agents are dual-use chemicals with both a civilian and a military purpose. Chlorine and ammonia are both used in large quantities for commercial applications, whereas phosgene is used within the chemical industry. Methods for producing choking agents are well known, but may be technically challenging. Choking agents require specialized equipment to produce, compress, and contain them. Choking agents were also manufactured for wartime use and were extensively used during World War I. The first major, successful, chemical attack of the war used chlorine gas at Ypres in 1915. Chlorine gas was later supplemented by phosgene use, which caused greater casualties.

Choking agents injure their victims through inhalation, with a comparatively mild effect on the skin. Exposure to low chemical concentrations causes chest discomfort or shortness of breath, irritation of nose and throat, and tearing eyes. High agent concentrations may quickly cause swelling of the lungs, respiratory failure, and possibly death. Symptoms of lung damage can occur up to 48 hours after inhalation of moderate concentrations and often do not manifest themselves until the lungs are aggravated by physical effort.

Victims of choking agents are generally treated symptomatically. Because lung damage may be exacerbated by exercise, victims are kept at rest until the danger of fluid in the lungs is past. Symptoms such as tightness of the chest and coughing are treated with immediate rest and comfort. Shallow breathing and insufficient oxygen may require supplemental oxygen.

Swelling and accumulation of fluids in the lungs are likely after exposure to a high dose of choking agent. Administration of corticosteroids has been recommended in cases of fluid accumulation, but their beneficial effects have not been proven. Rest, warmth, sedation, and oxygen are still the primary treatments, even in the case of marked edema.

Blood agents are chemicals that interfere with oxygen utilization at the cellular level. Hydrogen cyanide and cyanide salts are agents in this group. Hydrogen cyanide is a very volatile gas, smelling of almonds, whereas cyanide salts are odorless solids.

Hydrogen cyanide was considered for use as a chemical warfare agent, but was rarely used in military situations because its effectiveness was limited by its quick dispersion. The French manufactured hydrogen cyanide as a military agent during World War I. Hydrogen cyanide use has been attributed to both sides during the Iran–Iraq war.

Hydrogen cyanide and cyanide salts are now used as industrial chemicals, having applications in the chemical, electroplating, and mining industries. As with choking agents, methods for producing blood agents are relatively well known. However, the gaseous nature of hydrogen cyanide complicates the production and storage.

Blood agents act through inhalation or ingestion and impair cellular oxygen use. The central nervous system is especially susceptible to this effect, and blood agents usually cause death through oxygen starvation of brain cells. The symptoms of blood agent exposure depend on the agent concentration and the duration of exposure. In mild cases, there may be headache, dizziness, and nausea for several hours, followed by complete spontaneous recovery. Higher concentrations or longer exposure may lead to powerful gasping for breath, violent convulsions, and cardiac failure within a few minutes.

The effects of blood agents are reversed through treatment with specific antidotes—either amyl or sodium nitrite combined with sodium thiosulfate. The combination of these two chemicals removes cyanide, the active compound in blood agents, from the body. When symptoms such as convulsions or depressed breathing are present, ventilation with oxygen and administration of anticonvulsants are used. Cyanide is metabolized more readily than most chemical weapons; with prompt treatment, victims may recover from otherwise-fatal doses.

Many experts believe that it would be difficult for terrorist groups to use chemical agents as weapons of mass destruction.[23] Even VX, the most lethal of nerve agents, would require tons, spread uniformly and efficiently, to kill 50 percent of the people in a 100-kilometer area. On the other hand, chemical agents might be effectively used as weapons of terror in situations where limited or enclosed space might decrease the required amounts of chemicals. That is, the use of the weapon itself, even if casualties are few, could cause fear that would magnify the attack's effect beyond what would be expected based solely on the number of casualties.

There have been few examples of successful chemical terror attacks. In 1995, Aum Shinrikyo, a Japanese apocalyptic cult, used sarin on the Tokyo subway. The attack killed 12 people and sent more than 5,000 to the hospital with some degree of injury. This same cult reportedly carried out an attack in Matsumoto as well, where 7 people were killed and over 200 injured. Both of these attacks used G-series nerve agents, which are more toxic through inhalation than by contact. V-series agents employed in a similar manner might have caused greater fatalities.

In comparison, blister agents would likely be less lethal, but more injurious, if used in a similar manner. Blister agents are dermally active, so inhalation of the agent would not be necessary to cause injury. Additionally, because mustard agent vapor penetrates most fabrics, victims near the point of release might suffer grievously. Blister agents, although not likely to cause mass destruction, might cause mass terror and injury.

Choking agents are no longer considered to be useful military weapons, as chemical suits and masks provide high protection. As a weapon of mass destruction used against civilians, the comparatively low lethality of choking agents complicates their use because very large volumes would be needed. On the other hand, the industrial availability of some choking agents provides opportunities for acquisition and subsequent use of potentially very large volumes of such agents. For example, the United States produces approximately one billion pounds of chlorine a year for use in water treatment facilities. The potential vulnerability for chlorine-filled rail tank cars, by which chlorine is primarily transported, has been noted. Terrorist attack on industrial stores at chemical or water treatment facilities or during shipment has been raised as another potential source of concern.

Blood agents may be difficult to use as weapons of mass destruction for many of the same reasons as choking agents. The quick dispersal of blood agents, combined with the large amounts necessary to cause mass casualties, make such agents difficult to use on a mass scale. Even those blood agents that are industrially manufactured are often used on-site without being shipped. However, terrorist groups seem to be increasingly interested in these agents, perhaps because of criminal use of them.

Ramzi Yousef, convicted of the 1993 World Trade Center bombing, stated he had intended to include sodium cyanide in that bomb to create a cloud of cyanide gas. Although a small amount of cyanide was found in the supplies of the bombers, there was no evidence that this had been done. In 1995, following the sarin attack, members of Aum Shinrikyo attempted an attack in Tokyo by setting fire to a plastic bag of sodium cyanide positioned next to a bag of an acid. A similar combination of chemicals was discovered the following month in another station. Both devices were successfully disarmed. In 2002, Italian police arrested four Moroccan men possessing potassium ferrocyanide. It was reported that the men arrested planned to poison the water supply using the potassium ferrocyanide. It is questionable how effective this would have been, considering the volume of the water supply and the amount of potassium ferrocyanide found in their possession. A group calling itself September 11 threatened the use of cyanide to disrupt the America's Cup boat race in New Zealand.

It is believed that the Al-Qaeda terrorist group has produced and developed plans for the use of chemical weapons, including hydrogen cyanide. Osama bin Laden has stated that Al-Qaeda has a chemical capability. Ahmed Ressam, convicted in a plot to bomb the Los Angeles Airport, testified that he had received training in the use of hydrogen cyanide in Afghanistan at an Al-Qaeda training camp. The training described included the production of hydrogen cyanide using cyanide salts and acids, demonstrations of effectiveness of the agent by exposing dogs to it, and introducing the agent into building ventilation systems by placing a source near the air intakes. CNN also located and retrieved videotapes from Afghanistan that portray the results of testing of unknown chemical agents on dogs. It has been suggested that the chemical agent used in those videotapes was a blood agent, most likely hydrogen cyanide.

The use of chemical, biological, or toxin weapons in terror attacks could complicate emergency response due to the need to establish special care facilities for the victims, such as decontamination areas, and the need to protect first responders from the weapon's effects.[24] If first responders became victims through inadequate PPE (see following) or contamination of emergency vehicles, increased casualties and greater social disruption could result.

A nuclear weapon is the most destructive of all weapons of mass destruction, but obtaining one poses the greatest difficulty for terrorist groups.[25] The key obstacle to building such a weapon is the availability of a sufficient quantity of fissile material—either plutonium or highly enriched uranium. Some experts believe that if allowed access to the necessary quantities of fissile material, extraordinary capable groups could build a crude nuclear weapon.

Some experts point to Iraq's efforts to acquire a nuclear capability—a nation with economic resources, technical expertise, and motivation—to demonstrate the significant difficulty of building even a crude nuclear weapon. State sponsors of terrorists have been considered unlikely to turn over control of such weapons, once developed, to terrorist groups because of possible international retaliation or concern that the groups might leave their control. However, the problem of "loose nukes" (i.e., the possible leakage of nuclear weapons material and technical know-how from the former Soviet states) remains a cause of concern that some believe increases the likelihood of a terrorist group obtaining a nuclear capability. It is important to note that even if a terrorist group were to get hold of an assembled nuclear weapon covertly, the built-in safeguards and self-destruction mechanisms would pose a serious challenge to detonating the weapon. In addition, the size of most nuclear weapons makes them rather hard to transport, especially clandestinely. The most likely means for such transport is judged to be commercial shipping.

A much less difficult nuclear option is a radiological weapon, which uses conventional high explosives to disperse any type of radioactive material. These are officially known as a radiological dispersal device (RDD), but often referred to by the media and popular culture as a "dirty bomb." A "dirty bomb" is actually one type of RDD, in which explosives disperse the radioactive material, but in general RDDs do not require explosives.[26] Though unlikely to cause mass casualties, radiological weapons could still have very significant radiation contamination effects if well targeted.[27] Research indicates that RDDs have little effectiveness as military weapons because of their inability to incapacitate prepared soldiers. RDDs may pose a greater threat in a civilian setting. Although there may be few immediate health effects from the dispersed radiological material, long-term health risks, such as cancer, may increase, and there may be significant economic damage if there is an unwillingness to live or work in an area with a higher radiation level. Many experts contend that there is terrorist interest in constructing and using RDDs. No RDD has been used by a terrorist group, so it is not known how potent an RDD might be as a terror weapon.

Terrorist use of RDDs would most likely depend on public fear of *any* radiation rather than actual levels of radiation.[28] Terrorists could try to achieve several goals with RDDs in the following sequence: (1) Death and injuries. Any prompt casualties would most likely come only from the explosion of a dirty bomb; many experts believe these would be few in numbers. (2) Panic. Small amounts of radioactive material might cause as much panic as larger amounts. (3) Recruitment. The worldwide media coverage of an RDD attack would be a powerful advertisement for a terrorist group claiming responsibility. (4) Asset denial. Public concern over the presence of radioactive material might lead people to abandon a subway system, building, or university for months to years. (5) Economic disruption. If a port

BOX 5-4

HOMELAND SECURITY TACTICS BY EXAMPLE: THE IDAHO BUREAU OF HOMELAND SECURITY

Phillip Davis, Sam Houston State University

Regional Response Teams

Idaho's Regional Response Teams were designed as support units for hazmat incidents that exceed the resources of local response agencies. These specially trained teams are available to provide 24-hour coverage, seven days per week and are presently located in fire departments of Boise, Nampa/Caldwell, Lewiston, Pocatello, Coeur d'Alene, Magic Valley, and Idaho Falls/Jefferson County.

Services

Each Hazardous Materials Regional Response Team consists of three five-person response team units who provide 24-hour coverage seven days a week. Each unit consists of a team leader, assistant leader, intensive care paramedic, and two firefighters. Three alternates are on standby. The teams can provide the following services:

Provide emergency response anywhere in the state of Idaho or on special request to adjoining states; capable of both ground response or fly-in response and can be in almost any part of Idaho within a few hours.

Provide from 2 to 5 specialized technical support personnel and up to 10 on special request for serious releases.

Provide specialized equipment, resource information, and instrumentation to assist local responders.

Sample unknown chemicals remotely and safely and do field testing for identification with immediate results.

Contain, neutralize, overpack, and prepare for disposal many isolated spilled chemicals.

Transfer loads up to 100 gallons per minute or assist transfer teams in larger operations from unsafe storage containers.

Provide advanced life support to victims of releases, including rescuers, on scene and prepare them for transport without contaminating ambulances or medical facilities.

Provide expertise on the latest wet or dry decontamination techniques for both men and equipment at incidents.

Provide and set up booms for spills in waterways.

Assist in training, emergency planning, and disaster drills for industry and communities.

Assist in the cleanup of spills requiring the highest levels of protection; assist with obtaining contractors for cleanup.

Provide technical expertise that includes specialists, chemists, and resource people to assist in on-scene operation setup for local responders.

Source: Idaho Bureau of Homeland Security. Regional Response Teams. Retrieved from *http://www.bhs.idaho.gov/agency/ops/rrt.htm*

or the central area of a city were contaminated with radioactive material, commerce there might be suspended. (6) Long-term casualties. Inhalation of radioactive material or exposure to gamma sources could lead to such casualties, probably in small numbers.

PERSONAL PROTECTION EQUIPMENT (PPE)

The police response to a WMD attack is mostly contingent on adequate prevention of officers becoming casualties themselves and the level of preparedness officers have for these events. One police officer in a conference related to this topic described the police response to a WMD attack and the wearing of PPE this way:

> It's a timeliness issue. Are we saving a person's life now or going to get the equipment to put on first? What wins? The person does. It's as simple as that.[29]

Despite there being an element of truth to this statement, as police officers are trained that life is most important, this type of mentality must be overcome. If police favor a person's life over donning their protective gear first, they may not only be jeopardizing the person's life, but their own as well. Becoming part of the problem is not part of the solution. Training for these types of attacks is critical to preparing officers to work in this environment, and much of this is contingent on the officers having the proper PPE to be able to work and survive under these conditions.

The U.S. Conference of Mayors, in the aftermath of 9-11, addressed a key concern regarding the fielding of proper and adequate PPEs. The argued that "cities of all sizes have consistently raised concerns about the lack of availability of equipment such as protective suits, gas masks, detection devices, or protective drugs for first responders."[30] At the same time as the U.S. Conference of Mayors released their white paper on safety, the Rand Corporation sponsored a conference to analyze the experience of first responders, not only to the events of 9-11, but also of the Alfred P. Murrah Federal Building bombing in Oklahoma City and the anthrax attacks in the fall of 2001.[31] The most important conclusion of the Rand Corporation's report was when they explained that "the definition and roles of an *emergency responder* expanded greatly in the wake of the terrorist attacks, but few of the responders had adequate PPE, training, or information for such circumstances."[32] The Rand Corporation conference revealed that first responders, especially law enforcement, did not have the proper level of PPE available to them in their response to these terrorist attacks, they were inadequately trained or not trained at all to respond to such attacks, and they lacked the requisite knowledge to know how to effectively respond.

One realization about the terrorist attacks was that for first responders, they must understand the magnitude of the attacks and that like 9-11, there were multiple threats and multiple attacks.[33] Taken further, it should be recognized that although each of these attacks only lasted a short time, the response to the attacks was a long-term campaign. The term *first responders* is perhaps misleading. It sounds as if these individuals respond first and that someone will come in eventually to relieve them. In the case of 9-11, that couldn't have been further from the truth. Therefore, law enforcement should be thinking long-term responses to these types of attacks and must be prepared to implement rotation plans.

Another realization from the terrorist attacks was that when a WMD is used, it creates a hazardous environment above and beyond the contamination itself. Other considerations must be made for the rubble, debris, dust, smoke, heat, and stress of working long term in this type of environment. Although protective gear is assuredly needed for the biological, chemical, radiological, or nuclear attacks, they are also needed for operating in the hazardous environment that is created by a large-scale attack.

For law enforcement, however, having PPE in the first place is perhaps the first critical hurdle to overcome. Most police officers do not carry, have available, or have the necessary training on how to properly wear PPE.[34] Assuming they do have the PPE available, issues arise as to the condition of the PPE, whether or not it is the right PPE for the environment, and whether or not it is compatible for police duties. As the panelists of the conference hosted by RAND noted, "Most PPE is not designed or manufactured with the law-enforcement mission in mind."[35] In addition, the panelists noted that when police officers do carry PPE with them, it is usually stored in the trunk of the car, along with a large amount of other equipment, thus the packaging is exposed to possible tearing. Once the packaging is torn, the protection offered by the PPE is only 60 to 90 more days. Moreover, the panelists mentioned that police officers do not generally have the proper footwear, gloves, eye protection, hearing protection, or head protection for responding to these events and surviving in them during the aftermath. As one law enforcement official said, "You've got to understand what you're dealing with . . . we can equip our first responders to a certain level . . . but as managers, we have to understand what risks they are capably of dealing with or what hazards . . . if we put them in the wrong outfit and something happens to them, then we're going to get sued."[36] More importantly, officers may die.

Another area that police tend to be lacking in both equipment and training is in the proper protective masks. Simple painting masks and respirators are better than nothing, but in a WMD environment they are useless. Although many police departments secured military-style protective masks in the early 1990s, the rubber in them cracks, the filters must be replaced, and they must be maintained. In addition, even if these preventative measures have been taken, if officers do not have the masks readily available to them or do not know how to properly don and wear the protective masks, they quickly become casualties themselves.

Perhaps an even larger concern is the police ability to coordinate a WMD scene, prevent individuals from leaving, and moving all those contaminated to a decontamination site. One only has to watch the BBC movie *Dirty War* to quickly grasp the complexities

BOX 5-5

HOMELAND SECURITY TACTICS BY EXAMPLE: THE LOS ANGELES POLICE DEPARTMENT

Phillip Davis, Sam Houston State University

The Los Angeles Police Department has implemented several tactics with respect to homeland security following the terrorist attacks of September 11th, 2001. Their strategy has focused on three areas: Training, Interdiction, and Response.

Training:

All Department personnel have received an eight-hour block of training on Weapons of Mass Destruction (WMD). The training included information on the root of domestic and foreign Terrorism, recognition of precursor chemicals and equipment used in WMDs and response to WMD incidents. All field personnel have been issued protective equipment including nuclear, biological, and chemical protective gas masks. Training has been delivered to allied agencies at the Airport and Port of Los Angeles in unified operations. This training will continue until all parts of the City are integrated.

Currently in development are expanded training in response to WMD attacks, using the issued protective equipment, cooperative training for Law Enforcement and Fire Department managers in unified operations, training in terrorism awareness and suspicious activities reporting for the private sector and interactive first responder training based on the U.S. Marine Corps simulation technology.

Interdiction:

The Department's ability to investigate and interdict a terrorist act before it is carried out has been enhanced through the Department's involvement in the Los Angeles Terrorism Early Warning Group, the Los Angeles Task Force on Terrorism, and the establishment of a Terrorism Threat Assessment Center. The department's surveillance and analysis assets have been expanded to identify and disrupt active terrorist cells in the Los Angeles area before they can cause harm to our communities.

Response:

Bomb Squad, HazMat, SWAT and Air capabilities have been enhanced through training and technological advances. Real-time information is now available to responders via microwave links to the City's information backbone, allowing incident commanders to access critical information from the field. The Los Angeles Police Department is continuing to develop capabilities and deploy innovative technologies to keep Los Angeles the safest big city in the United States.

The LAPD has also undertaken operations such as Operation Archangel, in an effort to predict vulnerabilities.

Operation Archangel and DHS:

Archangel is a partnership between the City and County of Los Angeles, the California Department of Homeland Security and the U.S. Department of Homeland Security. Designed to identify critical locations in Los Angeles and develop a multiagency response. Archangel is geared toward facilitating the management of information and resources for the prevention, deterrence, response, and mitigation to major incidents. It develops interactive electronic target folders for critical locations in Los Angeles.

Source: LOS ANGELES POLICE DEPARTMENT PRESS RELEASE. Thursday, July 8, 2004. "Counter Terrorism And The LAPD" http://www.lapdonline.org/press_releases/2004/07/pr04369.htm

of a WMD scene and how quickly police resources can become overwhelmed in trying to channel people to a decontamination site. In addition, working in this type of environment with the PPE can be exhausting and fatiguing and replacements may not come quick enough. Moreover, the decontamination of the officers and the issuance of fresh PPE becomes critical to the police department's ability to properly respond. The key is obviously training. And, unfortunately the RAND panel "agreed that law enforcement is 'behind the curve,' compared with other emergency responders, in terms of receiving PPE training or information."[37]

FITNESS

A highly related aspect of responding to a catastrophic event is officer fitness and wellness. Although PPE is important on scene for officers, the ability to survive in the PPE in this environment will take an individual who is physically capable of handling the long-term exertions caused not only by the event, but also by working in the PPE. Although many have argued that police officers are more fit today than they were 20 or 30 years ago, there is the realization that once officers pass the physical fitness tests of the hiring process and graduate from the academy, there is little concern by most departments for the physical fitness of the officers.[38] Poor physical fitness can lead to the body's inability to handle stress and overexertion, leading to cardiovascular incidents that "are significant causes of injuries and death among police and EMS responders."[39] In addition, response to such large-scale events or terrorist encounters can lead to heavy emotional tolls on police officers. This is not only true of actual incidents, but it is

SWAT team members *(Source: PhotoEdit Inc. Photo by Dwayne Newton)*

also true of placing police officers on numerous alerts where they are working long shifts with no time off until the alert levels are reduced. This is causing both physical and mental fatigue on officers and in some cases is causing burnout and rises in sick days being used.[40] Physical fitness and mental fitness are highly related with one another, and therefore neither should be overlooked.

Police departments, if concerned with homeland security, must not only prepare its department in a number of ways, such as training and equipping its officers in new ways, but it must also physically prepare its officers to be able to work in this environment. Therefore, police departments should establish more incentives for officers to remain in good physical shape, they should provide training on proper nutrition, diet, and exercise; provide the facilities for officers to exercise; and provide the time to perform such exercise. Exercise, both anaerobic (e.g., weightlifting) and aerobic (e.g., running, martial arts), should be a continual part of the officers' in-service training. This should not be relegated to the fitness officer, the SWAT team, or the academy instructors, but rather a routine part of *all* officers' duties. In addition, to compliment the focus on the physical, police departments should develop stress programs for officers and their families.[41]

ANTITERRORISM UNITS

In many countries around the world, unlike in the United States, the threat of terrorism has been a very consistent part of policing. Police officers are often the first to respond to terrorist threats and attacks and are often the actual targets of the terrorists themselves.[42] According to a report by Raymond E. Foster, "The data indicates that police officers worldwide are on the front line in the war against terror," and that "they are the ones making arrests, guarding critical facilities and responding to the scenes of terrorist acts."[43] In fact, according to Foster's data, worldwide there were over 3,000 terrorist incidents in 2004 with over 1,000 officers being killed and another 1,300 wounded.[44] As Foster explained, "A closer look at terrorist acts reveals that among the incidents involving police officers, fatalities occur during attempts to arrest terrorists, guard duty of critical facilities, response to situations, the conducting of routine operations, such as traffic control, and off-duty ambushes."[45] Although the numbers remain almost nonexistent in the United States, this does not mean that police departments should not be thinking about their capabilities for affecting the arrest of terrorists or responding to an ongoing terrorist incident.

The response to these threats in other countries has been the development of antiterrorism units. Although these units are similar to America's special weapons and tactics (SWAT) teams, they are specifically trained to deal with terrorist incidents. Examples include the half-dozen antiterrorism units of the Polish police or the Nucleo Operativo Centrale di Sicurezza of the Italian National Police. These units bear some resemblance to the American SWAT teams, such as uniforms, weapons, and tactical training, but their sole focus is on the response to terrorist or potential terrorist incidents. Whereas the typical SWAT response may work well for a bank robber, a hostage situation, or high-risk warrant execution against gang members or common criminals, they may not be as effective against terrorists who have different motives, training, and capabilities. Hence the training of antiterrorism units must be tailored to a terrorist response.

SWAT teams in the United States have expanded over the past 30 years since their early development in the late 1960s. Recent research has found that in 1980, approximately 55 percent of police departments serving populations over 50,000 had SWAT teams.[46] By the 1990s, that number had risen to an estimated 90 percent.[47] Recent scholarship has taken to calling this the "militarization" of policing, arguing that increased SWAT teams demonstrates that police are becoming more militarylike in their response to crime.[48] Although the adoption of SWAT teams by America's police departments hardly qualifies the police as becoming more like the military, this frivolous argument aside, what is needed under policing for homeland security is a unit that is highly prepared to respond to terrorist incidents or intervene in terrorist operations. If this means America's police must become more "militarylike," then so be it.

Large-city police departments, having the luxury of greater resources and more SWAT teams already in place, should pick the best, brightest, and most capable team to begin developing it as an antiterrorism unit (ATU). For medium to large agencies that cannot afford this luxury, the existing SWAT teams should begin receiving training on how a response to terrorism will change the police tactics of the SWAT team, so that they can be better prepared to respond to these types of situations. Tactical training should focus on scenarios in specific terrorist threat locations, including airplanes, subway systems, train stations, and large stadium events. The most advanced weapons and technology should be dedicated to this unit for its preparation. In addition, opportunities for training should be seized and made available to the ATU, especially through training and association with other ATUs in the United States, such as the FBI Hostage Rescue Team (HRT) and the U.S. Secret Service Counter Assault Team (CAT), but also with international ATUs throughout the world, including the aforementioned Polish and Italian ATUs and others. In addition, training with America's special forces group should be encouraged, as the terrorist situations these units have actually responded to can provide enormous insight into a police ATU that is going to have far less real-world experience.

COMMUNITY

One other aspect of police tactics for homeland security that should be considered is the role of the community. Although there has been much talk and rhetoric regarding how homeland security can be achieved through community policing, little has been paid to the specifics.[49] The general argument for why homeland security can be achieved through the auspices of community policing has to do with the ties created with the community by the police under this philosophical approach to policing. It is envisioned that these strong ties will allow for an open communication between citizens and police and that when coming across terrorists, citizens will report them to the police. The argument contains a number of assumptions. The first is that under community policing, the community and police have built strong ties. In many cases, community policing has been weakly implemented, and strong ties with the community are lacking. Assuming that where community policing has been successful, the police and citizens do have strong ties, there is another assumption that citizens will know what to look for in terms of suspicious terrorist behavior. In general, citizens will not be able to identify terrorists because if terrorists are successful in their mission, they will blend into the local community. Like the response after the discovery of many serial killers, the discovery that certain people were terrorists is typically along the lines of, "He was a nice neighbor or a very quiet individual." In fact, taken further, it is most likely that citizens, in identifying individuals as potential terrorist suspects, will draw more heavily on racial and ethnic profiling than would the police, as this is most likely all they will have to go on.

This is not to say that the community cannot play a role in homeland security or that community policing practices should be entirely dropped in favor of homeland security. It is merely saying that citizens will most likely play a very different role. The role that would be most fitting under homeland security is that of citizen volunteers reestablishing a civil defense role, one that local police could draw on in case of not only terrorist attacks, but natural disasters as well. Citizens, working with the police on a volunteer basis, should begin collaborating in preparation for possible terrorist attacks and different scenarios that may occur based on threat.

A perfect example for the potential collaboration between police and citizens comes from a legitimate threat and an innovative means of preparing to deal with such a threat. The bombings of train/metro stations in both Spain and England highlighted a very real threat to America's infrastructure, its railways. Police responded with beefed up patrols, but that is a severe drain of resources. Under community policing, the concept of police and citizen collaboration may be to have citizens riding the subway be the "eyes and ears" for the police on their individual trains. Although this is not inherently a bad idea, as with cell phone technology today, these "eyes and ears" can communicate in a rapid manner. However, more than likely, as in the Spain and England bombings, there will be no warning signs that even trained citizens will be prepared for. Once the bomb is detonated, other than contacting the local police at that point, the concepts of community policing essentially end.

Under the old civil defense model, updated to homeland security, a very important function of the citizen–police collaboration would begin. Citizens, trained by the police, would begin securing the area, attending to those injured, evacuating the subways, and helping people to the rail platforms, where they can receive medical attention. They would be trained to recognize whether or not the bomb was a conventional bomb or a WMD. Quickly understanding the nature of the incident would help not only the police, but also all first responders in understanding what they are dealing with, whether or not they need to secure a large area, and whether or not decontamination is necessary. If decontamination is going to be required, having citizens onboard the trains assists in the process would create a more orderly situation.

This is, in fact, what the Washington D.C., Metropolitan Transit Authority Police did under a program financed by the U.S. Department of Homeland Security and through the cooperation of surrounding police departments.[50] Citizens who regularly rode the metro subway in the Washington, D.C., area were asked to serve as citizen volunteers by undergoing 20 hours of training and learning how to navigate the tracks in a dark subway tunnel (keeping in mind that the third rail is electrified). According to Lyndsey Layton, a reporter for the *Washington Post,* "Members of the community emergency response teams were given backpacks, or 'go-bags,' that include a yellow Day-Glo safety vest, a green hard hat, safety goggles, gloves, a medical mask, flashlight, duct tape and other supplies."[51] This team is encouraged to carry these "go-bags" with them when they ride the metro. In addition, it is the intent of the Metro transit police to begin training regular riders who would volunteer for preparation training. As Captain Delinsky of the Metro police explained, "We know there's a demand for the public to be involved."[52] This is the type of involvement that would serve the community best under a police–community partnership for homeland security and is reminiscent of the original concept of civil defense.

This would not be limited to trains and subways, but could be expanded to all types of transit systems. In addition, any type of location identified through both threat and risk assessments, especially those identified as particularly vulnerable, could benefit from this

BOX 5-6

HOMELAND SECURITY TACTICS BY EXAMPLE: CITY OF WHITE PLAINS NEW YORK

Since 9-11, the City of White Plains Public Safety has taken a proactive stance in preparing its agency for homeland security. It has ensured its officers are adequately trained in a variety of areas that support the both the Homeland Security Strategy and Police Operations. The following are examples of the types of training received:

WMD Hazmat Technicians Course, Anniston, Alabama, July 2003
>   Members of both the Police and Fire Bureaus attended training in Anniston, Alabama, hosted by the Department of Justice Office of Domestic Preparedness. The training included working in a live WMD environment, collecting specimens, analyzing air and agent quality, collection of evidence, full-scale evacuations and large-scale decontamination. Members worked with live VX and GB nerve agents and practiced with level

A and C protective suits as well as SCBA and APR respirators. Some members who underwent the training have received certification as Office of Domestic Preparedness WMD instructors.

Water Rescue Technician Course, July 2003

With the opening of Liberty Park in White Plains, members of both the Police and Fire Bureaus were trained as Water Rescue Technicians. Training included all aspects of water rescue, including drowning victims, unconscious persons in the water, capsized boats, use of flotation devices, fire equipment utilization, and rescue boat operations.

Basic SWAT Training, November 2003

Select members of the Police Bureau received 40 hours of SWAT training, which was instructed by members of the National Tactical Officers Association. Members were introduced to basic SWAT tactics and techniques which included, but were not limited to: historical overview of SWAT, team organization and structure, resolution of barricaded suspect situations, covert individual and team movement, searches and room clearing, chemical agents, less-lethal options, high-risk warrant service, and multiple field training exercises.

Incident Response to Terrorist Bombings, Soccoro, New Mexico, March 2004

Police members traveled to New Mexico in March of 2004 to attend an awareness level course developed by the New Mexico Institute of Mining and Technology in association with the U.S. Department of Homeland Security. Course studies included the recognition and identification of explosives and incendiaries, incident response, first responder priorities, rescue and recovery, medical treatment and evacuation, fire suppression, and evidence recovery. The course focused on all types of explosive devices, ranging from small pipe bombs to large (500-lb.) car bombs. Students learned intricacies of these devices by constructing them themselves. Explosives were detonated and mock crime scenes established for evidence collection practice.

Volunteer Division CERT Training, April 2004

All White Plains Volunteer Division members have been asked to complete the Community Emergency Response Team (CERT) training program. The CERT program is administered by the New York State Emergency Management Office. The goal of the CERT program is to provide volunteers with basic skills needed to respond to the community's immediate needs in the aftermath of a natural or man-made disaster. CERT represents a vital component of the Department's mission to ensure the safety of our residents and visitors. The 20-hour course encompasses nine training units: Emergency Preparedness, Fire Safety, Emergency Medical Operations I, Emergency Medical Operations II, Light Search and Rescue Operations, CERT Organization, Disaster Psychology, Terrorism and CERT, and Disaster Simulation.

Thirty-five Volunteer Firefighters and 8 Auxiliary Police Officers have completed the first CERT training program. The second CERT training program started in the beginning of June of 2004 with a goal of training another 60 volunteers by December 15, 2004. A database listing CERT personnel has been established with emergency contact information. A call-out procedure has been developed for CERT members and was tested in a limited call-out of Volunteer Fire Officers. The Volunteer Division is also developing mobilization procedures for CERT.

WMD/Nuclear Responder Operations Course, April 2004.

Members of both the Police and Fire Bureaus attended a four-day Weapons of Mass Destruction/Nuclear Responder Operations Course, which was held in downtown White Plains. The course, hosted by Bechtel Nevada Counter Terrorism Operations Support, was delivered to municipalities and jurisdictions throughout the United States and its territories approved by the Office for Domestic Preparedness.

Training focused on basic radiological detection, survey instruments, risk-based response, crime-scene preservation, personal protective equipment, radiological decontamination, and mitigation of radiological incidents. The course consisted of both classroom instruction and scenario-driven, hands-on, performance-oriented practical exercises. The exercises provided realistic weapons of mass destruction (WMD) scenarios with a culmination exercise that included radiological sources, smoke, pyrotechnics, emergency response vehicles and role players.

Interview and Interrogation Training, May 2004

All members of the Criminal Investigations Division attended an Interview and Interrogation Course instructed by Special Agents of the U.S. Justice Department's Drug Enforcement Administration. Many interview and interrogation techniques were discussed and demonstrated. Other subject matter included environmental preparation and how to differentiate types of nonverbal behavior.

Source: White Plains Public Safety. (2005). *White Plains Public Safety Homepage.* Available online at *http://www.ci.white-plains.ny.us/safety/counter.htm;* downloaded December 7, 2005.

program. If the police and other first responders could identify the location, then work together to identify the regulars and secure volunteers, citizen involvement in homeland security would create an added layer of preparedness and enhance capabilities for an ordered response. For instance, regular season ticket holders at stadiums across the United States could be identified and trained for emergency preparedness. Regular office workers in high-rise buildings could also be identified and trained. These and other locations could benefit from having these citizens prepared to help in the event of not only a terrorist attack, but any type of attack or natural disaster for that matter. Additional training could also enhance the citizens' ability to identify suspicious behaviors or events and report them to the police. Essentially these would be trained "eyes and ears," rather than encouraging the public-at-large to identify sleeper cells of Al-Qaeda living among us.

TRAINING

Training is critical in all areas of policing for homeland security. Earl Sweeney has pointed out that the key to tactical intelligence is the line officer.[53] Police officers on a daily basis come across numerous people through calls-for-service, traffic stops, and routine patrol. However, as Sweeney laments, "This country has a largely untapped and unrecognized source of intelligence on terrorists and potential terrorist acts: the local police

BOX 5-7

LAW ENFORCEMENT INTELLIGENCE UNIT

On March 29, 1956, representatives from 26 law enforcement agencies met in San Francisco and formed the Law Enforcement Intelligence Unit (LEIU). LEIU records and exchanges confidential criminal information that is not available through regular police communication channels.

LEIU has performed a valuable coordinating function among law enforcement agencies throughout the United States, Canada, and Australia. Its membership is divided geographically into four zones: the Eastern Zone, Central Zone, Northwestern Zone, and Southwestern Zone. Each zone has a chairperson and a vice chairperson. The governing body of LEIU is the executive board, which established police and oversees the admission of law enforcement agencies applying for membership. The board is composed of national officers, zone officers, the past general chairperson, a legal advisor, and a representative from the California Deparment of Justice (which is the Central Coordinating Agency for LEIU).

LEIU membership is open to state and local law enforcement agencies that have a criminal intelligence function. Applicants must be sponsored by a current member. LEIU has approximately 250 members.

LEIU holds one annual training conference on general matters and one on gaming issues. It has a central repository pointer index that its members can query confidentially. LEIU produces publications on intelligence issues of interest to its members. It also offers a gaming index containing names and identifiers of individuals applying for gaming licenses. An analyst is available to respond to members' inquiries for information on suspected criminals and their activities.

Source: Peterson, M. (2005). *Intelligence-Led Policing: The New Intelligence Architecture.* Washington, D.C.: Bureau of Justice Assistance, p. 31; Law Enforcement Intelligence Unit. (2005). *Law Enforcement Intelligence Unit Homepage.* Available online at *http://www.leiu-homepage.org/index.php*; downloaded December 7, 2005.

officer, the county deputy sheriff, and the state trooper or highway patrol officer."[54] Sweeney explained that officers can become a crucial element to America's gathering of intelligence, but that the "challenge is to train them in what to look for, what to report, and how and to whom to report it, ensuring that appropriate follow-up occurs and that these officers receive feedback and appreciation for this efforts."[55]

Sweeney advocates a number of proposals for law enforcement to play a major role in the prevention of terrorism. He advocates education and training of law enforcement to understand the modus operandi of terrorists. He also encourages an international and comparative perspective to learn how terrorists have plied their trade in other countries and to educate themselves on what has worked with other law enforcement agencies across the globe in preventing terrorism. Training on terrorism must, like all other police training, begin in the academy, become part of the standard roll-call training, and should be made available for officer annual recertification training. In addition, police departments must consider sending their officers to both state- and nation-sponsored training on terrorism, as well as those seminars sponsored by terrorism think tanks, law enforcement institutes, and colleges and universities. Moreover, Sweeney advocates the use of nontraditional approaches to

BOX 5-8

MAIL FRAUD

Paul M. Klenowski, Thiel College

Mail fraud is a unique form of white-collar crime that can range from very simple forms of deceptive mail schemes to very elaborate scams in which many perpetrators are involved in various different countries. As a result, there are few law enforcement agencies with resources in place that are tasked to gauge the true prevalence and scope of these types of crimes. The Federal Bureau of Investigation's National Incident-Based Reporting System (NIBRS) collects same data on mail fraud, but the statistics are mixed in with various other types of fraud offenses, making it impossible to decipher exactly how many instances of mail fraud were reported for any given year. To get the most accurate picture of mail fraud, it is then necessary to turn to the agency mandated by Congress to investigate and prosecute these types of offenses, the U.S. Postal Inspection Service.

The U.S. Postal Inspection Service is the law enforcement branch of the U.S. Postal Service, sanctioned by Congress and guided by federal statutes and regulations to enforce and investigate any law violation that specifically deals with the use of the U.S. Postal services. As it currently stands, there are well over 200 federal statutes related to crimes against the Postal Service and its distribution of the mail.

There are currently over 1900 postal inspectors in the United States who investigate any instance in which the U.S. mail is used to carry out various forms of crime. Of these 1900 investigators, 300 are specifically tasked to deal with fraudulent cases involving the mail. Also, the Postal Inspection Service has also created a new unit called the Deceptive Mail Enforcement Team, which seeks to identify those individuals or companies who administer false promotions and sweepstakes offerings that defraud customers by promising items (i.e., vacations, jewelry, cars) in exchange for personal information or coercing the individual into buying their product. Postal inspectors also work very closely with state and local law enforcement organizations and federal regulatory agencies to assist in combating the problem of mail fraud.

Postal inspectors base their case investigations on the quantity, frequency, pattern of activity, and various other facts regarding complaints received from the general public. In 2003 alone, the Postal Service took over 80,000 customer complaints resulting in roughly 1,500 criminal arrests.

According to the Postal Inspection Service statistics, on average, the inspectors investigate well over 3,000 mail fraud cases a year. In fiscal year 2003 alone, the number of cases investigated by inspectors was 3,150 and the number of mail fraudsters arrested and convicted was 1,453. Also, a great majority of these cases involved suspected international terrorist groups who were attempting to procure resources (money, weapons, identities, and passports) to further their illicit activities. With the skill and proficiency of the criminals becoming more refined coupled with new technological advances, the number of these cases will indeed continue to increase with each passing year. As a result, better means of prevention, detection, and prosecution coupled with research and analysis of how these crimes are committed is drastically needed to truly begin to understand the scope and prevalence of mail fraud in the United States.

antiterrorism training such as CDs, DVDs, and Web-based tutorials, as well as satellite broadcasts. The more educated officers can become on terrorism, antiterrorism, and counterterrorism, the better prepared they will be to protect the homeland.

Sweeney recognizes the limitations of classroom training and advocates practical training that can be conducted on a regular basis because, as he put it, "the skills needed to combat terrorism are perishable."[56] He cited that "some academies recently have added terrorist scenarios to their firearms training and vehicular pursuit simulators," whereas "others have included them in their officer survival scenarios in their basic and in-service programs."[57] These terrorist drills provide a coordinated, supervised activity that can test a single function within an agency.[58] In the two cases listed, it provides training to officers on deadly force encounters with terrorists and special concerns related to vehicle pursuits of terrorist suspects. These tactical drills can also teach officers how to react to suicide bombers, weapon of mass destruction detonation/dispersal, or crowd control at a decontamination site. The benefit is they are narrowly focused, provide instant feedback to the officers, can be performed in a realistic environment, and evaluate performance in isolation of other factors.

Another type of training that can benefit police officers is scenario-based training. Scenario-based training is essentially "an amalgamation of knowledge and skills-based training"[59] and is perhaps most critical for training in anti- and counterterrorism, as the number of actual situations will be extremely rare, thus limiting the amount of exposure an officer will have to tactical decision making in these events. These types of training exercises allow officers to employ their drill training to see how the various drills work in concert with one another. These can still remain on a limited scale, but are not relegated to the narrow focus of one specific skill.

Finally, the full-scale exercise is the most complex of the training exercises. These exercises are often multiagency and multijurisdictional exercises that can test many facets of emergency response and recovery.[60] They include many first responders operating under the incident command system (ICS) or unified command system (UCS) to effectively and efficiently respond to, and recover from, an incident. A full-scale exercise focuses on implementing and analyzing the plans, policies, and procedures previously developed to test

BOX 5-9

TOPOFF NATIONAL EXERCISE SERIES

TOPOFF (Top Officials National Exercise Series) is a congressionally mandated, national, biennial exercise series designed to assess the nation's capability to prevent, respond to, and recover from acts of terrorism. It examines relationship among federal, state, and local jurisdictions in response to a challenging series of integrated, geographically dispersed terrorist threats and acts. Participation in TOPOFF is by application and subsequent invitation. Department of Homeland Security (DHS) and the Office of Domestic Preparedness (ODP) manages the design, planning, conduct, and evaluation of the exercises. This exercise series is typically codirected by DHS/ODP and other federal agencies or departments. TOPOFF 2000 was codirected by DHS/ODP and the Federal Emergency Management Agency (FEMA).

TOPOFF 2, completed in May 2003, was codirected by DHS/ODP and the U.S. Department of State. TOPOFF 3 was a full-scale exercise that took place from April 4–8, 2005, and involved more than 10,000 participants representing more than 200 federal, state, local, tribal, private-sector, and international agencies and organizations and volunteer groups. The venues for the exercise included a simulated chemical attack in New London, Connecticut, and a simulated biological attack in Union and Middlesex Counties, New Jersey. The exercise took place over several days allowing police officers to respond to the initial 911 calls, fire personnel to conduct search and rescue operations, and hospitals to treat the injured (played by role players).

Source: Office of Domestic Preparedness. (2004). *Homeland Security Exercise and Evaluation Program.* *Vol. 1: Overview and Doctrine.* Washington, D.C.: U.S. Department of Homeland Security, p. 8.

their capabilities and adjust them accordingly. The events are projected through a scripted exercise scenario with built-in flexibility to allow updates to drive activity. It is conducted in a real-time, stressful environment that closely mirrors a real event. First responders and resources are mobilized and deployed to the scene where they conduct their actions as if a real incident had occurred. The full-scale exercise simulates the reality of operations in multiple functional areas by presenting complex and realistic problems requiring critical thinking, rapid problem solving, and effective responses by trained personnel in a highly stressful environment. The benefits of conducting a full-scale drill is that they allow agencies to assess organizational as well as individual performance, evaluate interagency cooperation, determine how best to allocate resources and personnel, assess equipment capabilities, work through the process of activating personnel and equipment, exercise the public information system, test communication systems and procedures, and analyze the effectiveness of memorandums of agreement, standard operating procedures (SOPs), plans, policies, and the overall strategy. A good example of these full-scale exercises is the federal government's TOPOFF exercise, which has consisted of not only federal responders, but state and local responders as well.

Although drills and scenario-based training can be developed and executed with relative ease, as they are dealing with more limited concepts and resources, larger scale, mutijurisdictional exercises, whether they are command staff training or full-scale exercises, require far more detailed planning and preparation. The planning process includes managing the project, convening a planning team, conducting planning conferences, identifying exercise design objectives, developing the scenario and documentation, assigning logistical tasks, and identifying the evaluation methodology.[61] As the tactical value for such an exercise is high, it is important to understand the process for building such an exercise.

To establish a foundation for designing, developing, conducting, and evaluating an exercise, project management is essential and involves the following tasks: developing a project management timeline and establishing milestones, identifying a planning team, and scheduling planning conferences. Timelines should be established through a memorandum of agreement by all vested parties and should begin with the actual exercise date that is between one and two years out. Utilizing backward planning, the specific

BOX 5-10

IDENTITY THEFT

Paul M. Klenowski, Thiel College

What Is Identity Theft?

The crime of identity theft occurs when individuals without permission transfer, take, or use the private information of others for their own personal and financial benefit. The types of information sought by these thieves include Social Security numbers, driver's license information, military records, passport and citizenship information, insurance records, tax returns, credit card numbers, and other types of financial account information. Identity theft is considered a "gateway" crime because it literally is used to open the gate of criminal activity to commit various other types of criminal offenses (e.g., passport fraud, credit card fraud, mail fraud, and embezzlement).

Prevalence

Today, the crime of identity theft is the fastest growing crime in the United States. In fact, according to the Federal Trade Commission in fiscal year 2003 alone, it had been estimated that over 10 million Americans had their identity stolen. Over a five-year period, the federal government has estimated that nearly 30 million American citizens have had their identities stolen and used for the commission of various forms of crime.

Law Enforcement Response

The need for stronger law enforcement efforts against identity theft is evident in the fact that only about 1 in 700 federal cases and 1 in 5,000 state and local cases results in the capture and successful prosecution of offenders by federal and state law enforcement officials. One of the most pressing issues facing law enforcement is the lack of training and resources available to aid in detection and investigation of these often complex cases of identity theft.

Today, all 50 U.S. states along with the federal government have established both laws and specialized investigative divisions to aid in the investigation and prosecution of identity theft cases. The U.S. Department of Justice now recognizes that all identity theft cases are serious offenses, even when no money is actually taken from a victim. On the federal level, violations of federal identity theft statutes are examined and investigated by the U.S. Secret Service (i.e., the only law enforcement agency in the country mandated by Congress to investigate all cases of identity theft), the Postal Inspector Service, and the Federal Bureau of Investigation. These federal cases tend to be high-dollar, high-profile cases that cross state and sometimes international lines and that fall under the auspices of federal jurisdiction. For example, many of the individuals that the Department of Justice and the Department of Homeland Security are still holding in conjunction with the terrorist attacks of September 11, 2001, are currently being incarcerated under federal identity theft and passport fraud statutes.

State and local cases, on the other hand, are usually investigated by specialized members of a multiagency task force within a particular region or state. These task forces are usually spearheaded by local and state district attorneys who look to collectively assemble experts in the various areas of detection, investigation, and prosecution of identity theft cases. These task force members usually have had numerous training courses and practical work experience in dealing with various forms of identity theft and fraud. It should also be mentioned that a majority of these state and local task forces have now joined with federal investigators and prosecutors to attempt to make a unified stance against these types of crimes. For example, the U.S. Secret Service has assisted in creating regional identity theft task forces that bring together various levels of law enforcement, prosecutorial staff, research analysts, scholars, and other government officials to join efforts in combating identity theft in America. The first task force of its kind created by the U.S. Secret Service began its operations in 1995 and was called the Electronic Crimes Task Force of New York. Today, every region of the United States has a task force of this type, and it has started to make a noticeable impact against identity theft in this country. Unfortunately, however, the victimization rate in United States continues to grow, ultimately meaning that more funding, training, and resources must continue to be funneled into our nation's efforts against the new crime epidemic of identity theft.

requirements can be detailed by specific dates as deadlines, thus creating the necessary milestones needed to work toward the final exercise. Once the various actors are all identified and a memorandum of agreement is signed to enter into the planning process, an exercise planning team should be identified.

The exercise planning team is responsible for designing, developing, conducting, and evaluating all aspects of an exercise. The planning team determines exercise design objectives, tailors the scenario to jurisdictional needs, and develops documents used in exercise evaluation, control, and simulation. Planning team members also help with developing and distributing preexercise materials and conducting exercise briefings and training sessions. Due to this high level of involvement, planning team members are ideal selections for observer/controllers and evaluators during the exercise itself.

The exercise planning team is managed by an exercise director. The team should be a manageable size and include a representative from each major participating jurisdiction and response agency. The membership of an exercise planning team should be modified to fit the type or scope of an exercise. The exercise planning team should use the ICS structure, so that the exercise, as it develops, will include perspectives from all the key ICS players. This helps it define each member's role, responsibilities, and functional area skills during the planning and execution of the exercise.

A series of planning conferences should be utilized throughout the planning process to ensure that the exercise remains on schedule and that all the vested parties have a chance to have their needs and concerns voiced. The first meeting is to develop the memorandum of agreement that an agency will be signing on and committing to the exercise. This concept and objectives meeting should be used to identify the type, scope, objectives, and purpose of the exercise. This is typically attended by the sponsoring agency, lead exercise planner, and senior officials from the various agencies that have signing authority.

Once the concept meeting results in a signed agreement, the initial planning conference (IPC) should be scheduled. The IPC lays the foundation for exercise development. It is used to gather input from the exercise planning team on the scope, design, objectives and scenario variables (e.g., hazard selection, venue). The IPC obtains the planning team's input on exercise location, schedule, duration, and other details required to develop exercise documentation. Planning team members should be assigned responsibility for the tasks outlined in the meeting.

At the halfway point between the initial planning conference and the exercise, there should be a midterm planning conference (MPC). The MPC presents an additional opportunity in the planning timeline to settle logistical and organizational issues that arise during planning such as staffing concepts, scheduling, logistics, administrative requirements, and reviewing draft documentation.

As the exercise approaches, a final planning conference (FPC) should be conducted, usually one to two weeks prior to the exercise. This is a forum to review the process and procedures for conducting the exercise, final drafts of all exercise materials, and all logistical requirements. There should be no major changes made to either the design or the scope of the exercise or to any supporting documentation.

Building on the exercise foundation, the design and development process should focus on identifying objectives, designing the scenario, creating documentation, coordinating logistics, planning exercise conduct, and selecting an evaluation and improvement methodology. The first of these, exercise objectives, defines specific goals, provides a framework for scenario development, guides individual organizational objective development, and provides exercise evaluation criteria. Generally, planners will limit the number of exercise objectives to enable timely execution, facilitate design of a reasonable scenario, and adequately support successful completion of exercise goals.

The actual scenario used provides the backdrop and story line that drives an exercise. The first step in designing the scenario is determining the type of threat/hazard (e.g., chemical, biological, radiological, nuclear, explosive, cyber, or other). Thought should be given to creating a scenario that involves local incidents and local facilities and is based on exercise objectives derived from the jurisdiction's risk and vulnerability assessments (see Chapter 4). For example, if the risk and vulnerability assessment identified a critical infrastructure at a local facility (such as a refinery, chemical plant, sport stadium) as a vulnerable target, the scenario could describe a terrorist event at that facility. Each type of hazard presents its own stengths and weaknesses for evaluating different aspects of prevention, response, and recovery and is applicable to different exercise objectives. Scenarios should not, however, include an "everything but the kitchen sink approach," in that they must be realistic.

The next step is to determine the venue (facility or site) that the scenario will affect. Venue selection should be based on the type of hazard used. For example, if a nonpersistent chemical agent (e.g., sarin) is selected, the venue should not be an open-air facility (e.g., a sport stadium) because of the agent's dissipating characteristics. Once this is completed, the next step is to begin collecting information to create a number of documents. These documents are often generated in concert together so that issues, as they relate to each other, are adequately identified. The five documents to be developed include the exercise plan, the controller and evaluator handbook, the master scenario events list, the exercise evaluation guidelines, and exercise policies.

The exercise plan (EXPLAN) is typically used for operations-based exercises. It provides an exercise synopsis and is published and distributed prior to the start of the exercise. In addition to addressing exercise objectives and scope, the EXPLAN assigns tasks and responsibilities for successful exercise execution. The EXPLAN should not contain detailed scenario information, such as the hazard to be employed. This document is generally intended for exercise players and observers.

The controller and evaluator handbook (C/E Handbook) supplements the EXPLAN, containing more detailed information about the exercise scenario and describing exercise controllers' and evaluators' roles and responsibilities. Because the C/E handbook contains information on the scenario and exercise administration, it should only be distributed to those individuals specifically designated as controllers and evaluators.

The master scenario events list (MSEL) is a chronological timeline of expected actions and scripted events to be injected into exercise play by controllers to generate or prompt player activity. It ensures necessary events happen so that all objectives are met.

The exercise evaluation guidelines (EEGs) are to help with exercise evaluation. These guides incorporate the critical tasks that should be completed in the exercise. The EEGs have been developed for use by experienced exercise evaluators, as well as by practitioners who are subject matter experts but have little or no exercise evaluation experience. EEGs provide evaluators with information on what they should expect to see, space to record observations, and questions to address after the exercise as a first step in the analysis process.

Finally, the exercise policies are developed to provide guidance or parameters of acceptable practices for designing, developing, conducting, and evaluating exercises. They are designed to prevent or, at a minimum, mitigate the impact of an action that may cause bodily harm to participants, destruction of property, or embarrassment to the local community and participating agencies. Agencies should develop policies appropriate to the type of exercise that address safety, media, cancellation, weather, and weapons safety.

After the design and development tasks are completed, the exercise takes place. Exercise conduct details include setup, briefings, facilitation/control, and wrap-up activities. In regard to setup, the planning team should visit the exercise site at least one day, if not several days, prior to the event to set up the site. On the day of the exercise, planning team members should arrive early before the scheduled start to handle any remaining logistical or administrative items pertaining to setup and to arrange for registration. Facilities must be available for presentations and briefings of all the exercise participants to discuss exercise policies and safety. In addition, for an operations-based exercise, planners must consider the assembly area, response routes, response operations area, parking, registration, observer/media accommodations, and a facility for the various volunteers playing roles in the exercise. Restrooms and water should be available to all participants, observers, and actors. All individuals permitted at the exercise should be wearing some form of identification. Perimeter security and site safety during both setup and the exercise are essential.

Once assembled, presentations and briefings should be used as a tool for delivering information to all participants. This may include briefings from controllers/evaluators, hospitals, actors, players, and observer/media. This is also the time to distribute exercise documentation, provide necessary administrative information, and answer any last-minute questions.

In the operations-based exercise, controllers will manage exercise play, set up and operate the exercise incident site, and possibly take the roles of response individuals and

BOX 5-11

FEDERAL LAW ENFORCEMENT TRAINING CENTER (FLETC)

Paul M. Klenowski, Thiel College

The Federal Law Enforcement Training Center, also known as FLETC, is a law enforcement partnership funded by the federal government and operating under the Department of Homeland Security. FLETC's mission is to offer high-quality professional law enforcement training at cost-efficient prices. This federal training center provides both federal law enforcement officers (excluding Federal Bureau of Investigation officers and agents) and state, local, and international police officers and agents with a multitude of training courses on a variety of different basic and specialty law enforcement topics.

Mission and Operations

As previously stated, FLETC was created to serve as a high-quality training center for federal law enforcement officers. Since its inception, the mission has expanded to include law enforcement officers at various levels throughout the United States and abroad. Currently, FLETC offers over 200 training programs and courses ranging from basic to advanced policing and investigative techniques to international courses regarding global terrorism. All these programs are continually evaluated and assessed through curriculum meetings and student evaluation reports to ensure that the quality of instruction remains extremely high, professional, and efficient. Based on the needs of a particular agency, FLETC officials also offer a unique selection of technical, clerical, and managerial support services to enhance the overall training needs of the participating agency.

FLETC instructors are experienced and highly trained professionals who have at least five years of law enforcement or investigative experience. Instructors range from federal officers and investigators on assignment from their respective agencies to state and local police officers who have specialized skills in a particular area (i.e., fingerprint analysis, forensic investigation) to civil instructors who have particular training in a law enforcement–related field (e.g., hand-to-hand combat, behavioral profiling, fraud investigation). Instructors include both full- and part-time faculty who are complemented by a full-time support staff.

It is also important to note that because both the Oklahoma City Federal building bombing and the terrorist attacks of 9/11, the Federal Training Center has seen a tremendous increase in issues involving terrorism. As a result, the need to create more specific courses centering on international and domestic terrorism has become one of the new operating goals of FLETC. With respect to international terrorism, FLETC has become an important venue for international officers and government officials to learn about the potential concerns regarding global terrorism.

History

FLETC officially took shape on March 2, 1970, and began its official operations in Washington D.C. Later in 1975, the center was relocated to its present headquarters near Brunswick, Georgia, in the small town of Glynco. The creation of FLETC was the result of a 1968 study conducted by an interagency task force comprised of various federal law enforcement agencies. The results of the study indicated that federal law enforcement officers reporting to the various federal agencies had no consistency in their formal law enforcement training. One of the major concerns with the study's findings centered on the fact that most federal law enforcement officers lacked the appropriate training, knowledge, and specific skill sets to do their job at even a minimum level of efficiency. In fact, most federal law enforcement training up to 1970 was conducted by part-time instructors, in dilapidated facilities, and with no consistent schedule of training courses or particular subject material.

To address this problem, the interagency task force proposed that a central Federal Law Enforcement Training Center be established. This proposed recommendation called for a centrally located state-of-the-art training facility that was to be operated and managed by a full-time staff that looked to offer high-quality programs ranging from basic law enforcement courses to highly specific investigative classes on a wide array of topics (e.g., money laundering investigation, drug identification, fraud investigation). Finally, in 1970, the federal interagency task force signed a federal Memorandum of Understanding for the Establishment of the Consolidated Federal Law Enforcement Training Center. It was further decided that the U.S. Treasury Department would provide both managerial and administrative support for the new facility because the department had already established a successful interbureau training organization known as the Treasury Law Enforcement Training School. At the conclusion of its first year of operation in 1970, FLETC graduated 848 police officers from the center. By the end of 1975, the number of graduates had climbed to well over 5,000 officers. Since 1970, more than 325,000 federal, state, local, and foreign law enforcement officers have successfully graduated from one of the many training courses and programs that FLETC has offered.

Organization

Today, FLETC is part of the Department of Homeland Security with a director who specifically answers to the Under Secretary for Border and Transportation Security. FLETC is governed by an eight-person interagency board of directors representing various federal law enforcement agencies throughout the country. Assisting the FLETC director is an executive staff comprising one deputy director, six assistant directors, a team of legal counsel, and a chief-of-staff operations.

Today, FLETC offers training to a majority of federal officers and agents from more than 80 different federal agencies. Along with federal law enforcement training, the center also provides instruction to hundreds of state, local, and international police agencies. On average, FLETC graduates more than 50,000 officers a year from their numerous training programs with an annual budget of more than $200 million. Currently, FLETC's 1,500-acre training center is now the largest in the United States and is now considered to be one of the elite training facilities in the world. Along with its main center in Glynco, Georgia, the center now has four satellite training campuses that offer a vast array of law enforcement courses. These FLETC centers are located in Cheltenham, Maryland, Charleston, South Carolina, Artesia, New Mexico, and Gaborone, Botswana, Africa.

agencies not actually participating in the exercise. For instance, if the agencies on scene request support from the Federal Bureau of Investigation, which is not a participant in the exercise, the controller/evaluators will serve as the representatives of this agency. Controllers also give key data to players and may prompt or initiate certain player actions based on the MSEL to ensure that objectives are met and the exercise maintains continuity. Controllers are the only participants who should provide information or direction to the players. All controllers should be accountable to one senior controller, who serves as the exercise director.

If the exercise proceeds well and the mission is being accomplished, the exercise should continue to play out and follow the MSEL. If certain agencies are not performing as expected and are deviating heavily from a standard response, the exercise can be halted for a midpoint debriefing or hot wash (see Assessment, following). Once a review of what is going well and what is going poorly is made, recommendations for improvements can be made prior to continuing with the exercise. Once the exercise is completed, both a debrief and hot wash should occur immediately, which should then be followed by an after-action analysis and formal report.

ASSESSMENT

After any major event, such as those that occurred on 9-11, agencies should conduct evaluations to determine what went well and what went poorly, and more specifically, how best to improve in the future. An after-action review, which is a professional discussion of an event, focused on performance standards, helps police officers to discover for themselves what happened, why it happened, and how to sustain strengths and improve on weaknesses. Ultimately, what should be produced from the more informal after-action review is a formal after-action report, such as the one published by the Arlington County Police Department, based on their response to the attack on the Pentagon on 9-11.[62] The most important element of the after-action report is the improvement plan. It should identify weaknesses in the response to the significant event and offer means to improve. This improvement plan should then become part of the operational plan to improve standard operating procedures, update or change the methods for deploying technology, or identify specific tactical training or changes to current training necessary.

Recognizing, however, that most agencies will not experience such major events as the Arlington County Police Department (The ACPD had also responded to the Air Florida Crash into the 14th Street Bridge on January 13, 1982), operational exercises can provide the necessary means of identifying strengths and weaknesses in an agency's ability to respond to a major incident, terrorist or natural, and improvement plans can be identified through debriefings and hot washes after these exercises. Therefore, any exercise should also use some form of evaluation and assessment, as well as after-action reports, to identify areas of improvement.

As evaluated practice activities, exercises provide a process for continuous improvement.[63] Evaluation is the cornerstone of exercises; it documents strengths and opportunities and improvement in a jurisdiction's preparedness. The evaluation process for all exercises includes a formal exercise evaluation, integrated analysis, and an after-action report and improvement plan that should begin with exercise planning and end when improvements have been implemented and validated through subsequent exercises. The methods used include debriefings, hot washes, after-action reports, and improvement plans.

A debrief is a forum for planners, facilitators, controllers, and evaluators to review and provide feedback on an exercise. It should be a facilitated discussion that allows each person an opportunity to provide an overview of the functional area they observed and document both strengths and areas for improvement. The debrief should be facilitated by the lead exercise planner or the exercise director. The results of the debriefing should be captured by a recorder for inclusion in the after-action report.

A hot wash occurs immediately following an exercise and allows players/responders the opportunity to provide immediate feedback. It enables controllers and evaluators to capture the events while they remain fresh in players' minds. The first aspect of the hot wash should focus on the scenario and the response to the exercise. It should explore what went well and what went poorly in the response to the exercises incident. The second aspect of the hot wash should attempt to ascertain players' level of satisfaction with the exercise and determine any issues or concerns and proposed improvement items. Again, like the debrief, every hot wash should have a recorder to capture the information for the after-action report.

The after-action report is used to provide feedback to participating jurisdictions on their performance during the exercise. The after-action report summarizes what happened and analyzes performance of the tasks identified through the planning process as critical and the demonstrated capacity to accomplish the overall exercise goal. The AAR includes recommendations for improvements based on the analysis, which will be addressed in the improvement plan.

To prepare the report, the exercise evaluation team will analyze data collected from the hot wash and debriefings, participant evaluations, and other sources (e.g., plans, procedures) and compare the actual results with the intended outcome. The level of detail in an AAR reflects the type and size of the exercise. AARs describe the exercise scenario, player activities, preliminary observations, major issues, and recommendations for improvement.

The improvement plan, which can be part of the AAR or separate, converts lessons learned from the exercise into concrete, measurable steps that result in improvement response capabilities. It is developed by the jurisdiction and specifically details the actions that will be taken to address each recommendation in the AAR, who or what agency will be responsible for taking the action, and the timeline for completion. This review process may identify needs for additional equipment, training, exercises, coordination, plans, and procedures that can be addressed through the homeland security strategy and operations.

CONCLUSION

In a forum related to the future of policing in the March–April 2005 issues of *The Futurist,* a panel of experts all agreed that homeland security has become the overriding strategy of policing.[64] They acknowledged the threat of terrorism, both international and domestic, as being a continued threat in the future, and they also stated a fear that domestic criminals may learn from the terrorists and begin employing their tactics. To best respond to these threats, the panelists agreed that police tactics, complimented by advances in technology, and better educated and trained officers will adequately prepare them for this new role. However, all the panelists were concerned about the availability of funding to adequately meet this new mission. In fact, one of the panelists, Judith Lewis, lamented that "the expectations of law enforcement as first responder for homeland security have put an almost unachievable burden on local law enforcement."[65] Although this burden may be heavy, to meet the demands of homeland security, it is imperative that policing focus on the police tactics necessary to accomplish the mission.

A homeland security strategy for police should drive police operations and ultimately police tactics. It is imperative that police tactics evolve and change to meet the demands. Policing must learn to prevent future terrorist attacks by applying intelligence gathering to its standard operating procedures. It must be adequately prepared to deal with large-scale events, WMD, officer safety, and a whole host of other preparatory concerns. In addition, it must be ready to respond by continually assessing its technology, training, and education on anti- and counterterrorism measures. But most important, it must ensure that tactically, police officers are prepared for their homeland security role. Remembering the words of Sun Tzu that "strategy without tactics is the slowest route to victory"[66] should mobilize police departments to concentrate much of their resources on police tactics for homeland security. However, it must also ensure that strategy ultimately drives tactics, for as the other part of Sun Tzu's utterance states: "Tactics without strategy is the noise before defeat."[67]

Roll Call of Those Police Officers Who Died on September 11, 2001

NEW YORK CITY POLICE DEPARTMENT

Sergeant John G. Coughlin
Sergeant Michael S. Curtin
Police Officer John D'Allara
Police Officer Vincent G. Danz
Police Officer Jerome M. Dominguez
Police Officer Stephen P. Driscoll
Police Officer Mark J. Ellis
Police Officer Robert Fazio
Sergeant Rodney C. Gillis
Police Officer Ronald P. Kloepfer
Police Officer Thomas M. Langone
Police Officer James P. Leahy
Police Officer Brian G. McDonnell
Police Officer John W. Perry
Police Officer Glen K. Pettit
Detective Claude D. Richards
Sergeant Timothy A. Roy
Police Officer Moira A. Smith
Police Officer Ramon Suarez

Police Officer Paul Talty
Police Officer Santos Valentin
Detective Joseph V. Vigiano
Police Officer Walter E. Weaver

PORT AUTHORITY POLICE DEPARTMENT NEW YORK/NEW JERSEY

Police Officer Christopher C. Amoroso
Police Officer Maurice Vincent Barry
Police Officer Liam Callahan
Lieutenant Robert D. Cirri, Sr.
Police Officer Clinton Davis, Sr.
Police Officer Donald A. Foreman
Police Officer Gregg John Froehner
Police Officer Thomas Edward Gorman
Police Officer Uhuru Gonja Houston
Police Officer George G. Howard
Police Officer Stephen Huczko, Jr.
Inspector Anthony P. Infante, Jr.
Police Officer Paul W. Jurgens
Sergeant Robert M. Kaulfers
Police Officer Paul Laszczynski
Police Officer David P. Lemagne
Police Officer John J. Lennon
Police Officer J. D. Levi
Police Officer James F. Lynch
Captain Kathy N. Mazza
Police Officer Donald J. McIntyre
Police Officer Walter Arthur McNeil
Superintendent Fred V. Morrone
Police Officer Joseph N. Navas
Police Officer James A. Nelson
Police Officer Alfonse J. Niedermeyer, III
Police Officer James W. Parham
Police Officer Dominick Pezzulo
Police Officer Bruce A. Reynolds
Police Officer Antonio Jose Rodrigues
Police Officer Richard Rodriguez
Chief James A. Romito
Police Officer John P. Skala
Police Officer Walwyn W. Stuart, Jr.
Police Officer Kenneth F. Tietjen
Police Officer Nathaniel Webb
Police Officer Michael T. Wholey

The President's Address to a Joint Session of Congress and the American People September 20, 2001

THE PRESIDENT: Mr. Speaker, Mr. President Pro Tempore, members of Congress, and fellow Americans:

In the normal course of events, Presidents come to this chamber to report on the state of the Union. Tonight, no such report is needed. It has already been delivered by the American people.

We have seen it in the courage of passengers, who rushed terrorists to save others on the ground—passengers like an exceptional man named Todd Beamer. And would you please help me to welcome his wife, Lisa Beamer, here tonight.

We have seen the state of our Union in the endurance of rescuers, working past exhaustion. We have seen the unfurling of flags, the lighting of candles, the giving of blood, the saying of prayers—in English, Hebrew, and Arabic. We have seen the decency of a loving and giving people who have made the grief of strangers their own.

My fellow citizens, for the last nine days, the entire world has seen for itself the state of our Union—and it is strong.

Tonight we are a country awakened to danger and called to defend freedom. Our grief has turned to anger, and anger to resolution. Whether we bring our enemies to justice, or bring justice to our enemies, justice will be done.

I thank the Congress for its leadership at such an important time. All of America was touched on the evening of the tragedy to see Republicans and Democrats joined together on the steps of this Capitol, singing "God Bless America." And you did more than sing;

you acted, by delivering $40 billion to rebuild our communities and meet the needs of our military.

Speaker Hastert, Minority Leader Gephardt, Majority Leader Daschle and Senator Lott, I thank you for your friendship, for your leadership and for your service to our country.

And on behalf of the American people, I thank the world for its outpouring of support. America will never forget the sounds of our National Anthem playing at Buckingham Palace, on the streets of Paris, and at Berlin's Brandenburg Gate.

We will not forget South Korean children gathering to pray outside our embassy in Seoul, or the prayers of sympathy offered at a mosque in Cairo. We will not forget moments of silence and days of mourning in Australia and Africa and Latin America.

Nor will we forget the citizens of 80 other nations who died with our own: dozens of Pakistanis; more than 130 Israelis; more than 250 citizens of India; men and women from El Salvador, Iran, Mexico and Japan; and hundreds of British citizens. America has no truer friend than Great Britain. Once again, we are joined together in a great cause—so honored the British Prime Minister has crossed an ocean to show his unity of purpose with America. Thank you for coming, friend.

On September the 11th, enemies of freedom committed an act of war against our country. Americans have known wars—but for the past 136 years, they have been wars on foreign soil, except for one Sunday in 1941. Americans have known the casualties of war—but not at the center of a great city on a peaceful morning. Americans have known surprise attacks—but never before on thousands of civilians. All of this was brought upon us in a single day—and night fell on a different world, a world where freedom itself is under attack.

Americans have many questions tonight. Americans are asking: Who attacked our country? The evidence we have gathered all points to a collection of loosely affiliated terrorist organizations known as al Qaeda. They are the same murderers indicted for bombing American embassies in Tanzania and Kenya, and responsible for bombing the USS Cole.

Al Qaeda is to terror what the mafia is to crime. But its goal is not making money; its goal is remaking the world—and imposing its radical beliefs on people everywhere.

The terrorists practice a fringe form of Islamic extremism that has been rejected by Muslim scholars and the vast majority of Muslim clerics—a fringe movement that perverts the peaceful teachings of Islam. The terrorists' directive commands them to kill Christians and Jews, to kill all Americans, and make no distinction among military and civilians, including women and children.

This group and its leader—a person named Osama bin Laden—are linked to many other organizations in different countries, including the Egyptian Islamic Jihad and the Islamic Movement of Uzbekistan. There are thousands of these terrorists in more than 60 countries. They are recruited from their own nations and neighborhoods and brought to camps in places like Afghanistan, where they are trained in the tactics of terror. They are sent back to their homes or sent to hide in countries around the world to plot evil and destruction.

The leadership of al Qaeda has great influence in Afghanistan and supports the Taliban regime in controlling most of that country. In Afghanistan, we see al Qaeda's vision for the world.

Afghanistan's people have been brutalized—many are starving and many have fled. Women are not allowed to attend school. You can be jailed for owning a television. Religion can be practiced only as their leaders dictate. A man can be jailed in Afghanistan if his beard is not long enough.

The United States respects the people of Afghanistan—after all, we are currently its largest source of humanitarian aid—but we condemn the Taliban regime. It is not only repressing its own people, it is threatening people everywhere by sponsoring and sheltering and supplying terrorists. By aiding and abetting murder, the Taliban regime is committing murder.

And tonight, the United States of America makes the following demands on the Taliban: Deliver to United States authorities all the leaders of al Qaeda who hide in your land. Release all foreign nationals, including American citizens, you have unjustly imprisoned. Protect foreign journalists, diplomats and aid workers in your country. Close immediately and permanently every terrorist training camp in Afghanistan, and hand over every terrorist, and every person in their support structure, to appropriate authorities. Give the United States full access to terrorist training camps, so we can make sure they are no longer operating.

These demands are not open to negotiation or discussion. The Taliban must act, and act immediately. They will hand over the terrorists, or they will share in their fate.

I also want to speak tonight directly to Muslims throughout the world. We respect your faith. It's practiced freely by many millions of Americans, and by millions more in countries that America counts as friends. Its teachings are good and peaceful, and those who commit evil in the name of Allah blaspheme the name of Allah. The terrorists are traitors to their own faith, trying, in effect, to hijack Islam itself. The enemy of America is not our many Muslim friends; it is not our many Arab friends. Our enemy is a radical network of terrorists, and every government that supports them.

Our war on terror begins with al Qaeda, but it does not end there. It will not end until every terrorist group of global reach has been found, stopped and defeated.

Americans are asking, why do they hate us? They hate what we see right here in this chamber—a democratically elected government. Their leaders are self-appointed. They hate our freedoms—our freedom of religion, our freedom of speech, our freedom to vote and assemble and disagree with each other.

They want to overthrow existing governments in many Muslim countries, such as Egypt, Saudi Arabia, and Jordan. They want to drive Israel out of the Middle East. They want to drive Christians and Jews out of vast regions of Asia and Africa.

These terrorists kill not merely to end lives, but to disrupt and end a way of life. With every atrocity, they hope that America grows fearful, retreating from the world and forsaking our friends. They stand against us, because we stand in their way.

We are not deceived by their pretenses to piety. We have seen their kind before. They are the heirs of all the murderous ideologies of the 20th century. By sacrificing human life to serve their radical visions—by abandoning every value except the will to power—they follow in the path of fascism, and Nazism, and totalitarianism. And they will follow that path all the way, to where it ends: in history's unmarked grave of discarded lies.

Americans are asking: How will we fight and win this war? We will direct every resource at our command—every means of diplomacy, every tool of intelligence, every instrument of law enforcement, every financial influence, and every necessary weapon of war—to the disruption and to the defeat of the global terror network.

This war will not be like the war against Iraq a decade ago, with a decisive liberation of territory and a swift conclusion. It will not look like the air war above Kosovo two years ago, where no ground troops were used and not a single American was lost in combat.

Our response involves far more than instant retaliation and isolated strikes. Americans should not expect one battle, but a lengthy campaign, unlike any other we have ever seen. It may include dramatic strikes, visible on TV, and covert operations, secret even in success. We will starve terrorists of funding, turn them one against another, drive them from place to place, until there is no refuge or no rest. And we will pursue nations that provide aid or safe haven to terrorism. Every nation, in every region, now has a decision to make. Either you are with us, or you are with the terrorists. From this day forward, any nation that continues to harbor or support terrorism will be regarded by the United States as a hostile regime.

Our nation has been put on notice: We are not immune from attack. We will take defensive measures against terrorism to protect Americans. Today, dozens of federal departments and agencies, as well as state and local governments, have responsibilities affecting homeland security. These efforts must be coordinated at the highest level. So tonight I announce the creation of a Cabinet-level position reporting directly to me—the Office of Homeland Security.

And tonight I also announce a distinguished American to lead this effort, to strengthen American security: a military veteran, an effective governor, a true patriot, a trusted friend—Pennsylvania's Tom Ridge. He will lead, oversee and coordinate a comprehensive national strategy to safeguard our country against terrorism, and respond to any attacks that may come.

These measures are essential. But the only way to defeat terrorism as a threat to our way of life is to stop it, eliminate it, and destroy it where it grows.

Many will be involved in this effort, from FBI agents to intelligence operatives to the reservists we have called to active duty. All deserve our thanks, and all have our prayers. And tonight, a few miles from the damaged Pentagon, I have a message for our military: Be ready. I've called the Armed Forces to alert, and there is a reason. The hour is coming when America will act, and you will make us proud.

This is not, however, just America's fight. And what is at stake is not just America's freedom. This is the world's fight. This is civilization's fight. This is the fight of all who believe in progress and pluralism, tolerance and freedom.

We ask every nation to join us. We will ask, and we will need, the help of police forces, intelligence services, and banking systems around the world. The United States is grateful that many nations and many international organizations have already responded—with sympathy and with support. Nations from Latin America, to Asia, to Africa, to Europe, to the Islamic world. Perhaps the NATO Charter reflects best the attitude of the world: An attack on one is an attack on all.

The civilized world is rallying to America's side. They understand that if this terror goes unpunished, their own cities, their own citizens may be next. Terror, unanswered, can not only bring down buildings, it can threaten the stability of legitimate governments. And you know what—we're not going to allow it.

Americans are asking: What is expected of us? I ask you to live your lives, and hug your children. I know many citizens have fears tonight, and I ask you to be calm and resolute, even in the face of a continuing threat.

I ask you to uphold the values of America, and remember why so many have come here. We are in a fight for our principles, and our first responsibility is to live by them. No one should be singled out for unfair treatment or unkind words because of their ethnic background or religious faith.

I ask you to continue to support the victims of this tragedy with your contributions. Those who want to give can go to a central source of information, libertyunites.org, to find the names of groups providing direct help in New York, Pennsylvania, and Virginia.

The thousands of FBI agents who are now at work in this investigation may need your cooperation, and I ask you to give it.

I ask for your patience, with the delays and inconveniences that may accompany tighter security; and for your patience in what will be a long struggle.

I ask your continued participation and confidence in the American economy. Terrorists attacked a symbol of American prosperity. They did not touch its source. America is successful because of the hard work, and creativity, and enterprise of our people. These were the true strengths of our economy before September 11th, and they are our strengths today.

And, finally, please continue praying for the victims of terror and their families, for those in uniform, and for our great country. Prayer has comforted us in sorrow, and will help strengthen us for the journey ahead.

Tonight I thank my fellow Americans for what you have already done and for what you will do. And ladies and gentlemen of the Congress, I thank you, their representatives, for what you have already done and for what we will do together.

Tonight, we face new and sudden national challenges. We will come together to improve air safety, to dramatically expand the number of air marshals on domestic flights, and take new measures to prevent hijacking. We will come together to promote stability and keep our airlines flying, with direct assistance during this emergency.

We will come together to give law enforcement the additional tools it needs to track down terror here at home. We will come together to strengthen our intelligence capabilities to know the plans of terrorists before they act, and find them before they strike.

We will come together to take active steps that strengthen America's economy, and put our people back to work.

Tonight we welcome two leaders who embody the extraordinary spirit of all New Yorkers: Governor George Pataki, and Mayor Rudolph Giuliani. As a symbol of America's resolve, my administration will work with Congress, and these two leaders, to show the world that we will rebuild New York City.

After all that has just passed—all the lives taken, and all the possibilities and hopes that died with them—it is natural to wonder if America's future is one of fear. Some speak of an age of terror. I know there are struggles ahead, and dangers to face. But this country will define our times, not be defined by them. As long as the United States of America is determined and strong, this will not be an age of terror; this will be an age of liberty, here and across the world.

Great harm has been done to us. We have suffered great loss. And in our grief and anger we have found our mission and our moment. Freedom and fear are at war. The advance of human freedom—the great achievement of our time, and the great hope of every time—now depends on us. Our nation—this generation—will lift a dark threat of violence from our people and our future. We will rally the world to this cause by our efforts, by our courage. We will not tire, we will not falter, and we will not fail.

It is my hope that in the months and years ahead, life will return almost to normal. We'll go back to our lives and routines, and that is good. Even grief recedes with time and grace. But our resolve must not pass. Each of us will remember what happened that day, and to whom it happened. We'll remember the moment the news came—where we were and what we were doing. Some will remember an image of a fire, or a story of rescue. Some will carry memories of a face and a voice gone forever.

And I will carry this: It is the police shield of a man named George Howard, who died at the World Trade Center trying to save others. It was given to me by his mom, Arlene, as a proud memorial to her son. This is my reminder of lives that ended, and a task that does not end.

I will not forget this wound to our country or those who inflicted it. I will not yield; I will not rest; I will not relent in waging this struggle for freedom and security for the American people.

The course of this conflict is not known, yet its outcome is certain. Freedom and fear, justice and cruelty, have always been at war, and we know that God is not neutral between them.

Fellow citizens, we'll meet violence with patient justice—assured of the rightness of our cause, and confident of the victories to come. In all that lies before us, may God grant us wisdom, and may He watch over the United States of America.

Thank you.

Executive Order Establishing the Office of Homeland Security and the Homeland Security Council October 8, 2001

By the authority vested in me as President by the Constitution and the laws of the United States of America, it is hereby ordered as follows:

Section 1. Establishment. I hereby establish within the Executive Office of the President an Office of Homeland Security (the "Office") to be headed by the Assistant to the President for Homeland Security.

Sec. 2. Mission. The mission of the Office shall be to develop and coordinate the implementation of a comprehensive national strategy to secure the United States from terrorist threats or attacks. The Office shall perform the functions necessary to carry out this mission, including the functions specified in section 3 of this order.

Sec. 3. Functions. The functions of the Office shall be to coordinate the executive branch's efforts to detect, prepare for, prevent, protect against, respond to, and recover from terrorist attacks within the United States.

(a) National Strategy. The Office shall work with executive departments and agencies, State and local governments, and private entities to ensure the adequacy of the national strategy for detecting, preparing for, preventing, protecting against, responding to, and recovering from terrorist threats or attacks within the United States and shall periodically review and coordinate revisions to that strategy as necessary.

(b) Detection. The Office shall identify priorities and coordinate efforts for collection and analysis of information within the United States regarding threats of terrorism against the United States and activities of terrorists or terrorist groups within the United

States. The Office also shall identify, in coordination with the Assistant to the President for National Security Affairs, priorities for collection of intelligence outside the United States regarding threats of terrorism within the United States.

(i) In performing these functions, the Office shall work with Federal, State, and local agencies, as appropriate, to:

(A) facilitate collection from State and local governments and private entities of information pertaining to terrorist threats or activities within the United States;

(B) coordinate and prioritize the requirements for foreign intelligence relating to terrorism within the United States of executive departments and agencies responsible for homeland security and provide these requirements and priorities to the Director of Central Intelligence and other agencies responsible for collection of foreign intelligence;

(C) coordinate efforts to ensure that all executive departments and agencies that have intelligence collection responsibilities have sufficient technological capabilities and resources to collect intelligence and data relating to terrorist activities or possible terrorist acts within the United States, working with the Assistant to the President for National Security Affairs, as appropriate;

(D) coordinate development of monitoring protocols and equipment for use in detecting the release of biological, chemical, and radiological hazards; and

(E) ensure that, to the extent permitted by law, all appropriate and necessary intelligence and law enforcement information relating to homeland security is disseminated to and exchanged among appropriate executive departments and agencies responsible for homeland security and, where appropriate for reasons of homeland security, promote exchange of such information with and among State and local governments and private entities.

(ii) Executive departments and agencies shall, to the extent permitted by law, make available to the Office all information relating to terrorist threats and activities within the United States.

(c) Preparedness. The Office of Homeland Security shall coordinate national efforts to prepare for and mitigate the consequences of terrorist threats or attacks within the United States. In performing this function, the Office shall work with Federal, State, and local agencies, and private entities, as appropriate, to:

(i) review and assess the adequacy of the portions of all Federal emergency response plans that pertain to terrorist threats or attacks within the United States;

(ii) coordinate domestic exercises and simulations designed to assess and practice systems that would be called upon to respond to a terrorist threat or attack within the United States and coordinate programs and activities for training Federal, State, and local employees who would be called upon to respond to such a threat or attack;

(iii) coordinate national efforts to ensure public health preparedness for a terrorist attack, including reviewing vaccination policies and reviewing the adequacy of and, if necessary, increasing vaccine and pharmaceutical stockpiles and hospital capacity;

(iv) coordinate Federal assistance to State and local authorities and nongovernmental organizations to prepare for and respond to terrorist threats or attacks within the United States;

(v) ensure that national preparedness programs and activities for terrorist threats or attacks are developed and are regularly evaluated under appropriate standards and that resources are allocated to improving and sustaining preparedness based on such evaluations; and

(vi) ensure the readiness and coordinated deployment of Federal response teams to respond to terrorist threats or attacks, working with the Assistant to the President for National Security Affairs, when appropriate.

(d) Prevention. The Office shall coordinate efforts to prevent terrorist attacks within the United States. In performing this function, the Office shall work with Federal, State, and local agencies, and private entities, as appropriate, to:

(i) facilitate the exchange of information among such agencies relating to immigration and visa matters and shipments of cargo; and, working with the Assistant to the President for National Security Affairs, ensure coordination among such agencies to prevent the entry of terrorists and terrorist materials and supplies into the United States and facilitate removal of such terrorists from the United States, when appropriate;

(ii) coordinate efforts to investigate terrorist threats and attacks within the United States; and

(iii) coordinate efforts to improve the security of United States borders, territorial waters, and airspace in order to prevent acts of terrorism within the United States, working with the Assistant to the President for National Security Affairs, when appropriate.

(e) Protection. The Office shall coordinate efforts to protect the United States and its critical infrastructure from the consequences of terrorist attacks. In performing this function, the Office shall work with Federal, State, and local agencies, and private entities, as appropriate, to:

(i) strengthen measures for protecting energy production, transmission, and distribution services and critical facilities; other utilities; telecommunications; facilities that produce, use, store, or dispose of nuclear material; and other critical infrastructure services and critical facilities within the United States from terrorist attack;

(ii) coordinate efforts to protect critical public and privately owned information systems within the United States from terrorist attack;

(iii) develop criteria for reviewing whether appropriate security measures are in place at major public and privately owned facilities within the United States;

(iv) coordinate domestic efforts to ensure that special events determined by appropriate senior officials to have national significance are protected from terrorist attack;

(v) coordinate efforts to protect transportation systems within the United States, including railways, highways, shipping, ports and waterways, and airports and civilian aircraft, from terrorist attack;

(vi) coordinate efforts to protect United States livestock, agriculture, and systems for the provision of water and food for human use and consumption from terrorist attack; and

(vii) coordinate efforts to prevent unauthorized access to, development of, and unlawful importation into the United States of, chemical, biological, radiological, nuclear, explosive, or other related materials that have the potential to be used in terrorist attacks.

(f) Response and Recovery. The Office shall coordinate efforts to respond to and promote recovery from terrorist threats or attacks within the United States. In performing this function, the Office shall work with Federal, State, and local agencies, and private entities, as appropriate, to:

(i) coordinate efforts to ensure rapid restoration of transportation systems, energy production, transmission, and distribution systems; telecommunications; other utilities; and other critical infrastructure facilities after disruption by a terrorist threat or attack;

(ii) coordinate efforts to ensure rapid restoration of public and private critical information systems after disruption by a terrorist threat or attack;

(iii) work with the National Economic Council to coordinate efforts to stabilize United States financial markets after a terrorist threat or attack and manage the immediate economic and financial consequences of the incident;

(iv) coordinate Federal plans and programs to provide medical, financial, and other assistance to victims of terrorist attacks and their families; and

(v) coordinate containment and removal of biological, chemical, radiological, explosive, or other hazardous materials in the event of a terrorist threat or attack involving such hazards and coordinate efforts to mitigate the effects of such an attack.

(g) Incident Management. The Assistant to the President for Homeland Security shall be the individual primarily responsible for coordinating the domestic response efforts of all departments and agencies in the event of an imminent terrorist threat and during and in the immediate aftermath of a terrorist attack within the United States and shall be the principal point of contact for and to the President with respect to coordination of such efforts. The Assistant to the President for Homeland Security shall coordinate with the Assistant to the President for National Security Affairs, as appropriate.

(h) Continuity of Government. The Assistant to the President for Homeland Security, in coordination with the Assistant to the President for National Security Affairs, shall review plans and preparations for ensuring the continuity of the Federal Government in the event of a terrorist attack that threatens the safety and security of the United States Government or its leadership.

(i) Public Affairs. The Office, subject to the direction of the White House Office of Communications, shall coordinate the strategy of the executive branch for communicating with the public in the event of a terrorist threat or attack within the United States. The Office also shall coordinate the development of programs for educating the public about the nature of terrorist threats and appropriate precautions and responses.

(j) Cooperation with State and Local Governments and Private Entities. The Office shall encourage and invite the participation of State and local governments and private entities, as appropriate, in carrying out the Office's functions.

(k) Review of Legal Authorities and Development of Legislative Proposals. The Office shall coordinate a periodic review and assessment of the legal authorities available to executive departments and agencies to permit them to perform the functions described in this order. When the Office determines that such legal authorities are inadequate, the Office shall develop, in consultation with executive departments and agencies, proposals for presidential action and legislative proposals for submission to the Office of Management and Budget to enhance the ability of executive departments and agencies to perform those functions. The Office shall work with State and local governments in assessing the adequacy of their legal authorities to permit them to detect, prepare for, prevent, protect against, and recover from terrorist threats and attacks.

(l) Budget Review. The Assistant to the President for Homeland Security, in consultation with the Director of the Office of Management and Budget (the "Director") and the heads of executive departments and agencies, shall identify programs that contribute to the Administration's strategy for homeland security and, in the development of the President's annual budget submission, shall review and provide advice to the heads of departments and agencies for such programs. The Assistant to the President for Homeland Security shall provide advice to the Director on the level and use of funding in departments and agencies for homeland security-related activities and, prior to the Director's forwarding of the proposed annual budget submission to the President for transmittal to the Congress, shall certify to the Director the funding levels that the Assistant to the President for Homeland Security believes are necessary and appropriate for the homeland security-related activities of the executive branch.

Sec. 4. Administration.

(a) The Office of Homeland Security shall be directed by the Assistant to the President for Homeland Security.

(b) The Office of Administration within the Executive Office of the President shall provide the Office of Homeland Security with such personnel, funding, and administrative support, to the extent permitted by law and subject to the availability of appropriations, as directed by the Chief of Staff to carry out the provisions of this order.

(c) Heads of executive departments and agencies are authorized, to the extent permitted by law, to detail or assign personnel of such departments and agencies to the Office of Homeland Security upon request of the Assistant to the President for Homeland Security, subject to the approval of the Chief of Staff.

Sec. 5. Establishment of Homeland Security Council.

(a) I hereby establish a Homeland Security Council (the "Council"), which shall be responsible for advising and assisting the President with respect to all aspects of homeland security. The Council shall serve as the mechanism for ensuring coordination of homeland security-related activities of executive departments and agencies and effective development and implementation of homeland security policies.

(b) The Council shall have as its members the President, the Vice President, the Secretary of the Treasury, the Secretary of Defense, the Attorney General, the Secretary of Health and Human Services, the Secretary of Transportation, the Director of the Federal Emergency Management Agency, the Director of the Federal Bureau of Investigation, the Director of Central Intelligence, the Assistant to the President for Homeland Security, and such other officers of the executive branch as the President may from time to time designate. The Chief of Staff, the Chief of Staff to the Vice President, the Assistant to the President for National Security Affairs, the Counsel to the President, and the Director of the Office of Management and Budget also are invited to attend any Council meeting. The Secretary of State, the Secretary of Agriculture, the Secretary of the Interior, the Secretary of Energy, the Secretary of Labor, the Secretary of Commerce, the Secretary of Veterans Affairs, the Administrator of the Environmental Protection Agency, the Assistant to the President for Economic Policy, and the Assistant to the President for Domestic Policy shall be invited to attend meetings pertaining to their responsibilities. The heads of other executive departments and agencies and other senior officials shall be invited to attend Council meetings when appropriate.

(c) The Council shall meet at the President's direction. When the President is absent from a meeting of the Council, at the President's direction the Vice President may preside. The Assistant to the President for Homeland Security shall be responsible, at the President's direction, for determining the agenda, ensuring that necessary papers are prepared, and recording Council actions and Presidential decisions.

Sec. 6. Original Classification Authority. I hereby delegate the authority to classify information originally as Top Secret, in accordance with Executive Order 12958 or any successor Executive Order, to the Assistant to the President for Homeland Security.

Sec. 7. Continuing Authorities. This order does not alter the existing authorities of United States Government departments and agencies. All executive departments and agencies are directed to assist the Council and the Assistant to the President for Homeland Security in carrying out the purposes of this order.

Sec. 8. General Provisions.

(a) This order does not create any right or benefit, substantive or procedural, enforceable at law or equity by a party against the United States, its departments, agencies or instrumentalities, its officers or employees, or any other person.

(b) References in this order to State and local governments shall be construed to include tribal governments and United States territories and other possessions.

(c) References to the "United States" shall be construed to include United States territories and possessions.

Sec. 9. Amendments to Executive Order 12656. Executive Order 12656 of November 18, 1988, as amended, is hereby further amended as follows:

(a) Section 101(a) is amended by adding at the end of the fourth sentence: ", except that the Homeland Security Council shall be responsible for administering such policy with respect to terrorist threats and attacks within the United States."

(b) Section 104(a) is amended by adding at the end: ", except that the Homeland Security Council is the principal forum for consideration of policy relating to terrorist threats and attacks within the United States."

(c) Section 104(b) is amended by inserting the words "and the Homeland Security Council" after the words "National Security Council."

(d) The first sentence of section 104(c) is amended by inserting the words "and the Homeland Security Council" after the words "National Security Council."

(e) The second sentence of section 104(c) is replaced with the following two sentences: "Pursuant to such procedures for the organization and management of the National Security Council and Homeland Security Council processes as the President may establish, the Director of the Federal Emergency Management Agency also shall assist in the implementation of and management of those processes as the President may establish. The Director of the Federal Emergency Management Agency also shall assist in the implementation of national security emergency preparedness policy by coordinating with the other Federal departments and agencies and with State and local governments, and by providing periodic reports to the National Security Council and the Homeland Security Council on implementation of national security emergency preparedness policy."

(f) Section 201(7) is amended by inserting the words "and the Homeland Security Council" after the words "National Security Council."

(g) Section 206 is amended by inserting the words "and the Homeland Security Council" after the words "National Security Council."

(h) Section 208 is amended by inserting the words "or the Homeland Security Council" after the words "National Security Council."

GEORGE W. BUSH

Endnotes

FRONTMATTER

1. Kayyem, J.N. (2002). *Beyond the Beltway: Focusing on Homeland Security. Recommendations for State and Local Domestic Preparedness Planning a Year after 9-11.* Boston: John F. Kennedy School of Government, Harvard University, p. vi.
2. Friedman, T. L. (2003). *Longitudes and Attitudes: The World in the Age of Terrorism.* New York: Anchor Books.
3. Oliver, W.M. (2005). "The Era of Homeland Security: September 11, 2001 to . . ." *Crime & Justice International,* March/April, pp. 9–17; Oliver, W.M. (2004). "The Homeland Security Juggernaut: The End of the Community Policing Era?" *Crime & Justice International* 20,no. 79: 4–10.

CHAPTER I

1. Friedman, T. L. (2003). "The Third Bubble." *New York Times,* Sunday, April 20, Section 4, p. 9; See also Friedman, T. L. (2003). *Longitudes and Attitudes.* New York: Anchor Books, pp. 316–317.
2. *ibid.*
3. *ibid.*
4. *ibid.*
5. This section is based largely on 9/11 Commission. (2004). *Final Report of the National Commission on Terrorist Attacks Upon the United States.* New York: W.W. Norton & Company; and Katzman, K. (2005). "Al Qaeda: Profile and Threat Assessment." *CRS Report for Congress,* February 10, pp. 1–3.
6. The Muslim Brotherhood was founded in 1928 in Egypt, and it has spawned numerous Islamist movements throughout the region since, some as branches of the Brotherhood, others with new names. For example, the Palestinian Islamist group Hamas traces its roots to the Palestinian branch of the Muslim Brotherhood.
7. Gunnaratna, R. (2002). *Inside Al Qaeda.* New York: Columbia University Press.
8. The September 11 Commission report says that U.S. officials obtained information in 2000 indicating that bin Laden received $1 million per year from his family from 1970 (two years

after his father's death) until 1994, when his citizenship was revoked by the Saudi government. See 9/11 Commission (2004). *Final Report of the National Commission on Terrorist Attacks Upon the United States.* New York: W.W. Norton & Company, p. 170.

9. Gunnaratna, R. (2002). *Inside Al Qaeda.* New York: Columbia University Press, p. 21.

10. 9/11 Commission. (2004). *Final Report of the National Commission on Terrorist Attacks Upon the United States.* New York, NY: W.W. Norton & Company, p. 67.

11. This section is based largely on 9/11 Commission. (2004). *Final Report of the National Commission on Terrorist Attacks Upon the United States.* New York: W.W. Norton & Company; and Katzman, K. (2005). "Al Qaeda: Profile and Threat Assessment." *CRS Report for Congress,* February 10, pp. 3–4.

12. 9/11 Commission. (2004). *Final Report of the National Commission on Terrorist Attacks Upon the United States.* New York: W.W. Norton & Company, pp. 139, 203–214.

13. This section is derived from the 9/11 Commission Report. To date there has not been a more precise telling of the events of September 11, 2001, therefore, rather than composing yet another version, this section draws directly on the report's version of events. See 9/11 Commission. (2004). *Final Report of the National Commission on Terrorist Attacks Upon the United States.* New York: W.W. Norton & Company, pp. 1–14.

14. This section is derived from the 9/11 Commission Report. See 9/11 Commission. (2004). *Final Report of the National Commission on Terrorist Attacks Upon the United States.* New York: W.W. Norton & Company, chapter 9.

15. 9/11 Commission. (2004). *Final Report of the National Commission on Terrorist Attacks Upon the United States.* New York: W.W. Norton & Company, p. 314.

16. This section is derived largely from Arlington County. (2002). *Arlington County After-Action Report.* Arlington County, VA: Arlington County.

17. *ibid.*

18. Arlington County. (2002). *Arlington County After-Action Report.* Arlington County, VA: Arlington County.

19. 9/11 Commission. (2004). *Final Report of the National Commission on Terrorist Attacks Upon the United States.* New York: W.W. Norton & Company, p. 315.

20. Arlington County. (2002). *Arlington County After-Action Report.* Arlington County, VA: Arlington County.

21. 9/11 Commission. (2004). *Final Report of the National Commission on Terrorist Attacks Upon the United States.* New York: W.W. Norton & Company, p. 315.

22. Arlington County. (2002). *Arlington County After-Action Report.* Arlington County, VA: Arlington County.

23. 9/11 Commission. (2004). *Final Report of the National Commission on Terrorist Attacks Upon the United States.* New York: W.W. Norton & Company, p. 315.

24. 9/11 Commission. (2004). *Final Report of the National Commission on Terrorist Attacks Upon the United States.* New York: W.W. Norton & Company, p. 314.

25. Henry, T. (2005). "Al-Qaeda's Resurgence." *The Atlantic Monthly,* June: 54–55.

26. Katzman, K. (2005). "Al Qaeda: Profile and Threat Assessment." *CRS Report for Congress,* February 10, p. 6.

27. Katzman, K. (2005). "Al Qaeda: Profile and Threat Assessment." *CRS Report for Congress,* February 10; Friedman, T. (2005). "The Calm Before the Storm?" *The New York Times,* April 13, p. 19.

28. Hill, S. and Ward, R. H. (2004). *Extremist Groups: An International Compilation of Terrorist Organizations, Violent Political Groups, and Issue Oriented Militant Movements.* 2nd ed. Huntsville, TX: OICJ Publications.

29. McVey, P. M. (2003). "The Local Role in Fighting Terrorism." In *Homeland Security: Best Practices for Local Government,* edited by Roger L. Kemp, 125–130. Washington, D.C.: International City/County Management Association, p. 126.

30. LaFree, G. (2005). "Developing a Criminological Agenda for the Study of Terrorism and Homeland Security." Beto Lecture Series. Huntsville, TX. February 23, 2005.

31. *ibid.*

32. McVey, P. M. (2003). "The Local Role in Fighting Terrorism." In *Homeland Security: Best Practices for Local Government,* edited by Roger L. Kemp, 125–130. Washington, D.C.: International City/County Management Association.

33. LaFree, G. (2005). "Developing a Criminological Agenda for the Study of Terrorism and Homeland Security." Beto Lecture Series. Huntsville, TX. February 23, 2005.

34. This section is based on an earlier article by the author. Oliver, W. M. (2005). "The Era of Homeland Security: September 11, 2001 to . . ." *Crime & Justice International* 21, no. 85 (March/April): 9–17.

35. Oliver, W. M. (2004). "The Homeland Security Juggernaut: The End of the Community Policing Era?" *Crime & Justice International* 20, no. 79: 4–10.

36. Bodero, D. D. (2002). "Law Enforcement's New Challenge to Investigate, Interdict, and Prevent Terrorism." *The Police Chief* 69, no. 2: 41–48.

37. Maguire, K. and Pastore, A. L. (2005). *Sourcebook of Criminal Justice Statistics.* [Online]. Available at http://www.albany.edu/sourcebook/; downloaded January 17, 2005. Table 2.1.

38. Maguire, K. and Pastore, A. L. (2005). *Sourcebook of Criminal Justice Statistics.* [Online]. Available at http://www.albany.edu/sourcebook/; downloaded January 17, 2005. Table 2.0009.

39. Maguire, K. and Pastore, A. L. (2005). *Sourcebook of Criminal Justice Statistics.* [Online]. Available at http://www.albany.edu/sourcebook/; downloaded January 17, 2005. Table 2.30.

40. Maguire, K. and Pastore, A. L. (2005). *Sourcebook of Criminal Justice Statistics.* [Online]. Available at http://www.albany.edu/sourcebook/; downloaded January 17, 2005. Table 2.0010.

41. Maguire, K. and Pastore, A. L. (2005). *Sourcebook of Criminal Justice Statistics.* [Online]. Available at http://www.albany.edu/sourcebook/; downloaded January 17, 2005. Table 2.0011.

42. Greene, J. R. (2000). "Community Policing in America: Changing the Nature, Structure, and Function of the Police." In *Criminal Justice 2000: Policies, Processes, and Decisions of the Criminal Justice System.* Vol. 3. Washington, D.C.: U.S. Department of Justice; Oliver, W. M. and Bartgis, E. (1998). "Community Policing: A Conceptual Framework." *Policing: An International Journal of Police Strategies & Management* 21, no. 3: 490–509; Pelfrey, W. V., Jr. (1998). "Precipitating Factors of Paradigmatic Shift in Policing: The Origin of the Community Policing Era." In *Community Policing: Contemporary Readings,* edited by G. P. Alpert and A. Piquero, 79–94. Prospect Heights, IL: Waveland Publishers.

43. Gowri, A. (2003). "Community Policing Is an Epicycle." *Policing: An International Journal of Police Strategies and Management* 26, no. 4: 591–611.

44. Oliver, W. M. (2000). "The Third Generation of Community Policing: Moving Through Innovation, Diffusion, and Institutionalization." *Police Quarterly* 3, no. 4: 367–388.

45. Yin, R. (1979). *Changing in Urban Bureaucracies: How New Practices Become Routinized.* Lexington, MA: Lexington Books.

46. Pelfrey, W. V., Jr. (1998). "Precipitating Factors of Paradigmatic Shift in Policing: The Origin of the Community Policing Era." In *Community Policing: Contemporary Readings.* Edited by G. P. Alpert and A. Piquero, 79–94. Prospect Heights, IL: Waveland Publishers, p. 90.

47. Kelling, G. L. and Moore, M. H. (1988). "The Evolving Strategy of Policing." *Perspectives on Policing,* No. 4. Washington, D.C.: National Institute of Justice.

48. Kelling, G. L. and Moore, M. H. (1991). "From Political to Reform to Community: The Evolving Strategy of Police." In *Community Policing: Rhetoric or Reality?* Edited by J. R. Greene and S. D. Mastrofski, 3–25, New York: Praeger Publishers, p. 23.

49. Greene, J. R. (2000). "Community Policing in America: Changing the Nature, Structure, and Function of the Police." In *Criminal Justice 2000: Policies, Processes, and Decisions of the Criminal Justice System.* Vol. 3. Washington, D.C.: U.S. Department of Justice.

50. Kelling, G. L. and Moore, M. H. (1988). "The Evolving Strategy of Policing." *Perspectives on Policing,* No. 4. Washington, D.C.: National Institute of Justice; Kelling, G. L. and Moore, M. H. (1991). "From Political to Reform to Community: The Evolving Strategy of Police." In *Community Policing: Rhetoric or Reality?* Edited by J. R. Greene and S. D. Mastrofski, 3–25. New York: Praeger Publishers

51. Chandler, 1962, as cited in Kelling, G. L. and Moore, M. H. (1991). "From Political to Reform to Community: The Evolving Strategy of Police." In *Community Policing: Rhetoric or Reality?* Edited by J. R. Greene and S. D. Mastrofski, 3–25. New York: Praeger Publishers, p. 3.

52. Kelling, G. L. and Moore, M. H. (1988). "The Evolving Strategy of Policing." *Perspectives on Policing,* No. 4. Washington, D.C.: National Institute of Justice; Kelling, G. L. and Moore, M. H. (1991). "From Political to Reform to Community: The Evolving Strategy of Police." In *Community Policing: Rhetoric or Reality?* Edited by J. R. Greene and S. D. Mastrofski, 3–25. New York: Praeger Publishers.

53. *ibid.*

54. Maguire, K. and Pastore, A. L. (2005). *Sourcebook of Criminal Justice Statistics.* [Online]. Available at http://www.albany.edu/sourcebook/; downloaded January 17, 2005. Table 2.0011.

55. Greene, J. R. (2000). "Community Policing in America: Changing the Nature, Structure, and Function of the Police." In *Criminal Justice 2000: Policies, Processes, and Decisions of the Criminal Justice System.* Vol. 3. Washington, D.C.: U.S. Department of Justice.

56. Greene, J. R. (2000). "Community Policing in America: Changing the Nature, Structure, and Function of the Police." In *Criminal Justice 2000: Policies, Processes, and Decisions of the Criminal Justice System.* Vol. 3. Washington, D.C.: U.S. Department of Justice, p. 309.

57. Greene, J. R. (2000). "Community Policing in America: Changing the Nature, Structure, and Function of the Police." In *Criminal Justice 2000: Policies, Processes, and Decisions of the Criminal Justice System.* Vol. 3. Washington, D.C.: U.S. Department of Justice.

58. Greene, J. R. (2000). "Community Policing in America: Changing the Nature, Structure, and Function of the Police." In *Criminal Justice 2000: Policies, Processes, and Decisions of the Criminal Justice System*. Vol. 3. Washington, D.C.: U.S. Department of Justice, p. 309.

59. Guzman, M. C. De. (2002). "The Changing Roles and Strategies of the Police in Time of Terror." *Academy of Criminal Justice Sciences Today*, Sept./Oct., pp. 8–13.

CHAPTER 2

1. United States Constitution. Article 4, Section 4. According to James Madison's notes, there was actually much debate over this specific clause during the Constitutional Convention. Luther Martin, a delegate to the convention from Maryland, "opposed it as giving a dangerous and unnecessary power. The consent of the State ought to precede the introduction of any extraneous force whatever." In addition, "Mr. Gerry was against letting loose the myromidons of the United States on a State without its own consent. The States will be the best Judges in such cases. More blood would have been spilt in Massachusetts in the late insurrection, if the General authority had intermeddled." Gouverneur Morris of Pennsylvania is also reported to have remarked, "We are acting a very strange part. We first form a strong man to protect us, and at the same time wish to tie his hands behind him." Finally, George Mason remarked, "If the General Government should have no right to suppress rebellions against particular States, it will be a bad situation indeed."

2. The state legislature was preferred to make the decision of calling for federal assistance because it was feared that a future insurrection might occur by way of a despotic governor attempting to assume dictatorial powers over the people of that state.

3. Cronin, T. E., Cronin, T. Z., and Milakovich, M. E. (1981). *U.S. v. Crime in the Streets*. Bloomington: Indiana University Press, p. 2; Mahoney, B. 1976. *The Politics of the Safe Streets Act, 1965–1973: A Case Study in Evolving Federalism and the National Legislative Process*. Ph.D. Dissertation, Columbia University, p. 12. See also the discussion by Hamilton in Federalist Papers Number 74, in Rossiter, C. (1961). *The Federalist Papers*. New York: New American Library, pp. 447–449.

4. Rossiter, C. (1961). *The Federalist Papers*. New York: New American Library, p. 276.

5. Rossiter, C. (1961). *The Federalist Papers*. New York: New American Library, p. 226.

6. Rossiter, C. (1961). *The Federalist Papers*. New York: New American Library, p. 120.

7. Hamilton would also state, in speaking before the New York Ratifying Convention on June 28, 1788, ". . . but the laws of Congress are restricted to a certain sphere, and when they depart from this sphere, they are no longer supreme or binding. In the same manner the states have certain independent powers, in which their laws are supreme: for example, in making and executing laws concerning the punishment of certain crimes, such as murder, theft, etc., the states cannot be controlled." In addition he would also explain, "the state officers will ever be important, because they are necessary and useful. Their powers are such as are extremely interesting among the people; such as affect their property, their liberty, and life. What is more important than the administration of justice and the executive of the civil and criminal laws?"

8. Friedman, L. M. (1993). *Crime and Punishment in American History*. New York: Basic Books, p. 262.

9. Calder, J. D. (1978). *Presidents and Crime Control: Some Limitations on Executive Police Making*. Ph.D. Dissertation, Claremont University. Calder explains that these

categories are purposely broad and that they were derived from reading several historical accounts, by noted historians and political scientists, of presidential intervention and justifications for such intervention.

10. The Tennessee Emergency Management Agency. (2005). "Tennessee Civil Defense History." Available online at http://www.tnema.org/Archives/EMHistory/TNCDHistory1-0.htm downloaded June 15, 2005.

11. *ibid.*

12. McCullough, D. (1987). *The Johnstown Flood.* New York: Simon & Schuster.

13. Oliver, W. M. (2003). *The Law & Order Presidency.* Upper Saddle River, NJ: Prentice Hall.

14. The Tennessee Emergency Management Agency. (2005). "Tennessee Civil Defense History." Available online at http://www.tnema.org/Archives/EMHistory/TNCDHistory10.htm; downloaded June 15, 2005.

15. National Archives and Records Administration. (2005). *Records of the Council of National Defense (CND).* Available online at http://www.archives.gov/research_room/federal_records_guide/print_friendly.html?page=council_of_national_defense_rg062_content.html&title=NARA%20%7C%20Research%20Room%20%7C%20Guide%20to%20Records%20of%20the%20Council%20of%20National%20Defense%20%5BCND%5D; downloaded July 12, 2005.

16. Primary Documents: D F Houston on U.S. War Readiness, 1917. (2004). Available online at http://www.firstworldwar.com/source/uspreparation_houston.htm; downloaded on July 12, 2005. The original source is listed as Source Records of the Great War, Vol. V, ed. Charles F. Horne, National Alumni 1923.

17. The Tennessee Emergency Management Agency. (2005). "Tennessee Civil Defense History." Available online at http://www.tnema.org/Archives/EMHistory/TNCDHistory10.htm; downloaded June 15, 2005. See also the Encyclopedia of Civil Defense and Emergency Management. (2005). Available online at http://www.richmond.edu/ ~wgreen/ECDnatdefcounI.html; downloaded July 12, 2005.

18. The Tennessee Emergency Management Agency. (2005). "Tennessee Civil Defense History." Available online at http://www.tnema.org/Archives/EMHistory/TNCDHistory1-0.htm; downloaded June 15, 2005.

19. Drabek, T. E. (1991). "The Evolution of Emergency Management." In *Emergency Management: Principles and Practices for Local Government.* Edited by Drabek, T. E. and Hoetmer, G. J., 3–29, Washington, D.C.: International City Management Association.

20. Hunter, L. C. (1959). *Organization of the Federal Government for National Security.* Available online through the National Defense University Library at http:// www.ndu.edu/library/ic3/L60-039.pdf; downloaded July 14, 2005.

21. Neel, C. H. (1959). *Organization for National Security.* Available online through the National Defense University Library at http://www.ndu.edu/library/ic2/L51-010.pdf; downloaded July 14, 2005.

22. Executive Order 10186, Establishing the Federal Civil Defense Administration in the Office for Emergency Management of the Executive Office of the President. Signed: December 1, 1950 by President Harry S Truman. Reference Federal Register page and date: 15 FR 8557, December 5, 1950. Available online at http://www.archives.gov/ federal_register/executive_orders/1950.html

23. The American Experience. (1999). *Race for the Superbomb.* Interview with historian Laura McEnaney. Transcripts available online at http://www.pbs.org/wgbh/ amex/bomb/filmmore/reference/interview/index.html; downloaded July 13, 2005.

24. 64 Stat. 1245

25. Sylves, R. and Cumming, W. R. (2004). "FEMA's Path to Homeland Security: 1979–2003." *Journal of Homeland Security and Emergency Management* 1, no. 2: 1–21.

26. The Tennessee Emergency Management Agency. (2005). "Tennessee Civil Defense History." Available online at http://www.tnema.org/Archives/EMHistory/TNCDHistory10.htm; downloaded June 15, 2005.

27. Drabek, T. E. (1991). "The Evolution of Emergency Management." In *Emergency Management: Principles and Practices for Local Government.* Edited by Drabek, T. E. and Hoetmer, G. J., 3–29, Washington, D.C.: International City Management Association.

28. Sylves, R. and Cumming, W. R. (2004). "FEMA's Path to Homeland Security: 1979–2003." *Journal of Homeland Security and Emergency Management* 1, no. 2: 1–21.

29. Federal Emergency Management Agency. (2003). *This is FEMA: A Look at the Federal Government's Primary Disaster Response and Recovery Resource.* Washington, D.C.: Department of Homeland Security.

30. The Tennessee Emergency Management Agency. (2005). "Tennessee Civil Defense History." Available online at http://www.tnema.org/Archives/ EMHistory/TNCDHistory10.htm; downloaded June 15, 2005.

31. Federal Emergency Management Agency. (2005). *FEMA History.* Available online at http://www.fema.gov/about/history.shtm; downloaded July 14, 2005.

32. General Accounting Office. (1993). *Disaster Assistance: DOD's Support for Hurricanes Andrew and Iniki and Typhoon Omar.* Available online at www.gao.gov/cgi-bin/getrpt? NSIAD-93-180; downloaded July 14, 2005; General Accounting Office. (1993). *Disaster Management: Improving the Nation's Response to Catastrophic Disasters.* Available online at http://archive.gao.gov/t2pbat5/149631.pdf; downloaded July 14, 2005.

33. Drabek, T. E. (1991). "The Evolution of Emergency Management." In *Emergency Management: Principles and Practices for Local Government.* Edited by Drabek, T. E. and Hoetmer, G. J., 3–29. Washington, D.C.: International City Management Association.

34. Osborne, D. and Gaebler, T. (1992). *Reinventing Government.* New York: Addison Wesley Publishing Company.

35. Sylves, R. & Cumming, W. R. (2004). "FEMA's Path to Homeland Security: 1979–2003." *Journal of Homeland Security and Emergency Management* 1, no. 2: 1–21.

36. The Tennessee Emergency Management Agency. (2005). "Tennessee Civil Defense History." Available online at http://www.tnema.org/Archives/EMHistory/TNCDHistory 10.htm; downloaded June 15, 2005.

37. Federal Emergency Management Agency. (2005). *Federal Emergency Management Agency History.* Available online at http://www.fema.gov/about/history.shtm; downloaded July 15, 2005.

38. Allbaugh, J. M. (2001). Testimony by the Director, Federal Emergency Management Agency Before the Committee on Environment and Public Works, U.S. Senate October 16, 2001. Transcript available online at http://www.yale.edu/lawweb/avalon/sept_11/fema_003.htm; downloaded July 14, 2005.

39. U.S. Northern Command. (2005). U.S. Norther Command Homepage. Available online at http://www.northcom.mil

40. O'Harrow, R., Jr. (2002). "Six Weeks in Autumn." *The Washington Post.* October 27, p. W06. Also available online at http://www.washingtonpost.com

41. *ibid.*

42. *ibid.*

43. *ibid.*

44. *ibid.*

45. The full text of the U.S.A. PATRIOT Act is available online through the Library of Congress at http://thomas.loc.gov/cgi-bin/bdquery/z?d107:h.r.03162:

46. See Doyle, C. (2002). "The USA PATRIOT Act: A Sketch." *CRS Report for Congress,* April 18 and the U.S.A. PATRIOT Act, available online through the Library of Congress at http://thomas.loc.gov/cgi-bin/bdquery/z?d107:h.r.03162:

47. Dempsey, J. X. (2005). "Patriot Act: Checks are Needed to Protect Rights." *National Public Radio Homepage.* Available online at http://www.npr.org/templates/story/ story.php?storyId=4763647; downloaded on July 29, 2005.

48. McDonald, H. (2005). "Patriot Act: Let Investigator's Do Their Job." *National Public Radio Homepage.* Available online at http://www.npr.org/templates/story/story.php?storyId=4763326; downloaded July 29, 2005.

49. Doyle, C. (2002). "The USA PATRIOT Act: A Sketch." *CRS Report for Congress,* April 18. And the U.S.A. PATRIOT Act, available online through the Library of Congress at http://thomas.loc.gov/cgi-bin/bdquery/z?d107:h.r.03162:

50. See Doyle, C. (2005). "USA PATRIOT Act Sunset: A Sketch." *CRS Report for Congress,* June 29; Doyle, C. (2005). "USA PATRIOT Act Sunset: Provisions That Expire on December 31, 2005." *CRS Report for Congress,* June 29; National Public Radio. (2005). "Debating the Patriot Act." Available online at http://www.npr.org/templates/story/ story.php?storyId=4759727&sourceCode=gaw; downloaded July 29, 2005.

51. Relyea, H. C. (2002). "Homeland Security: Department Organization and Management." *CRS Report for Congress,* August 7.

52. *ibid.*

53. Bush, G. W. (2002). "President Bush Signs Homeland Security Act." White House Homepage. Available online at http://www.whitehouse.gov/news/releases/2002/11/print/20021125-6.html#; downloaded August 9, 2005.

54. Department of Homeland Security. (2005). *Homeland Security Act of 2002.* Available online at http://www.dhs.gov/dhspublic/display?theme=46&content=410; White House. (2002). "Analysis for the Homeland Security Act of 2002." *White House Homepage.* Available online at http://www.whitehouse.gov/deptofhomeland/analysis/hsl-bill-analysis.pdf; downloaded August 9, 2005.

55. *ibid.*

56. *ibid.*

57. *ibid.*

58. *ibid.*

59. *ibid.*

60. *ibid.*

61. *ibid*

62. Department of Homeland Security. (2004). *Securing Our Homeland: U.S. Department of Homeland Security Strategic Plan.* Available online at http://www.dhs.gov/interweb/assetlibrary/DHS_StratPlan_FINAL_spread.pdf; downloaded January 14, 2005.

63. Department of Homeland Security. (2005). *Department of Homeland Security Homepage.* Available online at http://www.dhs.gov/dhspublic/index.jsp; downloaded August 2, 2005.

64. *ibid.*

65. *ibid.*

66. Transportation Security Administration. (2005). *Transportation Security Administration Homepage.* Available online at http://www.tsa.gov/public/; downloaded August 12, 2005.

67. Federal Law Enforcement Training Center. (2005). *Federal Law Enforcement Training Center Homepage.* Available online at http://www.fletc.gov/; downloaded on August 10, 2005.

68. Federal Emergency Management Administration. (2005). *Federal Emergency Management Administration Homepage.* Available online at http://www.fema.gov/; downloaded August 4, 2005.

69. Department of Homeland Security. (2005). *Department of Homeland Security Homepage.* Available online at http://www.dhs.gov/dhspublic/index.jsp; downloaded August 2, 2005.

70. Terrorist Threat Integration Center. (2005). *Terrorist Threat Integration Center Homepage.* Available online at http://www.fas.org/irp/agency/ttic/; downloaded August 12, 2005.

71. Department of Homeland Security. (2005). *Department of Homeland Security Homepage.* Available online at http://www.dhs.gov/dhspublic/index.jsp; downloaded August 2, 2005.

72. *ibid.*

73. *ibid.*

74. *ibid.*

75. *ibid.*

76. The Maritime Transportation Security Act of 2002. *U.S. Coast Guard Homepage.* Available online at http://www.uscg.mil/hq/g-m/mp/pdf/MTSA.pdf; downloaded August 12, 2005.

77. U.S. Coast Guard. (2002). *Maritime Strategy for Homeland Security.* Available online at http://www.uscg.mil/news/reportsandbudget/Maritime_strategy/USCG_Maritme_Strategy.pdf; downloaded August 12, 2005.

78. U.S. Coast Guard. (2005). *U.S. Coast Guard Homepage.* Available online at http:// www.uscg.mil/USCG.shtm; downloaded August 12, 2005.

79. U.S. Secret Service. (2005). *U.S. Secret Service Homepage.* Available online at http://www.secretservice.gov/; downloaded August 12, 2005.

80. Department of Homeland Security. (2005). *Department of Homeland Security Homepage.* Available online at http://www.dhs.gov/dhspublic/index.jsp; downloaded August 2, 2005.

81. United States Citizenship and Immigration Services. (2005). *Department of Homeland Security Homepage.* Available online at http://www.dhs.gov/dhspublic/index.jsp; downloaded August 12, 2005.

82. Department of Homeland Security. (2005). *Department of Homeland Security Homepage.* Available online at http://www.dhs.gov/dhspublic/index.jsp; downloaded August 2, 2005.

83. *ibid.*

84. Gortner, H. F., Mahler, J., and Nicholson, J. B. (1997). *Organization Theory: A Public Perspective.* 2nd ed. Fort Worth, TX: Harcourt Brace College Publishers.

85. Kingdon, J. C. (1995). *Agendas, Alternatives, and Public Policies.* 2nd ed. New York: HarperCollins College Publishers.

86. Barret, T. (2005). "House Approves Renewal of Patriot Act." *CNN Homepage.* Available online at http://www.cnn.com/2005/POLITICS/07/21/patriot.act/; downloaded August 16, 2005; Lichtbu, E. (2005). "Congress Nears Deal to Renew Antiterror Law." *The New York Times,* November 17, p. 17.

87. Department of Homeland Security. (2005). Department of Homeland Security Homepage. Available online at http://www.dhs.gov/dhspublic/index.jsp; downloaded August 2, 2005.

CHAPTER 3

1. Campbell, H. G. (2005). "Logic Models in Support of Homeland Security Strategy Development." *Journal of Homeland Security and Emergency Management* 2, no. 2: 1–7, p. 1.
2. *ibid.*
3. *ibid.*
4. McVey, P. M. (2003). "The Local Role in Fighting Terrorism." In *Homeland Security: Best Practices for Local Government,* edited by R. L. Kemp, 125–130. Washington, D.C.: International City/County Management Association.
5. McVey, P. M. (2003). "The Local Role in Fighting Terrorism." In *Homeland Security: Best Practices for Local Government,* edited by R. L. Kemp, 125–130, at page 125. Washington, D.C.: International City/County Management Association.
6. *ibid.*
7. Office of Homeland Security. (2002). *National Strategy for Homeland Security.* Washington, D.C.: U.S. G.P.O. Available online at http://www.whitehouse.gov/ homeland/ book/nat_strat_hls.pdf; downloaded January 4, 2005.
8. See Preface Office of Homeland Security. (2002). *National Strategy for Homeland Security.* Washington, D.C.: U.S. G.P.O. Available online at http://www.whitehouse.gov/ homeland/book/nat_strat_hls.pdf; downloaded January 4, 2005.
9. See Preface Office of Homeland Security. (2002). *National Strategy for Homeland Security.* Washington, D.C.: U.S. G.P.O. Available online at http:// www.whitehouse.gov/ homeland/book/nat_strat_hls.pdf; downloaded January 4, 2005.
10. Kemp, R. L. (2003). *Homeland Security: Best Practices for Local Government.* Washington, D.C.: International City/County Management Association.
11. International Association of Chiefs of Police. (2005). *From Hometown Security to Homeland Security.* Washington, D.C.: International Association of Chiefs of Police. Available online at http://www.theiacp.org/leg_policy/HomelandSecurityWP.PDF; downloaded on September 20, 2005.
12. Reese, S. (2005). "State and Local Homeland Security: Unresolved Issues for the 109th Congress." *CRS Report for Congress.* Washington, D.C.: Congressional Research Service. Available online at http://www.fas.org/sgp/crs/homesec/RL32941.pdf; downloaded September 20, 2005.
13. *ibid.*
14. Murphy, G. R. and Plotkin, M. R. (2003). *Protecting Your Community From Terrorism: The Strategies for Local Law Enforcement Series. Volume 1: Improving Local-Federal Partnerships.* Washington, D.C.: Police Executive Research Forum and the Office of Community Oriented Policing Services. Available online at http://www.cops.usdoj.gov/ mime/open.pdf?Item=1362; downloaded April 17, 2005.
15. Pelfrey, W. V. (2005). "The Cycle of Preparedness: Establishing a Framework to Prepare for Terrorist Threats." *Journal of Homeland Security and Emergency Management* 2, no. 1: 1–21.
16. Office of Homeland Security. (2002). *National Strategy for Homeland Security.* Washington, D.C.: U.S. G.P.O. Available online at http://www.whitehouse.gov/homeland/ book/nat_strat_hls.pdf; downloaded January 4, 2005, p. 2.
17. *ibid.*
18. White, J. R. (1998). *Terrorism: An Introduction.* 2nd ed. Belmont, CA: West/Wadsworth Publishing Company, chapter 1.
19. *ibid.*

20. Poland, J. M. (2005). *Understanding Terrorism: Groups, Strategies, and Responses.* Upper Saddle River, NJ: Prentice Hall, p. 9.

21. McVey, P. M. (2002). "An Effective Homeland Defense Partnership." *The Police Chief* 69 (4): 174–180, p. 174.

22. Jenkins, B. M. (1983). *New Modes of Conflict.* Santa Monica, CA: Rand Corporation.

23. Laqueur, W. (1999). *The New Terrorsim: Fanaticism an the Arms of Mass Destruction.* New York: Oxford University Press.

24. Heymann, P. B. (1998). *Terrorism and America: A Commonsense Strategy for a Democratic Society.* Cambridge, MA: The MIT Press, p. 6.

25. Friendlander, R. A. (1981). *Terrorism and the Law: What Price Safety?* Gaithersburg, MD: International Association of Chiefs of Police, p. 3.

26. National Advisory Committee on Criminal Justice Standards and Goals, Law Enforcement Assistance Administration. (1976). *Disorders and Terrorism.* Washington, D.C.: U.S. Government Printing Office, p. 3.

27. Federal Bureau of Investigation (2005). *FBI Homepage.* Available online at http://www.fbi.gov; See also Federal Bureau of Investigation (2002). *Terrorism in the United States: 2000/2001.* Washington, D.C.: U.S. Government Printing Office.

28. Dyson, W. (2005). *Terrorism: An Investigator's Handbook.* 2nd ed. Newark, NJ: Matthew Bender.

29. Federal Bureau of Investigation (2002). *Terrorism in the United States: 2000/2001.* Washington, D.C.: U.S. Government Printing Office. The definition is derived from 18 U.S.C. § 2331(5).

30. Federal Bureau of Investigation (2002). *Terrorism in the United States: 2000/2001.* Washington, D.C.: U.S. Government Printing Office. The definition is derived from [18 U.S.C. § 2331(1).

31. Office of Homeland Security. (2002). *National Strategy for Homeland Security.* Washington, D.C.: U.S. G.P.O. Available online at http://www.whitehouse.gov/homeland/book/nat_strat_hls.pdf; downloaded January 4, 2005, p. 2.

32. Office of Homeland Security. (2002). *National Strategy for Homeland Security.* Washington, D.C.: U.S. G.P.O. Available online at http://www.whitehouse.gov/homeland/book/nat_strat_hls.pdf; downloaded January 4, 2005, p. 7.

33. Office of Homeland Security. (2002). *National Strategy for Homeland Security.* Washington, D.C.: U.S. G.P.O. Available online at http://www.whitehouse.gov/homeland/book/nat_strat_hls.pdf; downloaded January 4, 2005, p. 12.

34. Office of Homeland Security. (2002). *National Strategy for Homeland Security.* Washington, D.C.: U.S. G.P.O. Available online at http://www.whitehouse.gov/homeland/book/nat_strat_hls.pdf; downloaded January 4, 2005, p. 21.

35. Office of Homeland Security. (2002). *National Strategy for Homeland Security.* Washington, D.C.: U.S. G.P.O. Available online at http://www.whitehouse.gov/homeland/book/nat_strat_hls.pdf; downloaded January 4, 2005, p. 25.

36. *ibid.*

37. Office of Homeland Security. (2002). *National Strategy for Homeland Security.* Washington, D.C.: U.S. G.P.O. Available online at http://www.whitehouse.gov/homeland/book/nat_strat_hls.pdf; downloaded January 4, 2005, p. 25–26.

38. Office of Homeland Security. (2002). *National Strategy for Homeland Security.* Washington, D.C.: U.S. G.P.O. Available online at http://www.whitehouse.gov/homeland/book/nat_strat_hls.pdf; downloaded January 4, 2005, p. 38.

39. Office of Homeland Security. (2002). *National Strategy for Homeland Security.* Washington, D.C.: U.S. G.P.O. Available online at http://www.whitehouse.gov/homeland/book/nat_strat_hls.pdf; downloaded January 4, 2005, p. 41.

40. Office of Homeland Security. (2002). *National Strategy for Homeland Security.* Washington, D.C.: U.S. G.P.O. Available online at http://www.whitehouse.gov/homeland/book/nat_strat_hls.pdf; downloaded January 4, 2005, p. 43.

41. *ibid.*

42. Brown, D. (2005). "Military's Role in a Flu Pandemic." *Washington Post.* Available online at http://www.washingtonpost.com; downloaded October 5, 2005.

43. Office of Homeland Security. (2002). *National Strategy for Homeland Security.* Washington, D.C.: U.S. G.P.O. Available online at http://www.whitehouse.gov/homeland/book/nat_strat_hls.pdf; downloaded January 4, 2005, p. 57.

44. International Association of Chiefs of Police. (2005). *From Hometown Security to Homeland Security.* Washington, D.C.: International Association of Chiefs of Police. Available online at http://www.theiacp.org/leg_policy/HomelandSecurityWP.PDF; downloaded on September 20, 2005.

45. International Association of Chiefs of Police. (2005). *From Hometown Security to Homeland Security.* Washington, D.C.: International Association of Chiefs of Police. Available online at http://www.theiacp.org/leg_policy/HomelandSecurityWP.PDF; downloaded on September 20, 2005, p. 1.

46. Office of Homeland Security. (2002). *National Strategy for Homeland Security.* Washington, D.C.: U.S. G.P.O. Available online at http://www.whitehouse.gov/homeland/book/nat_strat_hls.pdf; downloaded January 4, 2005, p. iii.

47. International Association of Chiefs of Police. (2005). *From Hometown Security to Homeland Security.* Washington, D.C.: International Association of Chiefs of Police. Available online at http://www.theiacp.org/leg_policy/HomelandSecurityWP.PDF; downloaded on September 20, 2005, p. 2.

48. International Association of Chiefs of Police. (2005). *From Hometown Security to Homeland Security.* Washington, D.C.: International Association of Chiefs of Police. Available online at http://www.theiacp.org/leg_policy/HomelandSecurityWP.PDF; downloaded on September 20, 2005, p. 3.

49. *ibid.*

50. International Association of Chiefs of Police. (2005). *From Hometown Security to Homeland Security.* Washington, D.C.: International Association of Chiefs of Police. Available online at http://www.theiacp.org/leg_policy/HomelandSecurityWP.PDF; downloaded on September 20, 2005, p. 5.

51. International Association of Chiefs of Police. (2005). *From Hometown Security to Homeland Security.* Washington, D.C.: International Association of Chiefs of Police. Available online at http://www.theiacp.org/leg_policy/HomelandSecurityWP.PDF; downloaded on September 20, 2005, p. 6.

52. International Association of Chiefs of Police. (2005). *From Hometown Security to Homeland Security.* Washington, D.C.: International Association of Chiefs of Police. Available online at http://www.theiacp.org/leg_policy/HomelandSecurityWP.PDF; downloaded on September 20, 2005, p. 7.

53. International Association of Chiefs of Police. (2005). *From Hometown Security to Homeland Security.* Washington, D.C.: International Association of Chiefs of Police.

Available online at http://www.theiacp.org/leg_policy/HomelandSecurityWP.PDF; downloaded on September 20, 2005, p. 3.

54. Kemp, R. L. (2003). *Homeland Security: Best Practices for Local Government.* Washington, D.C.: International City/County Management Association.

55. Kemp, R. L. (2003). *Homeland Security: Best Practices for Local Government.* Washington, D.C.: International City/County Management Association.

56. Bodrero, D. D. (2003). "Preventing Terrorist Acts: A New Challenge for Law Enforcement." In *Homeland Security: Best Practices for Local Government,* Edited by R. L. Kemp, 39–44. Washington, D.C.: International City/County Management Association.

57. Pelfrey, W. V. (2005). "The Cycle of Preparedness: Establishing a Framework to Prepare for Terrorist Threats." *Journal of Homeland Security and Emergency Management* 2, no. 1: 1–21; available online at http://www.bepress.com/jhsem/vol12/iss1/5

58. Pelfrey, W. V. (2005). "The Cycle of Preparedness: Establishing a Framework to Prepare for Terrorist Threats." *Journal of Homeland Security and Emergency Management* 2, no. 1: 1–21; available online at http://www.bepress.com/jhsem/vol12/iss1/5, p. 1.

59. Office of Domestic Preparedness. (2003). *The Office for Domestic Preparedness Guidelines for Homeland Security, June 2003: Prevention and Deterrence.* Washington, D.C.: U.S. Department of Homeland Security.

60. Office of Homeland Security. (2002). *National Strategy for Homeland Security.* Washington, D.C.: U.S. G.P.O. Available online at http://www.whitehouse.gov/homeland/book/nat_strat_hls.pdf; downloaded January 4, 2005.

61. Pelfrey, W. V. (2005). "The Cycle of Preparedness: Establishing a Framework to Prepare for Terrorist Threats." *Journal of Homeland Security and Emergency Management* 2, no. 1: 1–21; available online at http://www.bepress.com/jhsem/vol12/iss1/5, p. 7.

62. Office of Domestic Preparedness. (2003). *The Office of Domestic Preparedness Guidelines for Homeland Security June 2003: Prevention and Deterrence.* Washington, D.C.: U.S. Department of Homeland Security.

63. Office of Domestic Preparedness. (2003). *The Office of Domestic Preparedness Guide lines for Homeland Security June 2003: Prevention and Deterrence.* Washington, D.C.: U.S. Department of Homeland Security; Pelfrey, W. V. (2005). "The Cycle of Preparedness: Establishing a Framework to Prepare for Terrorist Threats." *Journal of Homeland Security and Emergency Management* 2, no. 1: 1–21; available online at http:// www.bepress.com/jhsem/vol12/iss1/5, p. 9.

64. Pelfrey, W. V. (2005). "The Cycle of Preparedness: Establishing a Framework to Prepare for Terrorist Threats." *Journal of Homeland Security and Emergency Management* 2, no. 1: 1–21; available online at http://www.bepress.com/jhsem/vol12/iss1/5, p. 10.

65. Office of Homeland Security. (2002). *National Strategy for Homeland Security.* Washington, D.C.: U.S. G.P.O. Available online at http://www.whitehouse.gov/homeland/book/nat_strat_hls.pdf; downloaded January 4, 2005.

66. Office of Homeland Security. (2002). *National Strategy for Homeland Security.* Washington, D.C.: U.S. G.P.O. Available online at http://www.whitehouse.gov/homeland/book/nat_strat_hls.pdf; downloaded January 4, 2005; Pelfrey, W. V. (2005). "The Cycle of Preparedness: Establishing a Framework to Prepare for Terrorist Threats." *Journal of Homeland Security and Emergency Management* 2, no. 1: 1–21; available online at http://www.bepress.com/jhsem/vol12/iss1/5, p. 10.

67. Pelfrey, W. V. (2005). "The Cycle of Preparedness: Establishing a Framework to Prepare for Terrorist Threats." *Journal of Homeland Security and Emergency Management* 2, no. 1: 1–21; available online at http://www.bepress.com/jhsem/vol12/iss1/5, p. 11.

68. *ibid.*

69. McVey, P. M. (2003). "The Local Role in Fighting Terrorism." In *Homeland Security: Best Practices for Local Government,* edited by R. L. Kemp, 125–130, at page 125. Washington, D.C.: International City/County Management Association.

70. *ibid.*

71. *ibid.*

72. International Association of Chiefs of Police. (2005). *From Hometown Security to Homeland Security.* Washington, D.C.: International Association of Chiefs of Police. Available online at http://www.theiacp.org/leg_policy/HomelandSecurityWP.PDF; downloaded on September 20, 2005, p. 3.

73. Office of Homeland Security. (2002). *National Strategy for Homeland Security.* Washington, D.C.: U.S. G.P.O. Available online at http://www.whitehouse.gov/homeland/book/nat_strat_hls.pdf; downloaded January 4, 2005, p. 2.

74. Pelfrey, W. V. (2005). "The Cycle of Preparedness: Establishing a Framework to Prepare for Terrorist Threats." *Journal of Homeland Security and Emergency Management* 2, no. 1: 1–21; available online at http://www.bepress.com/jhsem/vol12/iss1/5

75. Kemp, R. L., ed. (2003). *Homeland Security: Best Practices for Local Government.* Washington, D.C.: International City/County Management Association, p. 4.

76. *ibid.*

77. *ibid.*

CHAPTER 4

1. Cordner, G. W., Gaines, L. W., and Kappeler, V. E. (1996). *Police Operations: Analysis and Evaluations.* Cincinnati, OH: Anderson Publishing Company.

2. Oliver, W. M. (2003). *Community-Oriented Policing: A Systemic Approach to Policing.* 3rd ed. Upper Saddle River, NJ: Prentice Hall.

3. U.S. Department of Defense. (2001). *Joint Pub 1-02: Department of Defense Dictionary of Military Terms and Associated Terms.* Washington, D.C.: U.S. G.P.O., p. 275.

4. U.S. Department of Defense. (20002). *Joint Pub 5-001: Joint Doctrine for Campaign Planning.* Washington, D.C.: U.S. G.P.O.

5. Moore, M. H. (1990). In *Impossible Jobs in Public Management,* edited by E.C., Hargrove and J. C. Glidewell, 72–102. Lawrence, KS: University Press of Kansas.

6. Moore, M. H. (1990). In *Impossible Jobs in Public Management,* edited by E. C. Hargrove and J. C. Glidewell, 72–102. Lawrence, KS: University Press of Kansas, p. 82.

7. *ibid.*

8. National Commission on Terrorist Attacks Upon the United States. (2003). *The 9/11 Commission Report.* New York: W.W. Norton & Company, p. 396.

9. National Commission on Terrorist Attacks Upon the United States. (2003). *The 9/11 Commission Report.* New York: W.W. Norton & Company, p. 397.

10. Goldstein, H. (1990). *Problem-Oriented Policing.* New York: McGraw-Hill Publishing Company.

11. *ibid.*

12. *ibid.*

13. Eck, J. E. and Spelman, W. (1987). *Problem-Solving: Problem-Oriented Policing in New-port News.* Washington, D.C.: Police Executive Research Forum/U.S. Department of Justice and the National Institute of Justice.

14. Oliver, W. M. (2003). *Community-Oriented Policing: A Systemic Approach to Policing.* 3rd ed. Upper Saddle River, NJ: Prentice Hall.

15. Henry, V. E. (2002). *The COMPSTAT Paradigm: Management Accountability in Policing, Business and the Public Sector.* Flushing, NY: Looseleaf Law Publications, Inc., p. 147.

16. Henry, V. E. (2002). *The COMPSTAT Paradigm: Management Accountability in Policing, Business and the Public Sector.* Flushing, NY: Looseleaf Law Publications, Inc., pp. 147–148.

17. McDonald, P. P. (2004). "Implementing CompStat: Critical Points to Consider." *The Police Chief* 71(1): 1–6; available online at http://www.policechiefmagazine.org; downloaded July 14, 2004.

18. Henry, V. E. (2002). *The Compstat Paradigm: Management and Accountability in Policing Business and the Public Sector.* Flushing, NY: Looseleaf Law Publications, Inc.; Silverman, E. B. (1999). *NYPD Battles Crime: Innovative Strategies in Policing.* Boston, MA: Northeastern University Press.

19. Maple, J. & Mitchell, C. (2000). *The Crime Fighter: Putting the Bad Guys Out of Business.* New York: Broadway Publications.

20. Bratton, W., with Knobler, P. (1998). *The Turnaround: How America's Top Cop Reversed the Crime Epidemic.* New York: Random House Publishers.

21. Henry, V. E. (2002). *The Compstat Paradigm: Management and Accountability in Policing Business and the Public Sector.* Flushing, NY: Looseleaf Law Publications, Inc.; Silverman, E. B. (1999). *NYPD Battles Crime: Innovative Strategies in Policing.* Boston, MA: Northeastern University Press.

22. Henry, V. E. (2002). *The Compstat Paradigm: Management and Accountability in Policing Business and the Public Sector.* Flushing, NY: Looseleaf Law Publications, Inc., p. 20.

23. Silverman, E. B. (1999). *NYPD Battles Crime: Innovative Strategies in Policing.* Boston, MA: Northeastern University Press.

24. McDonald, P. P. (2004). "Implementing CompStat: Critical Points to Consider." *The Police Chief* 71(1): 1–6; available online at http://www.policechiefmagazine.org; downloaded July 14, 2004.

25. Henry, V. E. (2002). *The Compstat Paradigm: Management and Accountability in Policing Business and the Public Sector.* Flushing, NY: Looseleaf Law Publications, Inc., p. 21.

26. McDonald, P. P. (2004). "Implementing CompStat: Critical Points to Consider." *The Police Chief* 71(1): 1–6, available online at http://www.policechiefmagazine.org; downloaded July 14, 2004; Schick, W. (2004). "CompStat in the Los Angeles Police Department." *The Police Chief* 71(1): 1–7, available online at http://www.policechiefmagazine.org; downloaded July 14, 2004

27. Wilber, D. Q. (2004). "90 Minutes a Day that Shape Fight to Cut Crime." *Washington Post.* Available online at http://www.washingtonpost.com; downloaded June 1, 2004, p. B01.

28. Bush, G. W. (2003). *Homeland Security Presidential Directive/HSPD 5.* Available online at http://www.whitehouse.gov/news/releases/2003/02/20030228 9.html; downloaded on July 17, 2004.

29. Department of Homeland Security. (2005). *State and Urban Area Homeland Security Strategy: Guidance on Aligning Strategies with the National Preparedness Goal.* Available online at http://www.ojp.usdoj.gov/odp/ docs/StrategyGuidance_22JUL2005.pdf; downloaded on August 15, 2005.

30. LaTorrette, T., Peterson, D. J., Bartis, J. T., Jackson, B. A., and Houser, A. (2003). *Protecting Emergency Responders: Community Views of Safety and Health Risks and Personal Protection Needs. Volume 2.* Santa Monica, CA: RAND Corporation, p. 70.

31. FEMA. (2004). *NIMS and the Incident Command System.* Available online at www.fema.gov/nims; downloaded on July 13, 2005.

32. Arlington County. (2002). *Arlington County After-Action Report.* Arlington County, VA: Arlington County.

33. FEMA. (2005). *National Incident Management System: National Standard Curriculum Training Development Guidance.* Available online at http://www.fema.gov/pdf/nims/nsctd.pdf Downloaded August 15, 2005.

34. National Institute of Justice. (2003). "CCTV: Constant Cameras Track Violators." *NIJ Journal,* No. 249: 16–23.

35. International Association of Chiefs of Police. (2001). "The Use of CCTV/Video Cameras in Law Enforcement." *IACP Executive Brief.* Available online at http:// www.theiacp.org/documents/pdfs/Publications/UseofCCTV%2Epdf; downloaded November 1, 2004.

36. Maghan, J., O'Reilly, G. W., and Ho Shon, P. C. (2002). "Technology, Policing, and Implications of In-Car Videos." *Police Quarterly* 5(1): 25–42.

37. See Alpert, D. (2003). *GIS/GPS Law Enforcement Master Bibliography.* 2nd ed.Washington, D.C.: Police Executive Research Forum; Regional Community Policing Institute. (2004). *Global Positioning Satellite System (GPS).* Available online at http:// www.wsurcpi.org/tech/COPS%20Act%20GPS.pdf; downloaded on August 2, 2005.

38. LaTorrette, T., Peterson, D. J., Bartis, J. T., Jackson, B. A., and Houser, A. (2003). *Protecting Emergency Responders: Community Views of Safety and Health Risks and Personal Protection Needs. Volume 2.* Santa Monica, CA: RAND Corporation, pp. 79–80.

39. Stephens, D. W. and Hartmann, F. X. (2002). "The Policing Challenge." In *Beyond the Beltway: Focusing on Hometown Security,* edited by J. N. Kayyem, 15–22. Boston, MA: John F. Kennedy School of Government, Harvard University.

40. Pelfrey, W. V. (2005). "The Cycle of Preparedness: Establishing a Framework to Prepare for Terrorist Threats." *Journal of Homeland Security and Emergency Management* 2, no. 1: 1–21; available online at http://www.bepress.com/jhsem/vol12/iss1/5

41. *ibid.*

42. Arlington County. (2002). *Arlington County After-Action Report.* Arlington County, VA: Arlington County.

43. This section is derived from Lynn, Pl. (2005). *Mutual Aid: Multijurisdictional Partnerships for Meeting Regional Threats.* Washington, D.C.: Bureau of Justice Assistance.

44. Lynn, Pl. (2005). *Mutual Aid: Multijurisdictional Partnerships for Meeting Regional Threats.* Washington, D.C.: Bureau of Justice Assistance, pp. 13–20.

45. FEMA. (2004). *NIMS and the Incident Command System.* Available online at www.fema.gov/nims; downloaded on July 13, 2005.

46. Holmes, K. R. (2004). *The Heritage Foundation Homeland Security Task Force Executive Summary.* Washington, D.C.: The Heritage Foundation.

47. Holmes, K. R. (2004). *The Heritage Foundation Homeland Security Task Force Executive Summary.* Washington, D.C.: The Heritage Foundation, p. 54.

48. Roper, C. (1999). *Risk Management for Security Professionals.* Boston, MA: Butterworth-Heinemann, p. 43.

49. This section is derived from Moteff, J. (2004). "Risk Management and Critical Infrastructure Protection: Assessing, Integrating, and Managing Threats, Vulnerabilities and Consequences." *CRS Report for Congress.* Washington, D.C.: Congressional Research Service.

50. Moteff, J. (2004). "Risk Management and Critical Infrastructure Protection: Assessing, Integrating, and Managing Threats, Vulnerabilities and Consequences." *CRS Report for Congress.* Washington, D.C.: Congressional Research Service, p. 7.

51. Leson, J. (2005). *Assessing and Managing the Terrorism Threat.* Washington, D.C.: Bureau of Justice Assistance, p. 5.

52. Moteff, J. (2004). "Risk Management and Critical Infrastructure Protection: Assessing, Integrating, and Managing Threats, Vulnerabilities and Consequences." *CRS Report for Congress.* Washington, D.C.: Congressional Research Service.

53. Leson, J. (2005). *Assessing and Managing the Terrorism Threat.* Washington, D.C.: Bureau of Justice Assistance.

54. Leson, J. (2005). *Assessing and Managing the Terrorism Threat.* Washington, D.C.: Bureau of Justice Assistance, p. 6.

55. Moteff, J. (2004). "Risk Management and Critical Infrastructure Protection: Assessing, Integrating, and Managing Threats, Vulnerabilities and Consequences." *CRS Report for Congress.* Washington, D.C.: Congressional Research Service.

56. Leson, J. (2005). *Assessing and Managing the Terrorism Threat.* Washington, D.C.: Bureau of Justice Assistance.

57. Leson, J. (2005). *Assessing and Managing the Terrorism Threat.* Washington, D.C.: Bureau of Justice Assistance, p. 5.

58. Leson, J. (2005). *Assessing and Managing the Terrorism Threat.* Washington, D.C.: Bureau of Justice Assistance, p. 7.

59. Leson, J. (2005). *Assessing and Managing the Terrorism Threat.* Washington, D.C.: Bureau of Justice Assistance.

60. Moteff, J. (2004). "Risk Management and Critical Infrastructure Protection: Assessing, Integrating, and Managing Threats, Vulnerabilities and Consequences." *CRS Report for Congress.* Washington, D.C.: Congressional Research Service.

61. Roper, C. (1999). *Risk Management for Security Professionals.* Boston, MA: Butterworth-Heinemann, p. 63.

62. Moteff, J. (2004). "Risk Management and Critical Infrastructure Protection: Assessing, Integrating, and Managing Threats, Vulnerabilities and Consequences." *CRS Report for Congress.* Washington, D.C.: Congressional Research Service.

63. *ibid.*

64. Moteff, J. (2004). "Risk Management and Critical Infrastructure Protection: Assessing, Integrating, and Managing Threats, Vulnerabilities and Consequences." *CRS Report for Congress.* Washington, D.C.: Congressional Research Service, p. 9.

65. *ibid.*

66. Leson, J. (2005). *Assessing and Managing the Terrorism Threat.* Washington, D.C.: Bureau of Justice Assistance.

67. *ibid.*

68. Office for Domestic Preparedness. (2003). *The Office for Domestic Preparedness Guidelines for Homeland Security June 2003: Prevention and Deterrence.* Washington, D.C.: U.S. Department of Homeland Security.

69. Moteff, J. (2004). "Risk Management and Critical Infrastructure Protection: Assessing, Integrating, and Managing Threats, Vulnerabilities and Consequences." *CRS Report for Congress.* Washington, D.C.: Congressional Research Service.

70. Leson, J. (2005). *Assessing and Managing the Terrorism Threat.* Washington, D.C.: Bureau of Justice Assistance.

71. Moteff, J. (2004). "Risk Management and Critical Infrastructure Protection: Assessing, Integrating, and Managing Threats, Vulnerabilities and Consequences." *CRS Report for Congress.* Washington, D.C.: Congressional Research Service.

72. Carafano, J. J., Rosenzweig, P., and Kochems, A. (2005). "An Agenda for Increasing State and Local Government Efforts to Combat Terrorism." *Backgrounder,* No. 1826. Washington, D.C.: The Heritage Foundation; Marrin, S. (2003). "Homeland Security Intelligence: Just the Beginning." *Journal of Homeland Security,* November. Available online at http://www.homelandsecurity.org/journal/Articles/marrin.html; downloaded May 2, 2005; Moore, D. (2002). "Homeland Intelligence." Radio Interview with Professor Doug Moore, aired September 1, 2002. Available online at http://www.cjcenter.org/ media/radio/; accessed January 15, 2004.

73. Moore, D. (2002). "Homeland Intelligence." Radio Interview with Professor Doug Moore, aired September 1, 2002. Available online at http://www.cjcenter.org/media/ radio/; accessed January 15, 2004.

74. Peterson, M. (2005). *Intelligence-Led Policing: The New Intelligence Architecture.* Washington, D.C.: Bureau of Justice Assistance.

75. Carter, D. (2004). *Law Enforcement Intelligence: A Guide for State, Local, and Tribal Law Enforcement Agencies.* Washington, D.C.: U.S. Department of Justice; Peterson, M. (2005). *Intelligence-Led Policing: The New Intelligence Architecture.* Washington, D.C.: Bureau of Justice Assistance.

76. Carter, D. (2002). *Law Enforcement Intelligence: A Guide for State, Local, and Tribal Law Enforcement Agencies.* Washington, D.C.: U.S. Department of Justice.

77. Peterson, M. (2005). *Intelligence-Led Policing: The New Intelligence Architecture.* Washington, D.C.: Bureau of Justice Assistance, p. 3.

78. Global Intelligence Working Group. (2004). *Criminal Intelligence for the Chief Executive.* As quoted in Carter, D. (2002). *Law Enforcement Intelligence: A Guide for State, Local, and Tribal Law Enforcement Agencies.* Washington, D.C.: U.S. Department of Justice, p. 9.

79. Carter, D. L. (2002). *Law Enforcement Intelligence Operations.* 8th ed. Tallahassee, FL: SMC Sciences, Inc., as cited in Carter, D. (2002). *Law Enforcement Intelligence: A Guide for State, Local, and Tribal Law Enforcement Agencies.* Washington, D.C.: U.S. Department of Justice, p. 10.

80. Peterson, M. (2005). *Intelligence-Led Policing: The New Intelligence Architecture.* Washington, D.C.: Bureau of Justice Assistance.

81. *ibid.*

82. Peterson, M. (2005). *Intelligence-Led Policing: The New Intelligence Architecture.* Washington, D.C.: Bureau of Justice Assistance; see also Carter, D. (2002). *Law Enforcement Intelligence: A Guide for State, Local, and Tribal Law Enforcement Agencies.* Washington, D.C.: U.S. Department of Justice, Chapter 3.

83. Peterson, M. (2005). *Intelligence-Led Policing: The New Intelligence Architecture.* Washington, D.C.: Bureau of Justice Assistance; see also Carter, D. (2002). *Law Enforcement*

Intelligence: A Guide for State, Local, and Tribal Law Enforcement Agencies. Washington, D.C.: U.S. Department of Justice, Chapter 5.

84. Peterson, M. (2005). *Intelligence-Led Policing: The New Intelligence Architecture.* Washington, D.C.: Bureau of Justice Assistance; see also Carter, D. (2002). *Law Enforcement Intelligence: A Guide for State, Local, and Tribal Law Enforcement Agencies.* Washington, D.C.: U.S. Department of Justice.

85. Carter, D. (2002). *Law Enforcement Intelligence: A Guide for State, Local, and Tribal Law Enforcement Agencies.* Washington, D.C.: U.S. Department of Justice.

86. Carter, D. (2002). *Law Enforcement Intelligence: A Guide for State, Local, and Tribal Law Enforcement Agencies.* Washington, D.C.: U.S. Department of Justice, p. 2.

87. Moore, M. H. (1990). In *Impossible Jobs in Public Management,* edited by E. C. Hargrove and J. C. Glidewell, 72–102. Lawrence, KS: University Press of Kansas, p. 82.

CHAPTER 5

1. Bunker, R. J. (2005). *Training Key #581.* Washington, D.C.: International Association of Chiefs of Police; Bunker, R. J. (2005). *Training Key #582.* Washington, D.C.: International Association of Chiefs of Police.

2. Associated Press. (2005). "IACP Suggests Head Shots to Stop Suicide Bombers." Available online at http://www.policeone.com/news_internal.asp?view=117762; downloaded November 18, 2005.

3. *ibid.*

4. Bunker, R. J. (2005). *Training Key #581.* Washington, D.C.: International Association of Chiefs of Police; Bunker, R. J. (2005). *Training Key #582.* Washington, D.C.: International Association of Chiefs of Police.

5. Manning, P. K. (1997). *Police Work: The Social Organization of Policing.* 2nd ed. Prospect Heights, IL: Waveland Press, Inc.

6. Manning, P. K. (1997). *Police Work: The Social Organization of Policing.* 2nd ed. Prospect Heights, IL: Waveland Press, Inc., p. 44.

7. Manning, P. K. (1997). *Police Work: The Social Organization of Policing.* 2nd ed. Prospect Heights, IL: Waveland Press, Inc., p. 196.

8. Tzu, S. (1963). *The Art of War.* Translated by Samuel B. Griffith. London, England: Oxford University Press, p. 84.

9. U.S. Army Soldier and Biological Chemical Command's Improved Respond Program. (2003). *Law Enforcement Officers Guide for Responding to Chemical Terrorist Incidents.* Washington, D.C.: U.S Army Solider and Biological Chemical Command, Homeland Defense Business Unit. Available online at http://www.mipt.org/pdf/ leofficersguide-ChemicalIncidents.pdf; downloaded June 2004.

10. *ibid.*

11. *ibid.*

12. Buerger, M. E. and Levin, B. H. (2005). "The Future of Officer Safety in an Age of Terrorism." *FBI Law Enforcement Bulletin* 74(9). Available online at http://www.fbi.gov/publications/leb/2005/sept2005/sept05leb.htm; downloaded October, 14, 2005.

13. Houghton, B. K. and Schachter, J. M. (2005). "Coordinated Terrorist Attacks: Implications for Local Responders." *FBI Law Enforcement Bulletin* 74(5). Available online

at http://www.fbi.gov/publications/leb/2005/may2005/may05leb.htm; downloaded July 17, 2005.

14. *ibid.*

15. U.S. Army Soldier and Biological Chemical Command's Improved Respond Program. (2003). *Law Enforcement Officers Guide for Responding to Chemical Terrorist Incidents.* Washington, D.C.: U.S Army Solider and Biological Chemical Command, Homeland Defense Business Unit. Available online at http://www.mipt.org/pdf/ leofficersguideChemicalIncidents.pdf; downloaded June 2004.

16. U.S. Army Soldier and Biological Chemical Command's Improved Respond Program. (2003). *Law Enforcement Officers Guide for Responding to Chemical Terrorist Incidents.* Washington, D.C.: U.S Army Solider and Biological Chemical Command, Homeland Defense Business Unit. Available online at http://www.mipt.org/pdf/ leofficersguideChemicalIncidents.pdf; downloaded June 23, 2004.

17. Bowman, S. (2002). "Weapons of Mass Destruction: The Terrorist Threat." *CRS Report for Congress.* March 7. Washington, D.C.: Congressional Research Service.

18. Shea, D. A. (2004). "Terrorism: Background on Chemical, Biological, and Toxin Weapons and Options for Lessening Their Impact." *CRS Report for Congress.* December 1. Washington, D.C.: Congressional Research Service.

19. *ibid.*

20. *ibid.*

21. Shea, D. A. (2003). "High-Threat Chemical Agents: Characteristics, Effects, and Policy Implications." *CRS Report for Congress.* September 9. Washington, D.C.: Congressional Research Service.

22. *ibid.*

23. *ibid.*

24. Shea, D. A. (2004). "Terrorism: Background on Chemical, Biological, and Toxin Weapons and Options for Lessening Their Impact." *CRS Report for Congress.* December 1. Washington, D.C.: Congressional Research Service.

25. Bowman, S. (2002). "Weapons of Mass Destruction: The Terrorist Threat." *CRS Report for Congress.* March 7. Washington, D.C.: Congressional Research Service; see also Medalia, J. (2004). "Nuclear Terrorism: A Brief Review of Threats and Responses." *CRS Report for Congress.* September 22. Washington, D.C.: Congressional Research Service.

26. Shea, D. A. (2004). "Radiological Dispersal Devices: Select Issues in Consequence Management." *CRS Report for Congress.* March 10. Washington, D.C.: Congressional Research Service.

27. Bowman, S. (2002). "Weapons of Mass Destruction: The Terrorist Threat." *CRS Report for Congress.* March 7. Washington, D.C.: Congressional Research Service.

28. Medalia, J. (2004). "Terrorist 'Dirty Bombs': A Brief Primer." *CRS Report for Congress.* April 1. Washington, D.C.: Congressional Research Service.

29. Jackson, B. A., Peterson, D. J., Bartis, J. T., LaTourrette, T., Brahmakulam, I., Houser, A., and Sollinger, J. (2002). *Protecting Emergency Responders: Lessons Learned From Terrorist Attacks.* Santa Monica, CA: RAND Corporation, p. 52.

30. The United States Conference of Mayors. (2001). *A National Action Plan for Safety and Security in America's Cities.* Washington, D.C.: The United States Conference of Mayors, p. 11.

31. Jackson, B. A., Peterson, D. J., Bartis, J. T., LaTourrette, T., Brahmakulam, I., Houser, A., and Sollinger, J. (2002). *Protecting Emergency Responders: Lessons Learned From Terrorist Attacks.* Santa Monica, CA: RAND Corporation.

32. Jackson, B. A., Peterson, D. J., Bartis, J. T., LaTourrette, T., Brahmakulam, I., Houser, A., and Sollinger, J. (2002). *Protecting Emergency Responders: Lessons Learned From Terrorist Attacks.* Santa Monica, CA: RAND Corporation, p. xi.

33. Jackson, B. A., Peterson, D. J., Bartis, J. T., LaTourrette, T., Brahmakulam, I., Houser, A., and Sollinger, J. (2002). *Protecting Emergency Responders: Lessons Learned From Terrorist Attacks.* Santa Monica, CA: RAND Corporation, p. 52.

34. LaTorrette, T., Peterson, D. J., Bartis, J. T., Jackson, B. A., and Houser, A. (2003). *Protecting Emergency Responders: Community Views of Safety and Health Risks and Personal Protection Needs. Volume 2.* Santa Monica, CA: RAND Corporation.

35. Jackson, B. A., Peterson, D. J., Bartis, J. T., LaTourrette, T., Brahmakulam, I., Houser, A., and Sollinger, J. (2002). *Protecting Emergency Responders: Lessons Learned From Terrorist Attacks.* Santa Monica, CA: RAND Corporation, p. 26.

36. Jackson, B. A., Peterson, D. J., Bartis, J. T., LaTourrette, T., Brahmakulam, I., Houser, A., and Sollinger, J. (2002). *Protecting Emergency Responders: Lessons Learned From Terrorist Attacks.* Santa Monica, CA: RAND Corporation, p. 40.

37. Jackson, B. A., Peterson, D. J., Bartis, J. T., LaTourrette, T., Brahmakulam, I., Houser, A., and Sollinger, J. (2002). *Protecting Emergency Responders: Lessons Learned From Terrorist Attacks.* Santa Monica, CA: RAND Corporation, p. 41.

38. LaTorrette, T., Peterson, D. J., Bartis, J. T., Jackson, B. A., and Houser, A. (2003). *Protecting Emergency Responders: Community Views of Safety and Health Risks and Personal Protection Needs. Volume 2.* Santa Monica, CA: RAND Corporation.

39. LaTorrette, T., Peterson, D. J., Bartis, J. T., Jackson, B. A., and Houser, A. (2003). *Protecting Emergency Responders: Community Views of Safety and Health Risks and Personal Protection Needs. Volume 2.* Santa Monica, CA: RAND Corporation, p. 84.

40. Horwitz, S. (2004). "Police Show Strain From Endless Alerts." *The Washington Post,* October 18, A01.

41. Finn, P. and Tomz, J. E. (1997). *Developing a Law Enforcement Stress Program for Officers and Their Families.* Washington, D.C.: National Institute of Justice.

42. Foster, R. E. (2005). *Lessons Learned Overseas.* Policeone.com Homepage. Available online at http:// www.hitechcj.com/ itebuildercontent/sitebuilderfiles/lessons.learned.over seas.pdf; downloaded December 7, 2005.

43. *ibid.*

44. *ibid.*

45. *ibid.*

46. Kraska, P. B. and Cubellis, L. J. (1997). "Militarizing Mayberry and Beyond: Making Sense of American Paramilitary Policing." *Justice Quarterly* 14 (4):607–630.

47. *ibid.*

48. Kraska, P. B. (2001). *Militarizing the American Criminal Justice System: The Changing Roles of the Armed Forces and the Police.* Boston, MA: Northeastern University Press; Kraska, P. B. and Cubellis, L. J. (1997). "Militarizing Mayberry and Beyond: Making Sense of American Paramilitary Policing." *Justice Quarterly* 14 (4):607–630; Kraska, P. B. and Kappeler, V. E. (1997). "Militarizing American Police: The Rise and Normalization of Paramilitary Units." *Social Problems* 44 (1): 1–18; Kraska, P. B. and

Paulsen, D. J. (1997). "Grounded Research into U.S. Paramilitary Policing: Forging the Iron Fist Inside the Velvet Glove." *Policing and Society* 7 (2): 253–270.

49. See, for instance, Diamond, D. and Bucqueroux, B. (2005). *Community Policing Is Homeland Security*. Policing.com Homepage. Available online at http://www.policing.com/articles/pdf/terrorism.pdf; downloaded December 14, 2005; Docobo, J. (2005) "Community Policing as the Primary Prevention Strategy for Homeland Security at the Local Law Enforcement Level." *Homeland Security Affairs* 1 (1): Article 4. Available online at http://www.hsaj.org/hsa/volI/iss1/art4; downloaded December 7, 2005.

50. Layton, L. (2004). "Metro to Prepare Riders for Terror." *Washington Post,* September 2: B01.

51. *ibid.*

52. As cited in Layton, L. (2004). "Metro to Prepare Riders for Terror." *Washington Post,* September 2: B01.

53. Buerger, M. E. and Levin, B. H. (2005). "The Future of Officer Safety in an Age of Terrorism." *FBI Law Enforcement Bulletin* 74(9). Available online at http://www.fbi.gov/publications/leb/2005/sept2005/sept05leb.htm; downloaded October, 14, 2005.

54. Sweeney, E. M. (2005). "The Patrol Officer: America's Intelligence on the Ground." *FBI Law Enforcement Bulletin* 74(9). Available online at http:// www.fbi.gov/ publications/leb/2005/sept2005/sept05leb.htm; downloaded October, 14, 2005.

55. *ibid.*

56. *ibid.*

57. *ibid.*

58. Office of Domestic Preparedness. (2004). *Homeland Security Exercise and Evaluation Program. Vol. 1: Overview and Doctrine.* Washington, D.C.: U.S. Department of Homeland Security.

59. Lynch, M. D. (2005). "Developing a Scenario-Based Training Program." *FBI Law Enforcement Bulletin* 74(10). Available online at http://www.fbi.gov/publications/leb/2005/oct2005/ oct05leb.htm; downloaded October 14, 2005.

60. Office of Domestic Preparedness. (2004). *Homeland Security Exercise and Evaluation Program. Vol. 1: Overview and Doctrine.* Washington, D.C.: U.S. Department of Homeland Security.

61. *ibid.*

62. Arlington County. (2002). *Arlington County After-Action Report.* Arlington County, VA: Arlington County.

63. Office of Domestic Preparedness. (2004). *Homeland Security Exercise and Evaluation Program. Vol. 1: Overview and Doctrine.* Washington, D.C.: U.S. Department of Homeland Security.

64. Stephens, G. (2005). "Policing the Future: Law Enforcement's New Challenges." *The Futurist,* March–April: 51–57.

65. Stephens, G. (2005). "Policing the Future: Law Enforcement's New Challenges." *The Futurist,* March–April: 51–57 at p. 54.

66. Tzu, S. (1963). *The Art of War.* Translated by Samuel B. Griffith. London, England: Oxford University Press, p. 84.

67. *ibid.*

Index